Pot Smugglers: 5 East of the Light

By

Howard "Scooter" Alford

hsalford@charter.net

Dedication

This book is dedicated to all the people who have ever smoked the weed called cannabis sativa, marijuana or pot. The next time you smoke a joint, think about the process that took place for the weed to get from the growing fields of South America into your hands in the United States. This book is the true story of that process. This book is also dedicated to Joe Pegg (Pegleg), Jerry Smith (Black Fin), Brad Allen (Blue Eyes), all the people that worked in the Navy of Pegleg, and anyone that has ever hauled a load. You know who you are. This book is also dedicated to all those people who have gone on to their great reward: Mom & Dad, Len & Juanita, Howard & Edith, John S., Mom's, Steve J., Chrisy S., Steve M., Chip, Russell, the Colonel, Leroy, and Frankie. Many thanks to my old friend Mike Fay, who has never smoked pot, for his encouragement to write the book. Special thanks to the minstrels for writing all those great songs that were the soundtrack of our lives and turned us into folk heroes. Last but not least, this book is dedicated to my family, my children and especially to my loving ex-wife Patricia who stuck with me through thick and thin. You will always have a permanent place at the bottom of my heart.

Preface

It was the heady days of the late 1970's and marijuana smuggling from Colombia to South Florida was at its pinnacle. The War on Drugs was in its infancy and Port Everglades in Ft. Lauderdale was the prime entry point for the smugglers. Through the early to mid 1970's, there had been an evolution of smuggling organizations from Donald Steinberg to Black Tuna to "Big Ed" Hindelang to Joe Pegg. Known affectionately as Pegleg, Joe Pegg had grown his empire into a 50 boat armada with hundreds of employees. The Broward County authorities had heard rumors on the street of this 50 boat armada but it seemed too big to be believable. During one 12-month period in 1979-80, Pegleg and his Navy imported over 1.2 million pounds of pot into South Florida, the largest amount ever by any group in a 12-month period. This is the story of one man's journey from West Point Military Academy to The Coca-Cola Company, to the Miami Dolphins Ticket Office to an Admiral in the Navy of Pegleg. It is a story of love, friendship, respect, betrayal, and ultimately of redemption.

This is

POT SMUGGLERS: 5 EAST OF THE LIGHT

Table of Contents

Chapter 1
JR & the Dolphins
"Your services are no longer required by the Miami Dolphins.
You'll never work in the sports business again" – Joe Robbie

It's New Year's Eve 1977 and life could not be any better. Yesterday, I was fired from my job as the Assistant Ticket Director for the Miami Dolphins professional football team. I had done something really stupid! While returning to Ft. Lauderdale from Georgia with my infant daughter, I was hassled by a Police Officer at the Ft. Lauderdale airport I still have this thing about authority that is left over from my days as a "pretend" hippie of the 1960's. I decided to write a letter of complaint to the Chief of Police and sent it to him as well as a copy to all the County Commissioners. Just sending the letter itself was a mistake. The bigger mistake was sending it to them on official Miami Dolphins stationery. An internal investigation ensued and the incident came to the attention of the owner of the team Joe Robbie, affectionately known as "JR" to his friends and enemies alike.

Ole' JR wrote me a two-sentence letter that effectively ruined my career in professional sports. What really made me angry is that I didn't even get a signature on my pink slip. All I got was his initials "JR". I had already made up my mind that I was going to resign so I wasn't all broken up about the pink slip. I had typed my resignation over a month ago and was going to turn it in to my immediate boss, Rick Olson, as soon as the Super Bowl was over or the Dolphins were out of the hunt whichever came first. Rick was an okay guy and we got along fairly well. We had to get along because working in the Miami Dolphins Ticket Office in the bowels of the Orange Bowl was like being in combat every day. Each day was a constant procession of season ticket holders that wanted their seat locations upgraded. Somebody was always complaining about the location of their seats and it was always my fault if they couldn't be improved. I had been unhappy with the job for months and I didn't want to work for another football season for $165 per week.

December 30th was a day I'll never forget. My buddy, John Chesterfield, picked me up at my house around 8:00 AM to start our carpool to the Orange Bowl in downtown Miami. We went west on Commercial Boulevard then south on I-95 to the OB in downtown Miami. Commuting an hour each way from Miami to Ft. Lauderdale was no fun either. We had to be at our office at the Orange Bowl by 9 o'clock. John was the Ticket Director for the Ft. Lauderdale Strikers Soccer Team, also owned by Joe Robbie. During football season, the soccer staff worked with the football staff and vice-versa. That way, ole' JR got double duty out of us. That was good business on his part.

As soon as John and I got to the Orange Bowl, Rick Olson went to the Dolphins downtown office at 330 Biscayne Boulevard and disappeared for the rest of the day. Around 3:30 PM he returned and told the three ladies that worked with us, Jeannette, Ruby, and Cathy, that they could go home early. I should have known that something was up because Rick expected everyone to work overtime and sending them home early was sacrilegious. As soon as the ladies had gone, Rick asked John to go up front and work the ticket windows.

Rick said: "Howard, it's bad buddy, real bad."

I said: "Whaddaya mean Rick? What's bad?"

He said: "Come on over here and take a look at this."

I walked over to his desk and he handed me a sheet of paper that was folded in thirds. I opened the sheet of paper and read: "Your employment with the Miami Dolphins is terminated effective immediately. JR" For a minute, I was caught off guard and a little stunned. This was uncharacteristic of JR because he didn't like to fire people. If he fired you, you could draw Unemployment Compensation. If you quit instead of being fired, you weren't eligible for Unemployment. JR's m.o. was to make people so miserable, they would simply quit. But no, he'd fired me! Hallelujah, I was now eligible for Unemployment! When I finally caught my breath, I threw back my head and laughed. It was a long, deep, satisfying laugh that was filled with relief. I thought to myself: "Well, this nightmare is finally over."

When he heard me laugh, John stuck his head around the corner of the door to the front ticket windows, and, thinking that he'd missed a joke, said: "Hey you guys, what's so funny?"

I said: "Hey John, come over here and take a look at this. You ain't gonna believe it."

John said: "What? What is it?"

He took the memo out of my hand, read it, and all the blood drained out of his face. I laughed again, a bigger and more satisfying laugh than the last one.

He said: "What did you do man? You must have done something really bad?"

I laughed heartily again.

He said: "I can see that you're all broke up about it" and he started to laugh too. John loved working in professional sports, he just didn't like working for JR either. He was a lot more serious about his career than I was about mine. . I didn't have a career and I didn't give a damn. JR hadn't screwed me, he'd done me a favor. I picked up the phone, called my wife Pat, and told her JR had fired me.

She said: "Great! Come on home and I'll screw your eyeballs out." Wow, what a woman! Things were really looking up.

As soon as I'd hung up with Pat, Rick said: "Before you go home, clean out your desk and give me all your keys."

I said: "Faaaannnntastic, I'll do it now so I can get the hell out of here.

By 4:30, I was done. Rick and I bid our farewells, shook hands, and John and I split from the Orange Bowl. Instead of feeling sad or depressed, I felt like a new man. As John and I got into his car, I started to laugh uncontrollably. Before we even got out of the parking lot, John said: "You wanna smoke a joint?"

I said: "Sure, fire that mother up!" and we were stoned before we hit I-95. I felt like I'd had the weight of the world taken off of my shoulders. I turned on the radio to WSHE in Ft. Lauderdale, SHE's only Rock-n-Roll, and out of the dashboard speakers came the mellow voice of the DJ, Tommy Judge, spinning the next song. This had to be a sign from God as the high-octane rock-n-roll permeated the air.

I said: "John, do you hear that? That's a sign from God that things are looking up for me. Thank you Tommy Judge, thank you WSHE! Keep on rockin' guys, keep on rockin'!"

Shortly, we got onto I-95 heading north to Ft. Lauderdale and John said: "You still gonna have that New Year's Eve Party?"

I said: "Hell Yeah! Now I've really got something to celebrate."

The commute home that day went by in a flash and before I knew it, we were pulling up in my driveway on 18th Terrace. As I was getting out of the car, I asked John if he wanted to come over later and help me celebrate my unemployment.

He said: "No, we'll see you tomorrow night at your party. Besides, I've got to work tomorrow, remember?" We both laughed and John went home to his wife, the lovely Peggy.

As I walked up towards the house, I saw my wife and daughter looking as beautiful as ever standing in the front door. My wife had this mischievous grin on her face and after giving me a passionate kiss asked: "Are you okay?"

I said: "Sure I'm okay, I'm better than okay. Just a little tired, that's all."

She said: "Great! I'll feed you a good dinner and we'll go to bed early, okay?"

I said: "Sure, that sounds wonderful. I was counting on it!"

I was so stoned, I would have agreed to just about anything. I had no plans for tomorrow, no plans for the New Year, and no plans for anything. For some strange reason, it felt really good. All I knew was that I was really stoned and I didn't give a damn about much of anything. That pot John had was really good stuff. We always seemed to get the best pot in Ft. Lauderdale. Little did I know that very shortly, I would learn firsthand why we always got the best pot around.

After eating a superb supper, I played for a few minutes with my seven-month old daughter Sunshine, and then we put her to bed. Pat took me by the hand and led me into our bedroom. She slowly and suggestively removed my clothes and proceeded to make long, slow, wild passionate love to me. As I lay in a pot and sex induced stupor of post-orgasmic bliss, my wife cleaned me up with a warm washcloth. This has got to be about as close to Nirvana as a male human being can get in this lifetime. As I slipped into the arms of Morpheus, I was overcome with a tremendous certainty that 1978 was absolutely, positively, 100 percent for sure going to be better than 1977. It was almost as if it were fate. It had to be fate. My last thought before I fell asleep was: "Boy, it's amazing what some good pot and a good woman can do for your soul." I fell fast asleep and slept until noon.

Chapter 2
New Year's, a Threesome, & a Massacre
"Another year has passed me by, still I look at myself and cry,
what kind of man have I become?" – STYX

When I finally woke up around noon on New Year's Eve, I felt like a new man. The sun was shining bright, it was about 80 degrees, there were big, white, fluffy clouds in the sky, and I no longer worked for Joe Robbie. Pat was fixing me a bite to eat so I went out by the pool to sit in the sun like a lizard on a log until my lunch was ready. I sat in my jockey shorts and let the warm rays of the sun gradually awaken my body. Shortly, I started to break out in a sweat so I moved into the shade of the overhang, sat at the poolside table, and began to dig into my lunch. Once I'd finished my tuna salad on whole wheat, I took off my jockeys and lay naked in a lounge chair by the pool. As soon as I'd worked up a good sweat, I climbed into the floating chair in the pool and drifted aimlessly for the next two hours. For those of you who have never sunned yourself in the altogether, you must realize that there is an art form to this. The last thing in the world that you want to do is to get your private parts sunburned and put yourself out of commission for a couple of days, not to mention the pain. I learned the hard way that your hands just don't cut it when trying to keep yourself covered. The best and most practical thing to use to cover your private parts is your bathing suit folded strategically into a small triangle. This permits you to keep your private parts in the shade and safe from sunburn while you acquire that much-desired commodity, the ALL OVER TAN. Having your bathing suit close at hand is always a good idea in case the doorbell rings and the Morman missionaries have come for an unexpected visit. Don't laugh, this has happened to us on more than one occasion. So, we learned to keep our bathing suits close in case the doorbell rings and it's the Morman missionaries. We never did figure out if they were impressed with our ALL OVER TAN?

After drifting in the floating chair for nigh on to two hours, I'm just about ready to get out of the water. Pat sticks her head out of the pass-thru window to check on me.

She said: "Hey, I need some help, please."

I said: "Okay, what do you want me to do?"

She said: "How about blowing up the balloons?"

I said: "What are we having balloons for? Nobody cares about balloons."

She said: "I thought we'd put joints in the balloons and tape them to the ceiling. Then, if anyone wants to smoke a joint, all they have to do is bust a balloon and light up the joint."

I said: "Woman, that is genius, pure genius! How about if I roll the joints and you blow up the balloons?"

She said: "What do you think that I've been doing for the last two hours?"

I said: "Rolling joints?"

She said: "Right!"

I rolled out of the floating chair, slipped on my swimsuit, climbed out of the water, and dried off. I walked into the den and sat on the floor with my daughter who's playing pickup sticks with about twenty-four joints. I get cracking at blowing up about two dozen balloons and putting a joint in each one. Then, I tape them all to the ceiling so that the ceiling is covered with joint-filled balloons. We've only invited about thirty people to the party but with New Year's Parties, you never know. Three hundred people could show up and what could you do? Get them stoned and have a Happy New Year!

Pat has everything well under control. There is enough food to feed a small army. We've got twenty-four joints and an ounce of pot left over so we're okay there. We only have two cases of beer but plenty of liquor if we run out of beer. I think we're gonna be okay unless of course three hundred people show up.

By now, it's getting on to suppertime so I jump into the shower first and Pat follows me as soon as I'm out. We grab a bite to eat from all the food we've got for the party. I mix myself a rum and Coke and go into the den to watch television and wait for the first guests to arrive. Around 9-9:30, a group of four shows up and Pat brings them into the den. I shut off the tube and crank up the music, some classic rock-n-roll. Soon, two more people arrive and then four more. By 10:30, we've got around 20-25 people and the party's beginning to cook. I hear a balloon pop, the revelers discover the joints in the balloons, and the smell of cannabis sativa permeates the air. People are dancing, celebrating, and having a good time, it's a good party! All of our best friends are there: Rob and Janice, Jerry J. and his date, Ron and Lynn, and some tagalong guests who seem to be pretty good people. My best friend and ex-employer Jerry Smith hasn't shown yet and I'm beginning to wonder if he's gonna make it. I haven't seen him in months because of my work schedule with the Dolphins. Jerry was a Police Officer for ten years and left the force to open a Private Detective Agency. I worked for him as a Private Investigator before I went to work for the Dolphins. He's a great guy and he'd give you the shirt off his back if you needed it. He has done so many things for Pat and me that we could never repay him. For one thing, he gave me a job as a Private Detective when I needed a job. For another, he saved my daughter's life, literally. That sounds a little dramatic, I know, but here's what happened.

When Pat was about 4-5 months pregnant with Sunshine, we went to an Eric Clapton concert at the Hollywood Sportatorium, way out Hollywood Boulevard near the Everglades in the middle of nowhere. It was probably a foolish thing to do, but up until then, Pat had not had any trouble with her pregnancy. If our child were a girl, we had decided to name her Layla Sunshine after Clapton's song "Layla." We both loved the song and it was popular when we first met so it sort of became "our" song. At the time, we were driving an old Cadillac Fleetwood Brougham, black on black on black, that looked like a limousine it was so big. Jerry had repossessed the car for one of the local banks and then bought it from the bank for $500. Pat and I needed a car so Jerry sold it to us for $500.

During the concert, Pat started to bleed and we thought she was going to lose the baby. We left the concert early and when we got in the car, it wouldn't start. I was frantic! I had jumper cables but the concert was still going strong and we were the only people in the parking lot. I found a Broward County Deputy Sheriff and asked him if he would let me jump my car from his cruiser. He didn't want to help me at first but after I explained the situation with my wife, he agreed. I tried to start that Caddy for about ten minutes but I could hardly get it to turn over. Right about then, the concert let out and the Deputy Sheriff said that he had to go direct traffic on Hollywood Boulevard. In a couple of minutes, the people parked next to us came to their car so I asked them to give me a jump. I tried for another five minutes but that sucker wouldn't hardly turn over. It was stone dead! I finally gave up and decided to call Jerry because he had a tow truck that he used for repo's for the banks. By now, it was past midnight and I hated to call him but I didn't know what else to do.

I went to a payphone, dialed his number and, thank God, he answered. It was obvious that I'd woken him up and I apologized. I then explained the situation to him and asked him if he would come out to the Sportatorium and help us.

He said: "No sweat man, I'll be there as soon as I can but I expect it will take me an hour or more."

I hung up the phone and went back to the car to comfort Pat. She was trying to be cool about the situation but I could tell she thought she was going to lose the baby.

The Hollywood Sportatorium was about twenty-five miles west of Hollywood, Florida out a two-lane highway that was long, straight, and dark. When a concert is over, it becomes a one-way street going east because all the crazies from the show drive on both sides of the road back into Hollywood. I knew that it would be a bitch for Jerry to drive against the flow of traffic and I knew it would take him a while to get there. In about an hour and a half, which seemed like an eternity, Jerry finally showed up in his tow truck. By then, the parking lot was deserted and even the police had gone home. Pat and I were alone in that dark, lonely parking lot at two in the morning and it was a bit scary. It took Jerry every bit of thirty seconds to jump that Caddy and get it going, I couldn't believe it! I asked him to follow us home in case it quit running again and, of course, he cheerfully agreed. Boy, was it a long drive home! We finally got home around 3:00 AM with no more trouble. We called Pat's baby doctor first thing the next morning. He told her to go to bed for a week and not to get up except to go to the bathroom. In a couple of days, the bleeding had stopped and everything was all right. In May, our daughter was born and we named her Layla Sunshine and called her "Sunny" after my father "Sonny" with Sunny coming from Sunshine, of course. This little anecdote is just one example of all the times that Jerry has helped us out and bailed me out of trouble.

About 10:45, I look up and walking through the door is Jerry and his TWO girlfriends, Linda and Rita. That's right, TWO girlfriends. Jerry has been living with both ladies at the same time, Linda in the upstairs bedroom and Rita in the downstairs bedroom with Jerry alternating nights between the two of them. Don't ask me how he made it work but he did. The three of them looked like death warmed over. They looked like they'd been camping or something. They appeared to be totally exhausted like they'd been on a long trip or they'd been up for a couple of nights. Pat and I greeted them warmly because we were friends with both ladies regardless of the situation. Linda was a Delta Flight Attendant and a friend of Pat's from Delta. Pat had introduced Linda to Jerry while he was living with Rita. Linda and Jerry hit it off and she moved into the upstairs bedroom. Rita refused to leave and stayed in the downstairs bedroom. We all gave each other big hugs while exchanging New Year's greetings.

Jerry said: "You still got that TV in your bedroom?"

I said: "Yeah man, but why do you wanna watch TV on New Year's Eve?"

He said: "I just want to see the 11 o'clock news, that's all. Why don't you come watch it with us then we'll come party with you for awhile."

So, the four of us went back into my bedroom and turned on the TV. It was a couple of minutes before 11:00 so we chatted about old times and mostly talked about my job with the Dolphins. I told Jerry that I'd been fired the day before and that I was unemployed and looking for a job. I told him that I really felt like the New Year was going to be good for me because I hated working for Joe Robbie so much. In a minute, the 11 o'clock news came on with Ann Bishop and Chuck Dowdle. We instantly became absorbed in the news.

Ann Bishop wished everyone a Happy New Year and then started right in with the lead story: "Bales of marijuana are washing up on the beach at the Yankee Clipper Hotel on A1A in Ft. Lauderdale. The police have barricaded A1A from Las Olas Boulevard to the Intracoastal Waterway, no vehicle traffic is permitted until further notice, and all citizens are warned to stay away from this area. The police are working diligently to find and secure all contraband. Everyone is asked to cooperate by staying away from this area until further notice. It is reported that crowds of New Year's revelers are growing in this area and numerous pleasure boats are cruising in the area of the Yankee Clipper Hotel. The public is warned to stay out of this area or be subject to arrest if anyone is found in possession of contraband." Chuck Dowdle then went on to the next story.

Jerry turned to me and said: "What do you think about that?"

I said: "I think we ought to get in a boat and see if we can find us some free pot."

The threesome looked at each other and cracked up laughing.

Then Jerry said: "While you've been working for the Miami Dolphins, we've been smuggling pot. We brought in a load tonight but some of our friends had to dump their load just off the beach. They were running out of fuel and panicked. We were the last boat in the port before the cops threw up a blockade by the whistle buoy. I got on the radio and tried to warn the other boats that the heat had barricaded the port and were stopping and searching every boat. A friend of ours who we call 'Taterhead, heard my call on the radio but he was running out of fuel. I told him to go back out into the gulfstream and spend the night. I would get some fuel for him in jerry jugs and bring it to him in the morning or as soon as I saw the heat take the barricade off the port. That way, he could be safe and save his load. He panicked and dumped his load about 100 yards offshore right in front of the Yankee Clipper Hotel. That's 'Taterhead's pot that's washing up on the beach."

At first, I was truly amazed but the more Jerry talked, the more I realized that I should not have been surprised by anything that this man did. We talked for a few more minutes and Jerry told me some more about smuggling. Pat stuck her head in the door of the bedroom and said: "Hey you guys, you wanna come join the party or what?"

Jerry finished his little tale and said: "Since you don't have a job, why don't you come to work for me? I want to get a second boat and I'll teach you how to run it for me. There's a lot of money to be made smuggling pot. While you've been working for the Miami Dolphins for $165 a week, I've made over $2,000,000!!"

Well, needless to say, I was astounded! I told Jerry that I'd have to think about it because I had a wife and a kid to worry about. I told him that Pat made good money flying for Delta and that I wasn't going to start looking for a job for a couple of months. All I wanted to do was to lay back and spend some quality time with my wife and my daughter. Jerry said that he would touch base with me every so often and that if I changed my mind, he could really use me. He said they were doing trips all the time.

The four of us rejoined the party and we kicked in the New Year at midnight stoned out of our gourds. On top of being stoned, Jerry really had my head swimming. About 1:00 AM, he and his ladies left because they "had a boat we have to unload."

When the party finally broke up and all the guests had left, Pat and I climbed into bed. At this point, she didn't know anything. I started at the beginning with the 11 o'clock news and told her everything that Jerry had told me about smuggling. I said that Jerry wanted to buy a second boat and that he wanted me to work for him and run the new boat.

Pat said: "That damn Jerry, he's crazy ain't he?"

I said: "Yeah, he's crazy all right but he knows what he's doing."

She said: "Are you going to work for him?"

I said: "I don't know, would you care?"

She said: "You wouldn't listen to me anyway, would you?"

I said: "Sure I would."

She said: "Bull!!"

I grinned and said: "Good night my love and Happy New Year."

She said: "Good night to you too and Happy New Year."

I turned out the light and went to sleep while visions of sugarplums danced in my head. We slept soundly until Sunny woke us up the next morning. When we finally got up and got going, we went to the funky little restaurant on the pier at the end of Commercial Boulevard to eat breakfast. I bought a Ft. Lauderdale newspaper and found the story of the busts on the front page of the Metro Section. Four boats were busted and ten people were arrested with marijuana in Port Everglades last night. Thirty-four bales of marijuana had washed up on the beach at the Yankee Clipper Hotel and had been confiscated by the police. As of yet, there was no tally on the bales of marijuana found on the four boats that were busted. The authorities were heralding this as a "big bust." I was later to learn more details about this trip from Jerry and how the bust came to be referred to as the "New Year's Massacre." 1978 was not going to be a very good year for those ten people that were busted. It would turn out to be a great year for me!

Chapter 3
Joan, Cathy, & Pegleg
The idea of making a lot of money quick is very seductive.

The first few months of 1978 were really nice for me. Pat was flying three-day trips for Delta and I had become a househusband. When she was gone on a trip, I would take care of Sunshine, clean the house, do the shopping, and do all the things that a wife normally does. When she would come home from a trip, Sunshine would be happy, the house would be clean, and supper would be cooking. Pat told me that I was going to make somebody a good wife.

Jerry would drop by about every 2-3 weeks and ask me if I were ready to come to work for him yet.

He'd always say: "While you're trying to make up your mind about working for me, I've made another half-a-million dollars."

I had upgraded my resume, was going on interviews, and was halfheartedly trying to find a job. Good jobs were hard to find in Ft. Lauderdale for people with a college degree because the main economy was tourism. That B.S. Degree in Chemistry I had from the University of Georgia wasn't doing me much good. Pat and I were in a comfort zone and I was enjoying it to the hilt. We had a real good time for those first couple of months of the year.

About the middle of March, Jerry dropped by the house one day to see if we were ready to go to work for him yet. Pat and I were sitting out by the pool with our friend Rosanne who had stopped by for a visit. Jerry sat in the swing with Rose and held Sunshine and we talked while they were swinging. Finally, Jerry asked me if I were ready to go to work for him.

I said. "I really don't think so yet. I still don't know what I want to do."

He said: "Do you care if Pat comes to work for me?"

I said: "I don't really know, man. I would rather me come to work for you than I would her."

He said: "I need a girl to go on my boat real bad. Linda and Rita don't want to go anymore, they've had enough. I'm going to put them to work doing other things. So, I need at least one girl to replace them."

I said: "What about buying the second boat and letting me run it?"

He said: "I bought a 41 foot Columbia sailboat and that's what I'm doing trips with now. The fast boats are hot since the New Year's Massacre and we're not using them anymore for trips. The heat is watching for Searays, Magnums, and Cigarettes. I've still got the Searay Sundancer but I'm not doing trips in it anymore, I'm doing trips on the 41 Columbia. Sailboats are cool, fast boats are hot. I need crew for the sailboat real bad since Linda and Rita have retired. I especially need a girl to replace them. There's a trip coming up in three or four days and I'm putting my crew together for it. I've got a couple of guys already but I need a girl bad."

I told him that I would talk it over with Pat that night and call him the next day. That night, Pat and I discussed it at length. Pat was excited about going and it looked like she'd have time off between her three-day trips. I told her that I didn't want her to go if I couldn't go too. The next day, I went to see Jerry and I told him that both Pat and I wanted to go on the trip. I said that if I couldn't go, she couldn't go either. He hemmed and hawed a little bit but finally consented to letting us both go.

He said: "Okay, you know you both can go if you want but I can't pay you as much as the other guys are going to make on the trip. I'll pay Pat $5,000 because that's what the girls get to go and I'll pay you $5,000 too."

I said: "Fine, I'll be glad to go for $5,000."

At that point in our life, $5,000 was a whole lot of money especially if we both went and made $5,000 each. We had about $7,200 in a savings account at the bank that we'd saved over the course of our four-year marriage. It didn't seem like very much money if something bad were to happen like a serious medical problem. The opportunity to make $10,000 in three or four days was almost too good to pass up.

I left Jerry's house, drove home, and told Pat that we were both going on the trip. We were both excited! Now, we had a problem with getting someone to keep Sunshine while we were gone. We didn't have any relatives in Ft. Lauderdale, all the grandparents were in Georgia. We decided to call a Babysitter Service that we found in the yellow pages. The Sitter Service sent out a grandmotherly-type lady that we immediately liked and felt comfortable with. We told her that we were going sailing to the Bahamas for a couple of days and could she handle Sunny while we were gone? She laughed and said of course she could, she'd raised four kids of her own and now had grandchildren. We made the arrangements with her, worked everything out, and told her that we'd be going in a day or two. She promised to be ready when we called. Pat and I then began to go through withdrawal so to speak because we'd never left Sunshine overnight before much less for a couple of days. It really wasn't something that we'd considered up until then. We had to talk ourselves into the fact that it was going to be all right. We hoped like hell it was going to be all right.

In a couple of days, Jerry called and asked me to come over to his house. I drove over to this house, got out of my car, and knocked on the front door. Nobody answered so I opened the door and hollered "anybody home?" No answer. So, I walked through his house and went out the back door looking for him. He had a house on the New River that was just west of Cape Florida, a big bend in the river that looked like the shape of the State of Florida. At the dock was a sailboat named Cathy V, the 41 foot Columbia sailboat that we would be sailing to the Bahamas. Jerry was in the cockpit of the boat with some people. I walked over to the cockpit and Jerry did the introductions. There was a woman named Joan who Jerry was later to marry. There were two guys named Mike and Jimmy and I soon learned that Mike was 'Taterhead. So this was the crew for the trip: Jerry, Joan, Mike, Jimmy, Pat, and me. After the introductions, Jerry began to give us an orientation of the boat with it mostly directed toward Joan.

I said: "Jerry, what's going on? Aren't you going on this boat?"

He said: "No, I'm going on the middle boat that goes to the freighter. Joan is going to captain this boat."

I said: "Oh well, that changes things considerably. I don't know Joan, no offense Joan, but I don't know you and I've never been out of sight of land before in my life. Jerry, I trust you but I don't trust Joan because I don't know Joan. I don't know if I want to go if you're not going, in fact, I'm pretty sure I don't want to go and I don't want my wife to go either."

Jerry said. "Ah, don't be a sissy, Scooter. The boat's running fine, I just put a new engine in it. I just got back from a trip in this boat and it's running like a top. Joan's a boat person, she's got a lot of experience with boats, and there's no reason why you shouldn't go."

I said: "Well, let me think about it."

He said: "You better make a decision fast because we've gotta leave tomorrow."

I said: "Okay."

He said: "Let me finish this. You'd better pay attention 'cause you're gonna be on this boat, and you need to know this stuff."

So, he started going over the boat with us and explaining all the systems. Mike and Jimmy were powerboaters, in fact, they were the ones that dumped their load off the beach at the Yankee Clipper Hotel on New Year's Eve. They'd always run powerboats, that's all they knew, and they'd never worked a trip on a sailboat before. So, from that standpoint, we were all new to this boat. That didn't make me feel any better. Joan was also a powerboat person. When she'd been married, she and her husband had owned a 45 foot Hatteras in the Washington, D.C. area. She'd been on sailboats before but really didn't have much experience on them.

Jerry went through the boat from bow to stern with us and went over all the systems. I still wasn't sure at that point if Pat and I were going to go on the trip. When Jerry finished the orientation, I hung around for a little while and talked with Joan, Mike, and Jimmy. I tried to get to know them a little better so I would feel a little better about going without Jerry. I really didn't get good vibes from Joan and I wasn't sure if I wanted to go with her as the captain.

Shortly, a couple of guys drove up in a pickup truck and brother, did they look rough. In fact, they looked exactly like what you think criminals would look like. They had long hair and beards, and were wearing blue jeans, cowboy boots, and worn-out looking tee-shirts. They came around to the back of the house and had a talk with Jerry in the yard away from us. We couldn't hear any of their conversation. None of us knew who these guys were at the time and Jerry didn't introduce them to us. We figured that we weren't supposed to know them for whatever reason and we didn't ask. As it turned out, one of the guys was "the man", Joe Pegg, affectionately know as "Pegleg" to his friends. Joe could have been a twin to Keith Richards of the Rolling Stones. As soon as Pegleg and his friend left, I told Jerry that I was leaving and that I would call him later that night. I'd let him know then if Pat and I were going on the trip.

He said: "Okay, well you know we've gotta leave tomorrow now for sure and you gotta let me know tonight."

I said: "Fine, I'll go home, Pat and I will talk it over, and I'll give you a buzz."

As I drove home, I was reluctant, discouraged, and apprehensive. Pat and I talked it over and I told her that Jerry wasn't going on the sailboat, that he was going on the middle boat. That really put a wrench in our plans because we trusted Jerry but we sure as hell didn't trust people we didn't know. We discussed it back and forth and finally decided that we'd go on just this one trip. That way, we could make $10,000 and be able to breathe a little easier. Once the decision was made, I called Jerry and told him that after much discussion, Pat and I had decided to go on the trip.

He sounded very pleased and said: "Come on over to the house tomorrow afternoon around 3 o'clock. Bring your gear 'cause you'll be leaving then."

The first thing that we did was to call the babysitter and make the arrangements with her to keep Sunshine. The next thing that we did was to pack our duffle bags. We had already gone out and bought foul weather gear, Topsiders boat shoes, and some other things. We packed up everything in the duffle bags with some extra blue jeans and some warm clothes in case it got cold. Then, we went into the kitchen and began to cook supper. We didn't talk much as the excitement began to wane into a somber and fatalistic mood. After eating supper and putting Sunshine to bed, we crawled into bed early while struggling to keep our emotions in check. We contemplated the seriousness and the enormity of what we were about to do. I sure wish Jerry were going on the sailboat with us. The only reason we even considered smuggling is because we'd be doing it with Jerry. We fell asleep with visions of having another $10,000 in the bank in just a few days. We had some serious apprehension about leaving Sunshine and about going on a boat out of sight of land without Jerry Smith. The idea of making a lot of money quick is very seductive.

Chapter 4
'Taterhead and the Searays
Paranoia and fear are two emotions that really suck!

The babysitter arrived around 2:00 PM and we gave her a quick rundown of the supplies for Sunshine and the food we'd bought for the two of them. It went smoothly, we said our goodbyes, and headed for Jerry's house on S.W. 5th Place on the New River.

When we got to Jerry's house, all the rest of the crew were already there with the motor running warming up the Perkins diesel engine. Jerry gave us our last minute instructions: we were to sail a heading of 140 degrees to Gun Cay lighthouse in the Bahamas. He figured it would take us 10-12 hours if all went well and the boat ran good which he assured us it would. He said Joan knew how to handle the boat and 'Taterhead and Jimmy knew the area around Gun Cay like the back of their hand. He assured us that we wouldn't have any trouble, the weather report was favorable, and we were all optimistic about the adventure.

Okay, it was time to go, Jerry untied the lines from the dock cleats and threw them on the boat, pushed us away from the dock, and we were off! Joan was at the helm as we circled Cape Florida and headed east up the New River towards Port Everglades and the ocean. Soon, we came upon the 4th Avenue bridge near the public boat ramp and Hatteras Yachts, we blew our airhorn three times to get the bridgetender to open the bridge for us, and we began to circle in the River. The current there can be quite treacherous especially if the tide is running. You've got to keep a sailboat moving to avoid being pushed into the bridge or the seawall especially if the tide is running. So, we're circling in the River right in front of the public boat ramp. People were sitting on the seawall by the boat ramp fishing, crabbing, and watching us circle while we waited for the bridge to open.

'Taterhead and Jimmy had started snorting cocaine as soon as we left the dock. They had a little plastic, single tooter that they kept hitting with regularity and were laughing, cutting up, and having a good time. While we were going around in circles by the boat ramp, they told us a story about a trip they'd done recently in a 25 foot Searay Sundancer.

They had blasted over to Gun Cay from Ft. Lauderdale in about 2 ½-3 hours, gotten loaded with 1400 pounds of pot right under Gun Cay light in the shallow water, and spent the night anchored at Gun Cay. The next morning, they boogeyed for Ft. Lauderdale and got to the Port just before noon in a little over 3 hours. They came in the Cut into Port Everglades and there was a gray, Florida Marine Patrol boat with two officers, we call them "Grouper Troopers." As they came under the 17th Street bridge and passed the Gulf docks on the left, they continued north to where the New River begins and goes west through downtown Ft. Lauderdale. The Grouper Troopers started following them in the Port but there was a lot of boat traffic and quite a few boats between them and the Grouper Troopers. It is a "No Wake" zone in the Port, the Intracoastal, and all the way up New River past the 4th Avenue bridge so you had to cruise slowly at a dead idle.

As they turned left and headed west out New River, they could see the Grouper Trooper pass a boat behind them. The asspucker factor started to kick in. They cruised on up the River into the center of downtown Ft. Lauderdale, the River is quite narrow here with Yachts docked on each shoreline all the way through town. They checked behind them and the heat had passed another boat and were getting closer to them. They cruised on through the middle of town, went past Hatteras Yachts on the left, through the train trestle, went through 4th Avenue bridge, and made a hard left turn as the River turned. They looked behind them and the heat was passing the last boat between them. They were convinced that the Grouper Troopers were coming to get them, they admitted that they were all tooted up with cocaine, hyped up, and paranoid. As soon as they saw the gray boat pass the last boat between them, 'Taterhead shoved the throttles forward and floored it. Even with 1400 pounds of pot, the Mercruiser engines caused the Searay to jump and quickly got the boat up to top speed. As soon as 'Taterhead gunned it, the Grouper Trooper gunned it too because they felt sure the Searay was loaded with contraband. The asspucker factor was now maxed out as they were bearing down on the boat ramp at full speed.

It's a Saturday afternoon and there's a big crowd of people fishing, crabbing, and picnicking at the public boat ramp. Here comes 'Taterhead and Jimmy running flat out and headed right for the boat ramp. There's only one problem: NO TRAILER! The people that are fishing and crabbing closest to the boat ramp suddenly realize that this boat is coming up the boat ramp at full speed with no trailer. The people jump up and start screaming and running away from the boat ramp and it's mass pandemonium. There's fishing poles, and tackle, and crab nets, and arms and legs, and people going every which-a-way. 'Taterhead runs the boat right up the boat ramp, slides all the way across the parking lot, and comes to a stop on the grass under a tree. How the hell he didn't hit a parked car he doesn't know. As soon as the boat comes to rest under the tree, they jump off onto the ground, and take off running.

They run a couple of blocks until they get tired, then stop at a house, and ask the people if they can call a cab 'cause they've had car trouble. The people let them use their phone to call a cab, the cab comes, and takes them home.

The Grouper Troopers docked their boat, busted the Searay, and confiscated the load of pot but 'Taterhead and Jimmy got away. We're hearing this story while we're circling and waiting for the bridge to open and we're laughing hysterically. Pat and I had seen this story reported on the local news not too long ago and I said with incredulity: "That was you guys?" They just laughed and shook their heads "yes."

By this time, the bridge has opened and we've gone through downtown Ft. Lauderdale, and into the Port. So, 'Taterhead and Jimmy continue their story. There's another trip coming up for them so they went out and bought another 25 foot Searay Sundancer. They blasted over to Gun Cay, got another load of 1400 pounds of pot, spent the night at Gun, and brought the load home the next day. As they pass under the 17th Street bridge and approach the Gulf docks, that same Grouper Trooper was hanging out right in front of the Gulf docks. The officers see 'Taterhead and Jimmy in the new Searay Sundancer and pull them over.

One of the officers jumps on their boat and asks: "Can I see some identification?"

They said: "We don't have any ID. We never bring ID with us when we go on a boat. Haven't you seen that American Express commercial where the guy on the boat drops his wallet in the water?"

The officer said: "Okay, let me see the registration for the boat."

They said: "We don't have the registration for the boat, it's not our boat, we borrowed it from a friend."

The officer said: "Open up the Cuddy Cabin and let me take a look."

They said: "We don't have a key to the lock, it's not our boat, we just borrowed it from a friend to go for a ride this afternoon."

The Grouper Troopers are sure the boat is loaded with pot so they tell 'Taterhead to go down the canal by the Gulf docks to the Customs dock which is about halfway down the canal on the right. They pull up to the Customs dock, get on the dock, and act like they're tying their lines to the cleats on the dock. But they're not tying them up, they're just pretending. The Grouper Trooper pulls alongside their Searay, ties off to their port side, and turns off the motor.

Now, 'Taterhead and Jimmy are squatting down on the dock and as soon as the officer turns his engine off, they push the Searay and the gray boat away from the dock and the two boats drift out into the middle of the canal. 'Taterhead and Jimmy take off running. Before the officer can get his motor running and get both boats back to the dock, 'Taterhead and Jimmy are long gone. They ran down to Cordoba Road, went into Southport Raw Bar, and called a cab. The cab came and took them to the Dania Jai Alai Fronton where they were having an afternoon matinee. They called some friends who came and picked them up and brought them home. Needless to say, they didn't go out and buy another 25 foot Searay Sundancer or they wouldn't have been on the sailboat with us. Like Jerry said: Searays, Magnums, and Cigarettes were hot, sailboats were cool. I sure hope so!

We are just going out the Cut at Port Everglades and into the ocean as they are finishing up their stories. We have all had a couple of good laughs and I hope the remainder of the trip is light and funny. We all hope that we won't have any trouble with the heat like 'Taterhead and Jimmy but I wonder if it's a harbinger of things to come. This smuggling thing is really serious stuff. In any event, our journey has just begun.

Chapter 5
Getting' Religion in the Gulfstream
Being in 20 foot swells in the Gulfstream will cause you to make a deal with God.

We came through the Cut, out of the mouth of Port Everglades, turned right, and got on a heading of 140 degrees to Bimini and Gun Cay lighthouse, a trip of 54 nautical miles. Joan is still at the helm and we've got a sail of ten to twelve hours ahead of us. The seas are about two to three feet and I'm starting to feel a little queasy. I should've taken Dramamine before we left the dock but I didn't. If you wait until you're already seasick to take the Dramamine, it won't work. The boat was gently going up and down fore to aft which wasn't too bad but what made it worse was that the two to three foot seas were causing the boat to roll from left to right. The prevailing wind is out of the southeast but now the wind was turning counterclockwise and was blowing out of the northeast against the Gulfstream. The Gulfstream flows from south to north and when the wind blows against it, the sea gets rough, and that's what was happening now. I didn't know it at the time but it was gonna get worse.

Joan said: "Damn, where's this weather coming from? We're supposed to have beautiful weather for this trip. If this keeps up, it could get rough."

I said: "Great! That's just fucking great." You see, I get seasick in a bathtub.

I sat on the starboard side of the cockpit and let the air hit me in the face in hopes that I wouldn't get seasick but I think it was too late. By now, we're about an hour out of the Port and it seems like we aren't going anywhere. We keep looking over at the land and it seems like we're just off Dania Beach just south of the mouth of the Port. The top speed for our sailboat motoring is about six knots and the Gulfstream flows north about two to three knots. We're motoring south about six knots and it feels like we're standing still. It's starting to get dark now, it's about 8:00 PM, and the lights on the land are beginning to come on. The boat is going up and down, rolling side to side, and I'm seasick!

'Taterhead and Jimmy keep looking over at the land and saying: "Man, I don't believe this shit! We ain't ever gonna get away from Florida. If we were in our Searay, we'd be halfway to Gun Cay by now."

It finally got pitch dark around 9:00 PM and we could still see the lights on land behind us and to our right. We were farther out into the Gulfstream and it was getting rougher, the swells were about eight to ten feet, and the wind was blowing harder. We had the good sense to drop the mainsail which 'Taterhead and I did before it got any rougher. The wind had been picking up over the last couple of hours, the seas were building, and it was officially rough. I threw up for the first time, then twenty minutes later, I threw up again. Then, twenty minutes later, I threw up again, I wanted to die. It seems like I threw up every twenty minutes until we got to Gun Cay. I took Dramamine and threw them up. I put suppositories up my rectum but they didn't help. I took Emetrol by mouth and threw it up, nothing helped. The swells were now at least eighteen to twenty feet. The boat would be in a trough and you would look up and see this wall of water coming at the boat, it looked like it was higher than the mast of the sailboat which was forty-five feet high. You would think that the wall of water was going to crash down on the boat but the boat would just pop up on top of the swell and then go back down into another trough. That's what we were doing, going up to the top of a swell and then back down into a trough. At that point, I was really scared and started praying, seriously.

I would say: "Lord, if you'll just let me get back on land and see my daughter, I promise I'll never go out on a boat again for the rest of my life. I promise I'll go to church every Sunday." I repeated this a thousand times. I remembered the story of Jesus walking on water over to the Disciples in the boat. The Disciples thought their boat was sinking and the Bible says they were "sore afraid." I know what "sore afraid" is all about, I was damn sure "sore afraid." Nobody got seasick but me. Pat and Joan went downstairs and took a nap! I wish I could have taken a nap. By midnight, I was completely exhausted from the storm and from being seasick, I was worn out.

We were out in the middle of the Gulfstream now and it was dark, pitch black dark. You could hardly see the bow of the boat, there was no land anywhere, no lights of any kind. Finally we saw some lights and got excited, Bimini! We got our binoculars and everyone took a look at the lights hoping like crazy that it's Bimini. We're getting closer and closer to these lights and finally realize that it's a freighter, it's a huge freighter going from our left to right, north to south, and probably headed for the Port of Miami. It crossed our bow right in front of us and it looked like it was pretty damn close, like a couple of hundred yards close. It must have been at least 400-500 feet long, maybe more. It was just humongous looking out here in the middle of nowhere in the Gulfstream. It actually scared the hell out of us because we didn't think it could see us. We certainly weren't fast enough to get out of its way so we thought it was possible for us to get run over by a freighter. That got the adrenaline flowing and woke us up.

Finally, around 3:00 AM, we spotted a blinking light and we all got real excited, Gun Cay lighthouse! 'Taterhead and I were in the cockpit when we saw the light, he was at the helm. I went downstairs, woke everybody up, and we all got in the cockpit. Joan got the Bahamian Guide and looked at the lighthouse for Gun Cay, it blinks once every 10 seconds. We're watching the light and trying to time it with a watch while the boat is going up and down, up and down. The light is blinking and we've got a flashlight aimed at a watch trying to time the light. We can't get a fix on it, we're not sure if it's Gun Cay or not. I remember my ole' army training so I count: 1001, 1002, 1003, 1004, 1005. The damn light is blinking once every five seconds not once every ten seconds, it's not Gun Cay light.

Joan pulled out the Bahamian Guide again and looked up the lighthouse that blinks once every five seconds, it's Great Isaac's. Great Isaac's is actually just a platform that is north of Bimini about twenty miles. What has happened is that the Gulfstream has carried us twenty miles north of Bimini and we are going to Gun which is about ten miles south of Bimini. When we finally figured this out, we all got bummed because we realized that we weren't near the end of our voyage. We still have a long way to go.

I asked 'Taterhead: "How long is it gonna take us to get from Great Isaac's to Gun Cay?"

He said: "This boat is gonna take six hours." When he told me that I had six more hours, I didn't know if I could make it. I really didn't know if I could maintain my sanity for six more hours.

From Great Isaac's, we had to change our course from 140 degrees to170-180 degrees. We could steer due south, 180 degrees, until we got a visual sight on Bimini and then we could steer without having to stare at the compass so much. It is very tiring to run a boat by staring solely at the compass especially so in rough weather. 'Taterhead took the helm and he put the bow of the boat on a heading of 180 degrees. Now, we were motoring directly against the Gulfstream which may slow us down tremendously. Oh well, we didn't have a choice in the matter.

Around 4:00 AM, we spotted the lights on the houses on Bimini and the red lights on the radio tower on south Bimini. This improved our spirits considerably and gave us a visual fix to use to steer the boat. What we were able to do was to keep the lights of Bimini at about 11 o'clock to the bow of the boat, just to the left of the front of the boat. So, for the next couple of hours, we just kept motoring on a course of 180 degrees, due south, keeping the lights at about 11 o'clock. We must have been cruising pretty slowly because it seemed like we would never get up even with the lights of Bimini.

'Taterhead and I are in the cockpit alone and he's at the helm. A big, rogue wave crashes over the bow of the boat and the bow goes completely underwater. A wall of water goes over the windshield, under the top, and hits 'Taterhead right smack dab in the face and eyes.

He threw up his hands and said: "That's it, I can't take no more. You take the wheel, I'm going downstairs."

He got up, walked away from the helm, and disappeared into the main salon. I jumped up, took the wheel, got control of the boat, and continued following the shoreline of Bimini. What seemed like an eternity, Cathy finally got parallel with Bimini as we slowly made some headway going south. We must have been a couple of miles offshore but it appeared that we were only a couple of hundred yards offshore, the houses looked that close. This was my first experience judging distances over water at night.

I'm in the cockpit alone now still feeling seasick and just plain terrible but a little better mentally since I know for sure exactly where we are now. I can see the light at the end of the tunnel, maybe I'll make it? I'm cold, soaking wet, hungry, and miserable, this is not fun! It seems that the worst part of the storm has passed over us. The swells are down to eight to ten feet, still big but not near as big as they were in the middle of the Gulfstream when we saw the freighter. The rain has stopped and the wind has died somewhat, thank you Lord. It's beginning to get light and we're about halfway down the length of Bimini. I didn't know Bimini was that long of an island. I can see the red lights on the radio tower on south Bimini. I know that I'm in the right place going the right way. I am convinced in my mind that if I had to, I could swim ashore, not die, and somehow find my way back to the United States to see my daughter. I must be insane.

It's starting to get light now, I've been at the helm for about two hours, and I am at the point of total exhaustion. I haven't had a catnap of any kind, I've had nothing to eat, and I'm still feeling queasy and seasick. I am somehow barely able to keep from throwing up. Joan and Pat are awake, I can hear them talking downstairs. In a few minutes, they came up into the cockpit, they're eating a sandwich, and drinking a cup of coffee. They seemed to be in a pretty good mood especially since they'd slept a couple of hours.

Joan took the helm and said: "Do you want to go downstairs and try to sleep?"

I said: "I'll try but I don't know if I can."

Pat said: "Do you want some coffee?"

I said: "Yes, please."

She went below and came back in a minute with a fresh cup of coffee for me. I tried to drink it but it just didn't want to go down. I forced about half of the coffee down and threw the rest of it overboard. I sat in the cockpit and tried to relax now that I didn't have the helm. I went downstairs to see if I could sleep. 'Taterhead and Jimmy were in the aft stateroom sleeping like babies. I laid down on the floor of the main salon but the diesel fumes from the engine were so bad, I felt myself getting sick again so I went back upstairs into the cockpit. It's about 7:00 AM and we're at the southern end of Bimini, the water is considerably calmer, the swells are down to about five feet.

I asked Joan: "Where are we going?"

She said: "You see those islands in front of us?"

I said: "Yeah, I see the lighthouse too. Is that Gun Cay lighthouse?"

She said: "Yep, that's Gun Cay, that's where we're going."

The sky was getting lighter as the sunrise approached and I could barely see the blinking light on the lighthouse.

I asked: "How long do you think it's gonna take us to get there?"

She said: "Oh, we've got about two more hours."

I thought to myself: "That's great! I've got to be seasick for two more hours."

I sat on one side of the cockpit, Pat on the other, with Joan at the helm. I sort of half-reclined and closed my eyes trying hard not to throw-up again. As we got near the southern tip of Bimini, we could see the concrete ship at about 10 o'clock off our port bow. It is a big, concrete ship about 300-400 feet long that was sunk there on purpose during World War II and was used for practice bombing runs to train our pilots. It's been blown all to hell, got big holes all over it, and hardly resembles a ship at all now. As we passed the concrete ship, Gun Cay was coming into better view. On the northern tip of Gun is a beautiful horseshoe-shaped anchorage named Honeymoon Harbor. It is a very safe and famous anchorage for yachtsmen in the Bimini/Cat Cay area. We can see the water on the Bahamian Bank now and it is flat calm. The water is about ten to fourteen feet deep on the back side of Gun and I can't wait to get there into the calm water.

Joan said: "I can't believe it. There are no boats in Honeymoon Harbor, in fact, there are no boats at all at Gun, that's unusual. Every time I've been over here, there've always been one or two boats in Honeymoon Harbor."

We didn't know it at the time but there were a couple of places where we could have picked our way through the rocks and gotten into the shallow water of the Bahamian Bank. But, Jerry had told us to go through Gun Cay Cut and that's what we were gonna do. The Cut is directly under the pink lighthouse on the southern end of Gun Cay. It is a treacherous looking Cut the first time you see it. It appears to be about a twenty to thirty foot high bluff of wicked looking volcanic, lave rock. You wanted to be careful when you were coming through the Cut that you didn't get blown into the bluffs of Gun, it would destroy your boat. The southern end of the Cut is the northern tip of Cat Cay, and it is one beautiful island. Cat Cay is a private island that is owned by Rockwell International and the Rockwell family. There are numerous gorgeous homes on Cat Cay that belong to millionaire friends of the Rockwells. The northern tip of Cat Cay is a stunning, white sandy beach, not at all intimidating like the bluffs of Gun Cay.

The storm of the night before has blown through, it's cleared up, and we saw a beautiful orange sunrise. By 9:00 AM, we're about halfway down the length of Gun Cay and we've only got a couple of hundred yards more before we have to navigate the Cut.

Joan said: "You'd better go wake up 'Taterhead because he's gotta take the boat through the Cut. I don't know how, I've never done it before."

I go downstairs into the master stateroom in the rear, wake him up, tell him that we're at Gun, and that we're about ready to go through the Cut. We both return to the cockpit and he takes the helm from Joan.

I asked 'Taterhead: "You've done this before, huh?"

He said: "Oh yeah man, too many times, I've lost count. Don't worry, it's a piece of cake, a piece of cake."

I said: "Yeah, but you never took a sailboat through the Cut, have you?"

He said: "No, I never took a sailboat through the Cut but it's the same thing, no big deal. You take one boat through here, you can take any boat through here, you just gotta know how to do it."

I grabbed the Bahamian Guide to take a quick cram course in navigating Gun Cay Cut and to double-check 'Taterhead to make sure he knows what he's doing. After I quickly read the instructions, it looks like he's doing exactly what the guide recommends you do for a safe passage, I feel better. As we approach the southern tip of Gun, we're about twenty to thirty yards from the bluffs, they're off our port side to the left. Okay, here we go!

'Taterhead makes a left hand turn to port, keeps Cathy about twenty to thirty yards away from the bluffs, and brings the boat safely through the Cut and into the calm water. Wow, what a rush and what a relief! We motor about halfway down the island, 'Taterhead turns the boat into the wind facing the island, and Jimmy and I go on the bow to drop the anchor. 'Taterhead brings the boat in to about thirty yards from shore, we drop the anchor, and we fall back about ten yards, and then tie off the anchor line. We're here and I'm not seasick anymore. **So this is Gun Cay! Wow!!**

Chapter 6
5 East of the Light
Getting loaded for the first time.

It's a postcard, I'm looking at a picture postcard. Gun Cay is a long, low island with scrub brush, a little bit of elevation but not much. On the southern tip is the pink lighthouse with a small pink house for the lighthouse keeper. On the northern tip is Honeymoon Harbor, a beautiful horseshoe shaped, unspoiled anchorage with pristine white powder sand. It's about 9:00 AM and we are the only boat there. The adrenaline has stopped flowing and we are starting to get tired but we all feel pretty good.

Joan said: "Where do you think the other boats are?"

Nobody answered.

She said: "Oh shit, you don't think everybody got loaded last night except us and we've missed the trip. I'll bet we're not gonna get loaded."

We all get bummed out. I think: "Don't tell me I went through all that shit last night and I'm not gonna make any money. I'm gonna be pissed if we missed the fuckin' trip."

"Taterhead said: "Nah, we're not supposed to get loaded until tonight. We didn't miss it." We all realize he's right and we breath a sigh of relief. We wonder where the other boats are?

We sit in the cockpit and enjoy the view and the beautiful weather. We talk for a while and everybody asks each other if they're okay. We all decide: "Yea, I'm okay. Even though it was rough as a bitch last night, I'm okay now."

We decide that we're going to clean up a little bit, wash our face and brush our teeth and then we'll get some breakfast. The guys relent and let the girls go first so Pat and Joan disappear downstairs into the head. In a few minutes, it's our turn and what a difference it makes. Pat and Joan get in the galley and heat up some soup, make sandwiches, and coffee. We wolf down this feast in the cockpit and slowly start to relax. We begin to speculate on whether a boat or a plane will come and give us some word or we'll just have to wait until tonight to find out.

It hasn't been long since we finished breakfast and everyone is getting sleepy. We see a boat coming across the Bahamian Bank from south to north and it's throwing up a big wake.

Jimmy said: "Hey look, is that the Smith? I bet you that's the Smith. It's coming this way. Looka there, here it comes. It's coming this way." The Smith he is referring to is Joe Pegg's middle boat, the one he uses to offload from the freighters. Smith boats are custom made wooden boats that Joe likes. Almost all the other offloaders use 53 foot Hatteras Sportfishermen. The big aft deck of a Sportfisherman is ideal for loading marijuana. We all watch intently as the boat comes across the Bank and as it gets closer, we can see that it is indeed a Sportfisherman.

I said: "What if this is the Bahamian Police?"

'Taterhead said: "Ah, no, no, no. No Bahamian Police out here. There ain't no heat on the Bank. We're safe as long as we're on the Bank. Don't worry about it."

The boat is headed right directly at us and when it gets within about a hundred yards of us, it begins to slow down. About another fifty yards and it slows down to a dead idle. Now the wind is blowing over the land and east toward the bank so our bow is pointed at Gun Cay and our stern is pointed at the Bank. The boat pulls up to within ten feet of us and stops, the captain reverses the engines, and the boat starts turning around in it's own length. The captain is Pegleg! It's our guys. Pegleg looks pretty rough. He's got on a pair of cutoff blue jeans, no shirt, and boat shoes. He's drinking Jack Daniels out of the bottle at 10:00 AM. When the Smith's transom is facing our transom, Joe starts backing up slowly and the distance between our boats closes to about 3 feet. Low and behold, standing there on the stern of the boat is none other than Jerry Smith. Pegleg eases his boat closer to about a foot and Jerry steps from the transom of the Smith to the aft deck of Cathy V. 'Taterhead and I grab Jerry's arms and pull him aboard. Jerry comes over to each one of us individually and gives us a hug. He goes over to Joan and gives her a hug and a big kiss.

Jerry said: "Boy, we were really worried about you guys."

Joan said: "Yeah, we were really worried about us too. That was a hell of a storm last night."

Jerry said: "Yeah I know, we were in it. We loaded from the freighter in that storm."

Joan said: "No shit?!"

Jerry said: "Yeah, look at the starboard side of Joe's boat."

We looked at the right side of Joe's boat and the railing was completely gone. Every cleat on the right side was torn out of the wood and there were big holes in the deck where the cleats had been.

Jerry said: "Man, we were trying to load and the storm came right through. The freighter would go up and we'd go down and the lines would go "ping" and pull those cleats right out of the deck of the boat. They'd go flying through the air and I kept thinking that if they hit somebody in the head, it would kill 'em."

Joan said: "You mean you guys are loaded right now?"

He said: "Yeah, we're loaded right now. Everybody's loaded right now. All the middle boats are loaded. You guys are the first scam boat that showed up." Man, we couldn't believe it; we didn't do too bad.

Joan said: "You gotta be kiddin' me. We're the first boat here? How many boats are coming?'

Jerry said: "There's 12 scam boats and 3 middle boats to load 'em."

It took us 15 hours to get there and we were the first boat that made it. We didn't do bad at all!

Jerry said: "Is everything okay? Is everybody okay?"

Joan said: "Yeah we're okay, we're just really glad to see you."

Jimmy said: "You guys got any food we can eat? All we got is sandwich stuff and canned stuff. You got any steaks or anything?"

Jerry said: "We've got a freezer full of steaks. We'll give you some." So he hollers over to Joe's boat to one of the guys who opens the door to the Main Salon. We can see the bales of pot stacked solid to the ceiling. This guy crawls on top of the bales and disappears into the galley of their boat. In a minute he comes out onto the aft deck and throws us 5 steaks for supper that night.

Jerry said: "Okay look, we gotta go man. We gotta go back out onto the bank and get away from here so that if the heat flies around Gun, they won't see us. We'll see you guys tonight. We're gonna load you at 5 East of the Light. When it gets dark, we'll come into 5 East and we'll anchor. We'll call you on the radio and you can come out to us and get loaded.

I said: "How will you know when you're 5 East of the Light?"

He said: "We'll use our radar. Each circle on the radar screen is 5 miles. So, we can come into the first circle from Gun and that's 5 East."

I said: "Oh, that's pretty cool."

Jerry said: "Yeah radar is great. We couldn't do this without radar." Jerry hollers to Joe and he backs up the Smith to the transom of Cathy V. Jerry steps off our boat and onto the transom of the Smith. Joe gives his boat some throttle and they take off about half speed on a heading for Russell Beacon near Chub Cay. Chub is at the southern end of the chain of the Berry Islands.

It is a perfect day, temperature in the 80's and just enough wind to keep us cool. The water is flat calm. All day long, we sleep a little bit, clean up a little more, rest and relax. Around midday, the other scam boats begin to straggle into Gun Cay. We watch them come out of the north from the Bimini area, navigate the cut, come up by us in the middle of the island, and anchor. Everybody waves on both boats as they go by us and we give them big smiles. By mid-afternoon, there are 12 boats anchored at Gun Cay.

After we'd eaten and Jerry and Pegleg had left, we all went downstairs and took a quick shower to wash off the salt and the grime, and we brushed our teeth. That and a full stomach of food makes you feel fantastic. It was calm and I lay down in the aft stateroom and slept for 4-5 hours. It was some of the best sleep I've ever had.

Around 4:00 in the afternoon, we pulled out a little Hibachi grill, set it up on the aft deck, lit a fire, and began to grill those steaks. Man did they smell good! The girls opened a can of kernel corn and heated it up. We ate steak, corn, a piece of white bread, and a cold drink in the cockpit. We were all hungry from the salt air and the food was delicious. The water was just like glass as the wind laid down late afternoon. There was nary a ripple in the water; we looked over the side of the boat and could see our reflection in the water like a mirror. We saw a huge, magnificent sunset over Gun Cay that simply melted into the gulfstream like orange sherbet ice cream. This had to be an omen that everything would go well tonight.

After we'd eaten, cleaned up our trash, and stowed the Hibachi, it was beginning to get dark. It was time to tape down the inside of the boat. You have to prepare the boat to get loaded by using masking tape and painter's drop cloths. We put masking tape over all the cracks in the floor and the walls. We put a drop cloth down on the floor of the main salon and hung drop cloths on the walls. We taped the drop cloths together and tried to seal the inside of the boat. The residue from the bales is unbelievable and so is the waste. Bales get broken open in the loading process and pounds and pounds fall out on the floor. After we get loaded and we clean up the main salon, we throw the drop cloths, the pot, and any other trash in the Gulfstream as we're coming home.

Right at dusk, we see a boat coming across the Bank and we know that it's Pegleg. He is coming right at us at Gun and he comes in real close, closer than 5 miles it looks like to me. There are 2 other boats behind Joe; one is heading for Sylvia Beacon about 14 miles away and the other is going to the Concrete Ship. Joe anchors facing east and has his aft deck facing us at Gun. The boats are not even pulling on their anchor lines it is so calm. Joe turns on his spreader lights and lights up his boat like a Christmas Tree. With the naked eye, we can see people walking on the aft deck going in and out of the main salon. We use CB radios when we're on the Bank because too many people monitor their VHF radio. We've got our ears on, good buddy, and we're monitoring Channel 5.

Just then the radio crackles: "Mr. Boo, Mr. Boo, Pegleg, Pegleg; you got your ears on good buddy, kickit' back."

"Pegleg, Pegleg, Mr. Boo, Mr. Boo, that's a roger, kickit' back."

"Why don't you come on over and get on my port side."

"Roger that, I'll be there in a short-short."

We saw a guy go up on the front of a Chris Craft motor yacht and begin to pull their hook. When the anchor was up and stowed, the Chris Craft motored at dead idle over to Joe's boat and tied up to the port side. Joe called another boat and they cruise over and tie up to his starboard side. We can see a guy in the door of the main salon handing big bales to two guys on the aft deck. Each guy loads one of the boats on each side of them. The process continues back and forth, back and forth, until the 2 boats are loaded. As soon as the loading began, we grabbed our binoculars and watched; we could see the loading plain as day. They were close.

When they got through loading those 2 boats, it must have been around 10:00 PM.

We hear a voice from across the water: "Hey 'Taterhead, come on over." They didn't even call us on the radio; they just hollered to us over the water. Jimmy and I went up on the bow pulpit and pulled the anchor. 'Taterhead took the helm and drove the boat. We cruised over to Pegleg at half speed, about 3 knots, and were there in 5 minutes. We tied off to their starboard side, our port side. Another boat came over and tied up to Joe's port side.

I worked the cockpit, Joan worked the hatch, and Pat worked the main salon. 'Taterhead worked the forward cabin and Jimmy worked the master stateroom in the rear. Jerry loaded us himself on the middle boat. He would get a bale from the main salon, put it on his shoulder, and walk across the aft deck to Cathy V. He would hand the bale to me and put it on my thighs as I was sitting on the side of the cockpit. I would push the bale to Joan in the hatch who would push it down the stairs to Pat. Pat would drag it across the salon of the sailboat to 'Taterhead in the forward cabin and he would pack the bales in tight. Jerry would give me another bale and I would give it to Jimmy who was standing in the hatch to the master stateroom in the rear of the boat. Jimmy would disappear with the bale and pack them in tight in the rear stateroom. The process continued until we were packed to the gills in the fore and aft staterooms. We put nothing in the main salon, the galley, or the head and we ended up with about 5,500 pounds, almost 3 tons. It took about an hour to complete the task.

We didn't want to load the Columbia with anymore than about 6000 pounds because it would sit too low in the water and attract the attention of the heat in the port or the river. We had raised the water line about 6 inches so that when we were loaded, the boat would sit just right in the water with the added weight. The water line would be sitting just above the water level and it would look good sitting in the water. Also, we could leave the curtains open to the main salon, the galley, and the head. Then, if the heat rode past us in the port, they could look into the boat and see that the inside was empty. The water line would look good so hopefully they would think that the boat wasn't loaded. A 41 foot sailboat that is open in the main salon, galley, and head doesn't look like it can hold 3 tons of pot and that was the idea. That was the scam.

Once the loading was complete, we untied from the Smith, motored back over to Gun, and anchored in close to the island, about 50 yards offshore. We were hungry so we made sandwiches and got a cold drink. We sat in the cockpit, ate our snack, looked at the stars and talked about what just happened. I have never in my life seen so many stars in the sky. With no pollution and no lights from a city, there were literally billions of tiny stars between the big stars in the sky. I didn't know there were that many stars in the heavens. Some of the middle boats were still loading the scam boats and we could hear them talking on channel 5 on the CB. We decided to clean up a little by taking bucket baths. One by one, we accomplished this in the head. We were still pretty excited but the adrenaline had stopped flowing and we were getting tired.

We decided that we would sleep until daybreak and then leave for the Florida Coast so that we'd be at Port Everglades by middle of the afternoon. Joan, Pat and 'Taterhead went downstairs to sleep and Jimmy and I slept in the cockpit under the stars. The difference in the weather from one night to the other was day and night. The weather this night could not have been better and the weather last night could not have been worse. We came to learn that that's the way the weather was in the Devil's Triangle.

Around 5:00 AM, Joan woke up and got up all the rest of us. Jimmy and I went forward to the bow pulpit and pulled the anchor. 'Taterhead was at the helm and it was just beginning to get light. Morning had broken! He took the boat through Gun Cay Cut, out into the deep blue water of the gulfstream, and put us on a heading of 300 degrees to Port Everglades. On the heading to Ft. Lauderdale, you are going with the wind and the gulfstream so the trip home should take about 8-9 hours. By this time it's about 6:30 in the morning and Bimini is coming up on our starboard bow; we're about 10 miles offshore. Some of the Sportfishing boats are coming out of the Bimini Big Game Fishing Club and begin trolling the shelf for marlin, sailfish, and other sport fish. You can almost see a line in the water where the shallow green water turns into the deep blue water of the gulfstream. That's where the big game fish cruise looking for a smaller fish to fill their bellies. That's why the Sportfishermen troll right along that shelf.

The sun has risen right behind us over Bimini and it is a huge orange ball that floats right out of the water and into the sky. By 9:00 AM, we've lost sight of Bimini and we're making pretty good time. We spot a boat that's coming towards us at about 11 o'clock to our bow. It looks like it has a flashing light on the front of it. It looks like the flashing light on a policeboat. I was in the cockpit with Pat and 'Taterhead was at the helm. Joan and Jimmy were downstairs asleep. The boat was bearing down on us with a flashing light on the bow, it must be the heat. I went below and woke up Joan.

I said: "Joan, wake up! We think there's a police boat coming towards us. It's the heat."

She jumped up and said: "Oh shit. Everybody get their ID and get ready to throw them overboard."

We all got our ID's out of our duffle bags and put them in our pockets. If we saw for sure that it was the heat, we were gonna throw our ID's overboard. We all get in the cockpit and we're watching intently as this boat comes straight at us. As it gets closer, we can see that it's a power boat about 25 feet long and it has 2 guys in it.

Joan said: " Well, I'm the Captain, I'll take the wheel." She takes the helm from 'Taterhead.

As the boat gets closer to us, we realize that it's not a police boat. The flashing light we think we're seeing is the sun bouncing off the windshield. These 2 guys are well dressed and they look like they've been up all night long at a disco or a club. They're windblown all to hell. They make a big circle and pull up alongside us on our port side about 10 feet away.

The driver hollers: "Hey, we don't have a compass. Which way is Bimini?"

We all look at each other like "you've got to be shittin' me". What can we tell them: go down to the second stop light and turn right! How do you give people directions in the middle of the ocean if they don't have a compass? You can't see Bimini and you can't see Gun Cay either. There's no land anywhere that you can see to use as a point of reference. There's nothing but water, water everywhere.

I pointed right at the sun and said: "You just head straight towards the sun and you'll run right into it."

The driver hollers: "Thanks a lot!" He throws up his hand and waves, pushes the throttles forward, and they blast off toward Bimini. We all just look at each other and crack up laughing.

'Taterhead said: "Them guys are nuts! They're insane!"

I said: "Right. Like we're sane, we're okay; but they're nuts?" We all just cracked up laughing again.

After this little scare, we decide that we'd better get the boat cleaned up because there's pot and burlap residue all over the port side of the boat and in the cockpit. 'Taterhead, Jimmy and I got a bucket and a brush and started throwing buckets of water on the deck. We've got a rope tied on the handle of the bucket. You throw the bucket in the ocean, get a full bucket of water, haul the bucket up with the rope, and throw the water on the deck. Then, you take the brush and shove the water and residue towards the back of the boat and into the ocean. You continue this process until the boat is clean. Then, we got a bucket of soapy water and a hand brush to clean the soot off the transom from the diesel motor. I laid on my stomach and leaned over the transom, 'Taterhead and Jimmy held my legs so I wouldn't fall in the water, and I cleaned the soot off with the brush and the soapy water. Next, we got a bucket of fresh water and sponges and cleaned the salt off the cabin and the windows. When we're coming into the port, we want the boat to look clean like we've just been daysailing off Ft. Lauderdale Beach. We don't want the boat to look like it's just made a long, hard journey and get the attention of the Grouper Troopers.

After we get the boat cleaned up and standing tall, we put up the mainsail and the working jib and we continue motorsailing on our course to Florida. About middle of the day, we're out in the middle of the Gulfstream and we see this huge ship coming south towards us that is gonna pass very close to us. As it gets closer, we recognize it as a big, grey, U.S. Naval Battleship, it's got big guns on it. We think: "Oh oh, I hope they're not looking for drug smugglers or we're dead." The ship passes off our bow heading south for Miami or the Windward Passage maybe.

It isn't long and we sight land, it looks like the condos on the Florida Coast. Land Ho! Everybody gets real excited. We start looking for the smokestacks at the Electric Plant at Port Everglades. We grab the binoculars and scan the horizon. There they are, right in front of the bow of the boat on the heading we're traveling of 300 degrees. Now we can steer the boat by sight to the smokestacks instead of having to use the compass. It's a lot easier sailing by sight toward an object than it is to have to concentrate on the compass.

We've got our CB radio on to Channel 5 and we're listening to our channel boat talking to the other boats. Rita is in a 21 foot Boston Whaler Revenge acting as our channel boat. She's watching for the heat in the port, at the mouth of the cut, and in the ocean. If there's no heat around, the code is 10-10, green light, come on home. If there's heat, the code is 10-99, red light, stay out until the heat leaves and you get a 10-10. We can hear some of the other boats calling Rita and she's giving them a 10-10; there's no heat. We've got our sailing clothes on, sunvisors, and sunglasses. Our lines are coiled, the boat is clean, and we're looking good. We're looking like real sailors. Our sails are up and filled, the boat is heeled over, and we're making good time. We're all fired up now; this is it. We decide that it's time to call Rita and let her know we're coming home. Rita's CB handle is "Little Lady" and we're "Speedy Pete"

Joan grabs the microphone for the CB: "Little Lady, Little Lady, this is Speedy Pete. You got your ears on good buddy. Kickit' back."

"Speedy Pete, this is Little Lady, what's your 20?" Rita wants to know where we are, she wants to know our location.

Joan said: "We're about an hour and a half from the intersection, come back."

Rita said: "Roger that Speedy Pete. You've got a big 10-10 good buddy, it's clean and green." We all breathe a big sigh of relief. No heat around right now; of course this could change in the next hour and a half.

We figure we're about 10 miles from the mouth of Port Everglades. We can see the condos and the smokestacks real clearly now. It's a beautiful March Saturday afternoon and there are boats everywhere. There are literally hundreds of boats off Ft. Lauderdale Beach. We just start grinning because we'll blend in with the other boaters. We put the smokestacks at about 11 o'clock to our bow so that we'll come in a little north of the Port. What we want to do is sail south parallel to the beach and look like we're coming from the north into the Port. We actually came into the Sunrise Boulevard area, we came about, and we starting sailing south down the beach about 500 yards offshore. There are boats all around us everywhere.

We notice that there is a powerboat coming at us from the south with a guy standing on the front of it. As it gets closer, we can see that it is Rita in our channel boat with Jerry Smith standing on the bow holding onto a rope that is tied to the cleat. They circle around and pull up alongside us.

Jerry said: "Hey, you guys look like you know what you're doing." We all smile big smiles. "Man, everything's cool, there's no problems, we'll see you at the house." That makes us feel really good. We know that Jerry is doing everything he can possibly do to keep us safe. He and Rita head back to the mouth of the Port.

We sail on down the beach, go thru the Cut with our sails up, we're dead downwind so we go wing-n-wing with the mainsail and jib. We get into the Port and Joan turns the boat into the wind, the sails luff, and 'Taterhead and I drop the jib. Jimmy is there with a sailbag and stuffs the jib into the sailbag. 'Taterhead and I jump up on the cabin and drop the mainsail, roll it up on the boom, tie it off, and put a canvas cover over it. We pull the jib sheets through the blocks, roll them up, and stow them with the jib in the main salon. We're shipshape! Joan circles around for a couple of minutes until 17th Street Bridge opens. It is on a timer and opens automatically every 20 minutes.

Joan takes the boat through the bridge among about 50 other boats, power and sail. There's a policeboat right in front of the Gulf Docks, a Broward Sheriff's Office (BSO) boat, just sitting there not looking at anything in particular. We motor past the Gulf Docks, go to the left of the island, make a left hand turn, and head west up the New River. Rita has come up behind us in the channel boat and as soon as we turn up the River, she passes us and gets right in front of us. There is another man with her now, not Jerry. She leads us all the way through town, all the way up the River damn near to the end it seems to a house off Riverland Road. Linda is living in this house now and this is where Jerry unloads Cathy V. We pull up to the dock, tie the boat off, get our duffle bags, lock the doors and the hatch with a padlock, and everybody gets off the boat onto the dock.

It felt like the dock was moving, like I was still on the sailboat. But did I feel good! Rita had tied up her boat and gotten onto the dock too. She introduced us to the man with her "Jim".

She said: "Well, how did it go? How was your first trip?"

I said: " It was rough crossing over but it was calm coming home."

She said: "Well, you know that's the way it goes sometimes." We were all ready to get the hell out of there and go home and I guess Rita could tell. "There's a car in the driveway. We'll drive you up to Riverland Shopping Center and you can get a cab home. Jerry will call you later on about unloading." She and Jim drove us to the Shopping Center, we called a cab, and went home. What a relief!! What an adventure!!

Chapter 7
Unloading, Fu, and a Quarter
I want to run a middle boat.

When we got home and got to see Sunshine, it was one of the happiest moments of my life. We had a short talk with the babysitter who told us that Sunny was the perfect child and that everything had gone very well, she'd had no problems. We paid the babysitter, she left, and the three of us had a reunion of sorts.

I drew up a bathtub full of water and got in it with Sunny. It was really weird because I didn't have my land legs yet and the bathtub seemed to be moving like the sailboat. I swear there were waves in the tub with us. I bathed myself and Sunny and tried to adjust to being on land again, but I was still rocking back and forth like I was on the boat. I told Pat about my experience in the bathtub and when Sunny and I got out, she decided to take a shower instead of a bath.

We cooked a good meal for supper, ate, and I went to sleep around 6:00 because I had to unload Cathy V that night. I woke up around 10:00 PM and put some dark clothes on to unload in. I had some newer blue jeans that weren't faded and an old, black "Police" t-shirt that I'd gotten at a Police rock concert. I figured that was appropriate attire for the evening's work.

I drove over to Riverland Shopping Center and met Steve and 2 other guys around 11:00 PM. I left my car in the parking lot and we all went in their car to Linda's house. We went inside and began to set the house and the boat up for unloading. The master bedroom had a sliding glass door to the backyard which we were gonna use for entrance to the house. We would walk from the boat, across the yard, through the master bedroom, into the kitchen and laundry room, and into the garage. We had to move a few pieces of furniture and we put a drop cloth down on the carpet in the bedroom. Steve took one of the other guys and they went out to the sailboat to set it up. What they would do was unload bales from each cabin evenly into the main salon. You had to unload each cabin evenly or the boat would sit funny while you were unloading. They were able to unload about half of each cabin into the main salon in preparation for us to begin the unloading process.

When Steve and the other guy were finished, they came back into the house. By now it was around midnight. The neighbor directly across the canal from us had a spotlight that was on above a door to the rear of their house. It lit up Linda's backyard and thus was not conducive for our activities. We called Jerry on the telephone and told him about the light. He said that our neighbors had a teen-age daughter who had a 1:00 AM curfew, and that as soon as she came home from her date, she would turn the light off and it would be cool to unload.

Sure enough, about 2 minutes to 1:00, we could see the lights from a car coming down the street. The young lady comes home from her date right at 1:00 AM, gets a goodnight kiss at the backdoor, goes inside the house, and turns off the light. DARKNESS.

Steve and one of the guys go out to the sailboat. The other guy is gonna work the main salon, hand the bales to Steve in the cockpit, and he will hand them over the side of the boat to me and the other guy. We'll put the bales on our shoulder, walk through the yard, go into the house through the sliding glass doors, walk through the kitchen and laundry room into the garage, and stack the bales in the garage. We proceed to go through this process over and over again until all the bales were off the boat and in the garage. Most of the bales were between 40 and 50 pounds, and for a little guy like me, this was bust-ass work. We ended up with about 120 bales in the garage.

As soon as we had all the bales inside, we gave Jerry a call to let him know that this phase of the unloading was finished. This was the most dangerous part, walking through the yard with bales on your shoulder. Once this was done and all the bales were in the house, we could relax and breathe a little easier.

Now we had to weigh the bales and make a list for the dealer. We had a big balance scale that we used for this. We would weigh each bale, number each bale with a magic marker, and make a list putting the weight with each number. This took us until around 8:00 AM. When the weighing was complete, we loaded up the van, and called Jerry and told him we were ready to deliver the van. Jerry said that Steve would drive the first van and that he should take a quick shower and change clothes. You couldn't deliver a van to a public place covered in pot and burlap residue. Steve quickly showered and changed clothes. Jerry called right back and told Steve to take the van to Riverland Shopping Center, lock it up, and go inside the Floridian Restaurant. Sitting at a table eating breakfast would be our dealer "Fu" and his drivers. Jerry told me to shower and change clothes because I would be delivering the next van. Steve departed and was gone about 15-20 minutes. He returned with another van almost identical to the first one. We opened the garage door when he drove up and he backed the van into the garage. We loaded up the second van and luckily got all the remaining bales in the van. We didn't want to have to deliver a third van if we could help it.

We were ready to go so I called Jerry: "What am I supposed to do? Who do I give it to?"

Jerry said: "Drive the van up to Riverland, park it, lock it up, and go inside the restaurant. There'll be some guys sitting at a table eating breakfast. You'll know who they are and they'll know who you are. There'll be a little bitty weird guy named "Fu", he's our dealer. He's got long hair in a pony tail and a scraggly beard. Give him the keys. You can eat breakfast if you want and he'll drive you back to Linda's house when you're done."

I said: "That sounds great."

He said: "Okay, after you eat and get back to Linda's, tell Steve that they can go home. Clean up the house as best you can and Linda will get the rest of it. Call me as you're leaving the house so I can call Linda and tell her she can go home. I'll call you later today. Pat has got to get some help to clean up Cathy V this afternoon."

We hung up and I drove the van to Riverland Shopping Center, parked it, locked it, and went in the restaurant. Sure enough, there were 4 young guys sitting at a table and there was Fu, he was hard to miss. I walked over to their table, sat down, and casually handed him the keys to the van. He took them from me and handed them to one of the other guys. That guy got up and left, got in the van, and drove to Fu's warehouse to unload the pot.

Fu said: "Is everything okay?"

I said: "Yep, everything's fine."

He said: "Is that it? Is there any more?"

I said: "Nope, that's it. We got it all in 2 vans."

He said: "Good. You wanna eat breakfast?"

I said: "Nah, I'm ready to go home."

He said. "Okay, let's go." We all got up, Fu went to the cash register and paid for everyone's breakfast, and we left the restaurant.

Outside, Fu pointed to a small pickup truck and said: "Go sit in my truck and I'll be right there." He gave me the keys to his truck, I walked over to the truck and got in the passenger side. At my feet on the floorboard was a tennis bag. Fu was dressed in a tennis outfit so I assumed he was going to play some tennis today. He walked over to a van with his 2 guys, gave them some instructions, and they got in the van and left. He came and got in his truck and I handed him his keys.

He said: "Did you look in the bag?"

I said: "No."

He said: "Go ahead, open it up and take a look." I opened the tennis bag and it was full of bricks of money. My eyes almost bulged out. I'd never seen that much money before.

I said: "How much is that?"

He said: "It's a quarter."

I said: "A quarter? What's a quarter?"

He said: "It's a quarter million dollars! That's Jerry's middle boat fee." I thought to myself: "Holy shit, I want to run a middle boat."

He drove me over to Linda's house, I went in and told Steve we could go home. We called Jerry and told him we were leaving, and we all left in Steve's car. We drove back to Riverland Shopping Center, I got in my car and drove home.

When I got home, I went right to bed because I was exhausted. I slept 'till middle of the afternoon. Pat woke me up about 3:00 PM so I could keep Sunshine while she went to clean Cathy V. She fixed me a sandwich and then left to go to Linda's house. I ate my lunch and then began playing with my daughter.

It wasn't long and the phone rang, it's Jerry: "Well, how did it go?"

I said: "It went great. Everything went real smooth. I was surprised."

He said: "You ready to go again?"

I said: "You're kidding?"

He said: "No, we've got another one in 3 or 4 days so get ready."

I said: "Aw man, I don't know."

He said: "Come on man, there's nothing to it. The first one's always the hardest."

I said: "I wanted to get paid for the first one before I went on another one."

He said: "Well, maybe, maybe not. That all depends on our little buddy but don't worry about it. You'll get it all eventually. When they're out there, we gotta go get'em."

I said: "Well okay, we'll be talkin' at ya'"

When Pat got home from cleaning the boat, I asked: "You wanna go again?'

She asked: "How soon?"

I said: "3 or 4 days."

She said: "Aw man, I've gotta fly. You'll have to go without me unless it gets backed up."

I asked: "So it's okay if I go again without you?"

She said: "Yeah if you want to, it's okay with me. We'll just get the same babysitter."

I said: "You know, I'd really like to get paid for the first one before I go again but Jerry says it might not happen. Oh well, if I gotta go, I gotta go."

That night, I cooked steaks on the grill, we had a great meal, and now all I needed was a good night's sleep. We went to bed that night and made wild, passionate love. I feel asleep a very happy man, slept through the night, and woke up feeling like a new man. I had forgotten all about the problems we'd had on the first trip, the storm, and the seasickness. I was ready to go again. I had forgotten about all the promises I'd made to the Lord about getting on a boat again. All I'd wanted to do was make one trip, make $10,000, put it in the bank, and start looking for a job. Before I knew it, I had made one trip and was committed to do another trip. It seemed so easy to make $10,000 that I wanted to make $20,000. I guess we'd do just one more trip and then I'd start looking for a job.

Chapter 8
Penny, Sandbars & Candy Stripers
Toby and the Coast Guard

One more trip, that's all we were gonna do, one more trip. Jerry was gonna pay me $10,000 this time so that meant we'd have $25,000 after the second trip. Oh boy, what a nest egg! Then, I was gonna get serious about looking for a job. Pat had gone on a three-day trip for Delta and the babysitter was on standby. In a day or two, Jerry called and said it was gonna be a couple of more days before we had to leave. He asked me if we were still gonna go on the trip and I said "yes." That worked out well since Pat would be home from her trip, she would have four days off, and she would get to go too.

Pat got home from her trip, Jerry had called again, and said we were leaving the day after tomorrow which was gonna work out perfect for her. I asked Jerry if there were a better course we could take to Gun Cay so that we wouldn't have to motor directly against the Gulfstream. He suggested that we run down the coast to Miami, keeping close in to shore to stay out of the Gulfstream, to the whistle buoy at Government Cut in Miami. Then, we could take a direct course from Miami to Gun Cay. That way, we'd be crossing the Gulfstream at almost a right angle instead of going almost directly against it. The course from Miami to Gun Cay was 112 degrees so we could just steer a course of 110-115 degrees and be okay. We decided that we would leave around 10:00 AM so that hopefully we would at least have Gun Cay lighthouse in sight by the time it got dark. We would spend the night at Gun, lay over the next day, and get loaded the next night. If the trip got backed up another day, Jerry said he could bring Pat home on the middle boat so she could go out on her next three-day trip for Delta. The downside to that was she wouldn't get paid. One way or the other, we'd work it out.

I'd decided to go on a semi-fast to purge food from my body in hopes of keeping myself from getting seasick if it was rough. I was also gonna take Dramamine before I left the dock, I wasn't taking any chances this time. The weather was supposed to be nice so here's hoping. We got a good nights sleep albeit with much anticipation.

The babysitter arrived around 9:00 AM and we left the house shortly thereafter. We drove over to Linda's house, parked in her driveway, went out back to the boat, and climbed aboard. We met a guy named John who was the captain for this trip, a guy named Steve, and a girl with him. We got our gear squared away downstairs and pushed away from the dock just before 10 o'clock. Everyone was optimistic that we were gonna have a good trip. John was at the helm as we motored down the River through the middle of town to the Intracoastal Waterway. We turned right, went past the Gulf docks, through 17th Street Bridge, out the Cut, and into the ocean. The weather was absolutely gorgeous, it was perfect. There was almost no wind so we decided it would be pointless to put up the sails. We headed due south down Dania Beach in close to shore, past Hollywood Beach, and headed for Miami.

In about three hours, we spotted the whistle buoy at Government Cut so we made a left turn and got on a heading of 110-115 degrees for Gun Cay. We thought that there was a little bit of wind so our captain decided that he wanted to put up the mainsail. Steve and I crawled out of the cockpit, onto the deck, and hauled up the main. As it turned out, there wasn't enough wind to keep the sail full and it just flip-flopped back and forth. After about five minutes of flip-flopping, Steve and I dropped the main with much disgust. We all decided that it was time for lunch. The girls went downstairs into the galley and made sandwiches for us. We enjoyed a leisurely lunch in the shade of the cockpit while listening to our favorite rock-n-roll bands on tape.

After about three hours, the buildings of Miami disappeared behind us and we were once again out in the middle of the Gulfstream. Cathy V was running like a top and the weather remained perfect. Except for having no wind for sailing, it was a great day for boating and the trip thus far was very enjoyable. Steve and I took our turns at the helm and it was easy to keep the boat on course to Gun Cay. John kept checking the horizon with the binoculars in hopes of spotting either Gun Cay lighthouse or the radio tower on south Bimini. As the sun began to sink low in the west, we finally spotted the radio tower on the southern tip of Bimini at about 11 o'clock off our port bow. We knew then that we were on a good course for Gun and that we would spot the lighthouse soon. By then, it was around 8:00 PM and that big orange sun was beginning to melt into the ocean. John gave the girls a turn at the helm with instructions to keep the radio tower off the port bow until we spotted Gun Cay light. John and I pulled out the hibachi on the aft deck, lit a fire, and cooked steaks. Steve went down into the galley and heated up some vegetables on the portable propane burner. Just as it was getting dark, we were able to consume our feast in the cockpit along with a bottle of red wine. It was good food, good friends, good music, good times!

As we approached Gun Cay Cut just before midnight, John took the wheel and skillfully navigated the boat through the Cut and into shallow water. He took Cathy about 100 yards past the lighthouse, turned her into the wind, and Steve and I went on the bow pulpit and dropped the anchor. We let out a good bit of rope and tied it off. It was so calm that Cathy V hardly pulled on the anchor line at all.

As soon as Cathy had settled into her anchorage and we felt sure that she wasn't gonna drag her anchor, we folded the bimini top forward to the windshield, got a beer, sat in the cockpit, and looked at the stars. Steve produced a joint and we all shared in the product from the last trip. We took turns cleaning up a bit, washing our faces, brushing our teeth, and getting ready for bed. Steve and his lady retired to the aft stateroom while John, Pat, and I slept in the cockpit under the stars. I fell asleep with a silent prayer of thanks for the good weather because I hadn't gotten seasick.

We woke up early the next morning with the sunrise and Pat and I went into the galley and made a pot of coffee with the propane burner. While we were enjoying our brew in the cockpit, John informed us that Jerry was gonna load his boats at Sylvia Beacon instead of 5 east of the light. Pegleg was gonna load his boats at 10 miles east of the light and Jerry wanted to load us away from them. Jerry and Joe had decided that we were being a little too obvious in our loading procedures at 5 east of the light, especially if there were other pleasure boats at Gun Cay that weren't a part of our organization.

They had decided to move our rendezvous points a little further away from Gun Cay so we could be more discrete in our activities. As soon as it would get dark, the scam boats at Gun would motor out to 10 miles east of the light, the load boat would find them on the radar, and come to load them there. If there were pleasure boats at Gun, they wouldn't be able to see us load from ten miles away with binoculars or with the naked eye. Sylvia Beacon was fourteen miles from Gun so we'd be even further from Gun than the boats at 10 east. It was my impression that this was Jerry's influence on Joe. Jerry was very serious about smuggling, making money, and about our safety. I liked that a lot.

What John wanted to do was to motor over to Sylvia Beacon and have brunch when we got there. Then, he wanted to spend the afternoon sailing around in the vicinity of Sylvia Beacon and end up back there by sunset. We would eat, tape down, and wait for Jerry to come load us. We finished our coffee, John started the engine, and I went on the bow pulpit to pull the hook. As soon as I got the anchor up, John put us on a course of 112 degrees to Sylvia Beacon. At six knots, it was gonna take us about two and a half hours to go fourteen miles to Sylvia Beacon. Steve woke up when he heard the engine start and stuck his head out the hatch to the aft stateroom.

Steve said: "Hey, what's going on? Where are we going?"

John said: "We're going to my girlfriend's house."

Steve said: "Your girlfriend's house? Where's that?"

John said: "Sylvia Beacon."

Steve said: "Do you need my help?"

John said: "Nah, we've got it under control. Go back to sleep if you want."

Steve's head disappeared through the hatch. We motored about an hour on our course and I got the binoculars, went to the bow pulpit, and looked for Sylvia Beacon. I saw nothing but water, water everywhere. We motored another thirty minutes and I looked again. This time I thought I saw the mast of a sailboat. I looked again in fifteen minutes and there she was, Sylvia Beacon, at about 12:30 to our bow, and sure enough, there was a sailboat near Sylvia. In another thirty minutes, we arrived at Sylvia Beacon and anchored about fifty yards away from the other sailboat. We recognized the sailboat as a 37 foot Irwin center cockpit that belonged to a scammer who went by the handle of "Tin Man." The Tin Man had some weird disease that kept him from going on trips anymore. His girlfriend, Penny, ran the boat for him with an all-female crew.

Everyone was hungry and we decided to have bacon and eggs for brunch. Pat and the other lady went into the galley and began to cook. The smell of bacon wafting through the hatch made us all hungrier than we already were. In a minute, Pat stuck her head out of the hatch and said that she couldn't find any salt and pepper. She suggested that we call Penny on the radio and ask if we could borrow some from them.

I grabbed the CB microphone and said: "Tin Man, Tin Man, Speedy Pete, you got your ears on good buddy?"

There was silence for about thirty seconds and I was beginning to wonder if Penny had her radio on this early in the day. Finally, this pretty female voice responded.

She said: "Speedy Pete, this is the Tin Man; I've got a copy on you."

I told her we were cooking breakfast and asked if we could borrow some S&P.

She said: "Let me check, I'll be right back." There was silence for about a minute then she said: "Speedy Pete, that's a roger, we have a spare, we'll bring it over to you."

I said: "Tin Man, we'd be glad to come and get it."

She said: "Negative, we need to take a ride to cool off, you sit tight, we'll be right over."

I said: "Roger that Tin Man and thanks."

As we watched, the Irwin's motor started, a lady went on the bow of their boat, and began to pull their hook. Once the anchor was up, the Irwin made a wide circle, came in behind us, and pulled up close to about five feet on our starboard side slowly at a dead idle. Penny was at the helm, one lady was on the port catwalk outside the cockpit, and the other lady was still on the bow. They were wearing their bikini bottoms but all three of them were topless! As soon as their cockpit was opposite ours, the lady on the catwalk threw us the salt & pepper shakers underhanded. Steve made a great catch, we all waved to them, and they motored off back toward Sylvia Beacon. We wondered if they were going to load at Sylvia that night or if they were going somewhere else.

Bacon and eggs were ready and we ate with gusto. When we finished with brunch and the trash was stowed away, John announced that he wanted to do some sailing. It was hot and muggy and there was a nice breeze, good for sailing. Steve went up to the bow pulpit and began to pull the hook. I began to take the canvas cover off the mainsail. When the anchor was up and tied off, John turned the bow of the boat into the wind. Steve joined me at the foot of the mast and we hauled up the mainsail. We took the jib out of its sail bag, attached it to the rigging, and ran the sheets down each side of the boat to the winches on each side of the cockpit. Then, Steve and I hauled up the jib, tied it off, went into the cockpit, and pulled the sheets tight trimming the jib. John turned the boat off the wind, the sails filled with wind, and we began to pick up speed. John killed the engine, we were sailing, and it was quiet for a change. Nice! Now this is what boating is all about. We were zipping along about 7-7 ½ knots which was pretty fast for Cathy V. We were on no particular heading, we were just trying to sail the boat as fast as we could for our pleasure. It was a gorgeous day, the sky was deep blue, and there were big, white fluffy clouds that looked like they were painted on a canvas. After about an hour, I asked John to let me take the helm and he agreed reluctantly. I sailed the boat for about an hour and then Steve took a turn at the helm. The girls were on the aft deck in their bathing suits getting a suntan, not topless! The guys enjoyed a cold beer and then Steve produced a joint which we all shared. We listened to rock-n-roll tapes and enjoyed a pleasant, relaxed afternoon. After about three hours on this heading into the wind, it was time to head back toward Sylvia Beacon.

John took the wheel from Steve and said: "Prepare to come about!"

This means "wake up, we're about to change course, don't let the boom hit you in the head, and get ready to trim the sheets." John turned the bow into the wind and then kept turning until the wind "backed the jib" which brought the bow around even more. Steve and I trimmed the jib sheets and the jib filled with wind. We were now sailing downwind on a reach. We were only making about 5-5 ½ knots going downwind, it was a more lazy sail than the exhilarating sail going into the wind. We sailed on back to Sylvia Beacon and arrived around 6:00 PM. John turned the boat into the wind and Steve and I dropped the jib first and then the mainsail. While I folded up the mainsail onto the boom and put the sail cover on, Steve dropped the hook and then stuffed the jib back into its sail bag. We got the boat shipshape so we could eat and prepare to get loaded. It was as the cliché' goes "Just another shitty day in paradise."

Steve and I got the portable propane burner and duct taped it to the aft deck because he wanted to cook cube steak for us. He began to fry the cube steak while the girls opened up some canned vegetables in the galley. When the cube steak was about half done, Steve poured a can of Cream of Mushroom soup over the meat and let it simmer a few more minutes. When the steak was done, we set it aside and heated up the vegetables the girls had prepared. It was a great boat meal, easy, quick, and very tasty. When we were finished eating, the girls cleaned up the galley and we stowed the trash. We then got the drop cloths and began to tape down the main salon. We were almost done as the sun was going down so we all got into the cockpit to watch the sunset. The sun turned the white, fluffy clouds into orange sherbet and red colors and we knew we would have good weather for tomorrow: "Red sky in morning, sailors take warning. Red sky at night, sailors delight." As soon as the sun melted into the ocean, we all looked for the green flash but didn't see it. We went back downstairs and finished getting the main salon taped down. We had the radio on channel five and the boat was ready. We changed into our old jeans and t-shirts to load in and now we were ready.

We knew that Jerry and the other middle boats were probably headed for the freighter right at this moment, if it was out there. It would be about three to four hours before Jerry could load from the freighter and get to us at Sylvia Beacon, so, we had a little while to wait. We lay in the cockpit, looked at the stars, and snoozed. We listened to the static on the radio and we waited and waited. Every now and then, we'd see a shooting star and get excited. Someone would say: "Oh, I wish we'd get loaded tonight." It was a beautiful night, there was no wind, and the water was flat calm, not even a ripple in it. Cathy was hardly pulling on the anchor line. We could see Penny's Irwin and another sailboat too, a 44 foot Columbia aft cockpit that had arrived at Sylvia just before dark. I guess that this was Jerry's party for the night.

Shortly after midnight, the radio crackled and it was Jerry: "Speedy Pete, Speedy Pete, you got your ears on good buddy? This is Black Fin." We got excited!

John grabbed the microphone and said: "Black Fin, Black Fin, this is Speedy Pete. We copy, you comin' our way?"

Jerry said: "Sure am, good buddy. Turn your porch light on, I'm coming over and we're gonna party. I went downstairs and turned on our mast light. "I gotcha Speedy Pete, I'll see you in a short-short."

John said: "Roger that!"

John took charge and started giving orders. He told me to get on the bow of the boat and Steve to get on the stern. We got our lines out of the lockers and went to our positions to wait for the Hatteras. We're all looking east out into the darkness awaiting Jerry's arrival. We waited for about fifteen minutes which seemed like an eternity. Then, we heard this sound coming out of the darkness that sounded like a locomotive or a tornado, it sounded like it was gonna run right over us. It's going "whooooooo, whoooo, whooooo, whooooo." It's the sound of those big 12v71 TI Detroit Diesel engines on the Hatteras. We're all wondering if Jerry can see us or if he's gonna run all over us.

John grabbed the microphone and said: "Black Fin, Black Fin, Speedy Pete, you got a copy on me?"

Jerry said: "10-4."

John said: "Can you see us?"

Jerry said: "That's a big 10-4. I got you on my camera (his radar) and I can see your porch light. I'll be there in about two or three minutes."

John said: "That's a big 10-4, we're ready to party."

In about two minutes, out of the darkness came this 53-foot Hatteras with no lights on. All we could see was the shape of the hull coming out of the darkness, it was far out! The boat was sitting real low in the water; Jerry must be loaded to the gills. Those big diesels were straining hard to haul that load. Jerry brought his starboard side up to our port side and eased his bow into our bow. Somebody standing on his bow threw me a line; I caught it, and tied it off. Jerry reversed his gears and brought his aft deck in toward our stern. Somebody on his aft deck threw Steve a line and told him to hold it, not to tie it off yet. Jerry hollered to me to untie my line which I did. Jerry then eased his boat forward until his aft deck was even with our cockpit. He hollered to us to tie them off now and we did. Then, he told us to put a spring line on the boats just in case. It was calm and we probably didn't need it but we did it anyway for safety. Jerry shut his engines down, came down off the flybridge, hopped on Cathy, and greeted us all. We're all real excited and pumped up with adrenaline.

Jerry said: "You all ready?"

We said: "Yeah!"

Jerry looked through the hatch to see if we're taped down properly.

He said: "That looks good. Let's get this done."

John worked the cockpit, I worked the aft stateroom, and Steve worked the forward cabin. Pat worked the hatch and the other girl worked the main salon. The guys on the Hatteras had a fireman's line going on the aft deck. One guy worked the door, one guy was in the middle of the deck, and another guy was at the side of the boat. The guy in the door would hand a bale to the guy in the middle who would hand the bale to the guy at the side of the boat. He would hand the bale over the railing to John who would hand it to me in the aft hatch. I would take it through the hatch and pack it in the aft stateroom. The next bale John got would go to Pat in the hatch and she would push it through the hatch into the main salon. The other girl would drag it across the salon to Steve in the front who would pack it into the forward cabin. The guys who were working on the load boat were all big strong guys and they were pumped up on adrenaline. They were throwing those bales at John fast and furious and we were all bustin' our butts but we couldn't keep up with them. We finally had to tell them to slow down a little. But you have to remember that the name of the game for the middle boat is to get all your scam boats loaded by sunup. It they didn't get rid of all their pot by sunup, they had to lay over 'till the next night or finish loading in broad daylight which was a no-no. So they were busting their butts to get rid of all their pot so they wouldn't have to lay over and Jerry needed to go home to arrange for delivery of the pot to Fu.

We finished loading around 2:00 AM and we were packed to the gills. Jerry was happy because things were going well for his load boat. He had already loaded Mr. Boo's Chris Craft motor yacht at Russell Beacon near Chub Cay. Now, all he had to do was load the Tin Man and the 44-foot Columbia sailboat that were right here at Sylvia Beacon. He would be able to load them and be done long before dawn. Jerry started his engines, we untied the lines, the big Hatteras pulled away slowly behind us to avoid our anchor line, and went to load the Tin Man.

As soon as Jerry had pulled away, we all got a cold drink, and got into the cockpit to take a breather. We were hot, sweaty, dirty, and covered in pot and burlap residue. There were a number of bales that were busted open and the pot was ankle deep on the deck and in the cockpit. After we'd finished our drinks and cooled off a little bit, we started scooping up the pot with our hands and putting it inside a trash can bag. We were probably able to save three to four pounds of pot by scooping it up. Then, we got a bucket of water, some sponges and paper towels, and began cleaning up the rest of the residue in the cockpit. As soon as we'd done this, we got the cushions from where we'd stowed them in the main salon, and put them back in the cockpit. We took a broom and swept off the deck and got it clean. Then, we all took a quick "bucket bath" and put on clean clothes. It was getting near 3:00 AM and we decided to pull the hook and get on the road to Gun Cay.

Steve and I went up on the bow pulpit, pulled the anchor up, and tied it off. John pointed the bow at Gun Cay light which was a course of 292 degrees, the reciprocal of 112. We could see the glow of Cat Cay Yacht Club at about 11 o'clock to the bow and we could easily see the red lights of the radio tower on south Bimini at about 2 o'clock to the bow. John was able to steer the course to Gun Cay light visually without staring at the compass by keeping Cat Cay Yacht Club at 11 o'clock until we could see Gun Cay lighthouse. We were famished from loading so the girls went into the galley and fixed sandwiches for everyone. We got another cold drink and enjoyed our snack in the cockpit under the stars. We wanted to go through Gun Cay Cut at first light, get on our course of 300 degrees to Ft. Lauderdale, and be coming into Port Everglades around middle to late afternoon.

It wasn't long after we'd left Sylvia Beacon that we sighted Gun Cay light and John kept the bow of the boat pointed directly at the light. The girls had gone into the main salon to sleep and Steve and I lay on each side of the cockpit taking a catnap while John ran the boat. It was gradually beginning to get light as we were approaching Gun Cay Cut. John was having trouble staying awake but nevertheless, he took Cathy V through the Cut and put her on a course of 300 degrees to Ft. Lauderdale. I took the helm; John layed down in the cockpit, closed his eyes, and immediately fell asleep. The sunrise was peeping through the water over our right shoulder, it was calm, there was a little bit of wind and nary a cloud in the sky. There was no "red sky in morning" since there were no clouds in the sky, no reason to be alarmed, so it looked like we'd have good weather for the trip home. Steve was restless so he decided to get a bucket to throw water on the deck to clean off the residue from the loading. He proceeded with this task for about the next thirty minutes and he got the deck good and clean. The girls had awakened from their nap; they made a pot of coffee, and brought a cup to everyone. Steve and I were getting tired again so John took the helm and we went downstairs into the main salon to try and sleep.

By now, it was around 9:00 AM, the sun was up, and it was hot in the main salon so sleeping was difficult. Between the heat and the diesel fumes from the engine, Steve and I decided that a nap downstairs was out of the question. We went back upstairs into the cockpit and John informed us that we had a nice breeze out of the southeast and he wanted to put up the sails. We thought that we could raise the sails without doing a 180 and turning the boat into the wind and John agreed. Steve and I climbed onto the deck of the main salon and hoisted up the mainsail with no problem. We got the jib out of the main salon and hooked it to the forestay, ran the sheets down the deck on each side of the boat to the cockpit, and hoisted up the jib. We let both the main and the jib out a little to starboard and the sails filled nicely with the wind. As long as the wind didn't turn too much, we could sail a reach all the way into Ft. Lauderdale. That's what we did.

It was a very uneventful crossing and an easy trip home. The weather was great, the Gulfstream was calm, Cathy V ran like a top, and everything went smoothly. Around 2:00 PM we spotted the condos on the beach. We grabbed the binoculars and quickly found the smokestacks at the power plant at Port Everglades. We were dead-on the port, what a good feeling. We ran for about another hour and could hear Rita in the channel boat talking to the other scam boats on the radio as they came into the Cut.

I grabbed the CB microphone and said: "Little Lady, Little Lady, Speedy Pete, Speedy Pete, you got a copy on me? Kickit' back."

She said: "Hey Speedy Pete, this is Little Lady, I read you loud and clear. What's your 20?"

I said: "We're about an hour and a half from the intersection, come back."

She said: "Roger that. You've got a big 10-10 good buddy. It's clean and green."

I said: "Roger that. We'll see you in a short-short."

This is great, nobody's having problems, everybody's getting a green light, and it's almost too good to be true. We decide to come straight into the port instead of going north and sailing south down the beach. As we approached the mouth of the Cut, we saw Rita cruising around near the whistle buoy in her Boston Whaler Revenge, no Jerry this time. We are among hundreds of boats off Ft. Lauderdale Beach and Dania Beach. We're all smiles, what great cover for us.

We got up to the Cut and motor sailed down the Cut with our sails still up into Port Everglades. John turned the boat into the wind, the sails luff, and Steve and I drop the jib. We climb on the deck of the main salon and drop the mainsail. We roll the main up inside itself on the boom, tie it off, and put the canvas sail cover on it. We then go back to the jib, detach it from the forestay, and stuff it in its sail bag. We took the jib sheets and stowed them in the forward locker.

Just about then, the bells on 17th Street Bridge start ringing, the auto traffic is stopped, and the bridge begins to open. There are boats everywhere; there must be at least fifty boats in the Port going every which-a-way. There's about ten sailboats as well as that many Sportfishermen waiting for the bridge to open with all kinds of power boats running among the sailboats and Sportfishermen. As soon as the bridge is opened completely, we fall into line to take our turn going through the bridge. Rita has come into the Port in the channel boat and she gets in front of us. We motor through the bridge and get abreast of the Gulf docks. Pat, Steve, and I are sitting on the front of the deck of the main salon. A Boston Whaler pulls up alongside us on our starboard side, the man and woman are friends of ours, and they recognize Pat and me.

He hollers: "Hey! Howya doing man? You been sailing?" We shake our heads up and down. He said: "Good to see ya'. Let's get together."

We wave back at them and they smile back at us. I wonder if they can tell we are sitting low in the water or if our waterline looks good to them considering we are sitting on 5,500 pounds of pot. They keep looking our way like they want to continue the conversation. I hope that the boat doesn't look bad and they've noticed it.

I hollered back at them: "Yeah man, we'll call you, we'll call you."

He waved back at us, pushed his throttles forward, and took off north up the Intracoastal Waterway toward Bahia Mar Marina & Resort.

We are just beginning to breathe a little easier as we get further away from the Gulf docks. Rita turns around and heads south back towards the Port, she gives us a little wave as she goes by. We are coming up on the island where you turn left and start up New River to go through the middle of town. We are supposed to bear left at the island and stay in the middle of the channel because the water is deeper there. No one noticed that it was low tide but it wouldn't have been a problem if we had stayed to the left in the channel. But John must have been daydreaming because he went to the right at the island instead of bearing left. Pat and I immediately noticed that this wasn't the right way to go.

I turned around, faced the cockpit, and hollered: "John, what in the hell are you doing? You're supposed to go left."

He kinda shook his head, came back to reality and said: "Oh, I went the wrong way. That's okay, we'll go around the back side of the island, it won't matter."

I said: "John, you need to turn around and go back around the left side of the island."

He didn't say anything but kept going straight. We got up to the end of the island and were just starting to turn left when we ran hard aground and the boat came to a complete stop. Steve, Pat, and I are thrown forward and Steve almost goes overboard over the bow pulpit. The forestay hits him in the shoulder and his legs hit the bow pulpit. As his body is going over the bow pulpit, he grabs the forestay with both hands, and somehow keeps himself from going into the water. Pat and I are thrown on our hands and knees on the deck and we skid to a stop just behind the bow pulpit.

Pat and I seem to be okay and I ask Steve: "Are you okay?"

He said: "Yeah, but my shoulder hurts, it may be dislocated."

The three of us climb into the cockpit and just glare at John. He puts the gear into reverse and gives it full throttle. He turns the wheel to the left and then to the right but we are going nowhere, all we're doing is kicking up a lot of mud. John put the gear in forward, turns the wheel hard right, and gives it full throttle. The bow of the boat lifts up a little bit but we aren't going forward. John puts the gear in reverse again and gives it full throttle but all we do is kick up more mud. I decide to call Rita.

I said: "Little Lady, Speedy Pete, you got a copy?"

She said: "Speedy Pete, Little Lady, I copy."

I said: "Little Lady, we've got a problem. We've run aground right by the island, come back."

She said: "Okay, I'm coming back to help."

Two guys in a center console boat stop and ask us if we want them to tow us off. Jerry had told us not to let anybody tow us if we ran aground, especially if we were loaded, because it could crack the keel and cause the hull to leak. Then, the boat would have to go in the yard and get hauled out of the water and we'd probably miss some trips. What we should do is just wait for the tide to rise and float us off. So, we told the guys that we didn't want a tow but they could drive around us and make waves. Maybe with the boat rocking from the waves, it would be enough for us to back the boat off the sandbar. So the guys started driving around us making waves. John put the gear in reverse and gave it full throttle but all we did was kick up more mud. We are stuck!

Just then, we heard the motors of a helicopter coming from the north and saw a Coast Guard helicopter heading our way. Because of the Coast Guards' orange logo on their boats and aircraft, they are affectionately known as Candy Stripers. The 'copter is flying south down the Intracoastal Waterway from the Bahia Mar area. It flies right over to us and hovers low over our starboard side for about a minute. We can see the pilot looking out at us from the windshield of the 'copter. After what seemed like an eternity, the 'copter flew off and continued south towards the Port. By now, the asspucker factor was at the extreme.

Right about then, Rita showed up in the channel boat and pulled up along our starboard side. I told Rita to make circles around our boat making waves and we'll try to back off the sandbar. Rita begins circling our boat; John puts the gear in reverse, gives it full throttle, and tries to back us off the sandbar. We keep this up for a couple of minutes but all we're doing is kicking up mud. About that time, a Broward Sheriff's Office (BSO) boat shows up with an officer named Toby who Jerry knows and says is an okay guy. Toby eased his boat up to the rear of Cathy.

He hollered: "Hey, throw me a line and I'll try to pull you off."

Steve went onto the aft deck and threw Toby a line that he tied off to a cleat on the rear of his boat. He gave his boat full throttle and began to churn up water. John had our boat in reverse at full throttle and we're both churning up a lot of mud and water. Rita is driving around us making waves but we can't get off the sandbar. About that time, the Candy Stripers' helicopter returned and hovered over us watching this whole scene which is pretty wild at this point since we're loaded. After a couple of minutes of this, Toby pulled his throttles back into neutral and untied our line from his cleat. John pulled the throttle back on Cathy and put the gear into neutral.

Toby hollered: "I don't think I'm gonna be able to pull you off. You're gonna have to wait for high tide."

He put his boat into gear and headed off towards the Gulf docks. The helicopter also left and headed south towards the Port.

Rita pulled back up along our starboard side and I told her I'm going to throw her a line from our bow and that I want her to try to turn our boat 180 degrees so that it's facing south. Then, I want her to try to pull us off with our boat facing south. I went up on the bow, got a line, and tossed it to Rita who tied it off to a cleat on her stern. She then headed her boat east toward the middle of the Intracoastal Waterway and gave it full throttle. Cathy V slowly started to turn to starboard and as she does, Rita began to steer her boat south. Slowly but surely, Cathy comes around until our bow is facing south back toward the Port. John put her in gear and gave her full throttle. Rita was giving her Whaler full throttle and we're churning up a lot of water and mud. For about ten seconds, nothing happened. We're all thinking "come on baby, come on baby" and then we felt the boat move a couple of inches in the mud and stop.

I said: "Let's all go up on the bow pulpit and see if we can get our weight forward to raise the stern of the boat enough to get us off."

So, the four of us jumped out of the cockpit and ran up to the bow pulpit. Steve and I sat on the pulpit, held onto the forestay, and leaned backwards out over the water. The girls were right up against us on the pulpit. In a couple of seconds, we felt the boat move a couple of inches again, then a couple of inches again, then a couple of inches again, and then we broke free and are floating! Thank you Lord!

Rita saw that we were floating, put her boat in neutral, untied our line, and threw it in the water toward us. I pulled the line out of the water, rolled it up on my arm, and threw it on the deck. John went south around the island then went north to New River and took a left. Rita got in front of us, led us through town, and took us all the way to Linda's house. We tied up Cathy fore and aft, put a spring line on, got our duffle bags, and padlocked the doors and hatch. We made it again!

As we walked through the yard and around the side of the house to get in my car, the knot in my stomach began to unwind but I was still very pissed off at John for running aground. I drove to Riverland Shopping Center, dropped off John, Steve, and his lady at the restaurant to call a cab, and Pat and I drove home in silence. We paid the babysitter so she could go home then spent a little quality time with Sunshine. We were thinking what a great trip it had been until the fiasco on the sandbar with Toby and the Candy Striper.

Chapter 9
Green Stamps, Bricks & a NOD
Your first payday, really a mindblower.

We still had to unload Cathy V that night so I needed to get some food and catch a nap before going to Linda's house. I jumped in a hot shower and starting washing off the trip as well as the fear that was left from our encounter with Toby and the Candy Striper. I tell you that was a close call. I was still pissed off about it! I got out of the shower without turning off the water and Pat got in right behind me. I dried off quickly with an eye on Sunshine who was sitting in the middle of our bed playing. The phone rang, I answered and it was Jerry.

He said: "How'd it go?"

I said: "Well, it went okay 'till the end."

He said: "Yeah, I heard what happened." I guess Rita had talked to him and told him about our grounding.

I said: "Are you at a stand-up?" A stand-up is a pay phone. We try not to talk about anything of substance unless we're at a payphone, in case the phone is tapped.

He said: "Yeah."

I said: "It was a real drag man, scary as shit! It scared the hell out of me and Pat. It was a real nice trip until John ran us aground. He was daydreaming and went the wrong way. I told him to turn around but he wouldn't, then we ran aground, almost threw Steve in the water. Then Toby shows up in the BSO boat and then a fucking Coast Guard helicopter shows up and hovers over us watching everything. It was wild! Scary as shit. I'm still pissed! John's got a problem, man. I don't know about him."

Jerry said: "Well look at it this way. The heat was all around you and you didn't get busted. You guys must have looked pretty good to them or they'd have boarded you if they were suspicious. Y'all looked like nice, young professionals out for a daysail, not drug smugglers. That's the scam; it worked." I thought about that for a moment.

I said: "I never thought about it like that. I guess you're right. If we hadn't of looked good, Toby would have boarded us. It was still scary as shit man."

He said: "Y'all did good, man; real good. So, you ready to unload tonight?"

I said: "Yeah man, no problem. I'm meeting Steve and John at 10:30 at Riverland."

He said: "I've got a couple of guys who are gonna help you so you'll have a full crew to unload."

I said: "Good, that'll help."

He said: "Call me when you get everything in the house."

I said: "Okay, we'll talk to you then." We hung up.

Pat and I ate a nice supper, I grabbed a three-hour nap, woke up, put on my dark unloading clothes, and Pat drove me to Riverland Shopping Center. I met John, Steve and 2 other guys, we drove to Linda's house, and went in the side door to the garage which Linda had left unlocked for us. In the garage was a white Chevy Van and behind it was a Styrofoam ice chest filled with various drinks on ice; Coke, Sprite, Dr. Pepper and Gatorade. Next to it was a brown paper bag full of munchie food; candy bars, chips, and cookies. Linda was taking good care of us. We put a drop cloth down on the floor in the master bedroom, checked the backyard and sure enough, the spotlight was on at the neighbor's house across the canal; their teenage daughter must be out on a date. We can't begin to unload until she gets home for her 1:00 AM curfew and she turns the light off. We decided that we'd all catch a catnap until she gets home so we spread out on the beds and the sofas throughout the house.

She comes home from her date right at 1 o'clock, gets a goodnight kiss at the door, goes inside and turns off the light. Once again, DARKNESS. Steve and John have already gone out to Cathy and filled the main salon with bales. We begin the unloading process and get finished around 4:00 AM; having the extra guys helps it go faster and smoother. We call Jerry and tell him we've got all the pot in the house, then begin to weigh each bale, label it with a Magic Marker and make a list of each bale and the weight. When we've finished the weighing, we load the van and are just able to get half the bales inside. For this trip, we ended up hauling about 5,800 pounds. Steve goes to take a shower and change clothes since he'll drive the first van. I then call Jerry and tell him we're ready. He called Fu and then called us back.

He said: "You're going to the IHOP (International House of Pancakes) on State Road 84 and I-95 next to the Ramada Inn, you know the one?"

I said: "Yes, across from the Holiday Inn?"

He said: "Right. Fu will be there with his drivers eating breakfast just like before. Are you going to be able to get it all in 2 vans?"

I said: "Yes, I think so; we got half in the first one."

He said: "Good. Call me when you're done."

I said: "Okay, sure thing."

Steve was finished with his shower and dressed in clean clothes. I told him he was going to the IHOP on State Road 84 and he said "no problem". He left and returned about 20 minutes later in another van identical to the first one. By then, I had showered and had put on my clean clothes, while John and the other 2 guys were loading the 2nd van. I drove it to the IHOP, went inside and sat down at the table with Fu and the boys. I discreetly handed him the keys to the van.

He said: "Is that it?"

I said: "Yep, we're done."

He handed the keys to one of his drivers who got up, walked outside, got in the van and drove off to Fu's warehouse. I ordered breakfast, went outside to the payphone, called Jerry and told him we were done. He said: "Good. I'll call you later." I went back inside, ate heartily, and called Pat to come pick me up. In about 15 minutes, I saw Pat out the window as she drove up, I paid my bill, got in the car and we went home.

That night after we'd had a great supper, we were sitting in our den watching television and a car drives up. We look out the window and see that it's Jerry. I go to the front door to let him in and I'm excited 'cause I'm hoping he's bringing us money. I let him in and brought him back into the den. We started talking about the trip and the sandbar fiasco, I didn't know if he wanted to hear about it, but I told him the whole story in detail. He listened without saying a word.

Then he said: "You know, John's a pretty good guy, maybe he's just not captain's material. I can just let him crew on one of the boats." I didn't say anything.

He paused and said: "So, you ready to go again?"

I said: "Man, you gotta be kiddin' me. Ready to go again? We just got back. We're not gonna go again, are we?"

He said: "Yeah man, we've got another one in two days."

I said: "Man, I ain't even been paid for the first one and you want me to go on a third one?"

He said: "Don't worry about the money, man. I'm good for it. We'll get all our money as soon as Fu gets it from his dealers. Sometimes this happens; you'll have two or three right in a row. When they're out there, we gotta go get 'em. But when we do get paid, you'll feel like you've got all the money in the world."

I said: "Yeah, well I'd like to get paid for the first one before I go on the third one."

He said: "Aw, don't worry about it; you'll get all your money. So, how about it, are you gonna go again?"

I said: "Sure, I'll go again but Pat's not gonna be able to go 'cause she's gotta fly a three-day trip."

He said: "Well, you know, we'll have to make do. You just rest up and get ready 'cause we got one in two days and it's there. It ain't gonna get backed up."

I said: "Holy Moses!"

Jerry left shortly, Pat and I put Sunny to bed and we climbed into bed ourselves. I couldn't believe it; all I wanted to do was do one trip, make $10,000, then quit and look for a job. Now, I'd done two trips and was committed to do a third, and I hadn't gotten paid yet for the first one. I was beginning to wonder if I'd ever see green money. I fell asleep thinking about having $40,000 after the next trip. I think I was getting hooked!

The next morning, Jerry called and said: "Come on over to room 128 at the Ramada Inn on State Road 84 tonight at 7 o'clock."

I said: "Okay, see you tonight."

Pat and I spent a nice day together at home, swimming in the pool, playing with Sunshine, relaxing and having a good time. Pat had to go out on her trip the next day so we called the babysitter and made arrangements for her to come early in the morning. We ate an early supper and when we were finished, I drove over to the Ramada Inn, went up to room 128, knocked on the door and when it opened, I went inside.

The room was full of people, Jerry and Joan were there with Linda and Rita and all the people I'd worked the trips with along with some people I didn't know. In a couple of minutes some more people got there and once they'd arrived, Jerry asked for our attention. He said that he'd had a long meeting with Pegleg and that they had come up with some ways that they thought would make our operation better. Joe was impressed and pleased with the channel boat and the job that Rita was doing in spotting the Police boats. He said that all the scammers felt real good that Rita was watching out for them and keeping them informed of the whereabouts of the heat. They had decided that we actually needed two channel boats, one inside and one outside. Rita would continue to work the outside; the Port, the Cut, and up and down the beach. He introduced a guy named Gary who would work the inside; the Port, the Intracoastal Waterway north of 17th Street Bridge, and the New River. That way, if anyone had a mechanical problem and needed to be towed to the dock, Gary could give them the tow and get them safely to the house. Rita would be able to stay at her position and call the other boats in.

Jerry said that he had an old friend who was a pilot, who owned his own airplane and was going to fly surveillance for us. The day after we got loaded and were coming home, he was going to fly a circular route from Ft. Lauderdale to Gun Cay, to Miami to Pompano to look for Coast Guard Cutters and Grouper Troopers in the ocean. If he spotted a Cutter or a Grouper Trooper, he would call Rita and the scam boats so that we could change course and take evasive action if necessary. He would continue this route until all the scam boats were in the Port.

Jerry said that he and Joe were gonna buy a condominium at Point of America Condos, which was right at the mouth of the Cut on the beach. They were gonna set up a retired couple to live in the condo and it would be our base station for surveillance. The condo would have a VHF radio, a CB radio, a portable airplane radio, and a police scanner that the retired couple would use to coordinate our surveillance. They could communicate with Rita and Gary in the channel boats, the scam boats, and the airplane if necessary. Jerry knew the people at the electronics firm in Ft. Lauderdale that set up all the radios for the police. He was going to get us a police scanner with the secret police crystals so we could listen to them talk on the secret police channels. This would be especially helpful to us when we were unloading. If the police were watching one of our houses and were staging a bust, we could hear them talking during their staging, our people could stop unloading and leave the house so they wouldn't get busted. If the heat didn't bust the house by the next day, we could go back that night and finish the unloading. Wow! We were getting really sophisticated. Jerry's idea was that we would watch the cops watch us. These counter surveillance ideas were more Jerry's than Joe's and I felt like he was drawing on his ten years experience as a police officer.

Jerry also said that we were gonna change the frequency that we used when we were loading on the Bahamian Bank. He said there were too many boats using channel 5 so we were gonna load on channel 11. If there were other people using channel 11 that weren't with us, he would say "drop down" which normally meant go down one channel to channel 10. But what he wanted us to do was go UP one channel to channel 12 instead. That way, if the other people were trying to listen to us and they heard him say "drop down", they would go down to channel 10 or below, and hopefully, they wouldn't find us on channel 12. We would still use channel 5 coming home because the channel boats would be calling in all the other scam boats too, not just Jerry's group. So, we would all be on channel 5 coming home.

Jerry had a chart of the Bahamas showing Bimini and Gun Cay all the way east to the Berry Islands. He showed us where the middle boats would try to rendezvous with the freighters, either at the southern tip of the Berry's near Chub Cay or the northern tip of the Berry's near Great Stirrup Cay. He had a chart of Port Everglades, the Intracoastal

Waterway and New River and he used these to show us where the channel boats would be located and what their responsibility was. This gave everyone a better idea of the big picture and would hopefully make the organization more efficient and ultimately keep us from getting busted. It made us feel like Jerry and Joe were doing everything they could possibly do to keep us safe. It made us all feel very good!

Jerry ended the orientation by telling us that we needed to leave tomorrow for the trip. We would get loaded tomorrow night at five miles north of Sylvia Beacon. Jerry told me that I was going with Steve, who was the captain for this trip, and his brother Randy. There were no girls going with us. He said that he would put two of his guys on our boat to help us load. Steve and Randy said they were going to the grocery store to buy the food and drinks for us. They were gonna put the grub on Cathy and then go to bed. I told them I'd see them tomorrow morning at 10 o'clock. We said our goodbyes, the meeting broke up and everyone went home real happy and confidant.

As I was driving home, my head was spinning as I rehashed the meeting in my brain. It hadn't even been a month that I'd worked for Jerry and already I'd done two trips and was about to go on number three. It was beginning to sink in that this was one big-time operation, BIG-TIME. The first trip, there had been three middle boats that hauled 20,000 pounds each, 60,000 pounds total, 30 tons for the trip! The second trip, there had been two middle boats that hauled 40,000 pounds total, 20 tons for the trip! WOW! That's a lot of pot! This is serious bidness, very serious. I knew we were good but I knew we were lucky too, and I hoped our luck would hold.

When I got home, Pat was already asleep so I crawled into bed with her and went to sleep too. The next morning she woke up early to go on her trip. I got up with her and helped her get out the door. The babysitter would be here at 9 o'clock and then I'd be off too.

The babysitter arrived on time the next morning and after a short conversation with her, I drove over to Linda's House. I walked out back, got on the boat and stowed my gear. Steve and Randy were already there with the motor running and we pushed away from the dock shortly before 10 o'clock. We went out New River, into the Port, out the Cut and motored south to Miami. At the whistle buoy at Government Cut in Miami, we took a left and headed east to Gun Cay. It was good weather and we had a nice, easy crossing to Gun. Since we didn't have the girls with us, we decided not to cook on the hibachi. We made sandwiches and ate in the cockpit once we'd spotted Gun Cay light.

We got to Gun around 9:00 PM, went through the Cut, and got on the heading for Sylvia Beacon. We were supposed to load that night so with Steve at the helm, Randy and I taped down the main salon while we were running. We got to Sylvia around 11:30 PM, took a left and ran due north for 45 minutes to five miles north of Sylvia, our loading area. We arrived there around 12:15 AM, dropped the anchor, and made last minute preparations for getting loaded.

Black Fin showed up around 2:00 AM and loaded us to the gills. He put one of his guys on our boat to help us load; he worked the main salon. Steve worked the cockpit, Randy loaded the aft cabin and I loaded the forward cabin. It went smoothly and we were done in about an hour. As soon as Jerry untied and pulled away, Randy and I pulled the anchor and we got on the heading back to Gun. The wind was picking up a little bit and there was a slight chop on the Bank but nothing too serious. Randy and I pulled up the drop cloths in the main salon, stuffed them in trash bags and cleaned up the main salon. Everyone was ravenous from loading so we made sandwiches and enjoyed them and a cold drink in the cockpit. By now, we had Gun Cay light in sight and we headed straight for it. We decided that we would go through the Cut in the dark, we were old hands at it now, and try to get home as fast as we could. We got out our halogen spotlight, lit up the bluffs like broad daylight, and Steve skillfully took Cathy through the Cut and into the Gulfstream.

The wind was blowing rather stiffly out of the north and the seas were about 5-6 feet. Steve was at the helm and Randy and I were on each side of the cockpit trying to get a catnap. We were north of Bimini by the time the sun came up and we decided that we'd put up the sails to see if we could get Cathy to go faster. Steve turned the boat into the wind and Randy and I hoisted the mainsail and then the jib. We got back on our heading of 300 degrees and the boat heeled over to port quite a bit. In fact, water was coming over the railing! We were sailing along about 7 ½ -8 knots which had to be close to hull speed for a 41-foot Columbia sailboat. Looking back, I think we really had up too much sail but we didn't know it at the time. I took the helm and Steve lay down for a nap. Randy had brought a fishing pole to troll while we were going home. He put a spoon lure on the line, dropped it in the water, let out a good bit of line and put it in a rod holder on the aft railing. He then lay down in the cockpit and tried to take a nap too. It wasn't long before we heard the reel going "wheeeeeeeeeee" as it was running out.

Randy screamed: "I've got a fish, I've got a fish." He jumps up and grabs the rod. I put the motor in neutral and the boat slows to 3-4 knots. Randy starts reeling the fish in, gets it up to the back of the boat, and hoists it onto the aft deck. It's a beautiful Bull Dolphin all blue and green in color, it's about a ten-pound fish. He's real excited about it 'cause he says he's gonna have fresh fish to eat tonight. The fish is flopping all over the aft deck and almost flops over the side and back into the water. Randy pulls the fish into the cockpit and now it's flopping violently in the bottom of the cockpit. Steve and I say "Whoa" and pull our feet up under us to get them out of the way. Randy goes into the main salon and returns with an aluminum billy club and whacks the fish in the head a couple of times. The fish stops flopping. Randy takes the spoon out of the fish's mouth and puts the fish on ice in one of the coolers we've got in the main salon.

I start the engine and the boat picks up speed to about 7 1/2 –8 knots again. Randy is all fired up from catching the fish so I give him the helm and I lay down for a nap. We're motor sailing along and we're making really good time, we're all about half asleep when the radio crackles.

"Speedy Pete, Black Fin, you got your ears on good buddy?" We all wake up with a start not expecting to hear from Jerry.

Steve jumped up and went downstairs, grabbed the microphone and said: "Black Fin, this is Speedy Pete, what's your 20?"

Jerry said: "Look behind you, I'm right on your ass!" We looked behind us and were surprised that the big Hatteras was about 25 yards behind us. We couldn't believe it, because of the wind and motor noise, we never heard him coming. "I've got a present for you. Somebody get on the back of the boat. We're gonna throw it to you." I got out of the cockpit and went back on the aft deck. One of Jerry's guys was standing on the bow pulpit with a trash can bag about twice the size of a basketball. Jerry eased the Hatteras up to the rear of Cathy V.

He said: "Just hold your course and keep your speed. I'm gonna come up to you."

He brought the bow pulpit of his boat in to about two feet off the back of our boat. The guy on the bow pulpit throws the package at me, it hits the railing, I try to grab it but miss, and it falls in the water. Jerry slows the Hatteras down, the guy gets a boat hook and fishes the package out of the water. He goes back up to the bow pulpit and Jerry eases in close again. The guy throws again and this time the package hits our aft deck and I grab it.

Jerry said: "You guys look like you've got this sailing thing figured out." We're so tired, we don't say anything. "Okay, I'll see you at home." We open up the package and it's about 20 pounds of pot. We figure that this must have been what they had left over when they cleaned up their boat. Rather than throw away twenty pounds of good Colombian pot, he gave it to us. The middle boats always come in clean with no drugs in case they're boarded and searched. That way the heat can't confiscate the middle boat and the captain won't lose a $250-300,000 investment.

We made it to the Port in about 8 ½ hours, the quickest trip home I'd had thus far. Rita gave us a big 10-10, clean and green and we brought Cathy up the River to Linda's house without incident. We went back that night and unloaded with no problems. I think we hauled about 5,800 pounds this trip. We delivered the vans to Fu at the IHOP and everything went smoothly. I went home and crashed 'till the middle of the afternoon.

The phone rang, I answered and it was Jerry.

He said: "Hey, you wanna come over tonight?"

I said: "Sure, what's up?"

He said: "I've got green stamps!" Green stamps are what we called money.

I said: "Oh boy, great! What time?"

He said: "Oh, why don't you come over about 8:00."

I said: "Okay, great, see you then."

He said: "Look, when you come in the lobby, you'll have to sign in. Don't use your real name, make up an alias."

I told Pat that Jerry had green stamps. We both got excited! We had a nice supper, got through eating and cleaned up the kitchen. We got in our little five-speed Honda Civic, drove down Commercial Boulevard to A1A, went south on A1A to Las Olas Boulevard, turned right on Las Olas and into the parking lot of the Condominiums at One Las Olas Circle. We went in the lobby and walked up to the guard desk.

He said: "Who are you here to see?"

I said: "Mr. & Mrs. Smith."

He said: "Sign in please." I took the guest register and signed "Mr. & Mrs. Ben Dover." We got in the elevator and went up to Jerry's condo. Joan let us in and took us into the living room, there were hugs all around. They fixed drinks for us and we chit-chatted for a few minutes. I was actually a little nervous, I didn't know why.

Finally Jerry said: "Well, come on back here in the bedroom with me." We walked into the spare bedroom. There was a bed and a nightstand but the bed wasn't made. Jerry opened the sliding doors to the closet and pulled out a Samsonite suitcase, the biggest one they make. He threw it on the bed, opened the locks, and folded it open. It was full of money in plastic baggies on both sides of the suitcase. I have never seen this much money before like this. I was speechless! Inside each baggie was money stacked like bricks.

Finally, I said: "How much is this?"

Jerry said: "This is $600,000. Fu just brought it this afternoon." I thought to myself "Holy fucking shit! SIX HUNDRED THOUSAND DOLLARS!"

Jerry said: "Now, how much do I owe you?"

I said: "Well, you owe me five for the first trip and Pat five, so that's ten. For the second trip, you owe Pat five and you said you'd pay me ten. So that's fifteen plus ten is twenty-five for two trips. And for the third trip, you said you'd pay me fifteen and Pat didn't go. You owe me twenty-five plus fifteen, that's $40,000."

He said: "Okay, that sounds good to me." He had a little piece of paper that he made a mark on. "Okay look, each brick is $10,000. It's all twenty's. Each brick has five packs that are a bank count of 100 bills so each pack is $2,000. Five packs of $2,000 is $10,000. You get four bricks, that's $40,000. Understand?"

I said: "Yeah man, I understand."

He put four bricks on the bed, closed up the suitcase and put it back in the closet. He said: "Did you bring a bag?"

I said: "Pat's got a big purse."

He said: "It ain't gonna hold four bricks." He went in the kitchen and came back with a brown paper bag. He put the four bricks into the brown paper bag, we walked back out to the living room and I sat on the couch with Pat and put the bag between us. She looked into the bag and looked up at me.

I said: "That's $40,000." She looked astonished and didn't say anything. I had this shit-eating grin pasted on my face from ear to ear. I felt elated! Finally, PAYDAY!

Jerry said. "How 'bout another drink?"

I said: "Sure, why not." He and Joan fixed us another drink.

He said: "Come on back here in the bedroom with me. I wanna show you something." We went back into the master bedroom. He opened his closet door and pulled out this big black, round, oblong box. He took one end off by screwing it counterclockwise and pulled out what appeared to be a black photographer's lens. We went out on his balcony which overlooked the back of the Holiday Inn on Las Olas Boulevard.

I said: "What is that?"

He said: "It's a NOD."

I said: "What's a NOD?"

He said: "A night optical device, N-O-D, a NOD. You can see in the dark with it. All it needs is a little starlight to work. It magnifies starlight like a thousand times. I use it when I'm loading my scam boats. When I'm close to your boat, like about 50 yards away, I still can't see you in the dark. I look at you through the NOD and see how your bow and stern are oriented. That way, I can pull up to you safely and not damage the boats. I use my radar to find you and the NOD to get tied up to you. Here, take a look. Don't point it directly at a light, it will hurt your eyes. Look over there at a room in the Holiday Inn with no lights on. You can see inside the room in the dark. He handed me the NOD and I looked through it. The view through the NOD had a light green tint to it but you could see really well in the dark, almost like it was daylight.

I said: "This is really cool. I'd like to have one of these on Cathy V. How much does it cost?"

He said: "$5,000. You don't really need 'em on the scamboats but we use them a lot on the middle boats. The other night we were out here playing with it and we saw a couple in a room, they left the curtains open to the sliding glass doors, they didn't think anyone could see them. They got naked and started fucking on the bed. We could see 'em plain as day. Then, they stood up and started fucking standing up and this guy picks this girl up and starts twirling her all around the room. It was wild! Then he throws her on the bed and finishes fucking the shit out of her. We watched the whole thing. Joan got turned on by it so we went inside and Joan fucked my eyes out."

I said: "Lucky you!"

He said: "Listen, when you get home tonight, sit on your bed, take the bricks and count the money. Your first payday, it's a good memory. Smoke a joint and count your money. If you're short, I'll make it up to you. If you're over, keep it. Fu handles so much money, he has a counting machine that he uses to make the bricks. It's probably right on but every now and then, it's a little short like maybe $80 or $100. No big deal. So if you're short, I'll make it up to you." Jerry put the NOD back in its case and we went back in the living room with Pat and Joan. Sunny was getting a little restless and was ready for bed so we said our goodbyes.

Jerry said: "It's gonna be about a week before we have another trip so enjoy your rest and be ready."

We left their condo and went down the elevator to the lobby. I was holding Sunny and Pat had her purse over her shoulder and was holding the brown paper bag full of money. Boy, did we feel conspicuous! We walked through the lobby under the watchful eyes of the security guard, got in our little Honda and headed for home. Pat drove and I held Sunny and had the money at my feet in the floorboard. We locked the doors, we were really paranoid and we didn't say a thing 'till we were halfway home. I told Pat to be careful and not to have a wreck "cause I didn't feel like dealing with a cop with $40,000 in a brown paper bag at my feet."

We got home safely without having a wreck and put Sunny to bed. We went back in our bedroom, sat on the bed, smoked a joint, and counted our money. Pat counted two bricks and I counted two bricks. It was exactly $40,000, not over, not under, right on like

Jerry said. We put the bricks back together, put the money on the shelf in our walk-in closet and got ready for bed. We were giddy! We got into bed and made long, slow, wild passionate love. We fell asleep very happy and content. Life was good! My first payday, truly a day I'll never forget. It was one of the happiest days of my life.

Chapter 10
A Mako, Joulters & the 4th of July
The freighter breaks down and gets busted. Jen is HOT at Joulters.

That first payday was a real mindblower. It took Pat and I a couple of days to get used to the idea that we had a little money in our kitty. It was a tremendous feeling of elation and financial security. We had gone from having $7,200 in our savings account to a little over $45,000 in about five weeks. That was awesome! I didn't want to spend our money, I wanted to save it to have the security. We did buy a few things for the house and we each bought some clothes but I don't think we spent more than $1,000 total. A lot of people would go out and blow most or all of their money, just "piss it away". I was determined not to let that happen to us, I liked the feeling of security too much.

We also had a little lull in the action and we went a couple of weeks without having to go out again on another trip. Spring in South Florida is really nice and the weather had turned absolutely gorgeous. Pat was flying her three-day trips and when she was home, we swam in the pool, went to the beach and the park, and just relaxed and had a good time. Nevertheless, I was itching to go out again and make some more money.

The first week of June, Jerry called and said it was time to go again. Pat was off so she would be able to go. The crew was Steve, Randy, Steve's lady, Pat and me. We were to leave the day after Jerry called. We alerted the babysitter and made the arrangements with her. By now, everyone was use to the routine, especially Sunshine.

We met at the boat the next morning and pushed away from the dock a little before 10 o'clock. The weather was just perfect, we made an easy crossing, arrived at Gun Cay a little after dark, and laid over at Gun because we were a day early. We were supposed to load at five miles north of Sylvia Beacon so that was our destination for tomorrow. The next morning, after a nice breakfast of bacon and eggs, we pulled the anchor and went sailing on the Bahamian Bank. As the sun was sinking low in the west, we sailed to Sylvia Beacon, dropped the anchor, and cooked a steak dinner on the hibachi on the aft deck. After watching a beautiful, orange sherbet sunset, we taped down and prepared to get loaded. We pulled the anchor, motored due north for forty-five minutes, and dropped the anchor there.

We all sat in the cockpit, looked at the stars and talked. After three successful trips, we were feeling like veterans and our conversation exuded confidence. It was the time of year when there were shooting stars about one every minute. We lay in the cockpit with our heads back looking at the plethora of shooting stars. It was an unbelievable night. It got to be midnight, 1:00, 2:00, 3:00 then 4:00 and we hadn't heard anything from Black Fin. The girls had gone down into the main salon to sleep. We were beginning to figure out that we weren't gonna get loaded tonight.

Finally, around 4:30 AM, we got a call that was very faint and it wasn't Black Fin, it was one of the other scam boats out at Russell Beacon. Russell Beacon is 48 ½ miles from Gun Cay and we were 14 miles from Gun so that put us about 34 ½ miles from Russell. We could barely make out who they were and what they were saying to us.

What they were telling us was that we were not gonna have a party tonight. The three guys bedded down in the cockpit for the rest of the night.

The next morning, we were up early with the sunrise, we made a pot of coffee and enjoyed our brew in the cockpit. After coffee, we all jumped in the water to cool off and wake up. As the morning progressed, it got hot and muggy so we put up the Bimini top to shade the cockpit and give us some relief from the heat. There was almost no wind to speak of so we decided to swim again before going sailing. Randy had bought some diving gear so he jumped in with his mask, fins, and snorkel. Steve brought a raft which he blew up and lay on as Randy dove down to the bottom in search of shells. The girls and I took a quick swim and then got out of the water and back on the boat. The girls sat in the shade of the cockpit while I lay in the sun on the aft deck. I could hear Randy diving and then snorting through his snorkel as he surfaced. In a couple of minutes, I heard this noise that sounds like "aarrgg, aarrgg, aarrgg", I turned around just in time to see Randy leap out of the water, grab the back of the boat, and pull himself up onto the aft deck. Steve has his arms and legs pulled up on the raft as this big shadow goes through the water between him and the boat. It's a shark! Randy spits the snorkel out of his mouth and he's real excited.

He said: "Did you see that big, ole' shark? It went right by me when I was down on the bottom. I was screaming "shark" under water."

I said: "Man, I couldn't hear "shark." All I heard was "aarrgg, aarrgg, aarrgg."

Steve paddles his raft over to the boat, he climbs up the ladder, and gets on the aft deck with Randy.

Steve said: "Man, that thing scared the shit out of me. What kind of shark do you think it was?"

Randy said: "I don't know but I've got a fish book, I'll look it up."

He goes below, gets his fish book out of his duffle bag, looks up "Sharks" and decides that it's a Nurse Shark. He tells Steve that Nurse Sharks are vegetarians and they don't eat people. That makes Steve feel a little better but he's still not sure that the shark wouldn't bite him given half a chance.

After we settled down from the shark incident, we decided to eat lunch and then go sailing to keep cool. The girls made sandwiches and we enjoyed them with a cold drink in the shade of the cockpit. Randy and I pulled the anchor then hoisted the mainsail and we went sailing for the rest of the afternoon. There was hardly enough wind to keep the main from flip-flopping so we didn't put up the jib We listened to Jimmy Buffett tapes and other rock-n-roll tapes that we had. Everyone took a turn at the helm, even the girls, while we just tooled around all afternoon. Randy put a line in the water with a spoon lure and trolled in hopes of catching a fish for supper but we didn't get a bite. We ended up back at Sylvia Beacon for the sunset and Steve's famous cube steak.

After we finished supper and we'd stowed the trash, we pulled the anchor and motored back to five miles north of Sylvia. Randy and I did a touch-up on the tape job in the main salon. We got to five miles north and dropped the anchor. The girls went down into the main salon to sleep and the guys catnapped in the cockpit. We sat there all night long without hearing anything. Black Fin didn't show and nobody called us. By 4:30 AM, we knew we weren't gonna get loaded. We then tried to get some serious sleep.

We were up the next morning with the sunrise, we jumped in the water to take a quick swim to wake up. The water was real warm, just like a bathtub. We then cooked scrambled eggs for breakfast and while eating, we realized that we were running low on food. We concluded that we needed to bring enough food for a week in case we had to lay over for a few days like this trip. We pulled the anchor, motored back to Sylvia Beacon, and got on a course to Russell Beacon. We were only about thirty minutes out of Sylvia when the radio crackled. It was Jerry!

He said: "Speedy Pete, Black Fin, you got your ears on good buddy, kickit' back."

I grabbed the CB microphone and said: "Roger that, come back."

He said: "What's your 20?"

I said: "We're about three miles from my girlfriend's house. What's your 20?"

He said: "I'm about ten miles from you, I'll be there in a short-short, I'll talk to you when I get there."

I said: "Roger that."

In about fifteen minutes, we see a boat coming toward us from the east and it isn't long before Jerry pulls the Hatteras up alongside Cathy V. Joan takes the wheel, Jerry steps over to the side of the flybridge, and cups his hands to his mouth.

He said: "The freighter is not gonna show. Go home."

I said: "Okay."

He said: "I'll see you at home, I'll call you tomorrow."

I said: "Fine."

We come about and head back to Sylvia Beacon, then go to Gun, navigate the Cut, get on our heading to Ft. Lauderdale and motor sail home. We come through the Port, go up the River, and by the time we get to Linda's house, it's dark. We get our duffle bags, lock the doors, get off the boat and go home. DRY RUN.

The next day, I talked to Jerry to find out what happened. The first night, they were supposed to rendezvous near Chub Cay at the southern end of the Berry Islands and the freighter didn't show. The next night, they were supposed to rendezvous near Great Stirrup Cay at the northern tip of the Berry Islands and the freighter didn't show the second night either. Joe found out that the freighter called Colombia and got instructions to go north to another group on the East Coast. For some reason, we lost the trip.

Joe had his own pilot, a retired Air Force Colonel that we knew as "the Colonel." He would fly for Joe and find the freighters and then find the middle boats and tell them if the freighter were there or not. As he was flying across the Bahamian Bank back to Florida, he would tell the scam boats if they were going to party tonight or not. If there were no party that night, the scam boats wouldn't have to tape down and stay up all night waiting for the load boats that weren't gonna show anyway.

About a week later, Jerry called and said it's time to go again. Same crew. This time we bought food and drinks for a week. It was good weather and Cathy V ran like a top. We had a nice, easy crossing, and as we approached Gun Cay light, the Colonel flew over and told us we would be having a party tonight. We all got excited! We motored to

Sylvia Beacon, went due north to five miles north of Sylvia, and got loaded that night. Everything went real smooth. We motor sailed home. Jerry's pilot was flying for us now spotting Coast Guard Cutters and Grouper Troopers in the ocean. He would fly over us in the Gulfstream and dip his wings to the right and then to the left to let us know that it was him and that he was watching over us. Rita and Gary were in the channel boats watching out for the heat in the Port and the River. Rita was really doing a great job, she had her shit together. We were becoming a fine-tuned organization. We were professional and proud of it. We were good and we knew we were good. People in other groups were getting busted and we weren't. We must be doing something right.

All the scam boats got home safe. We unloaded Cathy V and delivered the pot to Fu. In a couple of days, Jerry called with green stamps and I had my second payday. Jerry had worked out a deal with Joe that if we had a dry run, everyone would get paid $1,000 for the effort. I also had unloaded another boat and gotten paid $2,500 for that. So, my second payday was $15,000 for me, $10,000 now for Pat, $2,500 for the extra unloading, and $2,000 for the dry run, a total of $29,500. Not too shabby! Our kitty had grown to almost $75,000.

It was the end of June, the phone rang, and it was Jerry. We're gonna do another one, the last one for the year, then we won't work again until September. We were all looking forward to a little vacation, maybe spend some of our money, relax and lay back. The crew was Steve and his lady, Pat and I. Only thing was that Pat had to fly a three-day trip over 4th of July weekend. Pat's best friend Jen had been wanting to go on trips so we called her and she jumped at the chance to make some quick money We were to leave on July 2nd to get loaded on July 3rd. We would be coming home on July 4th weekend so there'd be lots of boats everywhere, not only coming in to Port Everglades but also at Gun Cay and Honeymoon Harbor.

Jerry wanted us to load at Russell Beacon which was 48 ½ miles from Gun Cay on a course of 98 degrees. There had begun to be a little heat activity in the area of Bimini and Gun Cay, we had seen Coast Guard helicopters and airplanes flying around Gun. It looked like they were beginning to fly between Miami, Ft. Lauderdale, Bimini and Gun. Also, the middle boats were having to go further out to meet the freighters and were having trouble loading all the scam boats by sunrise. By loading at Russell Beacon, it would help the middle boats. That made it a long haul for a sailboat that only went 6-7 knots. It was an 11-12 hour trip to Gun and then another 8 hours across the Bahamian Bank to Russell Beacon, a 20-hour trip total.

We left Ft. Lauderdale the morning of July 2nd and had a pretty easy crossing. It was hot as a bugger with very little wind, but we hoisted the main to look good and motored all the way to Gun. After going through the Cut, we anchored about halfway down the island and spent the night at Gun. We awoke with the sunrise, ate some breakfast, and got on our course of 98 degrees to Russell Beacon. Steve and I were concerned that if we were off the least little bit with our navigation, that we'd miss Russell Beacon and wouldn't know 'till we ran into the Berry Islands. We decided to take two hour shifts at the helm because we had to concentrate on navigating with the compass, there were no visual sights to use to navigate. We also wouldn't let Jen or

Steve's lady take a turn at the helm which put a bridge in their nose, so to speak. Steve and I were really concentrating on keeping the boat on our course of 98 degrees.

We motored along for about 6 ½ hours, we didn't even put the mainsail up, and then I grabbed the binoculars and went up to the bow pulpit to look for Russell Beacon. Russell is just a platform with a light on it and we were really concerned that we would be able to find it. I scanned the horizon from 9 o'clock to 3 o'clock and, lo and behold, there it was at about 11 o'clock to our bow looking just like the drawing in the Bahamian Guide. We couldn't believe it! We found it.

As we're approaching Russell Beacon, we can see that there are already two other boats there. One of them was a 26 foot Permacraft that was on my first trip and the other was a 44 foot Columbia aft cockpit sailboat that went by "Apple Pie." He had loaded with us on a couple of trips around Sylvia Beacon, so it looked like this was Jerry's party. When we arrived at Russell, the two boats were about 30 yards apart so we anchored right between the two of them. We were so close that we could all talk to each other from boat to boat in a normal tone of voice. We decided that we would eat supper, tape down, and then raft off and wait for Jerry to call us. When Jerry called us, we would unhook from each other, spread out, and wait to get loaded.

Steve and I pulled out the hibachi and cooked steaks on the aft deck. Jen and Steve's lady fixed some veggies and a salad in the galley. We enjoyed a great meal in the cockpit as the sun set to the west over the Bahamian Bank. There were no islands that we could see and that big orange sun just melted into the water. It wasn't long before Apple Pie motored over and rafted off to my port; the Permacraft followed shortly and rafted off to my starboard. After everybody checked out each other's boat, we sat in the cockpit, talked and looked at the stars. Around 11 o'clock, the Permacraft untied from Cathy and anchored off to my starboard side about thirty yards away. We sat there and anxiously waited for the call from Jerry. Finally, around 3:00 AM, the radio crackles.

Jerry said: "Speedy Pete, Speedy Pete, Black Fin, Black Fin, you got a copy on me good buddy, kickit' back."

I grabbed the CB microphone and said: "Black Fin, Black Fin, Speedy Pete, yeah we got a copy on you, kickit' back."

He said: "Yeah Speedy Pete, Black Fin, we're not gonna be partying tonight, you copy that?"

I said: "That's a big 10-4, we copy, we will not party tonight, what about tomorrow?"

He said: "Don't know right now, we'll be talking to you about lunchtime."

I said: "10-4, we'll talk to you about lunchtime."

We decide that it's time to bed down and do some serious sleeping. Apple Pie and his crew get back onto their sailboat and we stayed rafted off to each other. Steve and his lady went down into the aft stateroom, Jen and I slept in the cockpit. The next morning, Jen and I woke up early and made a pot of coffee. Steve and his lady woke up shortly and we decided to cook breakfast on the aft deck using the portable propane burner. Jen and I whipped up bacon and eggs which we all enjoyed in the cockpit. It's beginning to get really hot and there was no wind to keep us cool. Around 11 o'clock, the radio crackles, it's Black Fin.

He said: "Speedy Pete, Speedy Pete, Black Fin, got your ears on good buddy? Kickit' back."

I said: "Black Fin, Speedy Pete, 10-4, we've got a copy on you, kickit' back."

He said: "We're heading at you and we'll be there in about forty five minutes, you copy that?"

I said: "10-4, we copy, what's up good buddy?"

He said: "I'll talk to you when we get there."

I said: "Roger that."

We figure that this was not good news and that we may have another dry run. Bummer! We sat there and waited, in about thirty minutes we see a boat coming at us, and in about forty five minutes, Jerry pulls up on our starboard side.

He hollered to us: "We're gonna raft off to you for a few minutes."

His guys are putting out bumpers on his port side and getting lines to throw to us. Jerry eases the Hatteras over to Cathy V, his guys throw us the lines, we grab them and tie them off. Everybody on our boat and on Apple Pie's boat gets on the Hatteras and we go into the main salon. Jerry's guys are sitting in the air conditioning, watching "Smoky and the Bandit" on video, and eating ice cream! It's like we died and went to heaven.

I asked Jerry: "What's happening man, are we gonna do it or not?"

He said: "Well, we got problems. The freighter's broke down and we're trying to fly the part to it with a helicopter. It's out in the ocean and it's floating. If we can get the part to it and get it fixed before it gets busted, we'll do it. If it gets busted first, we won't do it. While we're waiting, we might as well enjoy ourselves. We're in one of the prettiest places in the Bahamas."

I said: "What are we gonna do?"

He said: "We're going to Joulters, it's a little deserted island on the northern tip of Andros, about forty five minutes from here. We're gonna get in the water and see if we can shoot some fish or maybe get some lobster for supper tonight. It's a cool place, it used to be an old Pineapple Plantation and there are little shacks on the beach that the slaves lived in that're still there."

He gets on the radio, calls the Permacraft, tells them we are going off for the afternoon, and for them to keep an eye on the sailboats. They don't sound too happy that they're getting left behind. We untie from Cathy, Jen and I climb up onto the flybridge with Jerry, he starts the big Detroit Diesels, and we take a course for Northwest Channel Light. We run for about twenty minutes and I see an island off to our left.

I said: "What's that?"

Jerry said: "That's Chub Cay."

I said: "Why don't we go there?"

He said: "No man, they've got people there. They might have heat there too. We stay away from Chub if we can help it."

I see another island at about 12:30 to the bow. I said: "What's that?"

He said: "That's Joulters, that's where we're going."

He gets on the CB radio and says: "Blue Eyes, Blue Eyes, Black Fin, you got a copy on me good buddy, kickit' back."

In a minute we hear: "Black Fin, Blue Eyes: "Roger that, we copy, kickit' back."

Jerry said: "Blue Eyes, what's your 20, come back."

Blue Eyes said: "We're about ten from you out in the deep water doing some fishing. We're trying to catch us some supper for tonight."

Jerry said: "Roger that. We're gonna go over here in the shallows, maybe go on the beach and have a weenie roast. Why don't you come on over and join the party?"

Blue Eyes said: "Listen, I hear it's real shallow over there, come back?"

Jerry said: "That's a 10-4 but I know a way in where there's no coral and you won't do any damage to your boat, you copy that?"

Blue Eyes said: "10-4, whereabouts are you going in?"

Jerry said: "Down on the eastern end, it's all sand, no coral heads, come back?"

Blue Eyes said: "Maybe we'd better follow you in so we'll know the way."

Jerry said: "That's a big 10-4

Blue Eyes said: "Okay, we're gonna pull our lines in and we'll be over and meet you before you get into the real shallow water."

Black Fin said: "10-4, I'll be there in about 20 minutes."

Blue Eyes said: "Well by the time we get our lines in, we'll be over there about the same time. See you soon, good buddy."

By now, we're getting close to Joulters, we're maybe two miles from the beach, the water is just starting to get shallow, about fourteen feet deep. I grab Jerry's binoculars and take a look. It's a postcard, a white sand beach, coconut palms and about a dozen little wooden shacks. I gave the binoculars to Jen and she takes a look. It's just beautiful, one of the prettiest places I've ever seen in my life. The water is unbelievably clear, a light green color, clear as a swimming pool with a white sandy bottom.

Off to the east is another Sportfisherman that is coming our way, that must be Blue Eyes. Jerry pulls the throttles back, sets the engine speed at 1000 rpm's, and the boat slows to less than half speed. The depth gauge is showing eight feet, there's no grass and no coral heads, just beautiful white sand.

I said: "How shallow does it get in here?"

He said: "Oh, about four feet."

I said: "I thought you drew more than that?"

He said: "I'm supposed to draw four and a half but I've been showing three feet on my depth gauge before, been kicking up sand but haven't been touching the bottom. All it does is clean your props off."

I said: "You sure, huh? You've been in here before?"

He said: "Oh yeah, I've been in here a bunch. This is one of the prettiest places in the whole world. You ain't gonna believe it."

By now, we're about 500 yards off the beach, Blue Eyes has come in behind us, and he's about fifty yards back. Jerry pulls the throttles back all the way and we're easing forward at a dead idle. The depth gauge is showing five feet, then three feet and the alarm goes off on the depth gauge. Jerry pulls the gears straight up into neutral as the boat slides forward, we look behind us and the water is all milky looking from us kicking up sand.

I said: "What's that man?"

He said: "Oh, it's just a shifting sandbar, it's no big deal. Look, we're over it now. Look at the depth gauge, it's back to four feet."

Jerry pushes the gears forward and we continue ahead at dead idle. We turn around and look and Blue Eyes is just coasting over the sandbar too. The depth gauge goes to five feet then six feet, Jerry turns the boat into the wind, and one of the guys drops the anchor. We're about two hundred yards off the beach. Blue Eyes slides up to our starboard side, throws us some lines, we tie him off, and he and Black Fin shut down their engines. All's quiet except for the faint hum of the generators on each boat.

Jen goes below and changes into a two-piece bathing suit. When she comes back into the main salon, all the guys are bug-eyed looking at her awesome body. She is HOT! Jen and I get on Blue Eyes' Hatteras and meet him and the Cookie Monster, his right-hand man. We go inside the main salon, meet the rest of his guys, and check out the layout, a galley-up model. Jerry's Hatteras is a galley-down model which has a larger main salon that is better when you have a boatload of people because you have more room. Blue Eyes' people get on Jerry's Hatteras and check out his galley-down model.

We're anchored within swimming distance to some coral heads in about ten to twelve feet of water. Jerry wants to get in the water and go spearfishing around the coral heads to get us some fish for supper. He, Joan and two of his guys are on the aft deck getting their snorkeling gear and their spear guns together.

Jerry said: "Stay together now because sometimes there's sharks around here."

They all jumped in the water and swam off towards the front of the boat. Jen and I went up on the bow pulpit of the boat to watch. They swam over to these coral heads about thirty to forty yards away and started diving down, coming up and snorting like dolphin blowing the water out of their snorkels. In about ten minutes, we see them swimming as fast as they can back to the boat. Jerry is swimming backwards looking behind them as he swims. Jen and I go to the back of the boat onto the aft deck, Joan is the first one back. I grab one of her arms and pull her through the fish door. The other two guys follow her and pull themselves out of the water. Jerry is last and he leaps out of the water.

I said: "What happened? What's going on?"

Jerry said: "Man, there's a big ole' Mako shark over there. I speared a fish and that Mako came over and took that fish right off of my spear."

I said: "No shit? You sure it was a Mako?"

Jerry said: "Yeah man, I'm sure it was a Mako. They're mean mothers. Man, it's a little bit dangerous over there, don't look like we're gonna have any fish for supper tonight. I'll tell you what, we'll get in the dinghy and go down off the east end of Joulters. There's more coral head down there and some rocks. We might find some lobster. Maybe we can have some lobster tonight."

Joan said: "Well listen, if you're going out in the dinghy, how about taking me over to the beach."

I said: "Hey, that sounds good to me too. I'd like to go to the beach."

The five of us got in the dinghy and puttered off toward the beach. Jen stayed on the Hatteras in the air conditioning and watched the movie with the other guys. Jerry dropped off Joan and me on the beach and headed east toward the coral heads. It's about 4 o'clock and Jerry tells us he'll pick us up around 5 o'clock. It was a little weird standing on the beach because I felt like I was rocking from being on a boat for three days.

I said: "Joan, do you feel like being alone or do you want company?"

She said: "I feel like being alone."

I said: "Good, so do I. Which way do you want to go?"

She said: "I'll go that way" and pointed west.

I said: "Okay, I'll go that way" and pointed east. "I'll meet you back here at 5."

Joan took off walking toward the west and I took off walking toward the east. I decided to do a little exploring so I went up to one of the shacks and checked it out. There was a nice little porch on the front with a primitive wooden hammock that was suspended between two coconut palms. It was cool! I lay on the hammock for a while and listened to the wind blowing through the casuarinas trees. I closed my eyes and took a catnap for about thirty minutes. When I woke up, I walked back down to the beach, went east in ankle deep water and looked for seashells. It wasn't long before I saw Jerry and the guys coming in the dinghy. I did an about face and walked back until I met Joan on the beach. Jerry picked us up and we headed off for the boats. They had gotten three lobsters, enough to make a snack of lobster hors d'ouerves for everyone.

When we got back to the Hatteras, Jerry boiled the lobster, cut them up in small pieces, put them in melted butter, and gave everyone a taste of fresh lobster. It was wonderful! Then, he and Joan got in the galley and cooked supper. Jerry pan-fried some fish that he'd gotten the day before, they boiled some potatoes, and Joan made a big green salad in a wooden bowl. We had to eat in shifts because there were a dozen or so people. Some ate in the dinette, some ate in the main salon, and some went out of the aft deck. Jen and I ate in the air conditioning in the main salon and then went out on the aft deck to watch the sun go down. When Jerry had finished eating, he came out on the aft deck too.

I said: "What's the game plan, man? What are we gonna do? How do we find out about the freighter?"

Jerry said: "Joe and the Colonel are gonna fly over tomorrow and tell us whether we're gonna work or whether we can go home. We're just gonna spend the night here and wait to hear from him tomorrow. Y'all can sleep on the floor in the main salon in the air conditioning and I'll take you back to your boat tomorrow when we know what we're doing."

I said: "That sounds good to me."

After getting a good nights sleep in the air conditioning, we woke up and had a nice big breakfast to start our day. Jerry and Joan cooked bacon and scrambled eggs, we had toast, orange juice, and coffee. Jerry had turned on his portable airplane radio to channel 12345 and about mid-morning, the Colonel flew over. Joe told Jerry that he thought a Navy plane had spotted the freighter drifting in the ocean. We had not been able to get the part to them. He figured that the Navy called the Coast Guard because they saw a Cutter heading for the freighter so the freighter was gonna get busted. Joe said we should go home. So that's it, another dry run.

We untied from Blue Eyes, pulled our anchor, and headed back to Russell Beacon. Jerry put me, Steve and his lady back on Cathy V, Jen went home on the Hatteras with Jerry. We motorsailed Cathy back to Ft. Lauderdale, it took us about seventeen hours, and when we got home on July 5th, there were hundreds of boats everywhere. It's too bad we weren't loaded. We took Cathy to the dock, tied her up, walked away, and went home. Now it was time for a vacation.

When Pat got home from her three-day trip, I told her all about the dry run and the weekend at Joulters. We spent the next couple of days being lazy, swimming in the pool, going to the beach and having a good time with Sunshine. It was just starting to sink in exactly what we had done, in three and a half months we'd made over $75,000 tax-free. That was awesome! It was a great feeling of financial security to go from a kitty of $7,200 in March to over $75,000 in July. We'd been bitten and we wanted more. I had forgotten all about our idea of doing one trip and then looking for a job. We had both been seduced by Jerry and the money.

We talked and debated about what we should do. We relived each trip and had many hearty laughs when we spoke of the first trip and how bad it was crossing over. Toby and the Candy Stripers brought even more chuckles. This was so much fun and getting paid for it was even funner! We discussed our organization, the surveillance, the channel boats, the airplane, everything. We felt like Joe and Jerry were doing everything they could possibly do to keep us safe. We realized the risks we were taking but we thought we had them minimized. The people that were getting busted on scam boats were being given two years in prison and they were getting out in ten months with good time. People were saying "I can do ten months standing on my head." I think it was at this point in time that I started seriously thinking about getting busted and having to go to prison. It was a sobering thought, no fun there.

Pat and I talked and decided that if we could make a half-a-million or a million dollars before we got busted, and if we still had the money when we got out of prison, it would be worth it. That was a revelation! Once we got to this point in our thought process, we decided that we needed to make as much money as fast as we could and then retire from smuggling. This meant that if I wanted to make the big bucks, I had to buy my own scam boat and run it with my own people. That was the decision that we made, that's what we were gonna do. Like the saying "Go big or go home," we decided to GO BIG! When Jerry paid me for the dry run, I was gonna present my proposition to him. If I could run my own boat and get paid a percentage of what I hauled, I could make over a million bucks in the upcoming smuggling season. It sounded like a plan, Stan!

Chapter 11
Cancer, Laetrile, & a Drug Deal
"Oh mama I'm in fear of my life from the long arm of the law" – STYX

Pat and I needed to make a trip to Memphis to visit Pat's father, Howard, who was battling lung cancer and was losing the fight. He had endured numerous rounds of chemotherapy and now was down from 225 pounds to about 100 pounds, the chemo was burning him up but was not killing the cancer. We had seen a special on TV about a clinic in Montego Bay, Jamaica that was having success in treating cancer using laetrile and other drugs not approved by the FDA. We told Howard and his wife Edith about the clinic and they had recently made a pilgrimage to Montego Bay to get laetrile treatments for Howard. Their two-week stay at the clinic produced very positive results, many of the tumors in Howard's body were shrunk considerably, and the prognosis was good.

They had returned to Memphis with enough laetrile to last a brief period but now they were about out. Edith had called the clinic in Montego Bay and spoken to the administrator who gave her the name of a doctor in the Nashville, Tennessee area who they said could help. Edith could not go to Nashville herself because there was no one else to care for Howard while she'd be gone. Pat volunteered me for the mission to travel to Nashville and thus our visit to Memphis was necessary and imminent. Pat procured passes from Delta for us to fly to Memphis and for me to fly to Nashville. I called Jerry, told him of our plans to go to Memphis, and asked him if I could come over and have a talk.

He said: "Sure, come on over."

I drove over to his house with the intention of asking him to let me buy and run my own boat. When I arrived, he was glad to see me and immediately went and got $2,000 as payment for the dry run, $1,000 for me and $1,000 for Jen. I told him that Pat and I had done a lot of talking and thinking about smuggling and that we were very pleased with the organization and with the money we'd made. We wanted to continue working in the upcoming year and we wanted to make as much money as we could. In order to do that, I felt like I needed to run my own boat and to have my own people. I asked him if that would be all right with him and would he help me do that?

He said: "Sure, I'll sell you Cathy V if that's what you want."

I couldn't believe it, I couldn't believe he'd want to sell Cathy V. We had done all of our trips on Cathy and I knew her like the back of my hand. I was thrilled! We had never had one lick of trouble with Cathy, she'd never sucked air, and she'd never shut down on us. She was a very sound and reliable boat.

I said: "How much do you want for her?"

He said: "I paid $40,000 so I'll sell her to you for that."

I said: "Well, that's great! You've got a deal."

He said: "I'll front you the boat if you want and you can pay me after you make your first trip."

I said: "I appreciate that, I don't know if that's what I want to do but I appreciate the offer."

He said: "I'll do whatever you want to do, it doesn't matter to me."

I said: "How will you pay me for each trip, how much can I make per trip?"

He said: "I'll pay you 15% of the weight you haul but then I get 3% for you unloading at Linda's house. You'll net 12%.

I said: "Okay, so how much can I net per trip?"

He said: "You oughta' net $75-80,000 at least and maybe as much as 100."

I said: "Wow! That would be awesome!"

We shook hands and as far as I was concerned, we had a deal.

He said: "I'm putting Cathy in the yard. We're gonna change the cutlass bearing on the shaft, do a bottom job, and check her for leaks. I don't think she's leaking after John ran her aground but we're gonna check her out real well anyway. The yard bill shouldn't be very much and I'll pay for it. She should be back in the water in about a week. When are you going to Memphis?"

I said: "Well, we're flying on passes so we can go whenever there's space available but we were gonna try to leave tomorrow."

He said: "Maybe by the time you get back from Memphis, she'll be back in the water."

We said our goodbyes and I promised to call him as soon as we were back in Ft. Lauderdale from Memphis. I drove home and told Pat that we'd bought Cathy V. She was as happy as I was. That night, we called Edith in Memphis and told her to expect us tomorrow. We called Delta and checked the flights to Memphis for availability, packed our bags, and went to bed early.

We awoke early and arrived at the Ft. Lauderdale airport around 8 o'clock. The next flight to Memphis was wide open and even though we were flying stand-by, we were able to arrive in Memphis before noon. Edith picked us up and took us back to the house. We went back into the master bedroom to see Howard and in spite of his "chipper" attitude, he did not look good. In fact, he looked like death warmed over. He had a big tumor growing on his throat that was causing him problems with his breathing. It was ugly! Howard and Edith told us all about their visit to the clinic in Montego Bay, about the progress that Howard had made while there, and that the doctors at the clinic had given them a tremendous amount of hope. Edith gave me a big file of Howard's medical records from the doctor in Memphis along with a smaller file from the clinic in Montego Bay. Pat called Delta, checked on availability of flights to Nashville, and we made plans for me to fly to Nashville tomorrow.

I arrived in Nashville just before noon, rented a car, and got directions to this little town about thirty-five miles north of Nashville. By the time I drove to the town and found the doctor's office, it was around 1 o'clock. I went in, waited a short time, and then was shown into the doctor's private office. He came in, I stood up, we shook hands, and I introduced myself.

He said: "Do you have some identification?"

I said: "I've got my driver's license." I took it out of my wallet and handed it to him.

He said: "What is your relationship to the patient, Mr. Clark?"

I said: "He's my father-in-law."

He said: "How much do you know about laetrile and its' use."

I said: "Well, my wife and I saw a special on television about laetrile and about the clinic in Montego Bay, Jamaica. We told Howard and Edith about the clinic and they made a trip to Jamaica for treatment. They brought back some laetrile with them but now they're running out. The clinic in Montego Bay gave us your name and telephone number."

He said: "I don't believe that you're a police officer, are you?" I shook my head no. "Do you understand that the use of laetrile in the United States is not approved by the FDA and that I could go to jail and lose my license to practice medicine if I so much as have laetrile in my possession?"

I said: "Yes, I do."

He said: "And Mr. Clark lives in Memphis?" I shook my head yes. "If he lived in this area and could come to my office, I could give him the injections here but I suppose he can't travel here from Memphis?" I shook my head no. "Okay, I'm going to give you a telephone number in Memphis, it's a nurse there that works with us. Go to a payphone when you get back to Memphis and call her. Give her the number that you are calling from. She will go to a payphone and call you back and arrange to meet with you. Understand?"

I said: "Yes. Are you going to give me the laetrile to take to her or does she have it?"

He said: "She has her own supply and she'll give the injections if you want."

I said: "How much will this cost?"

He said: "The cost of the laetrile is nominal, it's not very expensive, and you pay her for that. There is no charge for her services."

I said: "How much do I owe you for this office visit?"

He said: "I don't charge for this."

I said: "You people are angels from heaven."

He said: "No, we're just simple people trying to help people that are dying."

I said: "Well, God bless you and thank you very much!"

I left his office, got in the rental car, and drove back to the Nashville airport. As I'm driving, I'm thinking to myself: "Here I am, I've been smuggling multi-ton loads of pot into South Florida, I've been breaking the law big-time. Now, I've got to go to Memphis and do a drug deal to get a drug that's illegal but that might save my father-in-law's life. Now, what's wrong with this picture?"

When I arrived back in Memphis, Edith picked me up at the airport, Pat stayed with Howard. Edith was very interested to hear how my trip went and what I had found out. I started at the beginning and told her about the doctor and how cautious he was. I told her he checked my identification and asked me if I were a police officer and that he impressed on me the fact that what we were doing was against the law.

Edith said: "What do we do now?"

I said: "Basically, what we've gotta do is, we've gotta do a drug deal."

She said: "We've never done anything like this before, have you? Can you help us?"

I said: "Sure Edith, that's why I'm here. What we have to do is go to a payphone and call the nurse. She'll take our number and then go to a payphone and call us back. Then, we'll arrange to meet somewhere and work out the arrangements. It shouldn't be too difficult."

She said: "Is it going to be dangerous?"

I said: "No, I don't think so. There's no chance of violence like with a drug deal for illegal street drugs. If she's being followed by the cops, they probably won't arrest her when she meets with us because we're not doing anything but talking in a public place. If they follow her to your house when she comes to give Howard the injections, they could arrest her then 'cause she'll have the laetrile with her, and they'll know that. They probably wouldn't arrest you and certainly not Howard, shame on them if they did. These seem to be very competent, cautious people. The lady probably knows if she's being watched or followed. Try not to worry about it, it'll be okay."

She said: "Okay Scooter, I'm trusting you with this."

We drove to the house and told Pat and Howard all the details. Then, Edith and I went to a payphone at a nearby shopping center and called the nurse. She took our number, we hung up, and in about five minutes, she called us back. We arranged to meet that evening at a nearby restaurant. Edith and I met the nurse at the appointed time, we had a cup of coffee, and a very frank discussion. We liked her very much. We arranged for her to come to the house tomorrow to give Howard his first injection of laetrile. Everything went very well and Edith and I returned home with a peace about us that we were doing everything we could possibly do to help save Howard's life.

Pat and I decided that we would stay two more days and then return to Ft. Lauderdale. The next day, the nurse arrived and gave Howard an injection of laetrile. There were no cops and nobody got busted, we all breathed a sigh of relief. Edith cooked us a nice supper and even Howard ate a little bit.

Over supper, Edith said: "Howard seems to be having a good day. Give me about thirty minutes to clean him up a little and I'll put some clean PJ's on him and sit him up in the chair. Then, we can all visit in the bedroom 'till he gets tired."

In about a half an hour, Edith came and got us and brought us back into the master bedroom. Howard was sitting up in a high-backed chair and he looked a little better, I think the nurse had given him hope. Pat and I and Sunshine sat on the floor at his feet and Edith sat on the foot of the bed. We talked about old times, told stories, and laughed and giggled. After about twenty minutes, Howard started getting tired, we could see it in his face. He asked Edith and Pat to leave the room because he wanted to talk to me alone. They looked at each other kind of funny but got up and left.

Howard said: "You know, when I first met you, I wasn't sure I was gonna like you, you know, with the long hair and all"

I said: "Yeah, I know. I didn't know if I was gonna like you either."

He said: "I wasn't sure you were good enough for my daughter. I think we got to know each other better that first time we played golf in Atlanta. After that, we started warming up to each other, didn't we?"

I said: "Yeah, we did. I think we both began to realize that we were a lot alike in a lot of ways."

He said: "Yeah, I think we are. This disease and staring at death every day makes you take a hard look at your life. I was such an idiot in so many ways and so many things that I did, all the partying and all the running around I did. I hurt the people that loved me the most. I just wanted to tell you not to do with your life what I did with mine, don't hurt the people that love you the most."

I said: "Hey man, don't beat yourself up. You were a good provider and y'all had a lot of good times. You need to tell Edith this."

He said: "I already have, she's forgiven me. I don't deserve Edith."

We talked for a few more minutes and then I went and got the girls. I helped Edith get Howard back in the bed, she tucked him in, and we left him alone to sleep. Before we went to bed that night, I told Pat about my conversation with Howard. I began to realize that he was telling me goodbye because he knew that he was dying. It was gonna take laetrile plus a miracle to keep that from happening. I resolved to do what he was asking me to do, not to hurt the people that love me the most. As I fell asleep that night, I felt good about the decisions that Pat and I had made about smuggling. I wanted to make as much money as fast as I could and to spend as much quality time with my family as was humanly possible. I didn't want to work for "the man" in that 9 to 5 rat race of life. After talking with Howard that night, I was convinced that we were on the right track. Even tho' we were on a break, I had many things that needed to be done once I got back to Ft. Lauderdale. For one thing, I had to get Cathy back in the water; for another, I had to talk to my friends and put together my crew for the upcoming trips. I was very optimistic that running my own boat was going to be good.

Pat, Sunny, and I flew back to Ft. Lauderdale after saying our goodbyes to Howard and Edith. We had a bad feeling that this was going to be the last time that we'd see Howard alive. The laetrile injections were too little too late, and we didn't get our miracle, Howard Clark died on August 6th at the age of 49.

Chapter 12
Go Big or Go Home
The idea is to make as much money as you can, as fast as you can,
and then retire and live happily ever after.

As soon as we returned to Ft. Lauderdale, I called Jerry and told him we were back. He said that Cathy was still in the yard out of the water and that she should be ready in a few more days. He had taken a close look at the keel and said that we hadn't done any damage to it when we ran aground, she was a tough old lady. I told him that I wanted to go ahead and pay him for Cathy before the first trip and he said that was fine with him. He suggested that I put my crew together and then do some daysailing once Cathy was back in the water so that everyone would be familiar with her once we started back working. I told him that was my immediate task for the days ahead.

I wanted my first hire to be a mechanic, at least someone that knew more about engines and mechanical systems than I did. Pat flew with another Delta Flight Attendant named Mindy who was married to a guy named Skip. Skip supposedly raced cars and knew how to turn a wrench and tinker with motors better than I did. We went to see them one evening, told them that we had been smuggling pot, and asked Skip if he wanted to come to work for me. He was out-of-work at the time and he jumped at the chance to make some good money fast. I really didn't like Skip that much and I think we had a personality conflict but he was the only mechanic I knew and I felt like I needed a mechanic. I told Skip that the boat was in the yard and that as soon as she was back in the water, I would get him familiar with her and we'd do some daysailing so he could learn to sail. He was excited and ready to go!

Next, I went and talked to a friend, Rob, that I'd worked rock concerts with and who I'd known for about three years. He worked for a rock promoter and I met him when I worked for Ticketron, we became good friends. He was a really good guy and very serious and professional about whatever he was doing, I liked that in him. I told Rob that we'd been smuggling for the past few months and had made some good money. I told him about the organization, the channel boats and the planes, and he was impressed. We had a long talk, discussed it at length, and he said he would have to think about it because he wasn't the type of person to jump into something this serious at the drop of a hat.

Now, I needed one or two women to round out my crew. Pat and I had a long, serious discussion about her continuing to go on the trips. I didn't want her going on any more trips because of Sunshine and because if the boat got busted and we were both on the same boat, then we'd both get busted. If we both went away to prison at the same time, someone would have to take care of Sunny, so I didn't want her to continue going on the trips. She didn't agree with me but she understood the line of reasoning. Pat's best friend, Jen, was my first choice for female crew especially since she'd gone on the 4th of July dry run. She already knew we were smuggling and she'd seen the operation even tho' the trip she made was a dry run. We asked her over to the house, told her that we'd bought Cathy V, and asked her to be a crew member. She really liked the people she'd met, she was impressed with the organization, and she said she was ready to go.

She was excited and I was too. Also, I'd heard from Rob and he'd agreed to go so it looked like my crew was set.

We had about a month or so before we were going to start working again and over the course of the next month, Skip and I did a lot of work on the boat and Skip familiarized himself with the engine and the mechanical systems. We waxed Cathy, shined up all the metal with polish, and did many things to make her look shipshape. I had a spray dodger and a new bimini top made for her so that in rough weather, we could stay fairly dry. We went daysailing three or four times and Skip, Rob, and Jen logged some quality time at the helm learning to sail. We'd pack a lunch and spend the afternoon sailing off Lauderdale beach on those dog days of summer afternoons. We got good and tanned and had some great times.

Finally, about the end of September, we got a call from Jerry who said it was time to go fishing. We had a meeting in a room at the Ramada Inn on State Road 84 and everyone was there including a few new people. Jerry gave us a briefing that lasted about two hours. He had charts of the Bahamas that he used to show everyone where he wanted us to be, where he would meet the freighters, and the course he would take to find us. It gave us all a better understanding of the big picture which in turn gave us confidence and made us better and more professional. The vibes among all the people in the room were unbelievably good and we felt like one big, happy family. We knew we had the channel boats and the planes looking out for us and we knew if we had problems on the water, that we could count on each other to help in any way possible. It was a good feeling! Jerry wrapped up the meeting, told us we needed to leave tomorrow, and said he'd see us over on the Bank.

I told Skip and Rob to meet me in the morning at 8 o'clock at Riverland Shopping Center and Jen and I took off to Skaggs Albertsons on Commercial Boulevard to buy groceries because it stayed open twenty-four hours. Jen and I each got a buggy, went up and down the aisles stuffing the buggy with food and drinks and just had a field day. When we had both buggies packed to the gills and stacked so high that stuff was falling off, we decided it was time to check out.

The cashier said: "What are you guys doing?"

I said: "Oh, we're having a party, we're having a bunch of friends come in for the weekend."

She said: "You look like you're gonna have some kind of party."

I said: "Yeah, it's gonna be fun!"

We took the food to my house and put all the perishables in the refrigerator. Jen went home and Pat and I went to bed and tried to get a good night's sleep. I was real apprehensive because it was my first trip running my own boat and I spent a restless night waiting for dawn so I could get up and get going.

We awoke early the next morning and after having coffee, we loaded up the perishables in the car with the other groceries. I kissed Pat and Sunny goodbye and went off to pick-up Jen. Boy was that weird leaving Pat at home. I knew she understood but I also knew that she really didn't understand either. I picked up Skip and Rob, we bought ice, drove over to Linda's house, and loaded the groceries and the ice on Cathy V. We pushed away from the dock mid-morning, went down the River into the Intracoastal and the Port, out the Cut into the ocean, and headed south for the whistle buoy in Miami.

When we got to the whistle buoy at Government Cut in Miami, we took a left and got on our heading of 112 degrees to Gun Cay. We actually steered 110-115 degrees and we tried to keep it on the high side to compensate for the gulfstream pushing us north. The weather was beautiful but with very little wind so we motored across the gulfstream without putting up the sails. After about three hours, the skyline of Miami disappeared behind us and our next landfall would be either Gun Cay Lighthouse or the radio tower on south Bimini. We were out of sight of land for a little less than five hours and when we sighted Gun Cay light as it was getting dark, we pulled out the hibachi and cooked steaks on the aft deck. Everyone was taking a two-hour stretch on the helm and it felt good to have a crew that was trained and competent. With Rob at the helm, Skip and I cooked the steaks on the aft deck while Jen heated up some canned vegetables and made a tossed salad in the galley. We enjoyed our feast under the stars in the cockpit.

We arrived at Gun Cay in about ten hours, went thru the Cut onto the Bank, and took a heading of 112 degrees for Sylvia Beacon which was where Jerry wanted to load us this trip. I let Jen take the helm and the three guys went into the main salon to tape down. We got the drop cloths and the duct tape and prepared the boat for loading. By now, Jen had Sylvia Beacon in sight and we could also see the mast lights of some other boats. As we approached Sylvia Beacon, we recognized Apple Pie and the Tin Man so this was Jerry's party.

I grabbed the CB microphone and said: "Apple Pie, Apple Pie, Speedy Pete, you got your ears on good buddy, kickit' back."

He said: "Speedy Pete, Apple Pie, roger that good buddy. Howya' doin' tonight?"

I said: "We're fine as wine good buddy. You hear from our friend yet?"

He said: "That's a negative good buddy, probably a little early for that."

I said: "Roger that. Okay, we'll be dropping our hook on your port side, we'll leave enough room in case the wind shifts and we swing around."

He said: "I appreciate that good buddy. You give us a shout if you need anything."

I said. "Roger that, the same goes for us."

Jen was still at the helm so I decided to let her learn how to run the boat while dropping the anchor. I told Skip and Rob to go up on the bow pulpit and drop the anchor while I stayed in the cockpit with Jen. I told Jen that when dropping the anchor or putting the sails up or down, you always turned the boat directly into the wind. I also explained to her that boats didn't have brakes so you had to use the gear to stop the boats forward motion or the rearward motion if the gear is in reverse. There was very little if any wind tonight so I told her to look at the other two boats and see which way they were facing. I told her to pull the throttle all the way back so the boat is going as slow as it can be going in gear and then turn directly into the wind and put the gear in neutral. When she turned the boat into the wind, the boat was sliding slowly forward so I told her to put the gear in reverse briefly to stop the forward motion. When she'd done this, the forward motion of the boat stopped.

I said: "Tell them to drop the anchor."

She hollered: "Drop the anchor" and we heard it splash in the water.

I then told her to put the gear in reverse again briefly to get the boat falling back on the anchor line. When she did this, the boat began to move backwards and the guys let out more anchor line. I then told her to put the gear in forward briefly to stop the rearward motion of the boat When she'd done this, the rearward motion of the boat stopped.

I said: "Tell them to tie it off."

She hollered: "Tie it off" and the guys tied off the anchor line to the cleat just behind the bow pulpit. She did a good job and we were anchored.

By now, it was about 1:00 AM. We all got a cold drink, sat in the cockpit and relaxed under the stars. After we finished our drinks, we reclined in the cockpit and tried to catnap until we heard from Jerry. Finally, about 3:00 AM the radio crackled and it was faint.

Jerry said: "Speedy Pete, Speedy Pete, Black Fin, you got your ears on good buddy, kickit' back."

I grabbed the CB microphone and said: "Black Fin, Black Fin, Speedy Pete, I copy good buddy, kickit' back."

He said: "Speedy Pete, we will not be partying tonight. We will party tomorrow night, do you copy?"

I said: "Roger that good buddy, we will party tomorrow night."

He said: "Spread the word for me, okay?"

I said: "Roger that, see you tomorrow night."

He said: "That's a roger."

I said: "Apple Pie, did you copy that last transmission?"

He said: "Roger that."

I said: "Tin Man, did you copy that last transmission?"

She said: "That's a roger."

I said: "We'll talk at'cha tomorrow."

My crew was disappointed and asked me if this meant that this trip was going to be a dry run. I told them that Jerry had a good tone in his voice and that he probably sent us over a day early in case anyone had a mechanical problem, they could get it squared away, still make it over and get loaded. That made them feel better. Jen went down into the aft stateroom to sleep and the three guys bedded down in the cockpit under a billion stars in the sky. It was a beautiful night even tho'we didn't get loaded!

We woke up early the next morning shortly after the sunrise, cooked a nice breakfast of bacon and eggs, put on our bathing suits, and jumped in the water for a swim. We were in about fourteen to fifteen feet of water and it was clear as a swimming pool. While we were lollygagging around the rear of Cathy, I pointed out the keel to my crew. Cathy drew four and a half feet and it was easy for my crew to see why in that clear water. I told them that was why you had to be careful in shallow water, because we had four and a half feet of keel under us. Being able to see the keel like that made an impression on them. After swimming for about twenty minutes, we climbed back on the boat, dried off, and prepared to go daysailing on the Bank.

I let Rob take the helm to teach him how to properly run the boat while pulling the anchor. Skip pulled the anchor and Jen helped with the line. Once we had the anchor up and tied off, Skip and Jen hoisted the mainsail and the jib. There was pretty good wind and we were able to turn the engine off and sail all day without the motor. We listened to rock-n-roll tapes.. We drank a few beers, smoked some pot, and had a nice relaxing day on the Bank. Late in the afternoon, we sailed back to Sylvia Beacon to cook supper and prepare to get loaded. I let Skip take the helm and I coached him in how to run the boat properly while dropping the sails and while anchoring. We cooked another great dinner, ate in the cockpit, cleaned up our trash, and touched up our tape-down job to prepare to get loaded. We had everything shipshape before it got dark and we all watched the orange sherbet sunset in the cockpit. We were playing tapes, talking, and having a good time while waiting for the load boat. As it got later, we reclined in the cockpit and tried to catnap and recharge our batteries from a day in the sun.

Finally, around 2:00 AM, the radio crackled.

"Speedy Pete, Speedy Pete, Black Fin, you got your ears on good buddy, kickit' back."

I said: "Black Fin, Speedy Pete, that's a roger, kickit' back."

Jerry said: "Turn your porch light on, I'll be there in a short-short, we're gonna have a big party."

I said: "Roger that." I turned on our mast light.

He said: "I gotcha Speedy Pete. Are you at your girlfriend's house?"

I said: "That's a roger."

He said: "You got some friends with you?"

I said: "That's a roger."

He said: "Good, I'll see you in a short-short."

I said: "We'll see you when you get here, good buddy."

We all got real excited and started stowing things away like the backgammon game, cassette tapes, drink cups, and other trash in the cockpit, and we stowed the cushions in the main salon up against the side of the boat. Then, everyone put on their old clothes for loading and came back up into the cockpit. I told Rob to get on the bow, Skip to get on the stern, and I got lines for them and also a spring line for the middle of the boat if Jerry wanted one for safety.

It wasn't long before we could hear those big Detroit Diesel engines out of the darkness, they were straining and pulling a load of weight, sounding like a freight train. In a few more minutes, we saw the shape of the Hatteras ease out of the darkness and

Jerry skillfully pulled her along our port side. He inched his bow in towards our bow and one of his guys threw Rob a line which he held and did not tie off yet. Jerry reversed his gears, putting the starboard motor in forward and the port motor in reverse, the Hatteras gracefully came alongside Cathy V to about three feet. One of the guys on his aft deck threw a line to Skip and he and Rob pulled the boats together and tied the lines off to cleats. I rigged up the spring line from a center cleat on Cathy to a bow and stern cleat on the Hatteras. Jerry gave me a thumbs up and shut down his engines. QUIET.

Jerry climbed down off the flybridge of the Hatteras and hopped on Cathy V. He gave me and Jen a hug and looked in the main salon at our tape-down job.

He said: "Hey man, it's good to work with people that know what they're doing. Y'all ready to load?"

I said: "Yeah man, we're good to go."

He said: "You want me to give you an extra guy to help you load?"

I said: "Yeah, we could use someone in the main salon."

He said: "Okay, that's no problem."

He told one of his guys to come on Cathy and help us load, he climbed over the railing, got on board, and went in the main salon. I worked the cockpit, Jen worked the hatch, Skip worked the forward cabin, and Rob worked the aft stateroom. The guys on Jerry's boat started handing me bales, some of them were big sons-a-bitches, about 80 pounds. I would put one through the aft hatch to Rob then give one to Jen at the hatch to the main salon. She would push it through the hatch and Jerry's guy would grab it and take it up front to Skip. For some reason, this was a very dirty load, many of the bales were broken open and we were getting pot and burlap residue all over us. It got in our hair, went down our shirts, got all over our arms, face and neck, and got in our nostrils. We were sweating up a storm and it was sticking to us like glue. We continued the loading routine until the fore and aft cabins were packed to the gills, we were done in about an hour, and Jerry was pleased.

He said: "Okay, we'll see you guys at home tomorrow. Good luck!"

We untied the lines, pushed the Hatteras away from Cathy, Jerry backed away behind us to avoid the anchor lines up front, and went to load Apple Pie and the Tin Man. As soon as Jerry had pulled away, Rob went on the aft deck, leaned over, and threw up. I think it was a combination of the heat, of breathing the pot and burlap residue, and a case of nerves. We all got in the cockpit with a cold drink and tried to cool off. There was pot everywhere, all over the deck, on the seats, and about ankle deep in the bottom of the cockpit.

As soon as we'd finished our drinks and cooled off, we got a trash can bag and starting using our hands to pick up the pot and put it in the bag to salvage as much as we could. I'll bet you we saved 10-15 pounds of good Colombian herb from the deck, the cockpit, and the main salon. We then got a bucket of water, sponges, and paper towels and cleaned up the cockpit and we put the cushions back on the seats in the cockpit. Rob was still feeling bad after throwing up and he lay down in the cockpit to take a catnap, he was soon snoring. Skip and I folded up the drop cloths in the main salon and put them in trash bags while Jen got in the galley and fixed us sandwiches. With the boat about as shipshape as we could get it for now, we went back up into the cockpit and ate our snack in hopes of getting some energy for the trip home.

I took the helm and sent Skip and Jen to pull the anchor up. Once it was up and tied off, I put the bow of Cathy on a heading to Gun Cay while Jen went below to shower. We were filthy dirty and needed to get the pot and burlap residue off of us and to get into clean clothes. When Jen had finished with her shower, Skip and then Rob followed. We were in sight of Gun Cay light so I gave Jen the helm while I showered. As we approached Gun Cay, I took the helm from Jen, brought Cathy through the Cut, and put her bow on a course of 300 degrees to Ft. Lauderdale as the sky began to turn light as morning was breaking. We were getting some weather as the wind blew out of the northeast and there were 4-5 foot swells that were rolling over our starboard side. I decided to keep the sails down and just motor back across the gulfstream to Florida.

We were taking water over our starboard side onto the deck so I went below into the main salon to check our bilge. I pulled off the hatch over the motor and damn if we didn't have water in the bilge above the bottom of the motor. The coupling on the shaft was leaking water pretty badly, it needed to be tightened. The bilge pump should have been working automatically so obviously either the float was stuck or there was debris in the diaphragm. Since it was a dirty load, there was a good chance that it was pot and burlap debris that was clogging up the float or the diaphragm, it shouldn't be too hard to fix. Nothing ever breaks on a boat in good weather, things only seem to break when it's rough as a bitch. I called Skip to come take a look and since I was beginning to feel seasick from being downstairs, I went back upstairs, stood in the doorway to the hatch, and let the wind hit me in the face. I told Skip to get the bilge pump working and pump out the water before it got any higher. He got down on his hands and knees, reached into the water, found the float, and lifted it up to manually get the bilge pump working. It didn't start pumping.

He said: "It's probably got trash in it that's stopping it up. I'll fix it when we get back to the dock."

I said: "Look man, I don't want the water to get any higher. If it gets up above the dipstick to the transmission, the water will get mixed with the transmission fluid and we could burn up the transmission. I don't want to burn up the transmission, we could miss a trip before we got it replaced. Will you just fix the fuckin' thing?"

He went and got an adjustable wrench and tightened up the coupling on the shaft and stopped the flow of water coming in to a slow drip. Then, he got a plastic cup and a bucket and he bailed out the water by hand into the bucket using the plastic cup. When he'd gotten as much water out as he could by hand, he came upstairs with the bucket of dirty bilge water and threw it overboard.

He said: "I'll check the water level once an hour and bail it by hand if I have to. I won't let the transmission burn up, I promise you."

I said: "Why don't you just fix the fuckin' pump like I asked you to?"

He said: "Man, I'll get sick and throw up before I can get it disassembled and fixed."

I said: "I get sick almost every trip, Rob's already gotten sick and thrown up. That's just part of smuggling, you gotta do what you gotta do and keep going, that's part of it."

He said: "I promise I won't let your transmission burn up, don't worry about it."

That pissed me off! I didn't like my hired help to tell me not to worry about something that I was obviously worried about. I couldn't believe that this asshole wouldn't do what I asked him to do. I guess that's what being the boss is all about, dealing with assholes.

We were about eight hours out of Gun when we spotted the Condos on the beach, grabbed the binoculars, and found the smokestacks at Port Everglades. We had heard some of the other boats talking to Rita in the channel boat and she was giving everyone a "big 10-10, it's clean and green." Our airplane flew over and dipped his wings right and left to let us know he was watching out for us. That made us feel good, our people were taking good care of us.

I grabbed the CB microphone and said: " Little Lady, Little Lady, this is Speedy Pete, you got a copy."

She said: "Speedy Pete, this is the Little Lady, what's your 20 good buddy?"

I said: "I'm about two hours from the intersection, come back."

She said: "Well, you got a big 10-10 good buddy, it's clean and green!"

I said: "Roger that, I'll see you in a short-short."

She said: "That's a roger, I'll be looking out for you."

We came in dead on the smokestacks at the Port. The boat was all cleaned up and looking good. As we approached the mouth of the Cut, I spotted Rita in her Boston Whaler Revenge about a hundred yards south of the Cut off Dania Beach. Jen went downstairs and changed into her two-piece bathing suit and as soon as we were in the Cut, she went up on the bow pulpit and held on to the front stay. I hoped that if we did see any heat, they would be looking at her beautiful body and not our waterline 'cause she was looking good!

I brought the boat through 17th Street bridge, past the Gulf docks, up the River through the middle of town, past Hatteras Yachts and the 4th Avenue bridge, and into the dock at Linda's house off Riverland Road without seeing a single Grouper Trooper. We tied up the boat bow and stern, put on a spring line, got our duffle bags, padlocked the hatch, and walked away. We made it again! We got in my car, drove to Riverland Shopping Center where I dropped off Skip and Rob, and then I dropped Jen off at her place, and I went home. We were going to meet back at Riverland tonight at 10 o'clock to unload Cathy.

When I got home, Pat and Sunny were waiting for me with a big hug and a kiss. I gave Pat a quick rundown of the trip and then I climbed in the shower to get the trip off of me. When I got out of the shower, I called Jerry and told him we were home and that everything went well. He had arranged for two additional guys to help us unload and I was pleased to hear that, it would make the unloading go faster and more efficiently. Pat had cooked me a nice supper and I ate heartily while giving her more details of the trip. I could tell that she really missed going on the trip with me. I told her all about Skip and the bilge pump incident and she said she wasn't surprised at all by the way he acted, I don't think she liked him much either. After I finished eating, I crawled into bed and slept soundly until Pat woke me up at 9:30.

As I was putting on my unloading clothes, Pat told me that Jen had called and talked to her about Skip. Jen said that Skip had come into the galley while she was making sandwiches, had kissed her, and tried to stick his tongue down her throat. Jen had pushed him away and told him to "grow up." Then, while he was getting his loading clothes out of his duffle bag, Skip showed Jen a pistol that he'd brought "for our protection." A few weeks earlier while we were working on the boat together, Skip had told me that he wanted to bring his pistol on the trip. I had told him then that Jerry expressly forbids firearms on the boats and that he could not bring his pistol on the trip. If you were caught in the commission of a felony with a weapon, it was a five-year minimum mandatory prison sentence. By bringing the pistol, Skip potentially put us all at risk for a five-year prison sentence. I was pissed! Mechanic or not, I made up my mind that this was Skip's last trip.

I kissed Pat goodbye and drove over to Jen's apartment to pick her up. She was going to be our lookout for the evening while we were unloading. She was going to sit in the bushes at the end of the street on Riverland Road and watch for cars and any heat that might come down the street while we were unloading. We had a CB base station in Linda's house and I had bought Jen a hand-held CB radio at Radio Shack which she would use to alert us if a car were coming. We would stop the unloading until we saw what the car was doing and we felt like the coast was clear. If the heat came down the street and Jen alerted us, we would run next door into the neighbor's yard and hopefully not get busted if the house and the boat went down. I paid her $1,000 to be our lookout for the night and figured that it was cheap insurance especially if it worked.

After picking up Jen, I drove to Riverland Shopping Center, picked up Rob and Skip, and drove to Linda's house. When we arrived and went in the side door to the garage, Jerry's other two guys were already there as well as a white van in the garage. I took Rob and we went out to Cathy to set her up for unloading. As soon as we got on the boat, I turned on the CB radio and did a radio check with Jen and the hand-held CB radio. Then, I told Jen to go to the CB base station and we did a radio check with it. All of our radios were working properly. Rob and I then began moving the bales evenly from the foreward and aft cabins into the main salon. When we'd gotten as many bales as we could into the main salon, we went back into the house to catnap and wait for the neighbor's daughter to come home at 1:00 AM from her date and cut off the spotlight over the door in the yard.

Sure enough, at 12:59 a car came down the street across the canal and it was the neighbor's daughter coming home from her date. After a goodnight kiss at the door, she went inside, turned off the spotlight, and it was darkness again. I sent Jen walking up the street to her post in the bushes on the corner at Riverland Road. Rob and I went out to Cathy, I worked the cockpit, and Rob worked the main salon. He would hand me a bale through the hatch and I would hand it over the railing to Skip and the other two guys who would put it on their shoulder and walk it through the yard into the house. We continued this efficient routine without incident and by 4:30, we had all the bales in the house. Rob and I got off Cathy and walked through the yard into the house.

I grabbed the CB base station's microphone and said: "Jen, we're done, come on home."

I called Jerry and told him we were finished unloading. He said to call him when we had the first van ready. In a minute, Jen walked in the side door to the garage and she locked the door behind her. Linda had left us a cooler full of drinks iced down along with a brown paper bag full of munchie food. We took a five-minute break, had a cold drink and a snack, and cooled off. Then we started weighing the bales and making a list. When the weighing was completed, we loaded the van and were able to get half the bales in the van so we knew we could deliver the load in two trips. As soon as we'd gotten the first van loaded, Skip grabbed a flashlight, started clowning around, and making hand shadows on the wall. Rob and I looked at each other and we were both thinking "what an asshole." By now, it was about 8 o'clock so I called Jerry and told him we were ready with the first van. He told me to shower, put my clean clothes on, and catch a catnap because Fu wouldn't be ready with his drivers until 9:00 AM.

At 9 o'clock, Jerry called and said Fu was at the IHOP on State Road 84. I drove the van over to the restaurant, went inside, sat at the table with Fu and the boys, and gave Fu the keys to the van. He gave the keys to one of his drivers who got up, went outside, got in the van, and drove off to go to their warehouse. Fu gave me a set of keys and I went outside, got in another white van, and drove back to Linda's house. Since I was clean, I let my four guys load up the rest of the bales into the van. I drove back to the IHOP, went inside, and gave the keys to Fu. He gave them to one of his drivers who left in it to go to the warehouse. Jerry was there by now and he gave me a ride back to Linda's house. I took Jen, Rob and Skip and we drove to Riverland Shopping Center where I dropped off Rob and Skip at their cars. I drove Jen to her apartment and went home myself. By the time I got home, I was feeling a tremendous rush of satisfaction and accomplishment at having completed my first trip on my own boat as the boss. It was a great feeling!

In about three days, Jerry called and said: "Why don't you come on over to my house, I've got some green stamps for you."

I said: "I'll be there within the hour."

I had gotten all my figures together and had run some rough numbers to see what I might make for the trip. Depending on what Fu paid us for the pot, I was hoping to make at least $80,000 net after paying my crew. I drove over to Jerry's house on S.W. 5th Place on New River and was a little nervous but I had high expectations. I knocked on the door and then opened it and went in, Jerry was in the kitchen, and we sat down at the kitchen table. I gave him a copy of my list with the bales and the weights that I had hauled. I got my calculator and he got his calculator and we started settling up. I had hauled 100 bales that was a total weight of 5,500 pounds of pot and sack weight. We were using three pounds sack weight for the bales so 5,500 pounds less 300 pounds sack weight is 5,200 pounds of pot. Jerry said Fu was paying us $220 per pound so my gross was 5,200 times $220 or $1,144,000. Jerry was paying me 12% of the gross of $1,144,000 so my gross was $137,280. I was ecstatic! I had to pay Jerry's two guys that helped me unload $2,500 each so that meant Jerry owed me $132,280. Jerry had a whiskey box full of money on the floor under the table. He pulled out the box from under the table and started putting bricks of money on the table. The money was all in $20's so each brick was $10,000, he put fourteen bricks on the table or $140,000. He took three packs of $2,000 out of one brick so that left $134,000. He got another pack of $2,000 and took $1,720 out of that pack, which left $132,280 for me.

He said: "You bring something to put this in?"

I said: "No, have you got a bag or a box?"

He said: "Both, which one do you want?"

I said: "It doesn't matter, give me a box."

He went into another room and came back with another whiskey box. I put all the bricks into the box and closed up the top. We shook hands.

I said: "I hope we can do this again real soon."

He said: "We're gonna do this a lot so be ready. You did real good man."

I said: "Thanks man, I won't let you down. I'm ready and I'll stay ready."

I grabbed my whiskey box full of money in a bear hug and walked out of the house to my car. I felt like the whole neighborhood was watching me carry my box full of money to my car. It was a weird feeling! I was driving my Honda Hatchback and it didn't have a trunk so I put my box in the front floorboard, left Jerry's house, and drove home. When I got home, I got the box out of the front floorboard, walked in the house and back into our bedroom. Pat was waiting for me and she followed me into our bedroom. I put the box of money on the floor, opened it up, and showed her the money, her eyes almost bulged out of her head.

She said: "How much is that?"

I said: "$132,000."

She said: "How much of it is ours?"

I said: "A little over $90,000 I think." She was flabbergasted! "I'm going to call Rob and Skip and go pay them. Why don't you call Jen and ask her over for supper and we'll pay her here at the house tonight?" She shook her head okay.

I went in the kitchen and got two brown paper grocery bags. I put $15,000 for Rob in one bag and $15,000 for Skip in the other bag. I owed Jen $7,500 for the trip plus $1,000 for being a lookout. That netted me $93,780 for my first trip, not too shabby!

I called Rob and Skip, they were both home, and I told them I had green stamps. I drove to Skip's house in Hollywood and paid him first, I didn't tell him he was fired. Then, I met Rob at the Holiday Inn at the Golden Glades Interchange in North Miami and paid him. We had a drink out by the pool and talked about the trip. I told him about Skip making a pass at Jen and about the pistol that he'd brought in his duffle bag, he couldn't believe it. I told him that Skip was done, that I wasn't going to use him again. He said: "Good, he's an asshole." I told Rob that he'd done real good and I was very pleased. I asked him if he wanted to keep going and do some more trips and he said "yes." When we'd finished our drinks, we shook hands, and both went home.

When I got back home, Pat and Jen were in the kitchen cooking supper with Sunny in a highchair. I gave Pat a hug and a kiss and gave Jen a hug and a kiss on the cheek.

I said: "Jen, come on back here in the bedroom with me."

She said: "I don't know if Pat would like that very much."

I said: "No silly, I want to pay you for the trip."

She said: "I know, I'm just kidding you."

We went back into the bedroom, I got my box full of money, and took out a brick of $10,000. I took a pack of $2,000, took out $500, put it under the rubber bands on the stack of $8,000 to make $8,500 and handed it to Jen. Pat came back with a camera and took a picture of me handing her the money as a memento for posterity. I told her that she'd done very well and that I was very pleased. I asked her if she wanted to keep going and do some more trips and she said "yes." I got a brown paper bag for her to put her money in, we finished cooking, and had a nice supper with a bottle of wine.

After we finished eating, we cleaned up the kitchen, visited a little more, and then Jen went home. We put Sunshine to bed and Pat and I went into the bedroom to count our money. We sat on the floor and took each brick apart and counted all the money in the whiskey box. It was exactly $93,780 just like it was supposed to be. We put all the bricks back together, put them in the whiskey box, and I put the box in our walk-in closet on the floor. It was a mindblower! I'd made more money in one trip than we'd made all last season with me doing six trips and Pat doing four. Our nest egg now was almost $130,000 and that made us both feel great! Now I needed to find another friend to replace Skip and I would start working on that tomorrow. I was optimistic and excited about the future and couldn't wait for the next trip. Pat and I smoked a joint, got naked, and made long, slow, wild passionate love. Money and happiness are an aphrodisiac!

Chapter 13
Money, Diligence, and Beatin' the Odds
"We were gambling with our souls, we were playing to win,
we were beatin' the odds again." – Molly Hatchett

When we woke up the next morning and were having our coffee out by the pool, the light went on in my brain that it wasn't safe nor smart to keep $130,000 CASH in a whiskey box in the walk-in closet in the house. Damn, having money was a problem, a nice problem, but still a problem! We decided that we'd go to our bank and get a safe deposit box and that we'd have a safe installed in the house. I called a locksmith I knew on Davie Boulevard who also sold and installed safes. He said he could install the safe for me as soon as we picked one out and paid for it, it was no problem. I asked him how secure would the safe be. He said that a floor safe was more secure than a wall safe because the floor safe was installed in the foundation of the house. A wall safe was installed in the dry wall and wood of the wall and was easy to get out and walk away with. To install a floor safe, he would have to bring a jackhammer, bust a hole in the foundation, mix up concrete, and install the safe in the foundation with the concrete. To get in a floor safe without the combination, someone would have to blow the door off with explosives or bring their own jackhammer and bust up the foundation to get it out, that made the floor safe more secure. I told him I definitely wanted the floor safe.

Pat and I showered, put on nice clothes, took Sunshine and went to our bank to rent a safe deposit box. On the way to the bank, we stopped by the locksmith's office and picked out a floor safe, paid $425 for it, and arranged for him to come that afternoon and complete the installation. We then drove to Century Bank on top of the tunnel on Las Olas Boulevard and U.S. 1 in downtown Ft. Lauderdale. I had $60,000 packed in a briefcase and Pat had $20,000 in a big purse. We rented a medium sized box, signed the signature cards, each got a key, and when finally left alone, we placed the $80,000, 8 bricks, inside the box almost filling it up. I realized immediately that we probably needed to get the biggest box they had which was like a drawer; but, I didn't want to exchange it today because I thought it would look funny to the lady that helped us. Damn, having money was a problem! We left the bank, drove home, had lunch, and waited for the locksmith to come and install the floor safe.

The locksmith arrived about 3 o'clock with a helper and the two of them carried the jackhammer into the house. Pat and I wondered what in the hell our neighbors must be thinking we were doing with a jackhammer in the house. Of course, the locksmith's van had his company name on it so it was reasonable to assume that they could add two and two and get four. We pulled the carpet and the padding out of the walk-in closet in our bedroom, the locksmith got the jackhammer, and went to work on the foundation. About ten minutes later, there was a nice hole in the foundation which soon became home to our new floor safe. Once the locksmith had left and we'd cleaned up the debris from the foundation and concrete work, we began putting the remaining money in the safe. We quickly realized that the bricks would not go in the safe so we began breaking down the bricks into the five packs of $2,000. By standing the packs on end and putting them in tight, we were able to get almost all of the money in the safe. I think we had two packs of $2,000 left over that wouldn't go in the safe so I put them in the inside pocket of a blue blazer that I had hanging in the closet. If Pat and I needed money, we could get it out of the blazer pocket until that ran out and we had to open the safe. I realized then that we probably should have gotten a bigger safe. Damn, having money was a problem!

I needed to find somebody to replace Skip, and Pat and I remembered that we had a friend, Ron, who was good with all things mechanical. He was good at making jewelry, he was a good auto mechanic, and he also had built his own motorcycle from scratch. I called him up, went to see him, and presented my situation to him. Ron loved to smoke pot and he was very intrigued with the thought of smuggling and making a lot of money fast. He was engaged to a real nice lady, Lynn, and he said he was sure Lynn would not let him go on the trips. Ron was from Ohio and I think he'd been busted back home when he was younger and been given probation. When he finished his probation, he'd moved to Florida. Ron said that he'd be glad to be my mechanic but that there was no way he could go on the trips.

We took a ride and went over to Linda's house 'cause I wanted him to see Cathy V. We started up the Perkins 4.154 diesel engine and Ron was impressed. He was most pleased to see that she had a Raycor water filter that kept water in the fuel from going through the injectors and blowing them up. He said it was a good engine and a good set-up. He showed me a few things about the engine that I didn't know and he showed me how to trouble-shoot some common problems that we might encounter. It made me feel good but I would have felt better if Ron would have been able to go on the trips with me. Ron promised to be available 24/7 and said he would come in the middle of the night if I needed him. I guess having a good mechanic on call 24/7 was the best I could do. It was starting to get dark so I drove Ron home and I went home myself.

Over supper that night, Pat and I talked about who we could get to replace Skip. While we were on vacation, one of my roommates from college, Ross, had come to visit us and we'd told him we'd been smuggling, that we were buying our own boat, and were gonna run our own operation. Ross was in the landscaping business so he was very flexible with his time and his lady was a nurse who made good money. I called him that night, told him there was something I wanted to talk to him about, and asked him to come visit me as soon as he could. We didn't talk any more than that on the phone but Ross knew what I wanted to talk to him about. He came to Ft. Lauderdale that weekend, I told him that I'd bought Cathy V, that I needed another crew member, and asked him if he wanted to come to work for me. He said "yes" he was ready to go.

Now my crew was set with Rob, Jen, and Ross. I really needed another lady in case a trip came up and Jen couldn't go 'cause she had to fly a trip for Delta. Pat and I talked about some other Flight Attendants that we knew but I wasn't sure about any of them. I talked to Rob about his lady Janice and asked him if she wanted to start going on trips. I had worked concerts with her and really liked her so she was my first choice. She was in school studying to be a teacher and Rob said that she might want to go if she wasn't in school when the trip came up. I told him to talk to her and to let me know.

We had a married couple, Jay and Rose, that we were good friends with, and I'd worked a job with Jay and we'd become close friends. They had two kids, Rose didn't work, and I thought they may be interested in going on trips, at least maybe Rose would. I called them up, went to see them and told them Pat and I had been smuggling pot, they were blown away. I told them that I needed people for my crew and that I especially needed female crew. Jay had a good job and I figured he probably couldn't go but if Rose wanted to go, I told them I could use her. They said they'd have to think about it and they'd let me know in a few days. I told them that we had a lot of trips coming up and that she could make a lot of money in a short period of time. They liked that!

In a couple of days, Jerry called and said it was time to go fishin'. I called Rob and he was ready to go but Janice wasn't able to go this time. I called Ross and he was ready to go. I called Jen and she couldn't go 'cause she had a trip to fly for Delta. I called Jay and Rose and Rose said she wasn't quite ready to go yet, maybe next time. It looked like the crew was gonna be me, Rob, and Ross with no ladies.

We left Ft. Lauderdale, went down the coast to Government Cut in Miami, took a left and got on our heading for Gun Cay. The seas were calm but we had pretty good wind out of the southwest so we put the sails up so we could teach Ross to sail. He had lots of experience with ski boats and pontoon boats on the lakes around Orlando but other than sailing on Hobie Cats, he had no experience on big sailboats. The trip took on a tone of on-the-job training for Ross; and, Rob and I tried to show him everything we knew and explain it to him in detail to shorten his learning curve. From his experience on Hobie Cats, Ross understood the principles of sailing and he quickly learned to sail Cathy V.

The weather was good, we had an easy crossing, and we arrived at Gun Cay around 10 o'clock in the evening, went through the Cut, and got on a heading to Sylvia Beacon. Jerry wanted to load us at five miles north of Sylvia Beacon because one of the other middle boats wanted to load his boats at Sylvia. I was at the helm and Rob and Ross began taping down the main salon in preparation to get loaded. When we arrived at Sylvia Beacon around 12:30, there were three other boats there, we didn't recognize any of them. We turned left and headed due north for about 45 minutes. We could see some mast lights ahead of us and we figured that this was Jerry's party at five miles north. When we got to their location, sure enough, it was Apple Pie and the Tin Man.

We anchored about thirty yards away from the other boats. I let Ross take the helm and showed him how to run the boat while Rob went forward to the bow pulpit to drop the anchor. Once anchored, we tried to catnap while waiting on the call from Jerry. Around 3:00 AM, we got a call on the radio from Mr. Boo at Russell Beacon and the word was that we were not gonna get loaded tonight, Jerry had sent us over a day early. We bedded down in the cockpit and the three of us slept until the sunrise woke us up.

We had coffee in the cockpit then put on our swim trunks and jumped in the water for a wake-up swim. We had a day to kill so we might as well enjoy it and have a good time. We got snorkeling gear and tooled around Cathy, checked out the keel, hung on the anchor line, and lollygagged around for about an hour. That made us hungry so we got back on the boat, decided that we didn't want to cook anything, and just made sandwiches that we enjoyed in the cockpit with a cold drink. We called Apple Pie on the radio, told him we were going sailing, and asked him if he wanted to have a friendly race. He agreed so we both pulled our anchors, put up our sails, and went sailing on the Bank for the rest of the day. We drank beer, smoked pot, listened to Jimmy Buffett and rock-n-roll tapes and had a great afternoon. We arrived back at five north of Sylvia about an hour before sunset, rafted off with Apple Pie, and cooked steaks on the aft deck. After eating our meal and watching an awesome sunset, we touched up our tape-down job, then catnapped in the cockpit while waiting on Black Fin.

Jerry called us around 2:00 AM and said he'd be there in a short-short to party. Apple Pie untied from Cathy and just layed off our stern until Jerry arrived. The Hatteras came out of the darkness, Jerry skillfully brought her starboard side along our port side, and we tied up to each other. Apple Pie came over and tied up to Jerry's port side with his starboard side. Since we were short of people, Jerry gave us two guys to work the main salon while Rob worked the aft stateroom and Ross worked the forward cabin. We got loaded to the gills in about an hour and then Jerry began to load Apple Pie. We untied from the Hatteras and headed back toward Gun Cay light.

After navigating the Cut, we hoisted the sails and motorsailed back to Ft. Lauderdale. Our airplane, Pegasus, flew over a couple of times, Rita gave us a big "10-10" and we made it home to Linda's dock without incident. Ross was very impressed with our countersurveillance and at how smoothly the trip went. I was glad for him that we had good weather for his first trip and not the rough weather that I'd had. I took Rob and Ross home with me where we showered, ate a meal of spaghetti that Pat had prepared, and we all got a couple of hours of sleep.

We went back to Linda's house where we unloaded the boat without incident with the help of two of Jerry's guys. After we weighed the bales and made a list, I delivered the vans to Fu at the IHOP on State Road 84. Our method of operation had been fine-tuned and our organization was running very smoothly. Ross thought that smuggling was a piece of cake. Rob went home to Miami and Ross came home with me and spent another night, then, went home to Orlando the next day.

In a couple of days, before we could get paid for the trip, Jerry called and said it was time to go fishin' again, that we needed to leave the next day. I called Rob and Ross who had only been home a day and I told him to come on back. Jen was able to go this time as well as Rob's girlfriend Janice. We were coming up on Columbus Day weekend which is a great weekend for boating, there'd be boats everywhere that would be good cover for us. Jen and I went to Skaggs Albertsons and bought groceries, drinks, and ice and took everything over to Linda's and loaded it onto Cathy. We were ready to go and all excited about having a full crew of five people this time.

The next day, we pushed away from the dock about mid-morning, went out the River into the Intracoastal and the Port, out the Cut, and headed south to Miami. Since it was her first trip, I let Janice take the helm 'cause all she had to do was steer south and keep the boat parallel to the shore. When we got to Miami, Janice gave the helm to Jen, we hoisted the sails and put Cathy's bow on the heading for Gun Cay. The seas were calm but we had nice wind for sailing and we made good time crossing over the

Gulfstream to Gun. As the sun was setting, we cooked steaks on the hibachi on the aft deck and enjoyed our feast in the cockpit as the sun melted into the ocean. When we arrived at Gun Cay light, I took the helm and brought Cathy through the Cut onto the Bank and put her bow on a course for Sylvia Beacon. My experienced crew went down into the main salon and starting taping down in preparation for loading. Our experience gave us confidence but we also were almost casual about our tasks because we thought we'd lay over tonight and not get loaded until tomorrow night. We got the main salon taped down and everything stowed away but we really felt like we were sent over a day early. When we arrived at Sylvia, there were boats there that I didn't recognize, so I headed due north to our loading point at five miles north of Sylvia. When we arrived there, we dropped our anchor and waited to hear from Jerry that we were not gonna party tonight. About 2:30 AM, the radio crackled and it was Black Fin.

"Speedy Pete, Speedy Pete, Black Fin, you got your ears on good buddy, kickit' back."

I said: "Black Fin, Speedy Pete, roger that good buddy, kickit' back."

He said: "Turn your porch light on good buddy, I'm coming to have a party."

I switched on my mast light.

He said: "I gotcha' Speedy Pete, I'll see you in a short-short."

I said: "Roger that good buddy."

We couldn't believe it, we were gonna get loaded the first night! We started scurrying around like crazy to get everything out of the cockpit and stowed away. We cleared the cockpit of trash, drink cups, cassette tapes, the backgammon game, and we moved the cushions downstairs up against the wall of the main salon. Then, everyone put on their old blue jeans and t-shirts to load in. It wasn't long before we heard those big Detroit Diesel engines out in the darkness and the form of the Hatteras came out of the darkness over to our port side. Jerry skillfully brought the Hatteras in close, his guys threw us lines, and we got the two boats tied up quickly.

I looked up on the cockpit of BJ and there sat my wife! What the fuck was my wife doing on the flybridge of Jerry Smith's boat? She was supposed to be home with Sunshine. Oh well, I'd have to deal with that when I got home!

I worked the cockpit, Rob was in the aft stateroom, Ross was in the forward cabin, and Jen and Janice worked the hatch and the main salon. The bales were exceptionally big this trip, they averaged almost eighty pounds, and they were unwieldy to say the least. I would sit on the side of the cockpit and one of the guys would throw a bale over the railing onto my thighs, I would push it to Jen in the hatch who would push it to Janice in the main salon. She would drag it to Ross in the forward stateroom. Then, they'd throw another bale on my thighs and I'd push it to Rob in the hatch to the aft stateroom. The bales were so heavy they actually bruised my thighs. We all worked like a well-trained crew and got Cathy loaded in about an hour. We untied the Hatteras, Jerry backed away behind us to avoid the anchor line, and went to load his other scam boats.

We all got in the cockpit with a cold drink and took a breather to cool off. It was a pretty clean load so we didn't have a lot of residue on the deck and in the cockpit. We got a bucket of water, sponges, and paper towels and cleaned up the cockpit. Then, we put the cushions back in the cockpit, pulled the anchor, and put the bow of the boat on a heading to Gun Cay. I was at the helm while my crew cleaned up the main salon, stowed the drop cloths in a trash bag, and began taking showers. After my crew were all showered and had on clean clothes, I took my shower and put on clean clothes.

As we approached Gun Cay, the sky was beginning to get light as the sunrise approached. I took Cathy through the Cut and put us on a heading to Ft. Lauderdale. Rob, Ross, and I pulled two-hour shifts at the helm and catnapped as much as we could while Jen and Janice slept in the main salon. The weather was just beautiful with calm seas and enough wind to keep our sails full. We sighted land about middle of the day, found the smokestacks at Port Everglades with the binoculars, and headed straight in toward the 'stacks. It was Columbus Day weekend and there were hundreds of boats everywhere, great cover for us and we were all smiles! We heard Rita talking to some of the other scam boats and she was giving them a "big 10-10, it's clean and green."

Our airplane flew over, dipped his wings, and called us on the CB radio.

"Speedy Pete, Speedy Pete, this is Pegasus, you copy me, come back?"

I grabbed the CB microphone: "Pegasus, this is Speedy Pete, we copy, come back."

Pegasus said: "Speedy Pete, there's a big bear about 200 feet long up at the north end of Lauderdale. He's heading north but just wanted you to be aware that he's out there, you copy, come back?"

I said: "Roger that Pegasus, is that bear a Candy Striper?"

Pegasus said: "That's a roger, Speedy Pete, a 200 foot long Candy Striper."

I said: "Okay Pegasus, 'preciate the heads-up, we'll alter our course to come in a little south and stay away from the north side."

Pegasus said: "That would be a good idea, Speedy Pete, I'll keep you posted if the situation changes."

I said: "Roger that, Pegasus, we appreciate the updates."

I told my crew: "Okay, we've got a 200 foot long Coast Guard Cutter up at the north end of Ft. Lauderdale that's heading north away from us. That's good that he's heading north but bad that he's out there at all." Nobody said anything, the asspucker factor just increased about 50% but still no reason to panic. "But, if he turns around and starts coming this way, there's no way we can outrun him at 6 ½ knots top speed."

Rob said: "Is there anything else we can do?"

I said: "Yeah, we can get in close to shore in the shallow water. If we see them put a dinghy in the water to come and board us, we can run Cathy up on the beach and run like hell." I'd learned that from 'Taterhead and Jimmy. I turned the wheel to the left, headed in close to the beach, and put the smokestacks at about 2 o'clock to my bow. We were still in deep water but the dropoff was in pretty close to shore off Dania Beach and I wanted to get us into about fifteen feet of water. That should put us about two hundred yards offshore and I hoped I could run Cathy up on Dania Beach if I had to. I decided to call Rita in the channel boat so I gave the helm to Rob and grabbed the CB microphone.

I said: "Little Lady, Little Lady, Speedy Pete, you got a copy, come back?"

She said: "Speedy Pete, Little Lady, I copy, what's your 20?"

I said: "I'm about 30 to 45 minutes from the intersection, come back."

She said: "You got a big 10-10 good buddy, it's clean and green from where I am, You know about that Candy Striper up north?"

I said: "Roger that, I'm coming into the intersection from the southside."

She said: "You better get here quick as you can before it decides to turn around "

I said: "I'm coming as hard as I can Little Lady."

She said: "Roger that, we'll be standing by for ya'."

I decided a little music might help to break the tension so I turned on WSHE on the radio and Tommy Judge was cranking out the rock-n-roll on the airwaves. Just then, the plane flew over again heading south.

He said: "Speedy Pete, Pegasus, you copy?"

I said: "Roger that, Pegasus, I copy."

He said: "That Candy Striper has turned around and he's coming your way. He's right off the dropoff in the deep water, he's in real close to shore, you copy?"

I said: "Roger that Pegasus, I'm coming as hard as I can."

He said: "It looks like he's gonna get to the intersection about the same time you do." The asspucker factor just went to the max!

I said: "Roger that, Pegasus, all I can do is keep coming like I'm doing."

He said: "Roger that, Speedy Pete, we're standing by."

Well, things got real serious real fast. I took the helm from Rob, pushed the throttle all the way forward, ran the engine up from 2000 to 2400 rpm's, and got Cathy up to about 7 ½ knots which was damn hear hull speed for a 41 foot Columbia sailboat. The wind was out of the southwest, Cathy was laid over on her starboard side, and we were booking! Cathy was cutting through the water like a knife and we were in a race with the Coast Guard Cutter to see who could get to Port Everglades first. The adrenaline was flowing, I could feel the blood pumping in my temples, the sky was blue, the clouds were white, the sea was green and it was intense!

I was locked in on the wheel and had the bow of Cathy pointed right at the rock jetty on the north side of the Cut. We were about twenty minutes from the mouth of the Cut which was about 2-3 miles away. We could see the Cutter up around the pier at Commercial Boulevard, steaming south, putting out a lot of black smoke, and bearing down on us. We felt sure they were coming to bust us because they were in very close to shore for a boat that size. Just then, Tommy Judge on WSHE played "Beatin' the Odds" by Molly Hatchett. "We were beatin' the odds, we were beatin' the odds, we were beatin' the odds again. We were gambling with our souls, we were playing to win, we were beatin' the odds again."

I thought to myself: *"No shit, Tommy Judge, I hope we beat the odds this time!"*

Just then, our plane flew over again.

He said: "Speedy Pete, Pegasus, you see that bear?"

I said: "Roger that."

He said: "He's coming right at you!"

I said: "I can see that but there's nothing I can do, I'm going as fast as I can."

He said: "You see that jetty?"

I said: "That's a roger."

He said: "You know there's a reef that extends out about 150-200 yards from the end of the jetty and the water is only about two feet deep?"

I said: "Roger that."

He said: "Well, you'd better change course or you'll be aground in about five minutes."

I said: "Roger that, we're about to change course now."

We were about a half a mile from the jetty and the reef in about thirteen feet of water. We had a little bit of time before we ran aground but not much. The Coast Guard Cutter was about a half a mile away and bearing down on us. Rita was sitting right at the mouth of the Cut but there was nothing she could do except watch the bust unfold. My crew had heard the conversation with our airplane and they were watching me intently.

Janice said: "What are you gonna do Scooter?"

I said: "I'm gonna run this son-of-a-bitch up on the jetty if I have to and we'll all jump off and run like hell. We'll walk away from this boat and this load if we have to."

The Cutter got closer and closer to us and we got closer and closer to running aground, it was touch-n-go at that point. I realized that the Cutter was gonna make it to the Cut before I did, we were gonna lose the race. I didn't know if the Cutter was going into the Port or not but I was sure it was gonna get to the mouth of the Cut before I did. About that time, I realized that the course the Cutter was on would take him behind Cathy, it was gonna pass behind us.

Lo and behold, The Coast Guard Cutter passed behind us about 100 yards, got right in the middle of the channel, and started going into Port Everglades. I had to make a decision right then and there that either I was gonna turn to port and get in the channel in front of the Cutter or I was gonna turn to starboard and get in the channel behind the Cutter. We had to do something NOW because we were bearing down on the reef.

I shouted to my crew: "Prepare to come about! Rob, you take the port line, Ross, you take the starboard line, ladies, get up at the front of the cockpit and stay out of the way. Keep your head down 'cause the boom's coming around."

The guys knew what we were about to do and Jen did too, I wasn't so sure about Janice but she was gonna learn fast.

I said: "Okay, here we go" and turned the wheel hard to the right until we did an about-face and were going south into the wind. The boom swung around from the right to the left and my well-trained crew trimmed the lines properly. We looked like we knew what we were doing, we looked like sailors, we looked like professional sailors.

Now, we were on a heading going out of the Port that put us almost parallel with the Cutter going in the opposite direction into the Port, and we're close, about 50 yards. The Cutter passes us and is almost in the mouth of the Cut. I start turning the wheel to the right to get in the channel where there's about 40 feet of water depth.

I said: "Prepare to come about!"

My crew jumps back into position as Cathy comes around to starboard, the boom swings back around again, nobody gets hit in the head, and Rob and Ross adjust the lines perfectly. Now, we're following the Coast Guard Cutter into Port Everglades.

Janice said: "What'd you do that for, Scooter?"

I said: "Well, I'd rather us smell their diesel smoke then have them smell our pot." Everybody cracked up laughing and the tension was broken, 'cause we knew the Cutter hadn't come to bust us. We were all breathing a lot easier by then. Rita cruised by in the channel boat and gave us a little wave. I'll bet she thought that we were gonna get somebody busted today, we thought that too. We came on into the Port following the U.S. Coast Guard Cutter Diligence, it looked like they were giving us an escort, we all laughed about it later. The Diligence got into the Port and docked while I turned Cathy into the wind and my crew skillfully dropped the sails. While we were dropping the sails, the bells went off on the bridge to stop the auto traffic so the bridge could open for the boats. There were at least a hundred boats in the Port going every which-a-way. Jen and Janice had on their two-piece bathing suits and were standing on the bow looking good. We were shipshape!

We went through the 17th Street bridge, past the Gulf docks, up the River through the middle of town, and into the dock at Linda's house. Boy, was that a relief! We got our duffle bags, padlocked the hatch and the doors, got off the boat, and went home. We made it again! "We were gambling with our souls, we were playing to win, we were beatin' the odds again."

When I got home, the first thing I did was talk to Pat about going on the trips. I told her that she was supposed to be home taking care of Sunshine, not going on trips with Jerry. All she was doing was breeding mistrust. I said: "You will not go on any more trips with Jerry or with anybody, are we clear?" She was not happy but she shook her head "yes".

That night, we went back to Linda's house and unloaded Cathy. Jerry gave me two guys like before, Jen was our lookout, and the unloading went smoothly. The next morning, I delivered the load in two vans to Fu and his boys at the IHOP on State Road 84. Our operation was running like clockwork, the airplane and the channel boat had been superb, and my crew had performed admirably. I couldn't wait 'till the next payday, it was gonna be big, I was gonna get paid for two trips at once. Go big or go home, I'd gone BIG! Oh boy!

Chapter 14
Lawyers, Lear Jets, and the Laundromat
Crime is not supposed to pay, but sometimes, crime pays well.

As soon as I'd gotten a good night's sleep and was rested, I'd started working on my lists of the bales and the weights for the two trips, and I wanted to be ready when Jerry called. I figured for the first trip that I would net right at $100,000 on 5600 pounds of pot because I just had the salaries for Rob and Ross, no ladies. For the second trip, I thought I would also net right at $100,000 because I'd hauled 5800 pounds of pot in those big bales. I really was hoping that I'd end up with $190-200,000 net for the two trips, not too shabby!

In a couple of days, Jerry called and said to come over to his house, he had green stamps. I drove over to his house on S.W. 5th Place in my little Honda Civic Hatchback and boy, was I excited! I knocked on the door, opened the door and said "Anybody home?" and Jerry said "Yeah, back here" so I walked to his den in the back of the house. He was sitting on the sofa and had some charts of the Bahamas lying on the coffee table.

He said: "Hey man, howya' doin'?"

I said: "Great, what's goin' on?"

He said: "Oh, I'm just looking at some islands in the Exumas and the Berrys, we may buy one."

I said: "Oh yeah, what are you gonna do with it?"

He said: "Well, it would be a good investment and we may need to use it sometime. Little Whale Cay near Chub is for sale for a million and a half, I may buy it by myself. Me and Joe are looking at a couple of islands in the Exumas that are about 3-5 million."

I said: "That would be really cool to own your own island."

He said: "Yeah it would, wouldn't it? So, let's see what you've got."

I handed him a copy of the lists for the two trips. He got his calculator, I got mine, and we started to settle up. For the first trip, I'd hauled 100 bales and 5600 pounds of pot and sack weight, that was 5300 pounds of pot. Fu was paying $220 per pound so that was a gross of $1,166,000. Jerry was paying me 12% so my gross was $139,920. I had $30,000 in salaries to Rob and Ross, $5,000 to the two guys that helped us unload, and $1,000 to Jen for being our lookout, so my net for the first trip was $103,920.

For the second trip, I'd hauled 80 bales and 5800 pounds of pot and sack weight that was 5560 pounds of pot. Fu was paying $230 per pound for this trip because the pot was primo Santa Marta Gold. It was a beautiful gold color and actually smelled like butter. So, that gross was $1,278,800 times 12% gave me a gross of $153,456. I had $45,000 in salaries, $5,000 to the two guys that helped us unload, and $1,000 to Jen as the lookout, a total of $51,000 in expenses. That netted me $102,456 for the second trip. For the two trips, my gross was $293,376 and my net was $206,376! I was thrilled!!

Jerry went into his downstairs bedroom and came back with that big Samsonite suitcase that I'd seen before at Joan's Condo on my first payday, it looked heavy as hell. He opened it up on the coffee table and it was full of bricks of money in baggies on both sides. He started taking bricks out of the suitcase and putting them on the sofa between us. He counted out thirty bricks, $300,000, then closed the suitcase and took it back in the bedroom. He came back with a box that toilet paper came in by the case; I guess a whiskey box wasn't big enough for thirty bricks. We started putting the bricks in the box and on the last brick, Jerry took out two packs of $2,000.

He said: "I'm gonna give you $296,000 'cause you did such a good job."

I said: "Wow, thanks a lot man, I appreciate that!"

He said: "What are you gonna do with all this money?"

I said: "I don't know man, put it in a safe deposit box I guess."

He said: "Don't you have a safe deposit box already?"

I said: "Yeah, I do."

He said: "Isn't it already full?"

I said: "Yeah, pretty much."

He said: "You keep making money like this, you're gonna need your own walk-in vault. That ain't the answer. How much money have you made?"

I said: "Well, do you mean gross or net after I pay my salaries?"

He said: "No, how much money have you made yourself, not everybody else?"

I said: "A little over $300,000."

He said: "I think that once you pass a quarter million dollars that you need to talk to a lawyer and get yourself set up offshore. You need to start putting your money in the bank and sheltering your money."

I said: "Well, I don't know any lawyers."

He said: "I'm using one, I'll set you up an appointment to go and talk to him. He'll help you out, he's real good, he's an expert in offshore."

I said: "What's this guy's name?"

He said: "Jim Dolan."

I said: "Well, get me an appointment with Jim Dolan and I'll go see him."

He said: "Okay, I'll call him later on and let you know."

I said: "Good. Listen man, there's something I want to talk to you about."

He said: "Okay, shoot, what is it?"

I said: "I'd like to buy another boat, can I do that, will Joe let you load me?"

He said: "Yeah man, that shouldn't be a problem, Joe is always short scammers. What do you want?"

I said: "I don't know, what do you think? Should I get a power boat and have one power and one sail or should I get another sailboat?"

He said: "You can get a power boat if you want but they're a lot more suspect than a sailboat. You know, a sailboat is a sailboat is a sailboat. All the people we see in the papers that are getting busted are using power boats. I think the heat is looking out for power boats more than sailboats. I don't know of a single sailboat that's gotten busted."

I said: "Okay then, I'll get another sailboat. I just wanta' be successful and not get busted. Do you know anybody that's got a sailboat they wanta' sell?"

He said: "Yeah, I know a guy that's got one. Let me check with him, I'll call him and see if he wants to sell it. What about people, you got people that can run it for you?"

I said: "I thought I would hire some new people and run the new boat myself with them. Rob and Ross can run Cathy, I've got them trained and they're experienced, they've got a couple of trips under their belts. I thought that the first trip, we would sail together and cross together but I'm sure they can find Gun Cay and Sylvia Beacon without my help. Is this new boat in pretty good shape? I don't want a piece-of-shit boat that's gonna break down on me, I'd rather pay a little more and get a good boat."

He said: "Yeah, I think the guy takes pretty good care of it. He does a lot of day sailing on weekends and he's been to the islands a couple of times. It should be in pretty good shape."

I said: "Is the boat being worked now, it's not hot is it?"

He said: "No man, the guys not a scammer, he's got a straight job, the boat's not hot."

I said: "That's good. How much will it cost?"

He said: "It'll probably cost about the same as Cathy, boats that size are going for $1,000 a foot. It doesn't really matter anyway, does it? You're gonna make so fuckin' much money with it, what difference is a couple of thousand dollars either way?"

I said: "Yeah, you're right. I guess in the big picture, a couple of thousand either way is no big deal. Do you think we can buy it before the next trip?"

He said: "Well, if he wants to sell it, we can get it from him immediately."

I said: "That would be great!"

By now, my head was swimming. I'd just made over $200,000, I'm buying another boat, and I'm going to see a lawyer so I can go offshore with my money. This was all coming at me pretty damn fast but hey, I'm flexible. I got ready to leave Jerry's house and realized that I couldn't carry my box of money by myself; it was too big and bulky, too heavy! We both laughed and Jerry said he'd give me a hand. We each picked up a corner of the box, walked through the house, out the door, and to the back of my little Honda. The box was too big to go in the floorboard in the front so I opened the hatchback, put the backseat down, and we put the box in the car. I wondered if the neighbors were watching. We shook hands and I drove home scared to death that somebody was gonna hit me, I drove like a little ole' lady.

When I got home, I went in the front door and hollered: "Honey, come here, I need your help!" Pat came to the front door, I turned around, walked to the back of the car, and she followed me. I opened the hatchback and grabbed one side of the box, she grabbed the other side, and we walked the box into the house and into our bedroom, we dropped the box on the floor in front of the bed.

I opened the top of the box and said: "Take a look at this." Her eyes got real big!

She said: "How much is that?"

I said: " $296,000."

She said: "How much is ours?"

I said: "TWO HUNDRED AND EIGHT THOUSAND DOLLARS!" She was speechless for about a minute.

Then she said: "What are we gonna do with it? The safe deposit box and the safe are full." Damn, having money was a problem!

I said. "We're going offshore." She didn't say anything for about a minute.

Then, she said: "What does that mean, we're going offshore, where's offshore?"

I said: "I think it means a tax haven somewhere like Switzerland or the Cayman Islands or the Netherlands. Jerry is getting me an appointment with his lawyer who's supposed to be an expert in offshore."

She said: "Why do we have to do that? Why can't we just put it in another safe deposit box?"

I said: "Every time we work a trip, we're gonna need another safe deposit box. Jerry says we can't keep getting safe deposit boxes at the bank 'cause it might raise their eyebrows, they might get suspicious and turn us in."

She said: "Turn us in to who?"

I said: "The authorities I guess, maybe the IRS. I don't want to get in trouble with the IRS, they're the ones that sent Al Capone to jail, remember?"

She said: "So, if we take the money offshore to a tax haven, how do we get it back if we need it?"

I said: "I don't know, I'm hoping the lawyer will tell me that tomorrow. All I know is, Jerry says we can't have a dozen safe deposit boxes at the bank, it'll make 'em suspicious and we don't want that. We can't convert our walk-in closet to a vault because if a bad person finds out, they'll come in with a gun and rob us, maybe kill us too. I'd give 'em the money and hope they wouldn't kill us but you never know. The smartest thing to do is go offshore, that's why Jerry told us to do it."

She said: "Howard, this is getting complicated, ain't it?" When Pat called me Howard instead of Scooter, I knew she was serious.

I said: "Yes it is. All I know to do is just deal with it as it comes up. Try not to worry, we'll just take it a step at a time and figure it out as best we can."

She said: "How much are you gonna take offshore when you go?"

I said: "Let's keep the safe and the safe deposit box full, and I'll take everything else offshore."

She said: "Well the safe and the safe deposit box are damn near full now. Are you gonna take everything in that box offshore?"

I said: "Yeah, why don't we keep $8,000 and I'll take $200,000 offshore. I don't know what else to do other than take some to Georgia and let my Mom and Dad keep it for us."

She said incredulously: "You're gonna tell your Mom and Dad you've been smuggling?"

I said: "I think we're gonna have to at some point. Oh yeah, we're buying another sailboat, Jerry's got a guy that wants to sell one and we're gonna buy it."

She said: "Howard, do you know what you're doing?"

I said: "Honey, look at that box of money. That is as real as it fuckin' gets. That box of money is for two trips. With two boats, we can make that much every trip, every trip woman, do you hear what I'm saying? We agreed that we wanted to make as much as we could, as fast as we could and then retire. To do that, we gotta have more boats."

She said: "Who's gonna run the new boat?"

I said: "I am, I'm gonna have to hire some new people to go with me on the new boat. Rob and Ross and Jen can run Cathy V. I'll train the new people on the new boat and then let them run it and we'll buy a third boat."

She said: "Howard, are you fuckin' crazy?"

I said: "Hell yeah, I'm crazy. You know I'm crazy, that's one reason you love me, right, 'cause I'm crazy?"

She said: "Howard, this is a lot to throw at me at one time."

I said: "It's a lot for me too. We'll just take it one step at a time. I'll go see the lawyer and we'll go from there. We'll just go with it, that's all we can do; we'll just go with it."

Just then, the phone rang and it was Jerry.

He said: "Hey man, howya' doin'?"

I said: "Pretty good, me and Pat are having a serious discussion, she's almost freakin' out on me, she thinks I'm fuckin' crazy."

He laughed and said: "Hey man, we're all fuckin' crazy to be in this crazy business, that's a given. Tell her to get a grip, that everything's gonna be all right. Listen, you've got an appointment at 11 o'clock tomorrow with Jim Dolan. Also, the guy wants to sell his sailboat and I told him we wanted it."

I said: "Great, how much?"

He said: "He asked for $45,000, I didn't want to beat him down so I told him that was fine."

I said: "Great, what kind of sailboat is it?"

He said: "It's a 41 foot Columbia Sloop just like Cathy V."

I said: "Are you shittin' me? I'm gonna own two 41 foot Columbia's? That's great; I love 41 foot Columbia's."

He said: "Yeah, I thought you'd like that. Look, I'll pay the guy for the boat and you can pay me back."

I said: "Super! Where can I put her?"

He said: "We'll put her at a dock in the boatyard for now. If we have to, we can flip-flop her with Cathy at Linda's house. I'm gonna buy some more houses so as soon as I can close on one, we can put her there."

I said: "That's awesome man. Thanks a lot for your help, I really appreciate it."

I hung up with Jerry and filled Pat in on our conversation. I told her that Jerry said to get a grip, that everything was gonna be all right. She was speechless and looked overwhelmed. Hell, I was overwhelmed too, that box of money overwhelmed me. With the money in the safe and the money in the box, we had almost $325,000 in the house, which was too much to have in one place! It was a little scary. I called Rob and arranged to meet him tomorrow afternoon after I'd met with Jim Dolan. I called Jen and asked her to come over after supper tonight. I called Ross and told him he could get his green stamps next time he came to town or he could make a special trip, whatever he wanted to do was okay with me. He said he'd get his green stamps the next time he came to town.

Pat and I went in the kitchen, put Sunshine in her highchair, and began to cook supper. We didn't talk very much, I think everything had pretty much been said. When supper was ready, we ate in the family room and watched the local news. There were no boats that were busted and there were no bales of marijuana washing up on the beach anywhere, it was a slow news night. Jen came over and I paid her $9,500, she stayed awhile and then went home. We put Sunny to bed and got ready for bed ourselves. We dragged our box of money into the walk-in closet and crawled in bed. We started fooling around and took it real slow to savor it. We made long, slow, wild passionate love and it was wonderful! Having money was a problem but damn, life was good when you had a bunch of it. I fell asleep apprehensive about going to see Jim Dolan tomorrow. I hope he is as good as Jerry says he is. We shall see, we shall see!

When I woke up the next morning and was having my coffee, I began to think about my meeting with Jim Dolan. I'd never had an appointment with a lawyer before and I didn't know what to expect. Jerry hadn't told me very much about Jim Dolan and I didn't know how much I should tell him. I didn't know how much Jim Dolan knew from Jerry. Did he know we were smuggling pot and breaking the law? Jerry said that Jim was "cool" and that he was really good but what did that mean? Did "cool" mean he was just a cool guy or did it mean he knew we were smuggling and he was "cool" with that? I decided to play it real straight and tell him as little as possible but still get the job done, that would be my approach.

I showered, put on one of my suits, and drove over to the offices of Dolan, Fertig, and Curtis, Attorneys-at-Law. When I arrived a little before 11 o'clock, I found their office and with a little nervousness, went inside and walked up to the receptionist.

I said: "Hi, I'm Scooter Alford; I've got an 11 o'clock appointment with Jim Dolan."

She said: "Okay, he's got somebody with him but if you'll have a seat, he'll be right with you, he's finishing up."

I sat down in the receptionist area and waited about five minutes. A door opened and two men walked out, they're talking and smiling, they shake hands and one man leaves.

This little man turns to me and says: "Hi, I'm Jim Dolan, come on into my office and let's talk." I walked into his office and sat down in front of his desk, he takes a seat in a big brown leather chair behind his desk. I am very apprehensive and I think he can sense it. I really don't know where to start.

I said: "Well, you know I'm a friend of Jerry Smith's. I've made a little bit of money and Jerry thinks I need to put some of my money offshore. He says you're the man I need to talk to for this. Is this something that you do and if so, can you help me?"

He said: "Yes, that is one of the things that I do so you've come to the right person. How much do you know about offshore banking and tax havens?"

I said: "Not very much so you'll have to educate me."

He said: "Okay, I know you've heard of Switzerland, right?" I shook my head yes. "That's the most famous tax haven in the world, only problem is it's too far away for us to use. In the western hemisphere, there's a couple: the Bahamas is one, there's the Cayman Islands, and there's the Netherlands Antilles in St. Martin. For various reasons, we don't like the Bahamas as a tax haven. We like the Cayman Islands and we like the Netherlands Antilles. Of the two, we like the Caymans the best. It's just on the other side of Cuba about an hour and a half away by plane. It's in the British Commonwealth so its laws are based on British Law just like here in America, so it's easier for us to understand than the Netherlands Antilles which is Dutch and based on Dutch Law. The Caymans is closer, it has strict privacy laws, its laws are based on British Law like our laws so we just feel more comfortable in the Caymans. Does that make sense?"

I said: "Yes, it does. So what do we have to do, go there and open a bank account? How do we do that?"

He said: "First, we have to form a corporation in the Cayman Islands then we'll open the bank account in the name of the corporation. We can handle all that for you. All we have to do is choose a name for the corporation, I'll write a letter to a lawyer in Georgetown that I work with, he'll form the Cayman Corporation for us, and then we'll fly down there, sign the papers, and open the bank account. Do you have a name for the corporation that you want to use?"

I said: "No, not really, I haven't thought about it. What about you, do you have a good name we can use?"

He thought for a couple of seconds and said: "What about Retoocs?"

I said: "Retoocs, what does Retoocs mean?"

He said: "It's Scooter backwards."

I said: " Well, that would be okay I guess." I thought for a minute. "How about Sunshine? My daughter's name is Sunshine and we live in the Sunshine. Do you think that's too obvious? Aren't we supposed to use a name that can't be connected to me to maintain the secrecy?"

He said: "I like Sunshine. How about Sunshine International Investments, Ltd. Everything in the Caymans is Limited. We could use that as our first choice and Retoocs International Investments, Ltd. as our second choice. We need one more name; they want us to give them three names." I thought for a minute.

I said: "How about Tres Hombres? It's the name of a ZZTop Album that I like that has a song called LaGrange on it. I'm from LaGrange, Georgia."

He said: "Okay, we'll use Tres Hombres International Investments, Ltd. That should do it. I'll draft a letter to the lawyer in Cayman and give him those three names, we should be able to get one of them, we'll probably get Sunshine. As soon as he gets approval from the government on the name, he'll contact me, we'll fly down to sign the papers and open the bank account. Does that sound all right?"

I said: "Yes, that sounds good. Now, how much is this gonna cost?"

He said: "It costs $1,800 to form the corporation and for the first year's annual fees. After that, it's $1,200 for the annual fees every year.

I said: "Okay, that sounds reasonable. Do I pay for these fees myself or what? How does that work?"

He said: "No, I'll pay for everything with a company check and then we'll bill you later. That's easier for you. You'll pay us for everything."

I said: "That sounds great. Anything else we need to do?"

He said: "No, not for now, that's it. I'll call you as soon as I hear from the lawyer in Cayman and we've got approval on the name. Then, we can fly to Cayman at your earliest convenience."

I said: "Okay, thank you very much. This has been very informative. I'll wait to hear from you."

I left Jim Dolan's office feeling great! That wasn't so hard. I drove to Miami and met Rob at the Holiday Inn at Calder Race Track and paid him and Janice for the last two trips. We had a drink around the pool, I told him that I'd bought another boat, and that I wanted him and Ross to run it for me. He said he thought they could handle it. We talked about the last trip and the encounter with the Coast Guard Cutter; we had a good laugh about it. He said everyone was impressed with the way the plane and the channel boat performed, that he and Janice thought we were gonna get busted, and they thought I did a super job running the boat. He said I performed admirably under pressure. I said: "Thanks, I appreciate the confidence." When we finished our drink, we shook hands warmly and departed for home, he went south and I went north.

I got on I-95 going north in the middle of 5 o'clock traffic, it reminded me of my commutes to the Miami Dolphins Ticket Office less than a year ago. I had sure come a long way in less than a year. I got off I-95 at Commercial Boulevard and drove my little Honda Civic Hatchback to our house on 18th Terrace. I went in and kissed Pat and Sunshine and then told Pat all about Jim Dolan. She was all ears!

In a couple of days, I got a call from Jim Dolan that he'd heard from the Cayman Attorney and everything was all right, we had gotten the name Sunshine International Investments, Ltd. We needed to go down to Cayman, sign the papers for the corporation, and open the bank account. He asked me when was it convenient for me to go and I told him I'd have to check with Jerry, that I'd get back with him shortly.

I called Jerry, told him what was happening, and asked him if he knew if anything was coming up, I certainly didn't want to miss a trip because I was out of town. He said he hadn't heard anything from Joe in a couple of days and that usually meant it would be at least 3-4 days before anything would happen. He said we were having a little lull in the action and that I should go ahead and take care of my business.

I called Jim Dolan, he was available, and his secretary put me through.

I said: "Jim, the sooner we can go the better."

He said: "Okay, good, let me see if I can get us a plane and we can go tomorrow."

I said: "Tomorrow would be fine."

He said: "I'll get back with you this afternoon."

We hung up and in a little while, he called back.

He said: "Okay, we've got a plane and we're gonna go down tomorrow. We've got an appointment with the lawyer and we'll come back the same day."

I said: "Can we get a flight?"

He said: "We're not going commercial."

I said: "Oh, we're not, how are we going?"

He said: "I chartered a Lear Jet."

I said: "Holy shit! What do you mean you chartered a Lear Jet?"

He said: "I called Tom Boye over at National Jets at Ft. Lauderdale's Private Jet Center and chartered us a Lear Jet 25."

I said: "Is that necessary?"

He said: "Well, yeah, you've gotta take money down there, right?"

I said: "Yeah, I guess I do."

He said: "Well, you don't want to take money on a commercial jet."

I said: "I don't? How come?"

He said: "If they find it when you're going through security, you're in a lot of trouble."

I said: "Why?"

He said: "Because you can't take $5,000 out of the U.S without declaring it and you don't want to declare it because if you declare it, you've got to pay tax on it. If you have to pay tax on it, it's defeating the purpose of taking it offshore."

I said: "Oh, I see. So, you mean if I take more than $5,000 out of the country, I'm supposed to declare it?"

He said: "Yeah, you're supposed to declare it on your Customs & Immigration Form. There's a specific place on the back of the Customs & Immigration Form that says "Are you or any member of your family carrying more than $5,000 U.S.?" If it's more than $5,000, you're supposed to declare it and if you declare it, they report it to the IRS and you have to pay tax on it. That's the whole purpose of us doing this, so you don't have to pay tax on it."

I said: "Aren't we gonna have to declare it when we go on this Lear Jet?"

He said: "No, they don't ask you any questions. There's no law that requires the private charter companies to make their customers fill out the Customs & Immigration Forms. Only the commercial airlines cooperate with the government and make their passengers fill out the forms. The private airlines don't have to do it so they don't, and if they did, they wouldn't have any business so they don't do it."

I said: "Okay, I see. So, how much is this Lear Jet gonna cost?"

He said: "Tom Boye gives me a deal, this one's gonna cost $2,000."

I said: "TWO THOUSAND DOLLARS? Man, do we have to do this?"

He said: "Scooter, it's the only way."

I said: "So, when we leave the country tomorrow, I'm gonna have more than $5,000 and I'm gonna be breaking the law?"

He said: "Yeah, you're gonna be breaking the law."

I said: "Is that the only way to do this?"

He said: "That's the only way. The only way to get the money offshore is to take it out of the country illegally because if you don't do that, then you have to pay taxes on the money. If you have to pay taxes, you're defeating the purpose of going offshore. Look at it this way, the costs of forming the Cayman Corporation and chartering the Lear Jet are small compared to paying the IRS 40-50% tax on your money."

I said: "Yeah, you've got that right! Okay, I see now. All right, I'll meet you at the private air terminal at Ft. Lauderdale airport at 9 o'clock tomorrow morning."

He said: "I'll see you at nine."

That night, I didn't sleep very well; this was all new to me. I had no idea what to expect tomorrow, I had to trust Jim Dolan. I had a very uneasy feeling because I knew so little about offshore banking and tax havens, but I had an inkling that I was about to get a good education. I was going to take a good part of all the money I'd made and go offshore, put it in a foreign bank account that was not insured by the FDIC, and give a foreign attorney signature power and control over the money and the bank account. I didn't like anybody having control of my money except me. My sleep that night was fitful and uneasy to say the least.

I woke up the next morning, had coffee, showered, and put on a suit, I was gonna play this very straight. I pulled the box of money out of the closet and into the middle of the floor in the bedroom. I got my briefcase and put 4 bricks, $40,000, inside and barely got it closed. I got a small, brown Samsonite suitcase and put 16 bricks, $160,000 inside, and barely got it closed. I kissed Pat and Sunny goodbye, picked up my briefcase and suitcase, got in my car, and drove to the private air terminal on the backside of Ft. Lauderdale International Airport.

I arrived about 8:55 AM, parked, got my briefcase and suitcase, and walked in the lobby of the building. I could see out the far window this beautiful little Lear Jet with red carpet running from the door of the building to the door of the Lear Jet. I thought to myself: "Wow, they rolled out the red carpet for me, literally!" Jim Dolan was waiting in the lobby and he was all smiles. He introduced me to the two pilots, Frank Gaines, the Iron Man, and the Golden Greek.

The Golden Greek said: "Mr. Alford, let me take your suitcase" and he took it out of my hand, walked out to the front of the Lear Jet, and started putting it in the baggage compartment in the nose of the plane.

I looked at Jim Dolan and said: "I'd feel a whole lot better if we could keep the suitcase inside the plane with us."

Jim knew the suitcase was full of money so he walked outside to the front of the plane, spoke to the Golden Greek, and he put the suitcase inside the plane. I walked outside and stood in the sunshine at the door to the airplane, it was a beautiful South Florida morning.

The Iron Man said: "Are we all set Mr. Alford? Are you ready to go?"

I shook my head yes. "Okay, climb aboard, watch your head and we'll get going."

I climbed up the ladder into the plane and took the first seat on the right. Jim Dolan came in after me and took the first seat on the left side of the airplane. The Iron Man climbed in and got in the left seat up front in the cockpit. The Golden Greek climbed in, shut the door behind him, locked it, and got in the right seat up front. The engines began turning, then caught, and started up. This was Cool!! The Iron Man pushed the throttles easily forward and we taxied slowly out to the end of the runway, took a left turn then another left and we were sitting at the end of the main runway. Both pilots turned their heads toward the back and looked at us through the door.

The Iron Man said: "Everybody strapped in and ready to go?"

Jim Dolan looked at me and said: "You ready, Scooter?"

I said: "Yeah, I'm ready."

He said: "Give them a thumbs up."

I gave them a thumbs up, they turned around, and the Iron Man pushed the throttles all the way forward. That son-of-a-gun started moving down the runway and Jim and I were pinned in our seats, we couldn't have gotten up if we'd wanted to. We're hurtling down the runway, the Iron Man pulls back on the wheel, and the nose of the plane turns and goes almost straight up. He took the plane up to cruising altitude at about a 75 degree angle; I know Jim Dolan told them to do that to give me a thrill, and what a thrill it was. We were lying down on our backs in our seats and I felt like an astronaut blasting off in the Space Shuttle. We were going straight up! These guys must be ex-fighter pilots because they were flying this Lear Jet like an F-14. It wasn't long at all before we leveled off at our cruising altitude traveling 450 miles per hour. We were riding on a bullet!

We had a pot of hot coffee, a box of Dunkin' Donuts, milk, orange juice, soft drinks, vodka, rum, bourbon, beer, cans of nuts, and potato chips. Jim and I got a cup of coffee and a donut and had breakfast at 48,000 feet traveling at 450 miles per hour, it was cool! We chitchatted about nothing in particular and in a few minutes, the Golden Greek told me to come forward and take a look. I went up into the cockpit and had a great aerial view of Cuba; we were flying right over the middle of the island in a corridor that the Cuban Government permitted commercial aircraft to use. I returned to my seat and asked Jim what Customs was going to be like in Cayman.

He said: "Man, don't worry about it; it'll be a piece of cake. They want your money, that's their livelihood. They're a tax haven, that's the reason they exist, for people like you to bring money to put in their banks. You know, there's over three hundred banks in this little bitty country. People come down here everyday bringing money to put in these banks. They're not gonna bother you at all. The only thing I did do is I brought some manila envelopes for us to put the money in so when they open your briefcase, they won't see all this money. They'll pick up the envelopes and feel them but they won't open them. They want to make sure you don't have any guns that you're trying to bring in, there's no guns allowed in the Cayman Islands. They'll ask you what's in the envelopes and you just tell them money. They have no problem with anything as long as it's money because they want your money. It's good for their banks and it's good for their country."

That was easy for me to understand but I still felt uneasy about it. Jim got the manila envelopes out of his briefcase, I got my briefcase, and we started putting the money inside the envelopes. We had to break down the $10,000 bricks into the five packs of $2,000 to get the money in the envelopes; the bricks were too big for the envelopes. When we finished with the money in my briefcase, I got my suitcase, and we broke down the bricks and stuffed the envelopes with the packs of $20 bills. It was lucky that Jim brought two dozen envelopes because we needed them all. After about an hour and a half of flying, the Golden Greek called me to come back up front. Out in front of the aircraft, I could see Grand Cayman, a thin u-shaped island a whole lot smaller than Cuba. It was a flat island but beautiful looking from the air; the water was the clearest, prettiest water I'd ever seen.

I went back to my seat, buckled in, and shortly, we made our approach and landed. We taxied over to the terminal, pulled to a stop, the Golden Greek opened the door, and we all got out of the cool A/C of the Lear Jet into the sweltering heat of Georgetown, Grand Cayman. Airport workers came over and asked us if we had any bags and we said no, we're not spending the night. I had my briefcase in one hand and my suitcase in the other and I surmised that they thought they were both full of money. We walked a short distance to the terminal, went inside, and walked up to the Immigration Desk. We filled out an Immigration Card, showed them our Passports, and told the Immigration Lady that we were only staying for the afternoon. As she stamped our Passports, she said that the next time we came for a visit, we must stay overnight and enjoy their Caymanian hospitality, and we promised we would.

We picked up our bags, bypassed the luggage carousels, and walked up to the counter at the Customs desks. I started getting real uneasy and got a knot in my stomach. Jim Dolan put his briefcase on the counter and opened it up so I put my briefcase and my suitcase on the counter and opened them up too. The Customs Officer gave a brief glance at Jim's briefcase then came straight to me.

He picked up a manila envelope, felt it, and said: "What's this?"

I said; "It's money."

He said: "Okay" and put a chalk line on all of our bags.

We closed our bags and walked out of there. That's it, a piece of cake! It took every bit of five minutes to go through Immigration and Customs, how nice!

When we went through the doors to the outside, we were on the curb and a taxi was sitting there. We got in the taxi and went to the offices of Bruce Campbell & Company about a block from the harbor in downtown Georgetown. When we arrived, Jim paid for the taxi, we went upstairs to Bruce Campbell & Company, walked in and

Jim told the receptionist that we had an appointment with Mr. John Goodwill, Esquire. I kid you not, that was his real name, John Goodwill. She buzzed him and he said to show us in, so we walked in his office, he and Jim shook hands and acted like old friends and Jim introduced me.

John Goodwill took us into a conference room, we sat down at the table, he pulled out a long sheet of paper from a folder, and started asking me questions. Hell, I didn't know the answers to almost any of them. He'd ask me a question, I'd look at Jim, and Jim would answer it. He'd ask me another question, I'd look at Jim, and Jim would answer it. We went through about fifteen questions like that and I don't think I answered but about one or two of the questions.

When John got through with all the questions, he said with a heavy English accent: "Jolly good. That seems to be all we need. You need to go to the bank and open the account and when you get the account opened, you need to come back and give me the information on the account and bring the signature cards so I can sign them. Once I sign the signature cards, you can take them back to the bank. Once you take the signature cards back to the bank, then everything will be done."

John Goodwill's secretary was typing up the papers for the bank with the answers we'd just given him to the questions he'd asked. She brought us a handful of papers that we needed to take to the bank. We shook hands, left his office, and walked about a block to the Royal Bank of Canada on the corner opposite the main Post Office.

We went in the lobby, walked up to the receptionist, and Jim said: "We have an appointment with Don Stewart." She walked to an office at the back left corner of the bank and came right back out with a man following her.

She said to Jim: "This is our Branch Manager, Mr. Don Stewart."

They shook hands and they're all smiles like they're old friends. Jim introduces me and Don brings us back into his office. We make small talk for a couple of minutes.

Then Don said: "Well, are you all ready to go, do you have everything in order to open the account?"

Jim said: "Yeah, we do. Here it is." Jim handed him the papers from John Goodwill.

Don said: "Why don't we go in the conference room, I'll get some of my people, we'll do the paper work, and get the account open."

Jim said: "Great!"

Don took us through a side door in his office into a nice, large conference room. Don went and got a young woman and a young man, the young woman seemed to have more authority than the young man. The woman takes the papers that we've given Don Stewart and she starts filling out some forms to open the bank account. She fills the forms out by hand, passes them across the table to me, I sign them, and give them back to her. Then, she gives me the signature cards and I tell her that I need to take them to my attorney to get his signature because he'll have access to the account. She told me that when I leave and get his signature, to bring the cards back to her and then they can get the account opened properly. She takes the forms, leaves the room, and comes back in a minute.

She said: "How much are you opening the account for?"
I said: "$200,000 U.S.
She said: "Do you have it here with you today?"
I said: "Yes."
She said: "May we have it?"
I said: "Yes."

I put my briefcase on the table, opened it, picked up a manila envelope, tore it open, and poured the money on the table. I handed an envelope to her and the young man, picked up one myself and tore it open, they tore their envelopes open, and we all simultaneously poured the money on the table. I closed my briefcase, put the suitcase on the table, opened it and picked up an envelope, handed one to the two of them, tore it open and poured the money on the table. Their eyes almost bulged out when they realized that it was all in $20's and it was physically a lot to count by hand.

The woman said: "Well, we're gonna need some help with this."

She left the conference room and in a minute, came back with two more women. The four of them sat around this conference table with me and Jim Dolan and began to count this money by hand. They told us that they've had a money-counting machine on order but it hadn't gotten there yet. They promised that the next time I came with a deposit, the machine would be there so the counting would go quicker. Bank policy required that each pack be counted by two people. One of them would count a pack of $2,000, put a band on the stack of 100 $20 bills, and initial it. Another person would take the stack of bills, count it, and initial it also. We sat there about an hour while they double-counted $200,000 U.S. It took a while! When they had finished double-counting all the money, the head lady made out a deposit slip, gave me a copy of the slip along with the signature cards. By then, it was around 1:30 P.M. and I was hungry.

I said to Jim: "Do you know of a good place to eat around here? Let's go get some lunch; we can go see John Goodwill after we eat lunch. Then, we can bring the signature cards back to the bank and go home."

He said: "Yeah, there's a place about a block from here, it's real good, it's down on the Harbor, let's go there."

We left the Royal Bank of Canada, took a left, and walked a block down to the Harbor. We walked up a flight of stairs to the Cayman Arms. The hostess brought us to a table at the front of the restaurant overlooking the Harbor. It was a beautiful view! I ordered a cheeseburger in paradise and a Pina Colada, I thought that was appropriate. As soon as we'd ordered and the waitress had left, I looked out at the Harbor and couldn't believe my eyes. There was only one boat in the Harbor and it was a 41 foot Columbia Sloop just like my two boats! I thought to myself: "Now, isn't this ironic? This has got to be some kind of omen!"

I said: "Jim, would you looky there, the only boat in the Harbor is a 41 foot Columbia sailboat just like mine. Isn't that ironic?"

He laughed and said: "Yeah, the guy's probably a scammer. He's probably down here laundering money."

I thought to myself: "Okay, I guess Jim knows we're scammers."

Jim said: "You know, this is a pretty amazing place."

I said: "Yeah, it really is, isn't it?"

The waitress brought our drinks and I began to drink my frozen Pina Colada, it was goooood!

He said: "You know, this place is just one big Laundromat."

I said: "Whaddaya mean?"

He said: "Well, they take dirty money and wash it and make it clean money, it's a Laundromat. That's all a tax haven is, a Laundromat, they clean money."

I said: "I've got this picture in my head of my money in a washing machine being washed with soap and water."

He said: "That's what the banks are, a washing machine. They wash dirty money and make it clean. They launder your money for you."

I said: "Okay, once my money is clean, how do I get it back to the U.S. so I can spend it or invest it without getting in trouble with the IRS?"

He said: "I can't help you with that. That's not one of my specialties. You'll have to see a tax attorney for that."

I said; "Do you know a good tax attorney?"

He said: "Oh yeah, one of the best. His name is Lou Dereuil (he pronounced it Doral, like Doral Country Club). He was Chief Counsel at the IRS branch in Miami for 14 years, now he's in private practice in Ft. Lauderdale; he's over on Bayview Drive. You remember that bust at Ireland's Inn over on Ft. Lauderdale Beach a while back?"

I said: "Vaguely, I remember seeing it in the Ft. Lauderdale newspaper."

He said: "There were three young guys in two adjoining rooms in Ireland's Inn; they were real young like 23-24 years old. Two of them were in one room with cocaine and a scale breaking down a kilo of cocaine. The other guy was in the adjoining room with two million dollars in a pillowcase, taking a nap, using the money as his pillow. The two guys with the cocaine were making a bunch of long distance phone calls to their buyers and ran up a long distance bill of about $300. The desk clerk called them and asked them to come down and pay for the phone calls. One of the young guys went down to the desk, pulled out a wad of $100 bills, and paid the phone bill. Seeing that big wad of $100 bills made the desk clerk suspicious and he called the police. The police sent a squad car with two uniformed police officers, they went up to the room, and knocked on the door. The two guys in the room with the cocaine didn't even say "Who is it?" They thought it was one of their buyers so they just opened the door. The police officers saw the cocaine and the scale, immediately arrested the two guys, and searched the room. While searching the room, they saw that the doors between the two rooms were open so they went in the adjoining room, woke up the guy sleeping, searched that room, and found the two million dollars in the pillowcase. They arrested that guy. The three guys retained a criminal attorney who promptly got the charges thrown out because the police officers didn't have a search warrant and the suspicious desk clerk wasn't enough probable cause to arrest them. After the criminal attorney got them out of jail, he called Lou Dereuil. Lou Dereuil got the two million dollars back in less than 72 hours. They lost the cocaine but Lou got the money back. THAT'S Lou Dereuil!"

I said: "Far out! I've got to meet this guy."

He said: "Okay, I'll call him and get you an appointment when we get back."

The waitress brought our food and I devoured my cheeseburger. When we'd finished eating and the waitress brought the check, I reached in my pocket to get some money to pay the bill and realized that I had no money at all in my pocket, zero! I couldn't believe that I'd forgotten to bring some walkaround money with me.

I said: "Jim, you're not gonna believe this but I don't have any money to pay the bill."

He looked at me for a second and then cracked up laughing: "Don't worry about it Scooter, I'll pay for lunch." We both cracked up laughing again!

We left the Cayman Arms, walked back to Bruce Campbell and Company, John Goodwill came out and signed the signature cards, and we took the cards back to the lady at the Royal Bank of Canada.

She said: "Mr. Alford, you didn't tell me what you wanted me to do with the deposit. Do you want a checking account, a money market account, or a Certificate of Deposit?"

I looked at Jim and he said: "Why don't you put it in a 30-Day Certificate of Deposit. It will roll automatically every 30 days until you get ready to do something with it. That way, it will draw interest and give you the most flexibility."

I said: "Okay, let's do that, I like flexibility. Put it in a 30-Day Certificate of Deposit and roll it automatically until you hear from me."

We left the bank, grabbed a cab from the taxi stand across from the drug store, and went to the airport. The Iron Man and the Golden Greek were sitting in the restaurant having a soft drink; they already had our paperwork filled out to depart. We turned in our Immigration Forms, walked out to our Lear Jet, and flew home. What an education that was in laundering money!

When we landed at Ft. Lauderdale International Airport, we taxied to the private Customs terminal and cleared private Customs; it was a piece of cake. We taxied over to the private air terminal; I got in my car and drove home. When I got home, I kissed Pat and Sunshine and Pat asked me how it went.

I said: "It went very well, it was amazing. Jim Dolan knows everybody."

She said: "How was the Lear Jet?"

I said: "Unbelievable, it was like riding on a bullet. Next time I go, I'm taking you and Sunshine and we'll spend the night. It's a beautiful place and the water is clearer than the water in the Bahamas. It's a real pretty place and everyone was very friendly, they were really nice people."

I proceeded to tell her the whole story from beginning to end. She listened with this look on her face like "I'm hearing this but I ain't believing it." Hell, it was hard for me to believe it and I'd just lived it. Life was truly amazing!

Chapter 15
Expanding, Dummies & Waterfront Homes
Buying houses like I was playing Monopoly.

Now that I'd bought a second boat, my immediate problem was getting some more people to crew on the two boats. Rob and Ross were gonna be co-captains on Cathy V so I needed some more guys to crew on the new boat, Audacious. My plan was to run Audacious myself with the new guys so I could train them myself, let Jen go with us since she was the most experienced female I had, and I'd let Janice and Rose go with Rob and Ross on Cathy V. The only problem was I didn't have any male friends in South Florida that I'd known long enough or trusted that I wanted to hire and I wasn't ready to go to Georgia to hire old friends from high school or college. I wanted to be sure that my new hires were people that I'd known a long time or someone close to me had known for a long time so my organization wouldn't be infiltrated by the local heat or the DEA.

My good friend John Chesterfield who I'd worked with at the Miami Dolphins had recently left the Dolphins organization to become the Ticket Director for the Tampa Bay Buccaneers in Tampa, Florida. He and his wife knew that Pat and I were smuggling and we'd kept in touch since he moved to Tampa. He'd told me a while back that if I ever needed some more people, that there were two brothers Mick and Dan, that he'd grown up with that would probably be available to work trips. They lived over near Cape Kennedy, they were both self-employed, and thus flexible and available to go on trips. I called and talked to John about them, told him to call them and have them call me, and I invited them to come to Ft. Lauderdale to meet with me.

Mick and Dan came to Ft. Lauderdale and we met, spent some time together, and I liked them right off the bat. I told them that I had bought a second boat, was expanding, and needed some people to go with me on the new boat. I gave them a little background information on the organization, told them that I would let them go on the boat with me for a couple of trips, that I would teach them how to run a boat, and get around in the islands. Once they were trained and competent, I may let them run "Audy" and I'd buy a third boat and hire some more people. I told them my pay scale and said: "How's all this sound? You wanna come to work for me?" They said "Yes, we're ready to go." They couldn't believe that they'd make $15,000 for one trip. With them coming on board, it looked like I had the nucleus for two complete crews.

It was at this time that the light went on in my brain and I realized that I would be paying Jerry at least $70,000 per trip to rent two houses to unload my two boats. Jerry was paying me 15% of what I hauled but I was paying him 3% to rent Linda's house which came out to $30-40,000 per trip for house rental. Jerry was making out like a bandit on house rental fees. I came to the realization that I needed to buy my own houses and pocket that 3%. I went to see Jerry and talked to him about it.

He said: "Well, if you want to buy your own houses, that's okay. I've got plenty of people that I can rent my houses to. I've got extra houses in case I lose one so I won't have to go running around trying to find a house to buy. You know it takes time to buy a house. I don't want a trip to come up and miss it 'cause I don't have a house to unload a boat."

I said: "I'd like to continue to rent Linda's house to unload Cathy V and I'd like to buy my own house to unload my new boat."

He said: "Fine, I think that's the best thing for you to do."

I said: "Do you have any realtors or any people that you use? How do you find your houses?"

He said: "I've got a realtor that I use, a girl I went to high school with, but, what I usually do is just go ride around neighborhoods that have waterfront property and that I think would be a good place to unload. I look for signs in the yard that are "For Sale by Owner" then I call them up. If they're listed through a realtor, then I call Danielle, she calls them up, makes an appointment, and goes to see them. If she thinks it's good and it'll work, then she'll make arrangements for me to go and have a look at it."

I said: "Oh, so Danielle knows what's going on?"

He said: "Oh yeah, she knows everything that's going on, in fact her brother is working for me."

I said: "Oh, okay, that's good. Well, can you get her to find me a good house?"

He said: "Yeah, I'll call her and tell her to find you something good."

In a couple of days, Jerry called and said it was time to go fishing. After I got his call, I went out to a payphone to call my people because I was worried about continuing to use my home phone. There was a bank of six pay phones in front of a restaurant on the corner of Commercial Boulevard and 18th Avenue close to my house. It was great 'cause I could talk on two payphones at the same time if I had to. I called Mick and Dan at their home near the Cape, they were ready to go. I called Ross in Orlando and he was ready. I called Rob and he was ready as well as Janice who was out of school for a while. I called Jen and she wasn't flying a trip for Delta and she was ready to go. I also called Jay and Rose and Rose was now ready to go.

I was gonna let Janice and Rose go with Rob and Ross on Cathy V and I would take Mick and Dan with Jen on Audacious. I wanted us to sail together and cross the gulfstream together so we could baby-sit each other in case of any mechanical problems. I felt good about Audy being in good mechanical shape but you never know so I wanted to be safe and travel together.

Everybody came to town, got motel rooms, and we had a meeting in Mick and Dan's room. I brought charts of the Florida coast, the Gulfstream, and the islands and told everybody exactly what I wanted them to do. We would follow each other down the coast to Miami, turn left and stay in sight of each other as we crossed the Gulfstream all the way to Gun, Sylvia, and to the fishing hole where we'd get loaded. Everybody understood what I wanted them to do and I was sure we were on the same page. I adjourned the meeting and we went to Skaggs Albertsons to buy food and drinks. When we'd done that, we took everything over to the boats and stowed it away then went home and got a good night's sleep.

The next morning, we got an early start and pushed away from the dock around 8 o'clock. We followed each other out the River, through the Port, and into the ocean. We hung a right and headed south to Miami and Government Cut. I gave Jen the helm and coached Mick and Dan as they hoisted the mainsail. Rob and Ross hoisted both the main and the jib. As we ran down the coast, I let Mick and Dan take a one-hour shift at the helm. The weather was nice and we had a good breeze blowing out of the southwest. As soon as we got to Government Cut, we took a left, and got on a heading for Gun Cay. Cathy V must have been doing about 7-7 ½ knots because she was gradually pulling away from us.

I grabbed the CB microphone and said: "Speedy Pete, this is Gearjammer, you got a copy on me good buddy, kickit' back."

Rob replied: "Gearjammer, this is Speedy Pete, we copy, come back."

I said: "You're getting' a little ahead of me good buddy, can you slow her down just a little?"

He said: "Roger that. What do you suggest?"

I said: "How many rpm's you makin'?"

He said: "2000."

I said: "Why don't you cut her back to 1500 and I'll see if we can catch up?"

He said: "Roger that, cuttin' her back to 1500 rpm's."

I told Mick and Dan that it was time to put up the jib. I gave the helm to Jen, we got the jib from the front stateroom, went to the bow of the boat, and began to hook the jib onto the forestay. Once that was done, we ran the sheets down the sides of the boat through the blocks and around the winches in the cockpit. Mick and Dan went to the front of the mast, Jen turned the bow dead into the wind until the mainsail luffed, and Mick and Dan hoisted the jib. I told Jen to turn left to port and as the wind filled the jib, I adjusted the sheets until the jib was tight and properly trimmed. By then, Mick and Dan had climbed back into the cockpit so I explained to them how to properly use the winches to trim the sheets.

We had a cloud formation directly in front of us and it looked like we were gonna have a localized squall, something that happens all the time in the devil's triangle. It looked like we were gonna be right in the middle of the storm. I lost my visual on Cathy V so I grabbed the CB microphone, called her, and got no answer; the squall must be blocking the radio signal. I told everyone that they'd either better go downstairs or put on their foul weather gear because we were gonna get wet. I put on my foul weather gear as did Mick and Dan, took the helm from Jen, and she went downstairs. Big drops of rain started hitting the deck of the boat and pretty soon, it was raining cats and dogs, you couldn't even see the front of the boat.

Just then, right in the middle of the rainstorm, that Perkins diesel engine just shut down on me, just quit running with no warning whatsoever.

I said: "Son of a bitch! Mick, take the wheel, I'll go downstairs and check it out"

I went downstairs into the main salon and it's hot and humid, I broke out in a sweat. I took off my foul weather gear and was in shorts and a t-shirt. I pulled the hatch off the motor to take a look and, sure enough, it wasn't running. I went back into the cockpit, put the gear in neutral, and pressed the starter button. The engine turned over, whined, but wouldn't start.

I said: "Jen, put my foul weather gear on and come up here and take the helm. Come on Mick and Dan, now's a good time to learn to bleed the injectors."

As soon as Jen came up into the cockpit and took the helm, the guys went back into the salon, got some wrenches, and started bleeding the injectors. I would crack a fitting, manually pump fuel into the engine, look for air bubbles, and then tighten-up the fitting. I showed both Mick and Dan exactly what I was doing and let them each bleed one fitting. On about the fourth fitting, when I manually pumped the fuel, I got air bubbles and said. "Aha! There's our problem." I went ahead and bled all the injectors even tho' I thought our problem was solved. I told Dan to go into the cockpit and press the starter button, got a can of freon, and sprayed it into the breather. When Dan pressed the starter button, the engine fired right up! We were all smiles and my crew thought that I was a genius.

By now, the squall had passed through, it had cleared up completely, and it was a beautiful day once again. That's the weather in the devil's triangle. There wasn't a cloud in the sky except for the squall behind us and the ocean was calm as glass, not even a ripple. The sails were flip-flopping so I decided to teach Mick and Dan how to drop the jib. We went up onto the bow of the boat, I told Mick to take the sheet at the mast and for Dan to pull the jib down when Mick loosened the sheet line. Once the jib was down, we stuffed it in the sailbag and took it back into the forward stateroom. We pulled the mainsail in tight so that if it flip-flopped, it wouldn't throw the boat around too much. Now that the squall had passed through, I still couldn't see Cathy V so I called them on the radio.

I said: "Speedy Pete, Gearjammer, you got a copy, kickit' back?"

Rob said: "Roger Gearjammer, we got a copy, come back."

I said: "What's your 20?"

He said: "We're about fifteen miles from the stoplight."

I said: "Do you have it in sight? Can you see it?"

He said: "That's a big 10-4!"

I could tell by the tone in his voice that they were very pleased with themselves for finding Gun Cay all by themselves. I remembered how pleased I was with myself the first time I found Gun Cay all by myself. Plus, they were ahead of me and were gonna beat me to the stoplight.

I said: "Why don't you go on down to your girlfriend's house and then go to the fishing hole and I'll meet you there later on."

He said: "Roger that, good buddy, we'll see you later, we'll be waiting on you."

I said: "That's a roger, Gearjammer standing by."

As soon as we sighted Gun Cay, I let Mick and Dan take turns at the helm in one hour shifts. When we arrived at Gun just before dark, I took the helm and showed my crew how to properly navigate Gun Cay Cut and get safely onto the bank. Then, I gave the helm back to Dan and Jen and I setup the Hibachi on the aft deck, lit the charcoal, and

I began to cook steaks, we were hungry! Jen cooked some vegetables on a propane burner since our stove was broken and she fixed us a tossed salad. We enjoyed our feast in the cockpit with a cold drink. When we'd finished eating and stowed the trash, I gave the helm to Jen and took Mick and Dan into the main salon to tape down. We got the drop cloths and the masking tape and I showed them how to prepare the boat for loading. I decided that we didn't need to go all the way to Sylvia Beacon, that we could get a fix on Cathy and cut the corner.

I grabbed the CB microphone and said: "Speedy Pete, Gearjammer, got a copy?"

He said: "That's a roger, we copy, come back."

I said: "Are you guys at the fishing hole?"

He said: "That's a big 10-4!"

I said: "You got your porch light on?"

He said: "Negative, we're just sitting here looking at the stars."

I said: "How about giving me a wink?" That means to get your spotlight, turn it on for about five seconds, and wave it around so I can get a fix on you.

He said: "Will do, give us a sec."

In about thirty seconds off to our left at about 11 o'clock, this big spotlight just lights up the sky.

I said: "I gotcha' Speedy Pete, I'll be there in a short-short."

He said: "We'll see you soon Gearjammer, we're standin' by."

I turned the bow of the boat left to port and headed directly toward the light. It was a beautiful, clear night and it wasn't long before I could see Cathy with the naked eye and with the binoculars. I pulled up parallel to Cathy about thirty yards away, Mick and Dan dropped the anchor, and we settled down in the cockpit to wait on the load boat.

About 2:00 A.M. the radio crackled and it was Jerry. We were all expecting him to tell us we weren't gonna load tonight and he'd see us tomorrow night.

He said: "Gearjammer, Gearjammer, Black Fin, you got your ears on good buddy, kickit' back."

I said: "Black Fin, Gearjammer, we got a copy on ya', kickit' back."

He said: "Turn your porch light on, I'm coming atcha', I'll be there in a short-short, we're gonna have a party." I turned on my mast light. "I gotcha' Gearjammer, see you soon."

I said: "Roger that Black Fin."

Boy, we all got excited! We made our last minute preparations, stowed the cushions in the main salon, and cleared the cockpit of trash, tapes, and stuff. Pretty soon, we heard Black Fin's big Detroit Diesels coming out of the darkness, they were pulling a load. When the form of the Sportfisherman came out of the darkness, my God, he was sitting low in the water, he was loaded to the gills. He pulled over to the port side of Audy, his guys threw us lines, we tied up, and started loading. He gave us one of his guys to work the main salon, Jen worked the hatch, and Mick and Dan worked the fore and aft staterooms. In about an hour, we had Audy packed to the gills with a good load.

I got on the load boat and went over to help load Cathy V. I worked the cockpit, Rob and Ross worked the staterooms, Janice worked the hatch and Rose worked the main salon. My competent crew was efficient and we got Cathy loaded in about an hour. Jerry brought me back over to Audy, wished us luck, and went off to find his other scam boats. Jen and the boys had everything stowed away, the drop cloths were in trash bags, all the tape was pulled off, and all the furniture back in place. They had all taken showers and Jen had made sandwiches, they were all sitting in the cockpit eating the snack. I was impressed! I ate my snack, took a quick shower, and put on clean clothes

I grabbed the CB microphone and said. "Speedy Pete, Gearjammer, you copy?"
He said: "That's a roger, come back."
I said: "How y'all doing?"
He said: "We just had a bite to eat, we're waiting on you."
I said: "Roger that, let's pull the hook and get on the highway. Let's go home."
He said: "That's a big 10-4!"

We pulled the anchor, got on a direct heading for Gun Cay light, and motored at 2000 rpm's all the way to the Cut; Cathy stayed about 100 yards behind Audy. We navigated the Cut, put our sails up, and put the bow on a heading for Ft. Lauderdale. It was a beautiful day and we had a nice, uneventful sail home. Our airplane flew over, dipped his wings, and told us it was "clean and green." Thank God, no Candy Stripers!

We came in right on the smokestacks at Port Everglades, Rita gave us "a big 10-10, it's clean and green" and we brought the boats into the Port, past the Gulf docks, and up the River. I was taking Audy to one of Jerry's other houses and Cathy was going to Linda's house to be unloaded the first night. Then, we were gonna flip-flop the boats and unload Audy at Linda's the second night.

Rob and Ross brought Cathy into Linda's, tied her up, locked the doors and hatch, and walked away. Rob, Ross and Janice went to the motel and Rose went home. I brought Audy into the other house off Riverland Road, we tied her up, locked the doors and the hatch, and walked away. Mick and Dan went to the motel and I took Jen and went home. I now had five guys counting myself so I had a full crew to unload the boats.

We met at Riverland Shopping Center at 10:00 PM, drove over to Linda's, went in the side door, and set her house up for unloading. Rob and I went out to Cathy and set her up for unloading, we moved bales evenly from the fore and aft cabins into the main salon. As soon as the neighbor's daughter came home from her date at 1:00 A.M. and cut off the yard light, we began unloading. Everything went smoothly, we got the bales weighed and a list made, and delivered the vans to Fu at the IHOP the next morning.

Now we had to flip-flop the two boats so we could unload Audy at Linda's house that night. I drove Rob and Ross over to Jerry's other house so they could bring Audy to Linda's. I went back to Linda's, got on Cathy, started moving her to Jerry's other house, and I passed Audy in the River. As soon as Rob and Ross got Audy to Linda's and got her tied up, they came and picked me up, and we all went home and to the motel to get some sleep 'cause we had to unload all over again that night. Pat was handling the cleanup crews for me and she had to get Cathy cleaned over at Jerry's other house. She had a couple of ladies that were happy to make $250 to clean up a boat if the ladies that went on the trip couldn't do it.

All the guys met at Riverland Shopping Center at 10:00 P.M. and went over to Linda's house and unloaded Audy. Everything went smoothly and we delivered the vans to Fu at the IHOP. As soon as the vans were delivered, we flip-flopped the boats so that Cathy was back at Linda's house then we all went home to sleep.

I'd just paid Jerry $70-80,000 to unload the two boats at Linda's and I quickly realized that flip-flopping boats like we did was not a good idea. It could be done if you had to do it but it really wasn't a good idea, each boat needed its own house to dock and to unload. If the neighbors at each house were watching closely, they could probably figure out what we were doing even tho' both boats were 41 Columbia's. Plus, my cleaning crew was going to clean two boats at the same house which might look funny. I decided that I needed two houses if I were gonna own two boats, each boat needed it's own house.

I woke up from my nap around suppertime and decided that I needed to call Jerry before I let my out-of-town people go home.

I said: "Are we gonna be going again soon or are we gonna have a couple of days rest?"

He said: "Man, I don't know. Joe told me we had a couple, three or four coming right away but he hasn't told me anything definite."

I said: "Well, should I let my people go home or should I keep them here?"

He said: "If they want to go home, you might as well let them but just tell them they might have to turn around and come right back."

I said: "Okay, fine. I want to get together with you tomorrow and meet your realtor and see if she's found any houses for me. I've just about decided that I need to get two houses, one for each boat."

He said: "Well, that's a pretty smart thing for you to do. I don't mind taking your 3% but you really need your own houses, that way we won't have any conflicts."

I said: "That's great, I'm glad you feel that way."

I called the motel and told Ross and Mick and Dan that they could go home but they might have to turn around and come back. They said that was no problem.

The next day, I met with Jerry's realtor Danielle.

I said: "Have you found any houses yet that would work for us?"

She said: "I've looked at three or four but one of them is real good, I'd like for you to look at it first. The only thing about it is it's free and clear, there's no mortgage on it so you'd have to take out a mortgage on it or pay for the whole thing."

I said: "Well, if it's a good house, I'd like to see it."

That afternoon, I put on some nice clothes, met Danielle, and we went to see this house. The owners had already moved out and the house was empty, it was beautiful. They were asking $195,000, we offered them $180,000 and they took it. Now, I needed a corporation to buy the house for me. I called Jim Dolan and made an appointment to see him the next day, I didn't tell him why. The next day, I went to see Jim.

He said: "What's on your mind?"

I said: "I want to buy a house and I want to form a corporation, I want the corporation to own the house."

He said: "I don't handle that type of thing. I'm strickly aviation and offshore but one of my partners handles real estate. You need to see Chris, Chris handles real estate for the firm."

I said: "Fine, can I see him today or am I gonna have to come back?"

He said: "Let me buzz him and see."

He buzzed Chris and said: "I think if you can wait for 20 or 30 minutes, you can see him then."

I said: "Sure, I'll be glad to wait, no problem."

I waited in Jim's office and we chitchatted. In about 20 minutes, there's a knock on the door and a man walks in, and Jim introduces us.

He said: "Scooter Alford, this is my partner Chris Fertig."

Chris said: "Come on in my office and let's talk."

We walked down the hall into Chris' office.

Chris said: "Now, tell me what you need."

I said: "Well, I want to buy this house and I want to form a corporation to own the house."

He said: "Is that necessary? What's the big deal? Why don't you just buy the house in your own name?"

I didn't know how much Chris knew so I didn't know what to tell him. I didn't know if Chris knew everything that Jim did or exactly what the situation was.

I said: "Look, I've made a little money and we've got it offshore, Jim helped us get set up offshore. I want to bring the money back and I don't want to bring it back to myself. So, I want to form a corporation and have the corporation own the house, and have the money brought from offshore, and have the corporation buy the house. That's the way I understand it. I'm looking for some direction so just help me out. Tell me what I need to do but I don't want to own the house individually."

He said: "Do you have a corporation name?"

I said: "No, I haven't thought about a corporation name."

He said: "Well, why don't you think one up?"

I said: "Right now?"

He said: "Just make one up, whatever you want, it doesn't matter."

I said: "I'm at a complete loss, I'm not good at these things, I don't know."

He said: "Where is the house?"

I said: "It's up the river off Riverland Road."

He said: "Is it on the water?"

I said: "Yeah, it's on the water."

He said: "How about Riverland Waterfront Properties, Inc?"

I said: "Shit, that sounds good to me!"

He said: "Okay, who is gonna be President of the corporation?"

I said: "Well, I don't know, what do you think I should do?"

He said: "I don't think you should be President of the corporation if you're sheltering money. Do you have anybody that can front the corporation for you?"

I said: "What do you mean by fronting the corporation for me?"

He said: "Do you have anybody, a member of your family or someone who is fairly well off, who might be President of the corporation in the event anything should happen. Anybody that would have enough legitimate income that it would be reasonable for them to own this house?"

I said: "No, my family's poor on both sides and I really don't have anybody to do that type of thing."

He said: "I really don't think it's wise for you to be President of the corporation if you know what I mean?" He looked me right in the eye when he said that.

I was beginning to get the feeling that Chris was pretty hip to the things that were going on, or that he had an idea what was going on, but I also got the feeling that he didn't want to know too much. In fact, as the conversation went on, he was very specific in telling me that I was to be very careful with him, that he was an attorney and all he did was legal work, and that I should not bring other problems to him that were not legal work. He'd be glad to do legal work for me but that he was not willing to do other things.

I said: "Okay, I won't ask you to do other things, no problem. I just want to buy this house, so if you can help me, fine, if not, I'll ask Jim to refer me to somebody else."

He said: "Oh no, I can help you with this problem. I just want you to know that I don't want to know about anything in advance. Do you know what I mean?"

I said: "Yeah, I know what you mean. Now, how do we solve this problem?"

He said: "Tell you what, you go home and figure out who you want to be President of this corporation. When you figure it out, call me and let me know. I'll have my secretary form the corporation with this person as President. When the documents are ready, I'll call you and you can come by and pick them up. Take them to this person, have him sign them, have them notarized, and bring them back to me. When you bring them back to me, we'll get them to the Secretary of State's office, have them filed, and we'll get the corporation going, get it active. As soon as the corporation's active, we'll buy the house, we'll close on the house, we'll represent you at the closing, and we'll take care of it for you."

I said: "Okay, that sounds great! Now, how do we handle the funds? The funds are offshore, what do we do?"

He said: "What's the price of the house, what have you agreed to pay for it?"

I said: "$180,000."

He said: "Why don't you send me $190,000, give me $10,000 extra? I'll give you the firm's checking account number and you arrange for a wire transfer to our trust account. We'll hold the money in our trust account until time for the closing. When it comes time for the closing, we'll write a check to the people for $180,000 from our trust account."

I said: "Great! Gee, it's that simple, huh?"

He said: "Well, you have to do some things in the proper order but basically, it's that simple. We can handle it for you."

I said: "God, this is great. I had no idea it would be this easy."

He said: "Give me a buzz tomorrow and let me know who the President of this corporation is gonna be."

I said: "Okay, I'll call you tomorrow. Thank you very much, I really appreciate it. This is great, it's almost too good to be true."

He said: "My pleasure."

I left the office of Dolan, Fertig, and Curtis and drove over to Jerry's house on S.W. 5th Place. I told Jerry that I'd just spent some time with Chris Fertig and I filled him in on what was going on. I told him I didn't have anyone that could be President for me.

He said: "Listen, a real person is not going to be President of the corporation."

I said: "A real person is not gonna be President? Well, who the hell is then?"

He said: "A fictitious person, you just make up a name."

I said: "Make up a name? You got to be kidding me?"

He said: "No man, that's the whole purpose of having a dummy corporation. You don't want a real person to be President of the corporation because if the house gets busted, the cops are gonna go arrest the President of the corporation. So, when they go looking for this person to arrest them if the house gets busted, then there is no person because they don't exist."

I said: "Well, if there's no real person, then you can't get the house back?"

He said: "Man, you ain't gonna get the house back anyway. If a house gets busted, it's gone. So, what you want to do is protect your own ass and you don't want to bring anybody else into it for sure."

I said: "Oh, I see, so that's how it's done, huh?"

He said: "Yeah man, that's how it's done."

I said: "Does it matter who is President?"

He said: "Hell no, man, just think up a name."

I said: "Okay, so if I think up a name, I tell Chris who the President is and then I've got to have a signature and it's got to be notarized."

He said: "That ain't no problem. You just disguise your handwriting and sign it and bring it over here to Rita, she's a notary, she'll notarize it for you."

I said: "No shit? She'll notarize it for me?"

He said: "Yeah man, just bring it over here, she'll notarize it for you."

I said: "God, that's unbelievable!"

The next day, I called Chris Fertig and told him the name I had thought up to be President of the corporation.

He said: "Okay, you can come by anytime this afternoon and pick up the documents. As soon as you get me back the documents with a signature that's been notarized, we'll file the documents and have the corporation formed. As soon as it's formed and becomes active, we'll set the closing for the house."

I said: "Fantastic, I'll come get the documents this afternoon, get them signed and notarized, and bring them back to you as soon as I can."

That afternoon, I stopped by the law offices, picked up the documents, and went over to Jerry's house to see Rita, she was still living with Jerry. She notarized the documents for me, put her seal on them, and signed them. It was that easy.

I said: "Where's Jerry?"

She said: "He's out, he had to go meet Joe."

I said: "Well, I'm gonna go check on my boats and then I'm gonna go home so if he needs me, tell him to give me a call."

I left Jerry's house, took the documents back to the law firm, and gave them to Chris' secretary.

I left the law firm, went over to Linda's to check on Cathy, and drove to the marina to check on Audy. Mick and Dan were still working hard on Audy and she was beginning to shape up really well. Ron had stopped by and had shown them how to bleed the injectors and do some trouble-shooting. He had taught them a lot and they were feeling more confident. I left the marina and drove home. When I got home, Pat told me that Jerry had called.

I said: "Oh yeah, what did he say?"

She said: "He said to call him, call him from a stand-up."

I drove up to the bank of payphones on the corner of Commercial Boulevard and 18th Avenue. Since I had so many people working for me now, it was necessary that I not use my home phone to call my people anymore. The heat could obtain a "pencil tap" of your phone without a court order. What a pencil tap did was enable the heat to see the phone numbers of every call that went out or in to your phone number, they could see who you called and who called you without a court order. So for safety's sake, I now must not use my home phone to call my people, I must use a payphone to avoid the "pencil tap." I didn't think that my phone was tapped at this time but for safety's sake, I needed to start using payphones. I called Jerry from the payphone.

He said: "Where are you?"

I said: "I'm at a stand-up."

He said: "Okay, we're gonna have a fishin' trip and a party this weekend. Are you gonna be able to go with us?"

I said: "Shoot yeah!"

He said: "What about your friends?"

I said: "Yeah man, we're ready."

He said: "Okay, I want you to leave tomorrow."

I said: "Okay, great! Is that it?"

He said: "I'll talk to you before you leave. If you haven't heard from me, call me. Somebody'll be here at the house that'll know where I am, where you can get a hold of me. But, plan on leaving tomorrow."

I said: "Fantastic, no problem."

I called Rob, Ross, Jen, and Rose, everyone was ready to go. I drove back over to the marina to see Mick and Dan. When I got to Audy, they looked kinda shocked.

Mick said: "What's up man? We didn't expect to see you again today."

I said: "I just talked to Jerry and it's time to go again."

They got real excited, Mick said: "Well man, we're ready. We've got a couple more things to do but we'll come back tonight or we'll fix it tomorrow on the way out, but we're ready. We've got all the big stuff done. Whose going?"

I said: "The same people as last time. Same crew, same way."

Mick said: "Aw great, man, we really learned a lot from you and we were really looking forward to going with you again. We were hoping we could go with you again."

I said: "Well, you're going with me so don't worry about it."

The next day, we pushed away from the dock early and the two boats followed each other out the River. We went down to Miami, crossed over the Gulfstream to Gun Cay, and then went due east out of Gun to ten miles east of Gun. I had talked to Jerry about loading at ten miles east of Gun to save us some traveling time. Instead of going to Sylvia Beacon and then north five miles, we would just go ten miles east of Gun and be in the same general vicinity to load, it would just save us some traveling time.

We got loaded the first night, came home, and everything worked out fine. We flip-flopped the boats at Linda's house two nights back to back and delivered the vans to Fu at the IHOP. Once we'd gotten the two boats unloaded and the pot delivered, Ross wanted to go home to Orlando. I called Jerry.

I said: "What's the story man?"

He said: "We're waiting on another one, it could be two days or a week, it could be two weeks, we just don't know. Tell him he can go home but he may have to turn around and come right back."

I said: "Okay, no problem, he'll come right back if he has to." Ross went home.

The next day, Jerry called and said: "It's time to go again. You ready?"

I said: "Yeah man, we're ready, we'll do it again. We're tired but that ain't no big deal. We can sleep when we're dead."

I went out to my bank of payphones and called Ross, told him to come on back, we were going again. He couldn't believe it. I called everybody else and everyone was ready to go. We had to leave tomorrow so we went out and bought food, drinks, and ice and loaded it on the boats.

The next morning, we pushed away from the dock early, followed each other out the River, crossed together to Gun Cay, and went to the fishing hole at ten miles east. We got loaded the first night again, came home together, got a big 10-10, clean and green from Rita, and brought the boats in to the docks safe. We made it again! We unloaded Cathy the first night, flip-flopped the boats the next day, and unloaded Audy the second night. We delivered the vans to Fu at the IHOP and everything went smoothly. I kept thinking to myself: "You have got to buy some houses and stop paying Jerry the 3%." I'd just paid Jerry between $210-240,000 for house rentals for the past three trips, that could have paid for a house right there. It was time I had my own houses.

As soon as I'd delivered the second van from Cathy and gotten a catnap, I'd called Chris Fertig to see what was happening with the corporation. The corporation was formed and active and we had a closing set up on the house. Now, I needed to wire transfer the money to Chris' trust account from Cayman. Also, I'd called Danielle and she'd found another house that she thought was great. I called Chris back and told him to form another corporation, that I was buying another house. I needed to get more money down to Cayman now so I could wire it back to Chris to pay for two houses. If I could get paid for the three trips we'd just done and take that money down to Cayman, I could kill two birds with one stone so I called Jerry.

I said: "Listen, I'm gonna have to go to the islands and transfer some money to buy these houses. Is there any problem with me leaving? I can go down and come back the same day if need be."

He said: "No, it looks like we're gonna have a week or so before we work again, we're gonna have some breathing space. You'd better go ahead and get your business taken care of because when we start back, we're gonna have another big push before we quit. We're gonna be taking a break about the middle of July. This will be the last break in the action until we break in July so if you're gonna do this, you'd better go ahead and get it done."

I said: "Okay, I may spend the night or I might just go down and come back but I won't be gone more than one night. Any word on green stamps?"

He said: "Let me make a phone call, I'll call Joe up and see if we've gotten any in yet. I'll give you a buzz tonight at home."

I said: "Good, because I need to make my plans to go to the islands and I could kill two birds with one stone if I could get some green stamps. Then, I could take some down there and I could wire the money back to buy the houses. That would be great if it would work out like that. But if it can't, that's no problem, I can cover it."

He said: "Okay man, no problem. I'll call Joe and call you back tonight."

That night, Jerry called and said: "I got the green stamps so why don't you come over in the morning, not too early."

I said: "Oh, that's fantastic! I'll be over about mid-morning."

I had already worked on my lists for each boat for each trip. I was gonna get paid for two boats for three trips, this was gonna be BIG! I was hoping that after paying my people, I would net between $550 and $600,000. This was gonna be awesome!!

The next morning, I woke up, had my coffee, showered, and drove over to Jerry's house about 10:30 A.M. We sat down at the kitchen table, got our calculators and my lists, and began to settle up, it took us a while. For each boat for each trip, I was grossing right at $150,000 and netting a little over $100,000 after paying my people. When all was said and done, Jerry owed me a little over $900,000!! I was in shock!! My net after paying my people was a little over $600,000!!

Jerry said: "Did you bring something to put this in?"

I said: "No, you'd better give me a big box."

Luckily, Jerry had gotten a lot of the money in 100's and 50's so that would help with the bulk. Still, it was gonna be a lot. Jerry came back with another case box that toilet paper came in. We started putting the money in the box until all the bricks were in the box and we closed the top.

I said: "Ain't this gonna look funny to your neighbors, me walking out of your house with this big box?"

He said: "It don't matter, man. All my neighbors know what's going on."

I said: "What the fuck you talking about?"

He said: "Aw man, I've got my next door neighbor counting money for me. This little old lady counts for me, I can't count all this money, I'm not about to count it. Every time they bring me a box full of money, I bring it over to her to make sure I don't get shorted. I pay her a half of one percent and she counts all the money for me. I've been getting shorted and the money I pay her is a lot less than what I've been getting shorted and it sort of allows her to make some money. She's part of this."

I said: "You are joking me?"

He said: "No man, I'm not kidding you."

I said: "Smith, you are crazy!"

He said: "They won't think anything of you walking out there with that box. They'll just say "there goes another guy with a big box full of money."

I said: "That's exactly what I don't want them to say."

He said: "No man, it's okay, believe me."

I said: "Okay, if you say so."

Jerry and I picked up my box of money, walked out to my Honda, put the box in the back, we shook hands, and I left his house driving like a little old lady. I was in shock, I'm just kinda in a daze. This is all unbelievable, I've got over $900,000 in a box in the back of my car. I get home, go in the front door, and holler to Pat: "Honey, come here, I need your help." She comes to the door and I walk to the back of the car, she follows me and we pick up the box and walk it into our bedroom and drop it on the floor.

I said: "Take a look at this!"

She said: "How much is it?"

I said: "NINE NUNDRED THOUSAND DOLLARS!!"

She said: "How much is ours?"

I said: "SIX HUNDRED THOUSAND DOLLARS!!"

She stood there incredulous for about a minute.

I said: "Honey, I think we're millionaires now."

She looked at me and was speechless.

Finally, she said: "What are you gonna do with it?"

I said: "I'm gonna go pay all my people and then we gotta go to Cayman."

She said: "Am I going this time?"

I said: "Yeah, you're going!"

I left the house, drove up to my bank of payphones, called everybody, and told them I had green stamps. Everyone was home and they all got real excited. I drove back home, got a whiskey box, and counted out all the money I needed to pay my people. I kept all the 100's and 50's for myself and paid everyone with bricks of 20's. This was one of the fun parts of my job and I really enjoyed making people's day. I spent the rest of the afternoon paying everyone and putting a big smile on their face. Of course, I had the biggest smile of all on my face. After all, I was a millionaire!!

Chapter 16
The Money Cayman Went
The money came, the money went; the money Cayman Went.

Now that I had over $600,000 in a cardboard box at my house, I needed to take it to Cayman and put it in the bank so that I could wire transfer some money to the law firm to pay for the houses that I was gonna buy. Also, I'd decided that it was time I went to see the tax attorney, Lou DeReuil, to get some advice on taxes, offshore banking, and avoiding problems before they came up. I didn't want to screw-up, get in trouble with the IRS, and then have to use Lou to get me out of the trouble; I wanted to avoid the trouble in the first place before it reared its' ugly head. I called Jim Dolan at the Law Firm and he'd gone for the day so I called him at home.

After exchanging pleasantries, he said: "What can I do for you?"

I said: "Well, I need to go back offshore to the bank. I've got some business I need to take care of down there, you know what I mean?"

He said: "Yeah sure, when do you want to go?"

I said: "I need to go as soon as possible, I'd like to go tomorrow. I was gonna charter a Lear Jet, who do I call?"

He said: "I'll tell you what; the Law Firm has just gotten a new airplane. It's not a Lear Jet but it's a King Air, it's a real nice airplane. We'll fly you down there and it'll be a helluva lot cheaper than a Lear Jet."

I said: "I don't really care how I go, I just need to go and want to know the best way to do it. Whose gonna fly me?"

He said: "I'll fly you, I've got a commercial pilot's license, I'm qualified. We're looking to fly our customers on law firm business, that's part of our service."

I said: "Well shit, that works out good then. That sounds great! I'd like to leave at 9:00 in the morning and come back the same day."

He said: "Okay, we can do that, that'll work out okay."

I said: "I was gonna take my wife and we were thinking about spending the night. Can you do that?"

He said: "I can't spend the night because I've got appointments the next day, I'd have to come back the same day. You could come home commercial the next day if you wanted to stay the night."

I said: "There's really no need for me to spend the night. In fact, I've got a lot of things that I need to be doing here so it's really better if I come back."

He said: "If you're not gonna spend the night, are you still gonna take your wife?"

I said: "Oh yeah, I promised my wife that the next time I went to the islands, I would take her and let her see how pretty it was."

He said: "Do you mind if I take my wife?"

I said: "No, not at all. It would be a nice trip. I'll be glad to have your wife come along."

He said: "Alright, fine, I'll see you tomorrow morning at 9:00 at the private aircraft terminal, same place we got the Lear Jet."

I said: "Fantastic, I'll see you then."

The next morning after the babysitter showed up to keep Sunshine, Pat and I drove to the private aircraft terminal with the $600,000 in my briefcase and a Samsonite suitcase. When we got to the terminal, I saw Jim's car in the parking lot and there was a big, twin-engine airplane sitting right in front of the building on the tarmac. I figured that was the King Air, all fueled up and ready to go. I parked the car in the parking lot, got my briefcase and the suitcase from the trunk, and we walked through the terminal and over to the airplane. I was still nervous and apprehensive about carrying a lot of money out of the country and I wondered if Customs was going to show up to search my bags and hassle me. I didn't want them to confiscate my $600,000! As Pat and I approached the plane, the door on the left side folded out and down from the fuselage. There's a guy that I didn't know walking around the outside of the airplane checking things out, I thought that he must be a worker at the private aircraft terminal. I go up the stairs, stick my head in the door and see Jim sitting in the left hand seat, his partner, Ed Curtis, sitting in the right hand seat, and a woman sitting in the rear of the plane. I smile at her and introduce myself and Pat, she introduces herself as Jody Dolan, Jim's wife. Pat and I sat in the two front seats and put my briefcase and my suitcase behind our seats on the floor. This guy that's walking around the plane comes up the steps into the cabin, closes the door and locks it.

Jim said: "Have you met my brother Tommy?"

I said: "No, I don't believe I have" and we shake hands.

Jim said: "I hope you don't mind if he goes with us?"

I was already nervous and this caught me completely off guard. I really did mind like "what the fuck, over?" I had a bad feeling and I chalked it up to being nervous about going offshore with this much money. I wish now that I would have spoken up and said something because there was no need for Tommy to be going. Here I was trying to be so careful and to do the right thing and my lawyer was being careless. Jim and Ed were my lawyers and I had attorney-client privilege with them, and I figured Jody was okay. But I didn't have attorney-client privilege with Tommy Dolan and he was going to witness me going to Cayman and to laundering money. Now that wasn't cool! But, I kept my mouth shut because I didn't want to cause any hard feelings and in retrospect, I wish I would have spoken up. My instincts were telling me that this was not a good idea to let Tommy Dolan go to Cayman with us and my instincts were right as would be proven in the future.

Jim and Ed started the engines, got clearance from the Control Tower, we taxied out to the runway, took off and got on a heading for Georgetown, Grand Cayman. I breathed a sigh of relief, we'd gotten the money past Customs again! As soon as we achieved our cruising altitude, Pat and I began to put the money in brown manila envelopes, that took a while. It wasn't long before Jim turned his head around and asked Pat and I to come up front into the cockpit. We squeezed in between he and Ed and got a good view of the island of Cuba through the front windshield of the airplane. Cuba is a big island and it looked beautiful from the air with mountains and lots of lush vegetation. In about 45 minutes or so, Jim called us back up front again and we got a good look at the island of Grand Cayman. It was flatter than Cuba, not much vegetation, but with beautiful water and a big sound in the middle of the u-shaped island.

We would later learn that this was North Sound. We made our approach, landed safely, and taxied to the left side of the terminal. Once the engines had stopped, Tommy opened the door, I got my briefcase and suitcase, and we walked into the terminal to Immigration. There were no commercial flights that had landed recently and the terminal was empty. We went up to a big, black Caymanian woman and handed her our Passports.

She said: "How long will you be staying in our country?"

I said: "We're just here for the day, we'll be leaving this afternoon."

She acted disappointed and said: "Next time you visit, you'll have to stay longer."

I said: "You can count on it" and she gave me a big smile. She stamped our Passports and handed them to us. We took a right and walked over to the Customs counter. I put my briefcase and my suitcase on the counter in front of a young Caymanian man and opened them up.

He picked up a manila envelope and said: "What is this?"

I said: "Money."

He said: "Okay, no problem." He put the manila envelope down, closed my briefcase and suitcase, and put a chalk mark on each one about two inches long. I picked up my briefcase and suitcase and we walked out of the terminal into the bright sunlight of Georgetown, Grand Cayman. Wow, was it bright! I put on my sunglasses and focused on a cab on the curb right in front of the door. We all piled in the cab and took a short five minute cab ride to the Royal Bank of Canada in downtown Georgetown. After I paid the cab driver, Pat, Jody, and Ed walked a half a block to Kirk's Freeport Plaza to look at Rolex watches and other expensive jewelry. Jim, Tommy, and I went into the bank and told the receptionist that we were there to see the Manager, Don Stewart, that he was expecting us. She walked quickly to his office at the back left corner of the bank and the two of them returned promptly. Don was all smiles.

He said: "Good to see you again. Come on back into my office." He led the three of us to his office and we all took a seat. He said: "You have a deposit for us today?"

I said: "Yes, I've got $600,000 U.S., most of it in 100's and 50's, some 20's."

He said: "Let's go into the conference room and I'll get some of my people to count it. We still haven't gotten that counting machine, maybe next time you come, we'll have it."

We all went into the conference room and I put my briefcase and suitcase on the table. Don went out and came back with three women and a man. They each took a manila envelope, tore it open, poured the money on the table and began double counting the money. This was gonna take a while. By now, it was lunchtime and I was hungry.

I said: "Jim, is there anyplace around here that I can get something to eat."

He said: "We can't leave these people here with this money, somebody's got to stay with it."

I said: "Oh, okay. I'm getting real hungry and I'm getting a headache from not eating and I just wanted a little snack to hold me until we can eat lunch."

He said: "If you don't mind, we can leave Tommy here while they count the money. We could go meet the girls and eat lunch and by the time we were done with lunch, they'd probably be finished counting the money. Then, you could do any other business you have and we could fly back to Ft. Lauderdale."

I said: "Gee, that sounds good to me." I figured that Tommy Dolan was already a party to my money laundering so it didn't matter at this stage. I knew the count was correct on the $600,000 so that shouldn't be a problem. So, what the hell, let's do lunch!

Jim and I left Tommy at the bank and we walked across the street to Kirk's Freeport Plaza. We found Jody and Pat looking at Gold Rolex Oyster Presidential watches. They were beautiful. The women's Oyster Presidential was about $8,000 U.S. and the men's was about $12,000 U.S. The girls and Ed were hungry too so we left Kirk's and walked a half a block to the Harbor and went upstairs to the Cayman Arms restaurant. Pat and I got a frozen Pina Colada and a cheeseburger. We looked out in the harbor and the only sailboat there was a 45 foot Columbia sloop open cockpit. Nobody said anything but I'm sure we were all thinking that this was a smuggler's boat. After we ate heartily and with gusto, I paid the bill and we headed back for the bank. About halfway there, we ran into Tommy who handed me a deposit slip for $600,000 U.S. I told Jim that I needed to go back to the bank for a second and he said they'd go to Kirk's and shop some more and for me to come to Kirk's when I was done. I walked into the bank and told the receptionist that I needed to see Don Stewart again. She went and got him and he came up front with a funny look on his face.

He said: "Is there anything wrong?"

I said: "No, I just need to wire transfer some money to Jim's trust account in Ft. Lauderdale."

He said: "How much do you want to transfer?"

I said: "Three hundred and eighty thousand U.S." I figured $190,000 for each house should cover it and leave some left over for the fees from the law firm.

I could see Don breathe a sigh of relief and said: "Is it the same account number as last time?"

I said: "Yes, do you still have it or should I give it to you?"

He said: "I've still got it. The transfer will be sent this afternoon."

I said: "Thank you very much. I enjoy doing business with you."

I walked out of the bank, crossed the street, and walked to Kirk's where I found the girls peering at the gold Rolex watches. Jim and Ed were looking at some watches for aviators. I walked over to the girls and said: "What have you found:"

Jody said: "Scooter, why don't you buy Pat a gold Rolex?" I could tell Jody really wanted a gold Rolex for herself.

Before I could say anything, Pat said: "I wouldn't wear it if he bought it for me."

Jody said: "Sure you would, you could wear it on special occasions."

Jim said: "Scooter, you just put $600,000 in the bank. Buy your wife something nice."

Before I could say anything, Pat said: "You guys, I don't like jewelry. I wouldn't even let Scooter buy me a diamond wedding ring. I don't feel comfortable wearing jewelry, that's just not me." I thought to myself: "Wow, what a woman! Next time we make love, I'm gonna make sure she has TWO orgasms!"

We left Kirk's and walked to the taxi stand on the side of the Bank of Nova Scotia, all piled in a cab and went to the airport. We cleared Immigration, got in the King Air and flew to Ft. Lauderdale. It was a good feeling. I was buying houses for real just like I did when I played Monopoly as a kid. I felt sure I'd be buying more houses and more boats in the near future. I was growing and it felt good! On the plane ride home, I'd told Jim Dolan that I was ready to see Lou DeReuil. He promised to call Lou first thing in the morning and make me an appointment as soon as possible. Now I had the Beatles song "Taxman" going around in my head. It was time I learned to avoid and beat the taxman if that was possible. And Lou DeReuil was "the man" to teach me. Oh boy, this was gonna be fun!

In about two and a half hours, Ft. Lauderdale came into view and Jim flew the King Air into the flight pattern, we landed and taxied over to private aircraft Customs. We all went in to the office, gave them our passports, and Jim did the paperwork to clear us and the airplane into the country. This was the second time in a month that I'd cleared Customs at the private aircraft Customs office and I quickly realized that my trips were being entered into the Customs computers and that this history could be used by the authorities if I were ever investigated. Not good! Also, it tied me to Jim Dolan and the Law Firm. Once the paperwork was completed and we were cleared, Jim, Ed, Tommy and Jody got in the plane and Jim taxied the plane across the airport to the hangar where it was kept. Pat and I went out of the Customs office, caught a cab, and went around the perimeter road to the private aircraft terminal to get our car that was there in the parking lot. I drove north to David Boulevard, took a left and went west toward I-95 to a convenience store across from the McDonalds where I knew they had a bank of pay telephones. I called our realtor, Danielle, and asked her where we stood with the closing on the house off Riverland Road. She said that the owners had come to Ft. Lauderdale and that they were ready to close at a moments notice. As soon as we had the money, we could close, the people were waiting on us. I told her that the money had been wire transferred that day and we should have it in a day or two. I told her that Chris Fertig would call me as soon as he received the funds into their trust account and I would call her to set up the closing. She sounded very pleased and I knew she was happy because she would be getting her commission as soon as we closed. I asked her if she'd found any more houses that would be suitable for me and she said that she'd looked at one off Cordova Road near Southport Raw Bar, one of our favorite haunts. She thought the house was perfect so we made a date to look at it tomorrow afternoon.

We left the payphone bank at the convenience store, drove west out Davie Boulevard, took a left onto Riverland Road, and went to Linda's house on 28th Terrace to check on Cathy 5. I then drove to the marina to check on Audy and then we called it a day and headed for the house. I drove east on 17th Street Causeway and then up the beach road, A1A, to Commercial Boulevard. I turned on the radio to WSHE and we rolled down the windows to smell the ocean, it was invigorating! Once again, "She's Only Rock-n-Roll" came through for us. The sounds of high-octane rock-n-roll came out of the speakers. I said to Pat: "Listen to that honey, they're playing that song for us.

She didn't say anything but gave me a shit-eating-grin that said it all: "You're crazy as hell, what we're doing is crazy as hell, but I like it!" I had two boats, soon to have two houses, seven employees, two lawyers, was doing offshore banking and I was a millionaire! Life was getting complicated and I liked it, I liked it a lot.

About 8:30 the next morning, Sunshine awoke and starting playing noisily in her bed. Pat went and got her and brought her back and put her in the bed with us. We were laying there in bed half-awake when the phone rang around 9:15. I hopped out of bed and grabbed it, it was Jim Dolan.

He said: "You've got a one o'clock appointment today with Lou DeReuil, can you do that?"

I said: "Yes, that's perfect. I'll see him and then I'm looking at another house with a realtor. After that, I'll come by the Law Firm to see Chris and I'll give you an update."

He said: "That would be fine. I'll see you this afternoon."

Pat had made coffee and we sat out by the pool in our underwear and let the sun awaken our bodies while we drank our coffee. We looked like lizards on a log. We spent the morning being lazy, laying around the pool, swimming naked and playing with Sunshine. I was holding Sunny in front of me and would get a mouth full of water and would spray the water on her face and chest. She was giggling and cackling and we were having a good ole' time. Pat came up behind me, pressed her boobs on my back, pressed her crotch on my buttocks and reached around me with her right hand and fondled my tu-tu. I thought "whoa" and I started getting hard.

I said: "Hey lady, you'd better quit or you might get bit!"

She said: "I was hoping I'd get that kinda reaction out of you."

I said: "Woman, what's gotten into you?"

She said: "I had a sexy dream early this morning."

I said: "Oh yeah, you wanta tell me about it?"

She said: "Well, it involves you and me naked on the front of a sailboat with a bottle of baby oil. There were knats flying around your balls, you got an erection, and I had to make it go down. I woke up and I was dripping wet. I was about to roll over and get on top of you when I heard Sunshine. I'm still wet and I want you bad, whadaya say big boy?"

I said: "I love it when you talk dirty to me. What'll we do with Sunshine? She's not ready for a nap."

She said: "We'll put her in her walker in front of the TV with a cartoon. That should keep her occupied."

I said: "You smooth-tongued woman, you've talked me into it!"

We got out of the pool, walked through the sliding glass doors into the bedroom, and I put Sunny in her walker. Pat put a cartoon video in the VHS and hit play. She took me by the hand and guided me over to the bed, I was rock-hard and standing at attention.

She said: "My Lord, look at you!" I just smiled.

We got in the bed, Pat got on top and we made wild, passionate love with vigor. It was awesome! When we were done, I rolled her over and I laid on top of her and gave her a big, wet, French kiss. We rested and cuddled for a brief period and then I found her vibrator which we kept hidden behind some books on the back of our bed. I said: "Don't go anywhere" and got up to plug her vibrator into the wall. She laughed and said jokingly: "Why would I go anywhere?" I got back in bed, found that mound I was looking for, turned on the vibrator, and put the rounded end on her trigger. Her body gave a little jump and then she closed her eyes and enjoyed the good vibrations. I wondered if that's what the Beach Boys meant when they sang "Good Vibrations?" She grabbed my wrists with both of her hands and squeezed so hard, I thought she would bruise me. It wasn't long before her body stiffened, her toes curled under, and she began to moan deep in her throat. She opened her eyes and pulled me down next to her on the bed. I kissed her long and deep again.

I said: "Let me put that thing back on your trigger."

She said: "No, it's so intense, I can't stand it."

I said: "That's the idea woman, I want you to not be able to stand it. Besides, I owe you one."

She said: "Why, did you have two?"

I said: "No, I only had one but I still owe you one."

She said: "You don't owe me nothing big boy. Now, you just lay back and enjoy the glow and I'll get a washcloth and clean us up." With that, she got up and went into the bathroom, got a warm washcloth, picked me up gingerly and gently washed me off with the warm washcloth. As I stated before, this is nirvana to a male of the species.

She said: "I'll go make you some lunch. You'd better get moving and put your clothes on, you've gotta go see the taxman" and she disappeared into the kitchen still buck naked. I got out of bed and started to dress into some nice clothes. I decided that I didn't need to wear a suit so I put on some long pants and an island shirt. I went into the kitchen and Pat gave me a wet kiss and pointed to the kitchen table where she'd prepared my favorite lunch: tuna salad on whole wheat with mayo, Nacho Cheese Doritos, and Coca-Cola over ice. I ate heartily then brushed my teeth, kissed Pat and Sunshine, and headed out the door to see Mr. Lou DeReuil, the Taxman. I thought to myself: "Wow, what a woman!" It is really very simple for a woman to keep a man happy: all she had to do was feed him and fuck him. She could get her man to do almost anything if she'd just feed him and fuck him. Ladies, let that be your mantra for a happy relationship: FEED HIM AND FUCK HIM! He'll do whatever you ask, whenever you ask.

Chapter 17
The Taxman Cometh
"My life's work is fighting those sons-a-bitches at the IRS!"
Lou DeReuil

I drove south on 18th Avenue and took a left on Commercial Boulevard, drove to U.S. 1 and took a right and went south to Sunrise Boulevard. I took a left on Sunrise and drove east to Bayview Drive, took a left on Bayview and then a right into the parking lot of the Bayview Building. I took the elevator up to the 4th floor law offices of Isley and DeReuil, went through the door into a small lobby that was filled with burgundy office furniture on dark lush carpeting with oiled, dark wooden walls. The décor oozed money and class. Straight ahead was an open door that revealed the conference room and to the right was a 4' X 4' window for the receptionist. I walked up to the counter at the window and told the receptionist that I had a 1 o'clock appointment with Lou DeReuil. She smiled and told me to take a seat in the conference room and that Mr. DeReuil would be right with me. I walked into a 12' X 15' conference room with a large oval table and about ten chairs. I took a seat and in about 30 seconds, a small, wiry-built man walks in the conference room and introduces himself. He looked like he could take care of himself in a street fight and I thought "a fighter, that's good!"

He said: "Hi, I'm Lou DeReuil."

I said: "Hello, I'm Scooter Alford. Jim Dolan has told me quite a bit about you."

He laughed and said: "I'm not sure if it's good when my reputation precedes me."

I said: "I could probably say the same thing." We both laughed together. "Your accent is from where?"

He said: "I'm from New Awlens originally. I went to St. Aloysius High School and Tulane for my undergraduate degree and then Tulane Law School."

I said: "My mother's from New Orleans and one of my cousins went to Aloysius and my mother went to Ursuline. So you're Catholic?"

He said: "Oh yeah, I'm a good cath-o-lic boy. Your mom and I were probably in school at the same time, Aloysius and Ursuline are only blocks apart. Small world ain't it? We probably passed on the street or rode the same bus sometime."

I said: "Jim tells me you were with the IRS for a while?"

He said: "You could say that. I went to work for them in 1955, got my LLM in 1958, and became a Senior Trial Attorney in 1963. I opened the Miami IRS office in 1964 and went into private practice with Hugh Isley in 1967, we've been here in Ft. Lauderdale ever since."

I said: "Wow, that's impressive! Man, am I glad I found you. Jim told me about that bust over at Ireland's Inn on Lauderdale Beach?"

He said: "Yeah, we got a good result out of that situation."

I said: "Did you really get the money back?"

He said: "Yeah we did, the Government had no right to keep the money."

I said: "Why not? There was cocaine in one room and two million dollars in an adjoining room, is that right?"

He said: "Yes, that's right, but the Government couldn't connect the two rooms."

I said: "How could that possibly be?"

He said: "Well, the two young guys in the room with the cocaine were stupid. When the cops knocked on the door, they should have said "Who is it?" instead, they opened the door and the cops saw the cocaine and the scale so they arrested them, read them their rights, and took them down and put them in the back of the police car. Then, they came back up to the room and started searching the room, but they didn't find anything other than the cocaine and the scale. They went over to the adjoining door and opened it expecting the door to the adjoining room to be locked. They pushed on the door and it opened! They looked in the adjoining room and saw another young guy sleeping on the bed. They entered the adjoining room, woke up the guy sleeping and asked him for some identification and he showed them his I.D. Then, they began to search his room. They looked in the drawers, under the bed, in the bathroom, under the mattress, and then under the pillows, they found the money. They arrested him, read him his rights, and asked him if he knew the two guys in the room next door. He was smart and said "No, I don't know them." They went downstairs to the police car and asked the two guys in the back if they knew the guy in the adjoining room, they said "no, we don't know him." The Government could not legally connect the two rooms and it's not against the law to keep a pile of cash in a pillowcase. That's the argument we made, the Judge accepted it, and we got the money back. The Government had to release him because he hadn't broken the law. The other two guys with the cocaine got a criminal lawyer who got their charges thrown out because there was not enough probable cause to arrest them. The bad news is the Government turned them in to the IRS and they taxed them on the 2 million dollars at the 40% tax rate. It cost them $800,000 to be stupid, but nobody had to go to prison."

I said: "That's an amazing story especially since nobody had to go to prison."

He said: "Yeah, they were happy with the result except for having to pay the tax."

I said: "Yeah, I'll bet that hurt!"

He said: "Now, how can I help you? Are you in trouble now, do you have a tax problem?"

I said: "No, I don't have a problem yet, and I want to keep it that way. That's why I'm here. How much has Jim Dolan told you about me?"

He said: "Not very much. He said you've made some money and he took you to the Cayman Islands and that you're doing offshore banking in the Caymans. That's all he's told me about you."

I said: "Okay, that's not very much. So, you're an attorney right? We've got attorney-client privilege?"

He said: "Yes, of course. I can't tell anybody anything you tell me, especially if it's those sons-a-bitches at the IRS."

I said: "Okay good. I've been smuggling marijuana from the Bahamas to Ft. Lauderdale by boat for the past year. The man I work for goes and meets freighters north of Nassau and then comes to me around Bimini and offloads to my boats. I've got two sailboats and one house and I'm getting another boat and another house real soon. I've paid cash for the boats from private individuals. I wire transferred money to Jim Dolan's Trust Account and he represented me at the closing on the house. I use the houses to unload the boats. In the past year, I've made a little over a million dollars. I've got a safe deposit box full of money here in Ft. Lauderdale and I've got a little over $400,000 in a 30-day CD at the Royal Bank of Canada in the Caymans. My wife and I have decided that we want to make as much money as quick as we can and then retire and live happily ever after. And of course, we don't want to be in trouble with the authorities or the IRS when we're done. I want you to tell me how to get the money from Cayman back here to the U.S. without getting into trouble with the IRS."

He said: "Jesus Christ Scooter! That sounds like a big operation you've got there."

I said: "Yeah Lou, it's big, it's pretty damn big. The man that does the freighters and owns the pot, Joe Pegg, does 3 freighters a week. Each freighter has either 40,000 or 60,000 pounds of pot. I've been doing maybe two trips every 4-6 weeks. I think I've done maybe 15 trips total and made a little over a million bucks. I hope to make another 2 or 3 million or more before I'm done."

He said: "I knew this was going on from the talk around town but I had no idea it was this big. I mean I knew it was big but I didn't know it was this big."

I said: "Well, who around this town is talking about it?"

He said: "Hell everybody! The realtors are getting rich selling waterfront homes. The cars dealers are getting rich selling cars and trucks and vans. The Mercedes Benz dealer is sold out and has a 3 month backlog of orders. The bars and restaurants have large groups of young people that pay huge tabs with 100 dollar bills. Hell, the Miami Federal Reserve Bank is the only Federal Reserve Bank in the country that has a surplus of cash, they're drowning in cash. I hear they're sitting on maybe 2 to 3 billion dollars in cash and they don't know what to do with it. You guys have given them a helluva problem. Washington don't know what to do. Every businessman in this town is trying to figure out how he can get a piece of this action. And here you are, you're right in the middle of it."

I said: "Yeah Lou, I'm up to my eyeballs in it."

He said: "Well, you've done the right thing by coming to me before you get in trouble. Jim Dolan has given you excellent advice. When you bought the house, how did you do it?"

I said: "Jim's partner Chris Fertig formed a Florida corporation called Riverland Waterfront Properties, Inc. and the President is a fictitious person. One of the girls that is part of our group is a Notary Public and she notarizes everything for us. That way, if the house gets busted, the owner won't get arrested because the owner ain't a real person, the cops won't be able to find them 'cause they don't exist. Each house will be owned by a different corporation so if one gets busted, it can't be connected to the other houses."

He said: "That's smart, that's good. Did Jim come up with that?"

I said: "I'm not sure who thought it up. It was probably Jim and Chris and Jerry Smith together. Jerry was a Lauderdale cop for ten years and he's real street smart and smart about the law from being a cop for ten years."

He said: "Who is this Jerry Smith, is that his real name?"

I said: "Yeah, that's his real name. He's the one that got me into smuggling. He was a cop for ten years and a good cop, not dirty. He got off the police force and started a private detective agency and I worked for him for about a year and a half as a private detective. We mostly repo'ed cars and trucks but I did other investigative work for him too. Then, in 1977, I went to work as the Assistant Ticket Director for the Miami Dolphins. While I was working for the Dolphins for $165 per week, Jerry was smuggling pot and he made over 2 million dollars. After I quit the Dolphins, Jerry was expanding so I went to work for him first crewing on one of his sailboats and then I bought my first boat and starting making the big bucks. A year later, here I am."

He said: "Okay, let me get this straight now. The law firm formed a corporation for you with a fictitious person as the President. Then, you and Jim flew to the Cayman Islands and you deposited money into an account at the Royal Bank of Canada. Then you wire transferred money back to Jim's trust account and Chris Fertig represented you at the closing on the house. Is that right so far?"

I said: "Yeah, pretty much, not exactly but close enough. It was a CD not an account."

He said: "So what happens if the house gets busted and the cops come to Chris Fertig as the closing attorney for the buyer trying to find the buyer so they can arrest him?"

I said: "Chris tells them a guy of average height and build came to see him and asked him to form a corporation to buy a house. Chris had his secretary draw up the paperwork for a corporation, the guy gave him the name of the corporation, came by the next day and got the paperwork, brought the paperwork back the next day with a notarized signature, and Chris' secretary filed the paperwork with the Secretary of State and got the corporation active. The money was wired into his trust account, Chris set the closing, and represented his client and closed on the house. Chris never saw him again. Chris only saw him on those two occasions, the guy paid Chris for his work, and that's all Chris knows. He never saw him or heard from him again."

He said: "That is genius! You guys got it figured out pretty good, you got it going good don't you?"

I said: "Well I hope so. We hope that'll work if the house gets busted. I think they call that plausible deniability."

He said: "So what else can I help you with?"

I said: "All right, let me ask you this: does what I've told you so far and what we've done so far meet with your approval or have we done something wrong?"

He said: "I couldn't give you any better advice than you've gotten from Jim Dolan and Chris Fertig. You haven't done anything that would raise any eyebrows that I can tell. Your scheme is very clever."

I said: "That's good to hear. So, wiring the money from Cayman to the law firm's trust account won't raise any eyebrows?"

He said: "No, not at all. There's thousands of people from Latin America that come to South Florida every year and buy houses. They wire the money in and buy the houses just like you did. It won't raise any red flags with the IRS. It happens legally thousands of times every year. Don't worry about that, that's the least of your worries."

I said: "Okay, that's good to hear, that makes me feel better."

He said: "What else do you want to do?"

I said: "I want to start a real estate and development company in Georgia with my father. Can I wire transfer the money from Cayman to Georgia and not get into trouble with the IRS? Won't the bank in Georgia know the money came from the Cayman Islands? I don't want the bank in Georgia to know the money is coming from Cayman. How do I handle that?"

He said: "Now you're really asking me hard questions. Let me think a minute. He paused for about a minute and then said: "First thing you have to do is have a company in Georgia, do you have a company now or do you need to form one?"

I said: "We need to form one, this is ground floor, this is start-up."

He said: "Okay, this is what I'd do; form a corporation in Florida and you can be President. Florida only requires one officer to be named in the Articles of Incorporation so you can be the President. Go to Sun Bank in Miami and open a checking account in the corporation's name. Sun Bank is the largest bank in Miami. They probably receive 50 to 100 million dollars a week, maybe more, in wire transfers from overseas. There's Latins, Arabs, Chinese, Indians, all kinds of foreigners that have money wired into Sun Bank in Miami on a regular basis. Keep your wire transfers in the 200-250 thousand dollar range, that won't raise any eyebrows whatsoever. Take the Articles of Incorporation from Florida to your lawyer in Georgia and tell him to have the Florida Corporation domesticated in the State of Georgia. That gives the Florida Corporation the right to do business in the State of Georgia. Basically, the Georgia Secretary of State blesses the Florida Corporation and gives it the right to do business in the State of Georgia. Once your Florida Corporation is domesticated in the State of Georgia, go to your bank in Georgia and open up a checking account in the corporation name. When you're ready to buy some real estate in Georgia, wire transfer the money to your account at Sun Bank in Miami. As soon as Sun Bank receives the wire, instruct them to wire the funds to the corporations' checking account in Georgia. Your banker in Georgia will see that the funds came from Sun Bank in Miami if he even checks. He really has no reason to check. All he'll know is that a couple of hundred thousand dollars came into your account and he'll be thrilled because it increases his daily float. He won't care where it came from, he'll just be glad he got it because it increased his float. Then, buy the real estate, close on it, and pay with a check from your checking account in Georgia. Nobody in Georgia will know that the money came from the Cayman Islands. It's nobody's business anyway but yours and your dads'."

I said: "That's great Lou! That is so fucking cool! Now what do I do if the Banker or a Realtor or somebody else asks me or my dad where the money is coming from, what do I tell them?"

He said: "You can tell them it's none of their business. But, if you want to give them an answer, tell them part of it is your money and you have some investors who want to invest in real estate in Georgia. That's all you need to say."

I said: "What if an IRS agent comes snooping around and asks us where the money came from."

He said: "First, be nice but firm. Tell him the same thing, you've put together a group of investors that want to invest in real estate in Georgia."

I said: "What if he wants to know the names of my investors?"

He said: "Tell him that they wish to remain anonymous but assure him that you will file all tax returns that are required and that you will pay all taxes owed in a timely manner. That should keep him at bay."

I said: "What if the IRS agent goes to Sun Bank in Miami and finds out the money was wire transferred from the Cayman Islands? What if he wants to know the names of my investors?"

He said: "Tell him the same thing, that your investors are not U.S. citizens and they wish to remain anonymous. Tell him that you met them in Cayman when you were down there scuba diving on vacation. You're not required to give him their names. Tell him that you will file all tax returns in a prompt manner and you will pay all taxes owed. That's all he can ask for, it will be a Mexican standoff. He won't have any reason to continue an investigation of you."

I said: "That's amazing! Now what about taxes, will we have to file a corporate tax return?"

He said: "Well, you'll have to pay sales tax, transfer tax, taxes like that when you buy the property. Then in March, you'll have to file the 1120S Tax Return for an "S" corporation. Tell Chris Fertig to file the IRS Form 2553 to make the corporation an "S" corporation. "S" corporations don't pay any corporate tax, the profits are passed through to the stockholders and they pay personal tax on the profits as dividends. I've got a CPA here in Ft. Lauderdale who prepares all my returns for me. He hates the IRS, he's a good guy, he's one of us. He'll prepare the return without wanting to know anymore than he needs to know to prepare the return. He won't ask any questions, he'll just get it done. Someday you should meet him, you'll like each other a lot."

I said: "I always like to meet the good guys. What about me filing a personal tax return?"

He said: "That's another hard question you're asking me. You can do one of three things: You can not file at all, you can file fraudulently, or you can declare all your income truthfully and pay a ton of money in tax. Filing fraudulently will get you five years in prison so you don't want to do that. The simple answer is to not file at all. Why don't you come see me at tax time next year and we'll figure something out then. Does your wife work?"

I said: "Yes, she's a Delta Flight Attendant, she makes decent money."

He said: "Okay, have her file "Married Filing Separate" and that won't make her a party to your potential problems. That'll keep her legal and protect her at the same time. My CPA can file her return for you and you and your wife could meet him at that time."

I said: "Lou, this is amazing, you are amazing!"

He said: "This is my life's work, fighting those sons-a-bitches at the IRS."

I said: "Well, I can't think of anything else. I'm sure I'll think of something as soon as I walk out the door."

He said: "You call me anytime you've got a question."

I said: "Great! I'll do that. Now what do I owe you for your time today?"

He said: "Aw, you don't owe me anything."

I said: "What?!?! I want to pay you for your time. I can't put a price tag on what this is worth to me."

He said: "You're like a breath of fresh air that just blew into my life. You're the first smuggler that I've met. Now, I'm connected to the biggest thing that's happening in this town. This was fun! Hey, you guys are famous. Someday, they'll be writing books and making movies about you. Just make sure that I'm in the book and the movie as one of the good guys."

I said: "Lou, if I've got any say-so in it, you'll be in the book and the movie. Thank you very much for your advice and for your friendship."

We shook hands warmly and I departed the law offices of Isley and DeReuil. As I got in my car and drove north on Bayview Drive to go to the payphones at the Public Tennis Courts, my head was swimming but I had a really good feeling inside. I felt sure the IRS would want a piece of me at some point. Not if me and Lou DeReuil could help it Mr. Taxman, not if we could help it!

Footnote: Lou Dereuil passed away on Wednesday, January 30, 2008 at his home in Ft. Lauderdale from Lou Gehrig's disease. We all lost a good friend, mentor, and advisor. He will be missed!

Chapter 18
Another House, Another Boat
The name of the game is grow or die!

It was just a couple of blocks north up Bayview to the public tennis courts and the payphone there; I was beginning to know where all the payphones were in Ft. Lauderdale. I called Danielle at her office, told her that I was free, and we arranged to meet ASAP at Southport Raw Bar which was about a block away from Cordova Road. I left the tennis courts and drove south on Bayview to Sunrise, took a right and went west to U.S. 1, took a left and went south on U.S. 1 past Sears and the Rolls Royce dealer, through the tunnel under New River, past Davie Boulevard to 17th Street Causeway. I took a left and went to the first stoplight, turned left at the Mayhew's Liquor Store, and drove to the end of the first block and took a right into the parking lot for Southport Raw Bar. I went in the big, wooden nautical door and as soon as my eyes adjusted to the light or lack of it, I saw Danielle sitting at a table to the right near the bar. As I walked over to her table, I noticed the jukebox was playing one of my favorite songs and Danielle was working on an order of steamed clams.

I sat down and said: "Did you play that song for me?"

She said: "Yeah, how'd you know?"

I said: "Just figured."

She said: "Here, help me eat these steamers. If I eat the whole order all by myself, I won't eat my supper tonight." I speared a steamer with a fork, drenched it in melted butter and popped it in my mouth, GOOD! "You're gonna love this house."

I said: "Good, tell me about it."

She said: "It's got lots of vegetation in the rear and you can walk in the back door, go through the kitchen into a large family room and through a door on the front into the garage. It's perfect for what you want it for. Across the street in the back is a small neighborhood park so you won't have to worry about nosy neighbors at night."

I said: "It sounds as good as the house off Riverland Road."

She said: "Better! And it's empty too."

I said: "What are they asking?"

She said: "$185,000. I think we should offer them $175,000 and if we get it, great. If they counter with $180,000, we should accept. It's in good shape and I think it's worth at least $200,000." By then, we had devoured the steamers. Our buxom waitress sauntered over with the bill which I grabbed and paid while Danielle grinned like a Cheshire cat.

I said: "Let's go take a look at this house." We walked out into the bright sunlight and simultaneously put on our sunglasses.

She said: "You wanta ride with me and leave your car here?"

I said: "Sure, why not" and we both got into her car.

She went north to the corner of Cordova Road, took a right, and we winded up Cordova to 7th Street. She took a right on 7th, crossed over a little bridge, drove about a third of the way down the street and turned left into a u-shaped driveway in front of a beautiful brick and wood house. I liked the curb appeal! We got out and walked to the front door, Danielle opened the door with the key and we walked inside into a nice, large living room. The rear wall was a large opening that connected to the kitchen across the rear of the house. We walked into the kitchen and faced left, there was a door to the right that went out into the backyard and a door to the left that went into the family room. She turned on the light in the family room and we walked back toward the front of the house to a door which she opened and showed me the access into the garage.

I said: "This is perfect Danielle" and she beamed.

We walked back into the kitchen and went out the door into the backyard which was surrounded by a hedge of ficus and red tip photinias. The interior of the backyard was full of blooming hibiscus and bougainvillea. It was stunning! We walked out onto the wooden dock and it appeared to be in good shape. I looked across the canal and saw the neighborhood park on the south side of the street. No neighbors to worry about there.

I said: "Danielle, this is great, good job in finding it. What about a mortgage?"

She said: "There's no mortgage, Scooter, it's free and clear. Is that a problem?"

I said: "No, not at all. I want it, so call the people and offer them $175 and let's see what they say. You can pay $185 if you have to, just don't let it get away 'cause I want it."

She said: "Scooter, I really think they'll take $175."

I said: "Whatever, just don't let it get away 'cause it's perfect."

She said: "I'll call the sellers this afternoon and let you know as soon as I get their answer. Do you want to look at the rest of the house, do you want to see the bedrooms?"

I said: "Yeah sure, let's walk through the house" so we walked through the hibiscus and bougainvillea back into the kitchen, into the living room, and looked at all the bedrooms and bathrooms. This was a really nice house and would be perfect for unloading a sailboat.

She said: "You wanta ride over to the park and take a look at the house from over there?"

I said: "Yeah, let's do that" so we locked up the house, got in Danielle's car and rode one block north to the park. You could hardly see the back of the house at all, the vegetation was so lush. On both sides of the house and all the way across the back by the dock, the hedges blocked the view almost completely. Unloading would be easy and safe here. I was pleased, very pleased.

Danielle drove me back to my car at Southport Raw Bar, she headed for her office to call the sellers and make my offer, and I headed for the law firm to see Chris Fertig. I left Southport Raw Bar and drove south to 17th Street Causeway, turned right and went west to U.S. 1, turned right and drove north to Davie Boulevard, turned left and went west on Davie to the law firm of Dolan, Fertig and Curtis.

I parked in the rear parking lot, took the elevator up to their offices, went in the large reception area, and gave the receptionist my best smile.

I said: "I'm here to see Chris, is he available?"

She said: "Go on down the hall to his office, he's waiting on you." I went down the hall to the right and walked into Chris' office."

He looked up and said: "Hi, I'm glad you're here, the wire transfer came through, we've got the money. I called Danielle but she wasn't in her office."

I said: "Yeah, I know, she was with me."

He said: "Oh, okay. Is everything okay with you?

I said: "Yes, everything is fine with me. We just looked at another house and Danielle is going to put in a bid on it for me. Now that we've got the money, let's get the Riverland house closed so I can get some people living in it. Then, we'll close on this new house off Cordova Road."

He said: "Well, should we form another corporation?"

I said: "Yeah, we're gonna have to do that too."

He said: "Well, think up a name."

I said: "How about Cordova Waterfront Properties, Inc. If that's taken, try 7th Street Waterfront Properties, Inc."

He said: "Who do you want to be President?"

I said: "Oh, maybe Jack Miehoff."

He said: "You serious?"

I said: "No, not really." I thought a minute and came up with a name a little less conspicuous. I was getting good at this now. "I'll come by tomorrow afternoon and pick up the Articles of Incorporation so I can get a notarized signature for you." I knew that he knew what I was talking about.

Chris called Danielle at her office and she answered.

He said: "We received the wire transfer in my trust account and we're ready to close. I called the sellers and set up the closing for tomorrow, can you do 2:00 P.M?"

I could hear Danielle talking to Chris but I couldn't make out what she was saying. It sounded like she was excited!

Chris said: "Yes, Scooter's here with me now, he's filled me in on everything. We've got enough funds to close on both houses. As soon as we close the Riverland house, I'll set up the closing on the Cordova house. Yes, I'll tell Scooter that the people accepted his offer of $175,000. He'll be happy to hear that. Okay, I'll see you tomorrow at 2:00 P.M." He hung up with Danielle.

He said: "Danielle's excited, could you tell?"

I said: "Yeah, she should be, she's got one big commission in the bank and another one coming soon. Hell I'm excited too, I've just bought two beautiful houses!" We both laughed. We chit-chatted a few minutes and I said: "Is Jim here?"

He said: "No, he's gone for the day."

I said: "Okay, you fill him in on what we're doing." We shook hands and I departed the law firm.

I drove over to Jerry's house on S.W. 5th Place on New River. I knocked on the front door, opened it and walked in, Jerry was in the kitchen, he never locked his doors. I told him that I'd just left Chris Fertig and filled him in on what I was doing.

He said: "That sounds good. Sounds like you've got your shit together."

I said: "Well, I'm trying man, I'm trying. I want to do this right from the beginning and avoid problems, not deal with them after they crop up."

He said: "Well it sounds like you've got a good start."

I said: "Listen, I'm gonna have two houses and two boats. What I'd like to do is buy a third boat. Will you have enough pot to load my third boat if I get one?"

He looked kinda funny and said: "Gee man, do you have enough people to handle three crews?"

I said: "Yeah man, I do. I've got four guys trained that are capable of being captains and that's not including me. I've got some more guys that I trust that want to work and I'll have to get some more women, but that shouldn't be a problem, Pat'll help me with that. All my guys know how to sail, they know the headings to and from Gun Cay, and they know how to bleed the injectors and clear the fuel lines if they get clogged. I feel confident that I could put together three good crews. Some of them have been through some rough weather, some of them haven't, but they can handle it when it happens, and the boats are running great. We love those Perkins Diesels, they're reliable. I'd like to continue to rent Linda's house from you and I'll unload two of my boats at my two houses. What I need to know is: Will Joe let me get a third boat and will you load all three of my boats with a full load?"

He said: "It ain't no problem with Joe, Joe always needs more scammers. Sounds like you've got it figured out pretty good. Yeah, okay, that sounds good to me. That'll work out good because I've got two other scammers besides you but one of them is unreliable. The other guy is pretty good and he'll go if he has to but he's kind of unreliable too. So, I think that between the two of them, one of them would be going all the time as my fourth scam boat along with your three boats."

I said: "Well, that sounds real good to me. I know that you have a lot on you and I see what you do just holding up your end, so you won't let Joe down. I think that I've done pretty well for you, I've always been there and never had any of my boats break down and left you in a bind sitting on pot. I'm trying hard not to let you down and I'm trying to help you as much as I can. The way that I feel I could help you the most is if you would let me run all four of your scam boats. If you need four scam boats to get rid of 20,000 pounds, I'll train enough people and I'll buy another scam boat in a couple of trips. I'll run all four scam boats for you and then all you'll have to worry about is running the middle boat. I don't even mind continuing to rent some houses from you if you want to make some money that way. That doesn't matter to me."

He said: "That sounds pretty good to me. I tell you what, what kind of boat do you want? Do you want to get a power boat now that you've got two sailboats?"

I said: "Well, I've thought about a power boat, but frankly, I've had so much success with these damn Columbia sailboats that I've really fallen in love with them. I feel like they're real good seagoing boats and I know they'll stand up in rough weather because we've been through some bitch of a storms and they've come through with flying colors. We've had minor problems with them sucking air and we've had the fuel lines clogged up with black algae that grows in the diesel fuel, but it's nothing we couldn't handle. I'm just real sold on sailboats and these damn Columbias are just so cheap, they do the job so well, and they look good doing it. I think I'll just stick with sailboats for now. I guess I'll start looking for another one."

He said: "I'll tell you what, I've got another 41 foot Columbia that I just got back from Customs. They had confiscated it illegally from behind my house about a year ago. Chris Fertig just got it back for me a couple of weeks ago."

I said: "What?!?! Are you telling me you're hot, have you got the heat on you?"

He said: "No, I don't think I'm hot. We've been working for a year since they confiscated the boat. Every time we go work and come home, we unload the boats and deliver the pot, nobody gets busted. If I were hot, somebody'd be getting busted. We've been working for a year since they confiscated the boat and nobody's gotten busted in my group or Joe's group for that matter. You've got to figure you're not hot if nobody's getting busted."

I said: "That makes sense, I guess. Why did Customs confiscate the boat?"

He said: "I really don't have an answer to that question, I don't know. Customs said in Court that they got an anonymous tip, they don't know who from. They came up New River in a Customs boat and boarded my boat. I had a mechanic that was working on the motor doing a minor tune-up but he wasn't there when Customs showed up. They boarded my boat and searched it and found a small bag of pot, less than an ounce. The boat had never been worked, I was getting it ready to work it. Customs took the boat and towed it down to the Customs docks down the canal from the Gulf docks. I put Chris Fertig on it and it took him a year to get it back."

I said: "Didn't they want to know whose pot it was?"

He said: "Yeah, they did. Chris told them that it belonged to the mechanic, not to me."

I said: "Didn't they want to know the name of the mechanic?"

He said: "Yeah, they did. Chris told them that all we knew was his first name and we didn't have a phone number for him, that I met him over at one of the marinas and he asked me for some work. I gave him my address and told him to come over and tune up the motor on my sailboat for me. That's all I know about him."

I said: "Is that true?"

He said: "Hell no, the mechanic is Rita's brother, Randy, the one you worked a couple of trips with."

I said: "Smith, you've got big balls, brother. Where is the boat now?"

He said: "Oh, it's in the same marina as your new sailboat, she's on "D" dock, right? My sailboat's on "B" dock, it's tore up bad. Customs let it sit for over a year and it's just gone to hell. But I'll tell you what, you've been so good since you've been working for me that I'll just give you the boat because it'll make me a lot of money. I'd like to just give it to you as a bonus."

I said: "I think I'd prefer it better if I just paid you for it. I don't like anybody giving me anything. I believe I'd just as soon pay you for it if you don't care."

He said: "Aw man, you don't have to pay me for it, just go ahead and take it. Really, the damn thing, the way it sits now, it's not worth very much. If you can take it and fix it up and get it cleaned up and use it, it'll make you some money and make me some money too. It'll be worth it to me because frankly, it's just a pain in the ass right now, it's another problem that I don't need."

I said: "Well, what about mechanically, how does it run?"

He said: "It runs good, it's got that Perkins 4.154 diesel engine in it that all your boats have got. Randy had it slightly pulled apart when it was confiscated. He'd done a minor tune-up and it ran out good he said. Cosmetically, it's real bad looking, real dirty and just groddy looking. All it needs is a good cleaning. You'll have to get your mechanic to put the engine back together 'cause Randy's gone back to the west coast of Florida for awhile."

I said: "Shit Jerry, that's a helluva good deal for me. If you want to give it to me then I'll take it, and I sure as hell appreciate it. I'll damn sure work it 'cause I love those Columbias."

He said: "Go on down to the marina and go to slip B-12 I think. If that's not a 41 Foot Columbia, it's right nearby B-12. It's got a blue-gray stripe on the cockpit and I call her Blue Mist. If you want her, you can have her." He gave me the key to the padlock on the hatch and the key to the ignition.

I said: "Yeah man, I want her. I'll get her standing tall and make us both some money with her." We shook hands warmly and I left his house and headed for the marina. I was stoked! Now I had three 41 foot Columbias and I didn't have to pay for the new boat, what a deal!

I drove south on Andrews Avenue to State Road 84, turned right and went west passing the big Cemetary until I turned right and wound through the neighborhood to the marina. I parked in the parking lot and walked out to "D" dock and found Audy's slip. I got on her, climbed in the cockpit and knelt down at the open hatch at the front of the cockpit. Mick and Dan were rewiring an overhead light and they gave me a big smile.

I said: "Come on and take a walk with me, I've got a new boat so let's go take a look at her and check her out."

Mick said: "No shit, whose gonna run her?"

I said: "Well, I haven't thought that far along yet but it's probably gonna be one of you guys. I'll let one of you captain Audy and the other one captain Blue Mist." They both beamed!

We climbed off of Audy and walked over to "B" dock and found slip B-12. Sure enough, there was a 41 foot Columbia with a wide, gray-blue stripe around the cockpit. We got onto Blue Mist, climbed in the cockpit and I opened the hatch with the key that Jerry had given me. We walked down the stairs into the main salon and My God, she was dirty, filthy, and groddy. She was so dirty it looked like you could get a disease if you stayed too long.

Dan said: "Lord have mercy, this is gonna take a lot of work."

I said: "Yeah, it sure is. We're gonna have to get on it so we can use her for the next trip. How's Audy coming along?"

Mick said: "Aw man, we've got all the big stuff, it's just piddly stuff that's left to do. We can finish it up when we go on the next trip if we have to. It's just stuff like fixing and rewiring the overhead lights and little stuff like that, nothing major. We've got everything working that we need. We've got all the instruments working, we've got the radios hooked up and working, the knot log works and the engine's running great. We've got it cleaned up real good too so we can start working on Blue Mist if that's what you want."

I said: "That's exactly what I want you to do. I want you to get her ready for the next trip which should be here in about a week. I'll have our mechanic, Ron, come over and go over the engine and get it running good. I want you to go over this lady from top to bottom and bow to stern. Change everything in her and make her new. Double-clamp all the hoses in the head and all the hoses on the thru-hull fittings. We don't want to blow a hose and be taking on water from a thru-hull fitting. Make sure the bilge pumps are working and change all the cotter pins in the rigging. They may be weak or rusted and will give way in rough weather. We don't want the boat coming apart on us in rough weather. Tie the boat up tight to the dock and haul the sails up and check them out and see if the sails are in good shape. Jerry told me that she had good sails but I want you to haul them up here in the marina and check them out. Take a close look at all the grommets on the sails and make sure none are torn or missing. If we have to, we'll take them off the boat and take them to a sailmaker to get sewn. That may take a few days so do that tomorrow and let's get an answer on the condition of the sails right away. We can motor all the way over and back if we have to so we won't miss the trip. If she breaks down or if there's a problem, it'll be your ass that's floating out in the middle of the Gulfstream, not mine. It'd be great if we could go daysailing and give her a seatrial."

Mick said: "I thought you would captain Blue Mist on her first trip and let one of us go with you?"

I said: "It may work out that way or it may not. I've been wanting to go on the middle boat to the freighter and see what that's all about. I may do that if Jerry'll let me. If that happens, I may let you, Mick, captain Audy and Dan can captain Blue Mist. Are you guys ready to be captains, can you handle it? A captain makes $25,000 per trip you know. Rob and Ross make $20,000 each as co-captains. Do you think you're ready for that?"

Mick said: "We kinda thought that we'd go on our first trip as co-captains like Rob and Ross. That way we'd have each other in case anything happens. I guess we could each captain a boat by ourselves if we had an experienced crew. We would want to cross the Gulfstream together and stay close to each other while we were crossing. That way, we could babysit each other during the crossing."

I said: "Yeah, that's a good idea, in fact, Cathy 5 could cross with you and we could have a Columbia caravan. Y'all could take care of each other in the event something happened. I'll give you my most experienced people to crew with you to help. All you have to do is find Gun Cay and go to the fishing hole to get loaded. It's impossible to miss America coming home going west. Do you think you can do that?"

Dan said: "Yeah man, we can do it. We'll have to get our confidence up a little more before the trip comes but we can do it."

I said: "Well, I've got confidence in both of you. I've taught you everything I know, so you know what I know. I've got faith in you."

Mick said: "We appreciate that, man, We'll try not to let you down."

We got back in the cockpit, closed the hatch and locked it, and climbed off Blue Mist back onto the dock. I gave the keys to Blue Mist to Mick. He and Dan went back to Audy to do a few more things and I headed for the house. I had a real good feeling about Mick and Dan but I wasn't so sure about Blue Mist. She was gonna take a lot of work and we needed to go daysailing a couple of times to get confident with her. I hope the weather is good the first time we work her. Boats don't break down in good weather. They only break down in bad weather when the weather puts a strain on them.

Like they say, it's lonely at the top. This was a lonely road that I was on but I had a good woman and a lot of good friends to help me walk down that road. Lord, please help us all!

Chapter 19
John and Mom's
"Hey, Hey, Tampa Bay, the Bucs know how to shine" – Original theme song of the
Tampa Bay Buccaneers Professional Football Team

The next morning, I slept late, got up, sat in the sun and had my coffee under the overhang, took a brief swim in the pool, put my clothes on, and went to the law firm to see Chris. I parked in the rear parking lot and took the elevator up to the fourth floor reception area. I gave the receptionist a big smile.

I said: "Is Chris here? I need to see him."

She said: "No, he's gone to lunch and then he's going to your closing at 2 o'clock. He should be back around 3 o'clock. Here, he left this for you" and she handed me a large manila envelope, it was the Articles of Incorporation for Cordova.

I said: "Thanks, this is what I was looking for." She smiled knowingly.

I departed the law firm and drove over to Jerry's house. Jerry wasn't there but Rita was and that's who I needed anyway. Rita got her Notary seal, I signed the fictitious name as President of the corporation, and Rita notarized the fake signature. I signed the name with a leftward tilt so that it would appear that the signor was left-handed. I didn't want a handwriting expert to be able to match my right-handed handwriting with the fake signature if the house got busted. Rita offered me lunch which I accepted and she fixed us both a sandwich. We sat at the kitchen table and ate while we chit-chatted about nothing in particular. Rita was a damn good woman, we were lucky to have her. After we finished lunch, I left Jerry's house and drove over to Riverland Road to Linda's house on 28th Terrace to check on Cathy 5. Then I drove over to 30th Terrace to my very soon to be new house, they should be closing on it now. I was blown away at how beautiful this house was. Someday, I want to live in a house this nice that's not a scam house. I sat in my car in the u-shaped driveway for about two minutes and got real good vibes from the house and the neighborhood.

I left 30th Terrace and drove back to the law firm, walked into the reception area, and gave the receptionist an inquisitive look.

She said: "He just got back from your closing, go on back." I walked down the hall to Chris' office.

He looked up and said: "It's done, you own the house, everything went smoothly. Danielle wants you to call her." I handed him the Articles of Incorporation for the Cordova house and he handed me the keys to the Riverland house.

I said: "Great, dial her number for me will you?" He dialed her number and handed me the phone. She answered and sounded breathless. "You been running?"

She said: "You keep me running, Scooter, and I like it!"

I said: "I'm glad to hear that! Listen, I've just brought the Articles of Incorporation for the Cordova house back to Chris. His secretary will send them to Tallahassee and as soon as the corporation is active, we'll close on the new house. It shouldn't be more than two or three days. We've already got the money in Chris' trust account so that won't be a holdup for us. We should be good to go as soon as the corporation is active. Keep on looking at houses for me 'cause I'm probably gonna want to buy another one in the near future, not right away but pretty soon."

She said: "Okay, I'll keep looking and if I find a really good one, I'll let you know and you can look at it. I'll call the Sellers on the Cordova house and put them on standby for their closing, I'll tell them it should just be a couple of days."

I said: "Good job, Danielle, you keep up the good work. I am very pleased." We said our goodbyes and I handed the phone to Chris.

Chris said: "Danielle's a good woman "

I said. "Yes she is, and so is Rita." I knew that he knew what I meant.

He said: "Have you found a tenant to live in your new house?"

I said: "No, but I'll start working on it now that we've closed."

He said: "When you find someone, give me their name and I'll draw up a lease to protect everyone. We'll have a lease on the dock from the owners of the boat and a lease on the house from the people that are renting it, they'll both rent from the corporation. The people that are renting the house won't know anything about the people that own the boat and are renting the dock. That way, if something happens and there's a problem with the house, the tenant in the house is protected. Do you understand what I'm talking about?" I thought to myself that Chris was double-talking me.

I said: "Yeah, I guess I know what you're telling me. We're gonna protect the tenant in the house with a lease in the event the house has legal problems, is that right?" Now, I was double-talking Chris.

He said: "That's right, if there's a problem at the house, the cops won't be able to arrest the tenant in the house because they didn't rent the dock out, the owners of the house rented the dock out. The cops will go looking for the owners of the house, do you understand?"

I said: "Yes, I understand now. How will the tenant not be arrested if there's a problem at the house?"

He said: "Let me be careful now. When the sailboat goes sailing to the Bahamas, the tenant will have to leave and go to Disneyworld or go visit some friends out of town. When the coast is clear, they can come back to the house. If there's a problem at the house, they don't ever come back, they go back home to where they came from and hope the cops never find them to ask them questions about the owners of the boat. Does that make sense?"

I said: "Yes it does. Is this what Jerry does with his houses?"

He said: "Yes it is. Jerry came up with the idea to have leases on the house and the dock. Me, as attorney for the corporation, draws up the leases, gets them signed by both parties, and keeps the leases in the file with the closing documents."

I said: "Okay, so what if the house gets busted and the cops find the tenant for the house? What does the tenant tell the cops?"

He said: "Scooter, I've got to be very careful in the way that I advise you. I am your attorney and it is my job to do legal work for you and I have no problem with doing your legal work, preparing documents, forming corporations, representing you at closings, etc. However, there is a line that I must not cross over. We are very near that line with this conversation." Chris was telling me that he wanted to maintain plausible deniability to protect himself, and I didn't have a problem with that, I just wanted to get the job done.

I said: "Okay Chris, I don't want you to cross the line either, so we agree on that. I just need to know what to tell my tenant. How about this: we are not having this conversation, this is off the record, okay? We are not having this conversation. Now, off the record, can you tell me what to tell my tenant?"

He said: "How about this, Scooter, I can tell you what Jerry tells his tenants."

I said: "Even better, what does Jerry tell his tenants?"

He said: "Jerry tells his tenants this: if the cops find them after the house gets busted, they tell the cops that they took a trip to Disneyworld. When they were ready to come home, they called one of their neighbors to touch base and the neighbor told them that the house had been busted for drugs. They tell the cops that they didn't hardly know the people on the boat at all. That they hid a key outside the house and they showed the people on the boat where the key was in case they needed to get in the house or the garage when they weren't home. That's all they know, they don't know any more than that. They didn't want to come back to Ft. Lauderdale and get in the middle of a hornet's nest so they went home to where they came from."

I said: "Will that fly, will it work?"

He said: "Scooter, that's their story and they're sticking to it."

I said: "Okay Chris, I'm sorry that I put you on the spot. I should have asked Jerry these questions, not you."

He said: "Yes, that would have been better."

Chris and I said our goodbyes and I departed the law firm and headed for the marina to see Mick and Dan and check on my boats. When I got to the marina, Mick and Dan were on Blue Mist working away. They had gotten her cleaned up with soap & water, brushes, and a hose. The inside of her looked a thousand times better and I actually felt like I wouldn't get sick now from the filth and the grode. The boys had been working hard, she really did look good. I was pleased and I told them so.

Mick said: "We've been working on this lady since early this morning. Man, she was some kind of dirty. Oh yeah, Ron came by and put the engine back together, she runs like a top. Ron was glad to see that Racor water filter. He said that should save us a lot of problems. He said we should put a can of Biobar in the fuel tank, that it would kill the black algae that is probably growing in the diesel fuel."

I said: "Okay, let's do that. Why don't you go to the marine store on 17th Street tomorrow and buy three cans, we'll use it on all the boats."

Mick said: "Ron said you didn't need to use it unless the boats were gonna sit for an extended period of time. He said, the way we went through diesel fuel, the black algae wouldn't have time to grow. He showed us some neat stuff about these engines, he really knows his stuff."

I said: "Yeah, I wish he would go on trips with us but his wife won't let him go. I'd really like to have him on the water with us."

Dan said: "Yeah, that would be great if we had a problem on a trip and he was out there with us."

I said: "Okay, we closed on my first house today so we'll be unloading Audacious there until I get my second house bought. We'll probably flip-flop Blue Mist with Audy the second night so I don't have to pay Jerry to rent a house. We'll keep unloading Cathy

5 at Linda's house for the time being. My problem now is that I need someone to live in my new house."

Mick said: "Well, what do you have in mind?"

I said: "Well, it's a $180,000 waterfront home in a great neighborhood. If you guys moved into it, everybody in the neighborhood would know that you're scammers. You don't have enough means or age on you to own an expensive house like this. It would be better if we had some older people, like our parents age, who could live in the house for us like it was their house. That would be real good cover for the neighborhood. I don't know anybody down here that's got any age on them so I'm kinda stumped. Do you guys have any ideas, do you know anybody that we might get to live in the house for us?"

Dan said: "Our friend John may be able to help us. His mother is real cool and she might come down here and live in it for you. She lives in Merritt Island near the Cape. Maybe you could talk to John and have John talk to her about it. I'll bet she'd do it."

I said: "God, that'd be great! How old is this lady?"

Mick said: "Late forties, I don't think she's fifty yet."

I said: "Is she pretty cool about pot and everything?"

Dan said: "Oh yeah, she's real cool about pot, that's no problem. We've smoked pot in front of her before, it's no big deal. In fact, she even smokes it herself sometimes."

I said: "Far out! What's this lady's name?"

Mick said: "Her name is Patsy but we call her Moms."

I said: "Do you think Moms would want to go on trips?"

Mick said: "I don't know, Scooter. Moms can't swim and she's scared of the water."

I said: "My Lord, I thought everybody could swim these days."

Dan said: "No Scooter, there's a lot of people in the world that can't swim and Moms is one of them."

I said: "Well, I'm gonna call John and ask him, first of all, if he has any objections, and if he doesn't, I'll ask him to call her and ask her if she wants to come to Ft. Lauderdale and live in a beautiful waterfront home. That would be great if she would."

I climbed off Blue Mist and walked up to the marina's office where there was a payphone just outside the front door. Luckily, I had a roll of quarters in my back pocket so I dialed John's work phone number then shoved a couple of dollars worth of quarters in the phone.

"Hello, Tampa Bay Buccaneers Ticket Office, this is Terry, how may I help you?"

I said: "Hey Terry, this is Scooter in Ft. Lauderdale calling John Chesterfield, is he available?"

He said: "Hey Scooter, John's told me all about you, I'm looking forward to meeting you sometime. John's on the phone right now, he shouldn't be too long."

I laughed and said: "Oh Lord, Terry, I don't know if it's good when your reputation precedes you. What has John told you about me?"

He said: "Just that you guys worked together at the Dolphins Ticket Office and he told me a couple of war stories. We were having a few beers one night and he had us in stitches with his stories about the Dolphins and the Strikers. Oh John's off the phone now, I'll put you through. Why don't you come visit us sometime and bring your golf clubs, we'll play a round of golf and drink some beer."

I said: "That sounds good, I'll try to come visit you soon" and Terry put me on hold.

John picked up and said: "This is John Chesterfield."

I said: "John, Scooter, what's going on my brother?"

He said: "Oh man, it's happening, you know the routine. What's going on with you?"

I said: "It's happening here too, it's happening big time. I just closed on a beautiful waterfront home off Riverland Road and I'm gonna keep a sailboat at the dock there. I've been talking with Mick and Dan because I need somebody to live in the house that has some age on them. They suggested Moms, they said she might want to come down from Merritt Island and live in the house for me. What do you think about that? Do you have any objections to your mother living in one of my houses?"

He said: "No, I don't see any problem with it. What's gonna happen when it comes time for a trip?"

I said: "Well, she'll have to take a short vacation, go to Disneyworld or come visit you, just leave town until the coast is clear."

He said: "Okay, that sounds like it'll work."

I said: "The house is owned by a corporation and we'll give Moms a lease so she'll rent the house from the corporation. Maybe she could use her maiden name and that would add a layer of protection for her. The corporation will rent the dock out to the people that own the sailboat so as far as the cops are concerned, Moms has no control over the dock in case something happens. You know what I'm talking about, right?"

He said: "Yeah man, I'm with you."

I said: "So, if something bad happens and the cops find Moms and start asking her hard questions, she tells them that the corporation rented the dock and she didn't meet the owners of the boat until they showed up at the dock and told her that they'd rented the dock from the corporation. That's all she knows, that's her story and she's sticking to it."

He said: "Will she have to pay rent?"

I said: "Hell no. If my lawyers want her to pay rent to make everything look proper, I'll just give her the money every month and she can get a money order and mail it to the lawyers. The lawyers will give it back to me, the money will just go in a circle, it's no big deal. I've got two really good lawyers here in Ft. Lauderdale and we're still working out the details. We're trying to do everything possible to protect people in the event the worst happens."

He said: "That sounds great to me, Scooter. Moms will probably love it. How much did you pay for the house?"

I said: "$180,000."

He said: "Is it nice?"

I said: "Hell yeah it's nice, what do you think? A $180,000 house on a deep water canal in Ft. Lauderdale, it's a helluva nice house."

He said: "Man, Moms would be in hog's heaven. I'll call her tonight when I get home and call you back as soon as I hang up with her."

I said: "Good, I need to know so I can get it going. I'll go out tomorrow and buy some furniture. She won't need to bring anything but her clothes and her personal items. I'll buy dishes and pots and pans too, sheets, pillows, everything. All she needs to do is come on down and bring her clothes."

He said: "Aw man, Moms will be in heaven."

I said: "Great, I'll talk to you tonight" and we hung up.

I walked back across the marina to the docks, went to "B" dock, and climbed in the cockpit of Blue Mist. I went down the stairs into the main salon and told Mick and Dan about my conversation with John. We all agreed that it would be great if Moms would come to Ft. Lauderdale and live in the house for me. After we talked awhile about the things they'd fixed and the things that still needed to be done, I left the marina and drove home to my lovely wife and daughter.

That night, the phone rang and it was John.

He said: "Yeah Scooter, Moms is all excited about coming to Ft. Lauderdale, she can't wait. She's been wanting to move away from Merritt Island anyway. She says that there ain't nothing there but a bunch of old people waiting around to die. She wants to come to Ft. Lauderdale where the excitement is."

I said: "My Lord John, she's about to jump into the middle of excitement with both feet." He laughed and I did too. "How soon can she come down?"

He said: "She can pack up and be down there in a couple of days at the most."

I said: "Great, as soon as she gets here, we should have the house set up for her. Pat and I will go buy her some furniture tomorrow so hopefully, it will be delivered by the time she gets here. Mick and Dan can help me get it set up. I'll give her some money when she gets here so she can go get whatever she needs. Don't worry, man, I'll take care of her. Just tell her to get on down here as soon as she can."

He said: "That's what I told her, Scooter. I gave her Mick and Dan's phone number so she can get with them when she first gets down there. She can bunk in with them if the house isn't ready."

I said: "Good, that'll work. I'm looking forward to meeting Moms. Thanks a lot, John, you've just helped me solve a big problem."

He said: "No, thank you. You've just made Moms day, month, and year. She's flying high thanks to you."

I said: "That's great. Okay, we'll be talkin' atcha."

We hung up and I filled Pat in on our conversation. I told her that we were gonna have to go furniture shopping for the new house tomorrow. She reminded me of that furniture store off Oakland Park Boulevard that had nice furniture from North Carolina. I told her that we'd go there tomorrow morning and see if we could get everything we needed there.

The next morning, Pat, Sunny, and I went to the furniture store after eating a light breakfast at the house. There was a young lady there that was the daughter of the owners, she managed the store for them. We remembered her from a previous visit and she remembered us too. Pat and I walked all around the store looking at everything, I think the lady didn't think we were gonna buy anything, that we were just looking again. Finally, we were in the living room area and I began making my choices and pointing to them.

I said: "I'll take that sofa, that love seat, those two end tables, that coffee table, and that étagère."

She said: "Oh, you're getting a new living room suite today?"

I said: "Actually, we're furnishing a new house." I didn't tell her that we weren't gonna live in the new house ourselves.

She said: "Oh how nice!" and her eyes gleamed, she knew we were there to spend money now! She wrote everything down on a pad as I pointed to it.

We walked over to the bedroom area and I said: "I'll take that bed, that chest-of-drawers, that mirror, and that end table." She wrote everything on her pad.

We walked over to the kitchen area and I said: "I'll take that kitchen table and chairs, and those open shelves." She wrote it all down on her pad. "I think that's all for today."

We followed her to a large wooden desk in the middle of the store, she sat down and began to enter all the prices into a calculator. I had brought $6,000 cash with me all in 20's and I hoped that it would be enough. She got a total on the calculator and tore off the paper printout. It came to a little over $4,000, I was surprised it wasn't more, we'd gotten a lot of nice furniture for $4,000!

She said: "Will that be cash, check, or credit card?"

I said: "Cash, do you take real money?"

She said: "We love real money, we just don't see very much of it. Real money makes things easy."

I said: "I like easy. When can you deliver it?"

She said: "Would tomorrow be all right, around 11:00 A.M.?"

I said: "Tomorrow at eleven would be perfect." I gave her the address of the house and began to pay her. I gave her two packs of 20's, that was $4,000, and got the third pack and took out the difference that I needed and handed it to her. I put the rest of the third pack in my back pocket. She wrote me out an itemized receipt and handed it to me.

Pat, Sunny, and I left the furniture store and drove back to our house on 18th Terrace. Pat fixed us some lunch and we ate under the overhang out by the pool. Then, I drove back to the marina and found Mick and Dan on Blue Mist. I told them that Moms was coming down to live in the house for us and they said: "Yeah, she called us last night all excited when she hung up with John." I told them that Pat and I had bought furniture this morning and that it was being delivered tomorrow morning at 11 o'clock and that I wanted them to meet me at the house to help with the furniture. They said "No problemo" and we talked about Blue Mist. She was coming along fine and they'd made a lot of progress. They said they'd hauled the sails up and they looked good to them. I asked them if they felt like she'd be ready to go on the next trip and they said "Yes". They wanted to know who was gonna go on what boats and I told them that the two of them would probably go on Blue Mist with me and one of our ladies. Rob would have to solo captain on Cathy 5 and Ross would have to solo captain on Audy. They thought that sounded pretty good and they were happy to be going again with me. I left the marina, called it a day and headed for the house.

The next morning, after having my coffee and a wake-up swim, I headed over to my new house and arrived around 10:30 A.M., Mick and Dan were waiting on me. We opened up the house, opened some windows in every room, and opened the sliding glass door from the living room to the back yard, the house cooled down quickly with the breeze. The furniture truck showed up and the guys started bringing the furniture into the house. I showed them where I wanted everything and all we had to do was just move things around and get the pieces centered and looking good. Moms was gonna love this!

Mick said: "I talked with Moms last night and cleared this with her. Would you mind if I lived in this house with Moms like I was her son? She's agreeable to it if it's okay with you."

I said: "What about Dan, what's he gonna do?"

He said: "He and Moms don't get along as well as Moms and I do and he's messy and I'm neat. Moms already said she didn't want to live with Dan. She's agreeable to letting me live with her if it's okay with you."

I said: "Yeah, I'm okay with that, I think it's a good idea. You understand that you can't have a bunch of people coming and going all the time. This is a scam house and we've gotta keep it cool, it's got to look good to the neighbors. We don't want to raise any eyebrows and draw any heat."

He said: "Yeah, I understand perfectly, I promise there won't be any problems. It'll just be me and Moms living as a family."

I said: "Okay, go ahead, get you some furniture and move in."

He said: "I've got a waterbed that I brought down with me that's in storage right now, that's all I need. I'll get a few more pieces of furniture and I'll be set."

I said: "Okay, good. Now what's Dan gonna do?"

He said: "He's just gonna keep living in the apartment that we've been renting. Then when we go on trips, Moms can stay in the apartment if she wants."

I said: "He's okay with that?"

He said: "He's fine with that."

I gave Mick a key to the front door and that put a big smile on his face. We closed up the windows and the sliding glass door and I left to go see Jerry and they went back to the marina. As I drove to S.W. 5th Place, I was very pleased that I owned this beautiful home and I had two really good people that were gonna live in it for me. I had a good feeling that it was gonna help me make a lot of money. That was the idea, brother, that was the idea!

Chapter 20
Goin' Against My Instincts
"You better listen to your instincts, they'll keep you alive." Dad

When I got over to Jerry's house on S.W. 5th Place, I filled him in on my new house and the people I had that were gonna live in it. I told him that Blue Mist was coming along fine, she should be ready for the next trip, and that I was waiting to close on my second house.

I said: "Any word from Joe on our next trip?"

He said: "One's coming soon but we haven't heard anything yet. It could be a couple of days, it could be a week, it could be ten days, we just don't know."

I said: "I'm gonna be ready with all three boats, are you gonna be able to load all three?"

He said: "Yeah, we'll load them, that's no problem. Have you got crews for all three?"

I said: "Yeah, I'm working it out right now but I've got my key people down, so don't worry, I won't let you down."

He said: "Okay, that's good. Now, you know Tommy, Tommy Dolan? Didn't he go to the islands with you last time you went down there to transfer money?"

I said: "Yeah, he went with us, I know him."

He said: "Well, he wants to work and I don't have any place to put him. How about letting him crew on one of your boats? If you need people, he'd be real good."

I said: "Jerry, I've been real careful about choosing my people and about who I use. All my people, I'm real pleased with, they're all real good people. They're very serious about what we're doing and about making money. They don't do any drugs, they smoke a little pot but they don't do anything heavy so I can count on them, they're reliable. Now, you're asking me to take somebody into my group and I don't know who the hell Tommy Dolan is other than Jim Dolan's younger brother. I guess it'll be okay because our lawyers know everything but it goes against my instincts."

He said: "You know, Jim's done an awful lot for both of us. He brought his brother down here from Philadelphia because he was starving to death up there, I think he was managing a tire store. Jim wants him to make some money and he asked me if I could put him to work, and I told him I would. Now that you've taken over the scam boats for me, I don't have anyplace to put him so I'd really appreciate it if you would let him crew on one of your boats."

I said: "Alright, I'll take him into my family and I'll use him but if you're gonna give him to me, then I want him to work for me. I want it understood that he works for me and not you, that I'm his boss. I'll talk to him and I'll have this understanding with him. After I get him trained and he does a couple of trips, I don't want you taking him away from me and letting him do something else like run his own scam boat for you. I want that understanding with you, I want your word on it."

He said: "I don't have a problem with that, he's yours just as long as you want him."

I said: "Okay, I can use him 'cause I definitely need crew members, I'm set on captains but I need crew. I want him working on the boats everyday just like Mick and

Dan so he can get familiar with the boat he'll be going on, and he'll have to unload the boat and deliver the vans just like everybody does."

He said: "No, that's no problem, he's coming down here to live and I'm sure he'll want to work on the boat."

I said: "Okay, I'll call him and talk to him and we'll get him together with Mick and Dan but now as far as I'm concerned, he's mine and he belongs to me. You're not gonna take him away from me." I said that like a statement not a question.

He said: "No, he's yours, I won't take him back."

I said: "Okay, as long as we've got that understanding right now, I'll take him into my family."

I had a gut feeling that this wasn't gonna work out. I was going against my instincts because they were telling me that this was wrong. All my people were like family, we were very close and we took care of each other and we helped each other out. Everybody was well trained and everybody worked together real well, and I was proud of that. I was taking Tommy Dolan into my family when he wasn't family and it was going against my instincts, and I knew it was wrong. I was later to be proved right and I should've listened to my instincts but I felt like I owed Jerry and I owed Jim Dolan. So, I agreed to do it against my better judgement and against my instincts. If you'll listen to your instincts, you'll usually be okay but if you go against your instincts, you'll have problems.

That night, I called Tommy Dolan and told him that I'd talked to Jerry. Without saying too much on the phone, I told him to meet me at the marina the next morning. He sounded pleased and excited!

The next morning, I met Tommy at the marina, we walked over to Blue Mist and I introduced him to Mick and Dan. I told them that he was my lawyer's brother and that he was gonna be working with us as a crewmember on one of the boats.

I said: "I want you to put him to work, show him what to do, and teach him about the boats like I taught you. He's gonna be working everyday with you 'cause you need help with Blue Mist." They were making pretty good progress but an extra set of hands never hurt. So Tommy worked with Dan on Blue Mist and it allowed Mick to go back and work on Audy.

I had decided that I was gonna keep Blue Mist behind the house off Riverland Road and keep Audy behind the house off Cordova Road. Since Mick was living in the house off Riverland, I didn't want the neighbors seeing him leave on the boat behind the house in case the house got busted. That would protect him in that the neighbors couldn't tell the cops that Mick was using the boat that was busted since he was living in the house. I'd just about made up my mind that I was gonna let Mick captain Audy and Dan captain Blue Mist when they were ready. If the next trip came up before I'd closed on the Cordova Road house, I'd flip-flop Blue Mist and Audy at the Riverland house if I had to. That would save me 3% house rental fee to Jerry, I could put that money in my pocket, not his. I'd still unload Cathy 5 at Linda's house and pay Jerry for that. For the next trip, I was gonna let Rob captain Cathy 5 and take Tommy Dolan as crew. Ross would captain Audy and take Dan as crew and I'd captain Blue Mist and take Mick as crew. Then hopefully in two trips, I'd let Mick captain Audy, Dan captain Blue Mist, and Rob and Ross co-captain Cathy 5. I was hoping to go on the middle boat with Jerry and learn the load boat routine. Then maybe next year, if Joe would let me, I could buy my own middle boat, load my own scam boats, and have my own operation. This seemed like the logical thing to do and the way to make the most money the fastest.

I could haul 20,000 pounds now with my three scam boats, they'd be heavy but I could do it. Or, I could buy a fourth scam boat. I could flip-flop four boats at two houses or I could buy a third house. Yeah, that was the thing to do, buy a third house. All I needed was the okay from Joe and I'd buy a 53 foot Hatteras Sportfisherman and I'd be good to go with my own organization. I wondered if I could do all that without hurting Jerry's feelings and without letting him down. All of this was in the back of my mind and the more I thought about it, the more it seemed to be the most obvious thing to do.

I went to the payphone at the marina's office and called Chris Fertig. He said that the corporation was active and we were ready to close on the Cordova house. Danielle had called the sellers, they were up north but were headed for Ft. Lauderdale, they were driving. As soon as they arrived in Ft. Lauderdale, we'd close. I said "Great!" and hung up with him. I called Pat and she said that Jerry had called and for me to call him.

I called Jerry and he said: "Where are you?"

I said: "I'm at the stand-up at the marina."

He said: "Good, it's time to go fishing. Come to the Ramada Inn on State Road 84 tonight at 7 o'clock and bring your captains."

I said: "Great! Is this a go?"

He said: "Yeah, roger that. It's out there, it ain't gonna get backed up."

I said: "When do you want us to leave?"

He said: "You can leave right after the meeting if you want and cross tonight or you can leave in the morning, it's up to you."

I said: "Okay, I'll see you at seven." We hung up.

I called Rob in Miami and he and Janice were able to go. Only thing was, he had a concert to work and he wouldn't be able to leave until midnight or one o'clock. I told him that the new guy, Tommy Dolan was going with him. I called Ross in Orlando and he said he could leave within the hour. I told him he was captaining Audy with Dan. I called Jen and Rose and they were ready to go. I walked back to Blue Mist and told Dan and Tommy we were leaving tonight after our meeting. Mick saw me walking back to Blue Mist, he came over, and I told him we were leaving tonight after the meeting.

That night, I picked up Mick and Dan at the Riverland house and we went to the room at the Ramada Inn on S.R. 84. There were two other guys there that were gonna run the other two scam boats, that meant that Jerry would be loading five scam boats. Now if Jerry got a full load of 20,000 pounds, that means that each scam boat would only get 4,000 pounds. So, instead of my three boats hauling 15,000 pounds, I was only gonna haul 12,000 pounds. Most of the time, the load boats only got 18,000 to 19,500 pounds, they hardly ever got a full load of 20,000 pounds. It looked like I was gonna get shorted and I was a little shocked to say the least. I'd been busting my ass to get three boats ready so I could haul 15,000 pounds and now it looked like I was gonna get shorted. I was shocked that Jerry would do this to me.

Jerry introduced everyone and one of the other scammers was Apple Pie but the other one I didn't know. He gave us an orientation, told us we would talk on channel 5 on the bank to load and we would talk on channel 11 in the Gulfstream coming home and to Rita at the Port. We talked to the surveillance plane on the same channels. He said he wanted to load all five boats at 10 miles east of Gun Cay lighthouse, that another group would be loading at Sylvia Beacon. He said that as he was running from Russell Beacon toward Gun Cay lighthouse, he could look on his radar and see five boats clumped together at 10 miles east of Gun and come right to us. He wanted the first boat to get to 10 miles east of Gun and then help the other boats get there too by giving them a wink with their searchlight. That way, he could load us all, bam-bam-bam, and get done before the sun started coming up. You didn't want to have to load in broad daylight and you didn't want to have to lay over 'till the next night and sit on pot for 24 hours.

I said: "If you get a full load, and you are loading five scam boats, then somebody's gonna get shorted and get loaded light. The most each boat can get is 4,000 pounds if you load us all evenly. What's up with that?"

He said: "No, don't worry about that. Blue Eyes is loading the boats at Sylvia Beacon and he's only gonna have three scam boats. He'll have plenty enough pot to load one of you. Everybody's gonna get a full load, there'll be plenty of pot for everyone."

I said: "Oh, I see. So, Blue Eyes will load one of us with a full load."

He said: "That's right, there's plenty of pot for everyone."

We finished the orientation around 9 o'clock, Jerry adjourned the meeting, and we headed for the boats in the marina. The ladies had gone to buy groceries, drinks, and ice and the crew members were on the boats waiting for the captains to come and push away from the dock. Audy and Blue Mist would go ahead and travel together and Cathy 5 would follow as soon as Rob finished working the concert in Miami. It was time for another adventure and what an adventure it would turn out to be!

Chapter 21
Nightmare Off Dania Beach
This fucking boat is gonna kill somebody before we get it fixed.

When we got to the marina, Mick and I went to Blue Mist and Dan went to Audy. Ross was on Audy and he had the engine running and warming up. Rose was sitting in the cockpit of Blue Mist and she had the food, drinks, and ice stowed away. Mick and I stowed our seabags in the main salon and I started the engine on Blue Mist and then walked over to Audy.

I asked Ross: "Are you all ready to go? You got everything you need?"

He said: "Yeah, we're just about ready, maybe another five minutes or so."

I said: "Good, as soon as you're ready, cast off and go ahead because we're ready too. As soon as you get out of the marina basin, we'll cast off our lines and we'll follow you up the river. That way, we can go through the bridges together and the bridge tenders won't have to open the bridges twice."

He said: "Roger that."

In a few minutes, we saw Dan and Jen casting off their lines, Ross pulled Audy into the basin and idled out the marina into New River. Mick and Rose threw our lines on the dock and we cast off and followed Audy up the river. As we got to each bridge, Ross blew the airhorn three times, the bridge tenders opened the bridges, and we went through the middle of downtown Ft. Lauderdale into the Intracoastal Waterway, turned right and motored down to the Gulf docks and 17th Street bridge which is on a timer. In just a few minutes, the bells started ringing, traffic stopped, the bridge opened, and we motored through Port Everglades and the Cut and into the ocean. We hung a right and headed due south to the whistle buoy at Government Cut in Miami.

We must have had a front that moved in on us because it was a little rough, about 5 to 6 foot rollers. The Gulfstream was flowing south to north, the wind was blowing out of the north towards the south, and it was making those rollers on the Stream. I had taken some Bonine before I left the dock so I was hoping I wouldn't get seasick and throw-up. I decided that it wasn't a good idea to put up the sails and that we should just motor all the way over to Gun Cay unless it calmed down a little.

Mick and Dan had taken to calling me the "Little Big Man" and I liked it, so that was the handle I was using on the radio now. I let Mick take the helm and I grabbed the microphone to the CB radio.

I said: "Gearjammer, Little Big Man, you got a copy on me, good buddy, kickit back."

The sweet voice of Jen answered: "Little Big Man, this is Gearjammer, we got a copy on you, kickit back."

I said: "Listen, I think it's a little rough so let's not put up the sails, we'll just motor all the way unless it calms down a little, come back."

She said: "My captain says "Roger that" come back."

I said: "Okay, that's a Roger. Now you guys don't get too far ahead of me 'cause I don't have a lot of confidence in this boat yet, come back."

She said: "That's a Roger, Little Big Man. You let us know if we're getting too far ahead."

I said: "Roger that Gearjammer. Little Big Man standing by."

She said: "Gearjammer standing by."

By now, it was two in the morning, Audy was pulling ahead of me but I could still see his mastlight, and we hadn't even gotten down to the Dania Pier. I was staying in close to shore to try to stay out of the Gulfstream but Dania Beach was still on my right and we didn't seem to be making any headway. The beam on Audy was one foot less than Blue Mist so she was making better headway than I was. We were probably making about 6 knots but the Gulfstream was moving north about 5 knots against us so we were going nowhere fast. By now, it was about 3 o'clock in the morning, Audy was almost out of sight, when the radio crackled.

It was Rob on Cathy 5, he said: "Little Big Man, Speedy Pete, you got your ears on good buddy, kickit back."

I gave the helm to Mick and said: "Roger that, Speedy Pete, it's good to hear from you. What's your 20?"

He said: "I just came out of the Cut and I'm heading south off Dania Beach. What's your 20?"

I said: "I'm about halfway down Dania Beach, I haven't gotten to the Pier yet, come back."

He said: "Oh, is that you in front of me? I can see your mast light, come back."

I said: "Yeah, that's me."

He said: "What's the problem man, you having problems?"

I said: "No, nothing other than not making any headway against the stream."

He said: "Where's Gearjammer, what's his 20?"

I said: "He's probably coming up on the whistle buoy right about now."

He said: "Wow! I thought you guys would be halfway there by now."

I said: "This weather is kicking our butts!"

He said: "Do you want me to try and go ahead or do you want me to stay with you, come back?"

I said: "Why don't we stay together. Your boat has the same beam as mine so you probably won't make much headway either. I don't have a lot of faith in this boat yet so you stay with me, okay?"

He said: "That's a Roger!"

We motored on for another hour and Mick and I both got seasick and threw-up. Rose said she would be okay. The waves had gotten a little bigger, they were probably about 8-10 feet high now. We were just north of the Dania Pier about one hundred yards offshore. We were getting wet in the cockpit now and the three of us had put on our foul weather gear. It was getting rougher and it felt like we were on a roller coaster. We would go up the wave and down into the trough, up the wave and down into the trough. Mick and I had each gotten sick a couple more times. This was no fun!

Just then, we heard something go "PING!" and something hit the right side of the roof of the main salon. I thought "Son-of-a-bitch! What the fuck is that?" One of the three riggings on the starboard side that ran to the top of the mast had come loose and was flailing around and hitting the side of the main salon. As the boat was going up and down on the waves, the loose rigging was flailing out to the right and then it would swing back to the left and hit the top of the main salon with a big "boink" noise.

I said: "Oh shit, Mick, we've got to grab that rigging before it hits one of us in the head and kills us."

He said: "Here, you take the wheel and I'll go get it."

I said: "Now you be careful, man, and don't fall overboard."

He said: "Don't worry, I'm gonna crawl up the catwalk on my all fours holding on to the handrail."

I said: "Okay, that's good. Let me turn the boat directly into the wind. If you do fall overboard, swim to the back of the boat and I'll throw you a line and we'll pull you up on the aft deck."

He said: "Scooter, I ain't planning on falling overboard."

I said: "Okay, just be careful."

I turned the bow of the boat directly into the wind which was just about due East. The boat was going up the wave and down into the trough, it was rough! Mick climbed out of the cockpit onto the catwalk, got down on his all fours, and crawled up to the middle of the boat where the rigging was attached into a baseplate. The loose rigging came swinging at him and he grabbed it!

He said: "What do we do with it now?"

I said: "Hang on a sec, Rose, go get me a roll of duct tape" and she disappeared into the main salon and came back quickly with a new roll of duct tape and handed it to me. "Mick, see if you can get the end of the rigging to match up with the baseplate." I was hoping we could jury-rig it with some wire if the holes lined up.

He pulled the rigging down towards the deck and said: "Man, it misses coming together by about an inch, it ain't even close."

I said: "Rose, come take the wheel and keep the bow headed directly into the wind. I'm gonna go help Mick tie this thing down."

She said: "God Scooter, I don't know if I can do this."

I said: "Rose, yes you can. It'll only take about a minute, here, take the wheel" and she got behind the wheel. "Look at the compass, it's pointing at ninety degrees. Feel the wind on your face, just keep the bow on ninety degrees and the wind directly on your face. You can do this."

She said: "Okay Scooter, I'll do my best."

I said: "Rose, it'll only be for a minute, we'll do it fast."

I crawled out of the cockpit onto the catwalk, I had the duct tape in my left hand and I was holding onto the handrail with my right hand. The boat was going up and down, and up and down like a rollercoaster. I crawled on my all fours up to where Mick was in the middle of the boat and just as I got to him, a big wave went under the boat and the boat starting going down into the trough. It threw me into him and the top of my head hit him squarely in the nose. He screamed "Oh, shit!" and I screamed "son-of-a-bitch!" 'cause it hurt like hell. He fell over on his back and I fell on top of him, but he didn't lose his grip on the rigging. We both pulled ourselves back up to our all-fours and he held the rigging against the middle post for the handrail while I duct-taped the rigging to the post. We both simultaneously looked up at the top of the mast and even though the boat was going up and down, forward and aft, it looked like the mast was moving left and right about two feet each way.

I said: "Oh shit Mick, we're gonna crack this mast in half and have a dismasting. This damn boat! We should have left this fucking thing at the dock. We should have sea-trialed her before we took her on this trip."

He said: "What do you think happened, Scooter?"

I said. "I'll betcha that the cotter pin broke under the stress from the storm. It was probably rusted and weakened. That's why I told you guys to change all the cotter pins. Nothing ever breaks on a boat in good weather, shit only happens in a storm when the boat is under stress."

He said: "I'm sorry, man, that's one of the few things that we didn't get to do."

I said: "Don't worry about it now, let's get back in the cockpit" and we both crawled on all-fours down the catwalk to the cockpit, rolled over the side into the cockpit, and Mick took the wheel from Rose.

I got on the radio and said: "Speedy Pete, you got a copy, come back?"

Rob said: "Roger that, Little Big Man, come back."

I said: "Man, we've got serious problems over here. One of the starboard rigging just pulled loose from the baseplate. I'm afraid we could be dismasted. Don't you leave me."

He said: "Don't worry, my man, I won't leave you." Cathy 5 looked like she was about 50 yards away from Blue Mist, maybe a little closer. By now, it was after five in the morning and the sky was just starting to get light a little bit. In the maneuvering while we were fastening down the rigging to the handrail, we had moved out over the dropoff into the deep water and we were about 300 yards offshore.

Just when I thought things couldn't get any worse, they did, the engine just up and quit! It must have been that damn black algae that was stopping up the injectors. I pushed the start button, it started and stopped. I pushed the button again, it started and stopped again. I tried one more time, it started and stopped again. I thought: "Holy shit, now I don't have power, can I control the boat?" No! A wave came through and pushed the bow to port to about 10 o'clock. Then we went in the trough and another wave pushed our bow around almost 180 degrees. Now the bow of the boat was facing the beach. Another wave came through us and we surfed on the wave until it passed through and we went into the trough. Now with each wave, the boat is surfing and we are getting closer and closer to the beach. Without power, we can barely maintain control of the boat's attitude.

I grabbed the CB microphone and said: "Speedy Pete, you copy, you still there?"

He said: "Roger that, Little Big Man, what do you want me to do."

I said: "The engine has shut down and I don't have any power, I can barely control the boat. Come alongside me on my starboard side and we'll throw you a line, you'll have to tow us."

He said: "Roger that, I'm on my way."

It seemed like two or three minutes, maybe four or five minutes before he was along my starboard side. Cathy is surfing with every wave and we are getting closer and closer to the beach, we've crossed back over the dropoff and we're in shallow water now.

Mick has taken the helm and I've gotten a rope and am standing on the catwalk in front of the rigging. Tommy Dolan is standing on the aft deck of Cathy 5 and we're about 15 feet apart, maybe 20 feet. I throw the line underhanded to Tommy and it hits him in the chest and he misses it! Fuck!! I pull the rope in from the water and coil it up on my shoulder and arm into a circle.

I holler to Rob: "Try to pull in front of us and get a little closer but be careful so that when we surf on a wave, we won't have a collision with you. Stay just off to my starboard side."

Rob pulls Cathy 5 slightly ahead of Blue Mist and we are about 10 feet apart. I throw the line underhanded to Tommy but just as I throw it, a wave causes Cathy to surf away from Blue Mist and we miss again. Shit!! I pulled the line in again and rolled it up on my arm and shoulder again. Rob has either slowed Cathy down or put her in neutral because we are really close this time, about 5 feet apart. I am just about ready to throw the line to Tommy when a big wave causes Blue Mist to go up high and surf. As she is coming down off the wave, the back of Cathy is going up and I think we're gonna collide. I sit down real fast on the front of the boat and catch the aft deck of Cathy with my feet and legs and fend us off. We came really close and could have damaged the bow pulpit of Blue Mist if we had collided.

I went back into the cockpit and grabbed the CB microphone.

I said: "Speedy Pete, try to get close again on my starboard side but stay far enough away so I won't hit you when we surf on the waves. When my boat starts surfing and gets close to your boat, I'm gonna jump from my boat to the back of your boat. I'm gonna jump on your aft deck and bring the line with me so tell Tommy to get off the aft deck."

He said: "Ten-four, now you be careful" and there was incredulity in his voice.

I said: "Roger that."

I told Mick: "Try to keep the boat in a straight line as best you can because I'm gonna stand on the bow pulpit and jump on the aft deck of Cathy with the line. Then, I'm gonna tow you in toward the beach into about 15 feet of water and I want you to drop your anchor. Let out a good bit of anchor line so it'll catch and not drag the anchor. We don't want the boat to end up on the beach. When you've got the anchor tied off, wait to make sure the anchor ain't dragging. Once you're sure the anchor ain't dragging, you can untie the line from Cathy. Holler to me that you're ready and I'll pull Cathy up alongside Blue Mist and you and Rose can get on Cathy with us."

He said: "Okay man, you be careful, you can get killed doing this."

I said: "Yeah I know, I'll be as careful as I can be."

I got out of the cockpit and duck-walked up to the bow of Blue Mist. I picked up the coiled rope and tied it off on the cleat next to the bow pulpit. I let out about 15 feet of rope so that when I jumped, it wouldn't be jerked out of my hand if it got tight. I put the rope under the railing on the bow pulpit and then stood on the bow pulpit and held onto the bow rigging with my left hand with the coiled rope in my right hand. The bow of Blue Mist is going up and down about 10 feet and it's a wild roller coaster ride! Rob has maneuvered Cathy just in front of Blue Mist at about 1 o'clock.

The next big wave comes, Blue Mist surfs and then starts going down into the trough and gets pretty close to Cathy. Before the wave takes Cathy up above me, I jump! I push off with my legs from the bow pulpit as hard as I can and I freefall onto the aft deck of Cathy and land like a frog. Wham! I land on my all fours and there's pain in both knees. I get up just in time as the line in my hand tightens. I pull on the line and Blue Mist follows obediently. I put the line under the rear railing and tie it off on a cleat. I climb in the cockpit as the crew of Cathy 5 looks at me with amazement!

I take the helm from Rob and start towing Blue Mist in towards the beach. When we got into about 20 feet of water, I started a turn to starboard and slowly turned both boats around 180 degrees until we were headed due east directly away from the beach.

I grabbed the CB microphone and said: "Rose, you take the wheel and Mick, go up on the bow and drop the anchor."

By now, it's about 6:30 in the morning and we can see fairly well as morning has broken. I see Rose take the wheel and Mick goes up to the anchor locker and gets the anchor out with a bunch of line. Mick goes on to the bow pulpit, puts the anchor under the railing, and drops it in the water, SPLASH! I put Cathy 5's gear in neutral and the waves start pushing us back toward the beach letting out the anchor line on Blue Mist. Mick is letting the anchor line run through his hands and after about 40 to 50 feet of line has run out, I tell Rose on the radio: "Tell Mick that he can tie it off." She hollers to Mick and he ties off the anchor rope to the cleat on the bow pulpit. Then, he squatted down and held the anchor line with his right hand to see if it was dragging. It wasn't dragging so he walked back and got in the cockpit with Rose.

I grabbed the CB microphone and said: "Mick, you copy?"

Mick said: "Roger that, come back."

I said: "Good job Mick. Now, you've got to go back up front and untie us so we can come and pick you up. Get your bumpers and put them out on your port side. I'll come right up next to you on your port side so we can get you guys on Cathy."

He said: "Roger that" and he went back on the bow of Blue Mist and untied the line we'd used to tow them. Tommy pulled the line in as soon as it hit the water so it wouldn't get tangled in the propeller. Rose had disappeared into the main salon to get the bumpers and by the time Mick had returned to the cockpit, she was back up top with the bumpers. They hung three bumpers on the port railing in strategic positions about ten feet apart.

I made a circle to starboard, went behind Blue Mist to avoid her anchor line, and eased up to her port side to within about 2 feet. I put the throttle in neutral, Rob and Tommy grabbed the hand railing on Blue Mist, and Mick and Rose jumped onto Cathy 5. I gave Cathy some throttle, ran her up to 2000 rpm's, and put her bow on a direct course for the mouth of the Cut.

We motored down the Cut into Port Everglades and just as we got into the basin, the bells on the bridge started ringing and the bridge opened for us. We motored through 17th Street bridge and cruised over to the Gulf docks and docked Cathy on the outside of the docks. By now, it was a little after 7 A.M. I went to the pay phone outside the office and called Jerry.

After three rings, he answered and I said: "Hey man, I've got problems with Blue Mist. We blew a rigging off the baseplate on the starboard side, I think the cotter pin gave way. Then, the engine shut down and wouldn't start. Cathy was with me so we anchored Blue Mist off Dania Beach, everybody got on Cathy, and we're at the Gulf docks now."

He said: "It sounds like a nightmare, man?"

I said: "Yeah man, it was a nightmare off Dania Beach."

He said: "That's too bad, the weather's supposed to be good today, maybe you should have gotten a good night's sleep and left this morning."

I said: "Yeah, that's probably what we should have done. I'm sorry I'm gonna let you down."

He said: "That's no problem, there'll be enough folks out there to take care of business, don't worry about it. You know, she'd probably have run like a top if it'd been good weather. Boats never break down in good weather. You'd better change all those cotter pins before you go sailing next time."

I said: "Yeah, that'll be a priority as soon as we get back. I'm gonna call Pat and get her to get our mechanic and have them go get Blue Mist and bring her back to the marina. Can Rita run them out there in her Whaler?"

He said: "Yeah, that's no problem, I'll tell her before I leave. She can follow them all the way up the river to the marina or tow them if they can't get her running."

I said: "That's great! I'll tell Pat to get with her and work it out. Okay, I'll see you tonight. Have a safe crossing." We said our goodbyes and hung up.

I called my house and after five rings, Pat answered sleepily.

I said: "Honey, it's me, are you awake?"

She said: "I am now, what's the matter, is something wrong?"

I said: "Yeah, that damn new boat started coming apart on us. We broke a rigging on the starboard side and then the motor quit. Luckily, Cathy was with us so we left the boat anchored off Dania Beach. I'm at the Gulf docks and we're all on Cathy. You need to call Ron and get him to go with you, you're gonna have to go get the boat and take it back to the marina. I talked to Jerry and he said Rita will take you out there in her Whaler. Call Ron now and catch him before he goes to work. Do it this morning, we don't want to leave the boat off Dania Beach, somebody could steal it or vandalize it or the heat could confiscate it. We don't need that. Rita will follow you all the way to the marina and if the engine quits again, she can tow you to the dock at the marina. I hope Ron can get it running so you can drive it. Do you think you can do this?"

She said: "God, Howard, I don't know, I guess so. I'm sure glad you made me drive the boat up the River the last time we went daysailing. I can leave Sunshine with Sid and Betty across the street, they won't mind babysitting for a few hours. All right, let me call Ron and we'll get right on it, then I'll get with Rita."

I said: "Good, that's good, you can do this, honey. Just keep the boat in the middle of the River, don't cut the corners 'cause that's where it gets shallow, that's where the sand and the muck accumulate. Keep it in the middle of the River and you'll be all right, you can do this."

She said: "Yeah, I can do it if I have to, I'm gonna have to have Ron with me. What are you guys doing, are you leaving now?"

I said: "Yeah, we're leaving as soon as I hang up with you."

She said: "Howard, you be careful, I love you. I'll take care of Blue Mist." We said our goodbyes and we hung up. I thought: "What a good woman!"

I got back on Cathy and we had about ten minutes before the bridge opened on the timer. Everyone was sitting in the cockpit having a snack and they'd made one for me. They all looked at me kind of funny like "what kind of crazy man are you?" I filled them in on what was happening as I ate my snack. The bridge finally opened and we went through and out into the ocean. By now, it was around 8 o'clock and the storm had passed through. The wind wasn't blowing hard at all, the sun was out and shining brightly, there was blue sky and no clouds, it was a gorgeous South Florida day. We motored down to the whistle buoy at Government Cut in Miami, hung a left and had an uneventful crossing to Gun Cay. Everybody took a turn at the wheel and got a couple of hours sleep to boot.

When we navigated Gun Cay Cut and got on the Bahamian Bank, we could see the masts of our sailboat friends at 10 east of the light with the naked eye, we headed straight for them. When we got to the fishing hole and got anchored, we were so close that we could talk across the water to Audy. I told them about our nightmare off Dania Beach. We cooked steaks on the aft deck, ate our supper, and taped down. Jerry showed up around 3 o'clock and gave us all a good load, I think we got just under 5000 pounds each. Blue Eyes came north from Sylvia Beacon with extra pot, he'd loaded his boats heavy but had an extra 2000 pounds, so he gave each one of us another 500 pounds each, about 10 more bales each. We ended up with around 5400 pounds on each boat.

Once we'd cleaned up the boat after loading, we ate a snack, and caught a couple of hours of sleep, more a catnap really. As soon as the sun came up, we got on a direct course for Gun Cay lighthouse, went through the Cut, and got on our heading of 300 degrees for Ft. Lauderdale. It was a beautiful day and both boats put up the main and the jib and we had a friendly race to the Cut. Audy pulled ahead and won because she had a foot less beam than Cathy. Our airplane, Pegasus, flew over a couple of times, dipped his wings "Hello" and told us on the radio that everything was "clean and green." Rita met us off Dania Beach and escorted us into the Port. We brought the boats up the River, Cathy went to Linda's house and Audy went to my new house off Riverland Road. We unloaded the boats that night without incident and delivered the pot to Fu at the IHOP on State Road 84 the next morning. Everything worked like clockwork, we'd done it again without getting busted. It was another good trip and another good payday. The nightmare off Dania Beach made it a most memorable trip, a bad memory, but a memory nonetheless.

Chapter 22
Growin' Pains, Politics, and Bullshit
I'll tell you one thing, I'm damn tired of getting shorted.

As soon as I'd gotten some sleep, I got a bite to eat and started working on the figures for my boats. I'd hauled right at 5100 pounds on each boat after deducting sack weight. When I got the third boat, Jerry had agreed to pay me 18%, he said I'd earned it. I was only making 15% on Cathy 5 'cause I had to pay Jerry 3% to unload at Linda's house. But, I was making 18% on Audy 'cause I was unloading her at my house off Riverland Road. Jerry was getting 20% from Joe for what he hauled so he was making 5% from Cathy 5 and 2% from Audy plus his $250,000 middle boat fee. He was doing all right without having to take the chance of getting busted coming home or when we unloaded but he'd paid his dues so I guess he deserved it. After doing my calculations for the two boats, I was still netting out about $250,000. I was pleased with this but disappointed that Blue Mist didn't make the trip. I would have netted about $150,000 more from Blue Mist so my total net would have been a little over $400,000. That's what I'd been working and bustin' my ass for. Oh well, hopefully next trip!

I called Chris Fertig and he said that we'd closed on the house off Cordova Road while we were on the trip. Now I needed somebody to live in it so we could get a lease for them and for the sailboat. I told Chris that I'd start working on getting a tenant for the house. Moms had come to Ft. Lauderdale and she had moved into the house off Riverland Road. She had some I.D. in her maiden name so I gave that to Chris so he could prepare a lease for her. Also, even though she couldn't swim and was scared of the water, she wanted to go on trips and make some money so that gave me another lady for my crews.

I called my mechanic, Ron, and talked to him about Blue Mist. He had cleared all the fuel lines and bled the injectors to get her running. He said that there was a huge amount of black algae all through the fuel system and the engine. He had found someone that came to the dock and pumped out the fuel tank with a 55 gallon drum, a pump, and a filter, all for $50.00. I told him to go ahead and get all three boats pumped just to be safe. We had to solve the fuel problems on Blue Mist and the other two boats before the next trip. Ron met the guy at all three boats, had them pumped, and said the gunk that came out of the fuel tank in Blue Mist was unbelievable.

Pat and I had been brainstorming for days trying to figure out who we could get to live in my new house off Cordova Road. Pat's Mom, Juanita, lived in Atlanta with a man named Leonard and he had just gotten a job in Miami working as an Engineer building the new Rapid Transit System. Pat and I called Juanita "WaWa" and we called Len "Wen" and we talked about Wen and WaWa maybe living in the new house. Pat called WaWa one night and presented the proposition to them. We of course had told them that we were smuggling months ago when we had helped Howard and Edith get the laetrile for his cancer. It was a coincidence that just when I needed people to live in my new scam house, they would be moving to the area and needing a place to live, and Wen had a real job. Wen said he was flying to Miami in a few days to finalize his paperwork and that he would look at the house when he came down, but, they were agreeable to living in a scam house. When he flew down to Miami, we got together with him and showed him the house and he was thrilled and accepted our proposition on the spot, so that solved that problem. I put Audy behind the house on Cordova and kept Blue Mist behind the house off Riverland. Cathy 5 was still behind Linda's house.

In a couple of days, I talked to Jerry and he had green stamps and said to come on over. I drove over to his house on S.W. 5th Place, knocked on the door, opened it and went into his kitchen. Jerry was sitting at the kitchen table with Blue Eyes and they had the table covered with charts of the Bahamas.

I said: "Hey guys, what's going on?"

Jerry said: "You know Brad don'tcha?"

I said: "Yeah, we met last 4th of July out at Joulters and he's loaded me a couple of times. Howya doin' Blue Eyes?"

Brad said: "We're doing great. Jerry and I are just looking at some charts and planning a strategy for these trips that are coming up."

I said: "We gonna be busy, I hope."

Jerry said: "Yeah man, Joe says he's got 8 or 10 freighters coming. We're gonna be real busy!"

I said: "Allright! I want to make some money."

Jerry said: "Let's see what you've got from the last trip. Fu is paying us $220 per pound for this trip."

I gave Jerry my figures for the two boats; both of them hauled 5400 pounds each less sack weight was a net of 5100 pounds per boat. I got paid 18% for Audy 'cause she unloaded at my house off Riverland. I got paid 15% for Cathy 'cause she unloaded at Linda's house and I had to pay Jerry 3% for using Linda's house. My gross before salaries was a little over $372,000 and after salaries, my net was a little over $257,000.

Jerry said: "I gave Herb $2,500 for taking Pat out to get Blue Mist. Rita thought it might be too rough for her boat handling abilities so I called Herb."

I said: "Damn, that's a lot for towing a boat that wasn't even loaded. If it'd been loaded, that'd be a different story. $500 would have been plenty."

Jerry said: "Scooter, don't be a greedy motherfucker. You just made a quarter million bucks. You can afford $2,500 for the tow."

I was completely aghast at that statement! I didn't know what to say. I looked at Blue Eyes and he looked back at me with this look like "Say something, Scooter. Stick up for yourself." I thought: "what the fuck over, you just made a quarter million dollars. Let it go."

I said: "Okay Jerry, tell Herb that Pat and I say "thanks" for the tow. So, any word on the next trip?"

Jerry said: "It could be a couple of days, it could be a week, it could be ten days. When it comes, it'll be the first of many so rest up, you're gonna need it."

I said: "I'm ready, my boats are ready, and my people are ready." I shook hands with Jerry and Brad, Jerry got me a whiskey box for my money, and I left the house and drove to the convenience store on Davie Boulevard to use the payphone. I called all my people that were local and told them I had green stamps, everyone was excited.

I called Pat and when she answered, I said: "What's happening, anything I need to know?"

She said: "Yeah, Blue Eyes called, he's coming by the house around 3 o'clock, he wants to talk to you."

I said: "Fine, I'm going to distribute green stamps and I'll be home by 3 o'clock." I hung up with Pat and went to pay my people.

I got home around 2:30 and it wasn't long before Blue Eyes pulled up in my driveway. I greeted him at the door, we shook hands warmly, and I led him into my family room, the converted two-car garage at the front of the house. Pat brought us each a glass of Coca-Cola over ice and some chocolate chip cookies for a snack.

Brad said: "Scooter, do you know what's going on?"

I said: "I don't know man, I think so. What do you mean? You tell me what's going on."

He said: "Scooter, Jerry is fucking you bad. First of all, charging you anything for that tow is bullshit. Even if the boat were loaded, he shouldn't be charging you for a tow, that's just part of smuggling. If a boat is broken down, you get in another boat and go get it, you don't get charged for a tow, that's bullshit."

I said: "I could see $500 but $2,500 is a little high to me."

He said: "Scooter, it's not so much the money as it is the principle of the thing. He should be taking care of you, you're his scammer. He should be doing anything he can to see that you're successful. I can't believe he called you a greedy motherfucker. You know, if people like you, they say you're a good businessman. If they don't like you, they say you're a greedy motherfucker. Does that mean Jerry doesn't like you? If he don't like you, then he's a stupid motherfucker because you and your people are really good scammers. You make his life easy 'cause you're always where you're supposed to be. He never has to go looking for you. I can't tell you how many nights I've had to lay over with pot because I couldn't find my scammers because they were lost and didn't know where the fuck they were. As far as I know, Jerry's never had to lay over with pot 'cause you're always where you're supposed to be. Jerry's a stupid motherfucker and he's the greedy motherfucker, not you. He's jealous of you because you're making more money than he is, that's why he's screwing you. Hell, you're the one taking the risk of getting busted coming in the port with a load. You should make more money 'cause you're taking the risk of getting busted. You ought to talk to Joe and he'd put a stop to it. Jerry has screwed you out of a helluva lot of money."

I said: "Brad, I'm a millionaire because of Jerry Smith. We're only talking about $2,500 for the tow. That's no big deal in the big picture of things. Why do you say he's screwing me out of a helluva lot of money?"

He said: "Scooter, Joe's scammers get paid 20% of what they haul. You should be getting paid 20% but you're not, Jerry is screwing you by charging you 5% to load you. That ain't Kosher, man. Now, charging you 3% to use his houses to unload, that's okay, that's the going rate. But you should have been making 17% net from the gitgo. How many trips have you made?"

I said: "I don't know, maybe fifteen."

He said: "If you go back and figure up what you hauled for those fifteen trips and multiply by 3%, you'll see that Jerry fucked you out of a lot of money, probably more than a million bucks. If you've got a million bucks now, you should have two million. Joe would be pissed if he knew this, this ain't right."

I said: "I knew Jerry was getting 20% from Joe plus his middle boat fee but Jerry always made out like he was paying me the going rate. I thought that's the way it was. What do you think I should do about it? Should I talk to Joe? I don't know Joe's phone number."

He said: "Next time I talk to Joe, I'm gonna tell him what's going on, that Jerry's been screwing you. I guarantee you that Joe is gonna be pissed."

I said: "I don't want to piss Jerry off, then he'll really screw me."

He said: "Scooter, fuck Jerry. I would like for you and your people to be my scammers exclusively. You are the best I've ever seen and I've seen 'em all. I promise you that I'll load your boats with 20,000 pounds every trip. You'll make a ton of money working with me. When I talk to Joe, I want to tell him that we are working together and that you've left Jerry. Is that okay with you?"

I said: "Brad, I really appreciate the confidence you have in me and I appreciate what you've told me. Let me think about it and we'll see what happens. I'm not quite ready to leave Jerry yet. Let me work a couple of more trips and then let's talk about it again. I need to buy another boat so I can haul 20,000 pounds on four boats. I'll probably buy another house for the new boat too."

He said: "Do you know that Joe is very impressed with you?"

I said: "What the fuck have I done to impress Joe?"

He said: "Everything you've done has impressed Joe. Smuggling is constantly evolving and you're showing all the rest of us what the future of smuggling is going to be. You've got your own boats, your own houses, and good people as scammers and good people living in your houses. You're the future, man; you're blazing a trail for all the rest of us."

I said: "Wow, man, I had no idea. I'm just trying to make as much money as fast as I can and then retire and live happily ever after."

He said: "Yeah, ain't we all! You gotta understand what Joe's been doing up 'till now. First he's got all the middle boats like me who don't have any scammers. Then, he's got all these independent contractors who have their own boats. Some have houses and some don't. When a trip comes up, Joe's got to call the middle boats. Then he's got to call all the scammers and he's got to arrange for most of them to unload in rented houses. Then, he's got to coordinate with his pilot to go and find the freighters. Then, we go do the trip and come home. Then Joe's got to arrange for everyone to deliver the pot to Fu. Then Joe's got to get paid from Fu and then pay all of us. On top of all that, Joe's got to deal with the Colombians. Joe's got way too much to do. What he wants, and what we want too, is for Joe to deal with the Colombians and coordinate the trips. All the rest of it, he wants to delegate to us. What you're doing is what Joe wants all the middle boats to do. He wants us to have our own boats, our own houses, our own vans, and our own organization. You're showing us all how to do that. That's why Joe is so impressed with you and that's why Jerry is a stupid motherfucker. Because he's an ex-cop, he doesn't have any friends except cops and ex-cops and that's why he doesn't have any scammers except you. You're worth your weight in gold to Jerry and he should be taking real good care of you. Instead, he's fucking you out of money at every opportunity. He's stupid and he's greedy, not you."

I said: "Man, I had no idea. I've tried to stay out of the politics of smuggling, I hate politics. All I want to do is work and make money and hide my money in the islands."

He said: "Yeah, don't we all. But sometimes, the politics pulls you into it and you've got to deal with it to survive. You know there's a lot of people that don't like Jerry?"

I said: "No man, Jerry's basically a nice guy. Why don't people like him?"

He said: "You know the Tin Man, right?"

I said: "Never met him but I know who he is."

He said: "Well, the Tin Man is convinced that he's an undercover cop working inside Joe's organization to bring us all down. He is constantly telling Joe not to trust Jerry, that he's the heat. Jerry pissed him off once and the Tin Man hasn't trusted him since."

I said: "What happened, do you know?"

He said: "Yeah, Jerry loaded his sailboat once and when he came to settle with Jerry and get paid, Jerry tried to fuck him like he's been fucking you. The Tin Man stuck his finger in Jerry's face and told him if he didn't get every dime coming to him, that he was gonna kill him. Jerry paid him what he was supposed to pay him. The Tin Man has hated Jerry ever since and told Joe he didn't want Jerry loading his boats any more, he didn't want to work with Jerry in any way, shape, or form. He's convinced Jerry is an undercover cop."

I said: "Wow man, now that's bad blood!"

He said: "Yeah, no shit! So, what's happening is that I've got to buy my own scam boats and my own houses and get set up like you. But that's gonna take some time. Until then, I want to load you exclusively on all of Joe's trips. Then, as soon as I'm all setup, you can get a 53 foot Hatteras, run your own organization from top to bottom, and you and I will do trips together like me and Jerry are doing now. Plus, you'll work a whole lot more trips with me and make a whole lot more money than if you work for Joe exclusively."

I said: "So, are you tellin' me that you work for people other than Joe?"

He said: "I work for everybody, Scooter, everybody."

I said: "Oh yeah, like who?"

He said: "That's on a need to know basis and you don't need to know right now. We'll have this conversation again in the very near future."

I said: "Why does Joe let you work for other people than him?"

He said: "He can't stop me from working and making money with anyone I choose. Anyway, Joe needs me and he's gonna need you real damn soon. The Colombians are putting pressure on Joe to do bigger trips. They've got pot sitting in warehouses on the docks in Colombia, the humidity is making the pot wet, and the pot is rotting. It doesn't do them any good if it rots so they want to get it up here to Joe. Joe's gonna need all the people he can get when these big trips start coming so he needs me and he needs you. Until then, I wanta work with you and load your scam boats."

I said: "Brad, you're throwing a lot of shit at me this afternoon and I don't think I'm ready for it. I guess I'd better get ready, but I ain't quite ready right now. Let me work another trip or two with Jerry and let's see how things go and then let's talk again. Is that okay with you?"

He said: "Yeah sure, Scooter, if that's what you want. But you're gonna be making 18% with Jerry and you should be making 20%. He'll be fucking you out of 2%. I'm gonna talk to Joe for you and get you 20%. If it pisses Jerry off, then split up with him and work with me. I'll load you with 20,000 pounds every trip and pay you 20%. That's $880,000 gross and you'll probably net out $600,000 every trip after expenses. What's wrong with that?"

I said: "Not a damn thing, that's what I've been bustin' my ass for and trying to get to that point! So, how come you don't have a problem working trips with Jerry."

He said: "I don't have a problem dealing with Jerry as a middle boat captain. He knows more about boats, engines, and electronics than anyone I know. If I have a problem when we're on the Bank, Jerry'll be there to help, he's good about that. And I don't think Jerry's the heat."

I said: "Jerry ain't the heat, I'd know."

He said: "So, we ain't got nothing to worry about then, do we?"

I said: "No, just the heat in the port when we're coming home."

He said: "Yeah man, that's the most dangerous part and that's why the scammers should make the most money, they take the biggest risk."

I said: "Well my friend, it has been a very enlightening afternoon. You've given me a lot to think about."

He said: "Okay man, we'll talk again real soon. Don't worry about pissing Jerry off, FUCK JERRY. You can come to work for me and make a whole lot more money with less hassle."

We shook hands warmly and Brad left my house to go see Joe and talk to him about me. I was apprehensive but I was also excited. Pat came in the den and gave me a funny smile.

I said: "Did you hear any of that?"

She said: "Enough. I knew Jerry was screwing us but I didn't know it was that bad. What are you gonna do now?"

I said: "We're just gonna go work the next trip and see what happens. Maybe Joe'll make Jerry pay me 20%, that'll be an improvement. After the next trip, we'll see what happens and if Jerry screws me again, I'll talk to Brad and we'll make the break with Jerry. It's gonna happen sooner or later 'cause Jerry ain't gonna change. Brad's right, Jerry's stupid, he doesn't appreciate me and my people. I knew he'd been screwing me but it took Brad to slap me in the face with it to make me realize it. Me and Jerry are done, it's just a matter of time."

Pat came over to me, put her arms around me, and gave me a big wet kiss. She said: "Hey, you wanta fool around?"

I said: "Woman, does a hee haw haw have a hangdown?"

We went in the bedroom and made long, slow, wild passionate love. It was amazing!

Chapter 23
Calmin' the Wind and the Sea
"And they (the Disciples) were afraid. And Jesus awoke and rebuked the wind and the raging waves, and they ceased, and there was calm."   Luke 8, 24-25

In a few days, Jerry called and it was time to go fishing again, the first of many that were coming. I went to my bank of payphones and called all my people. I was excited because I was gonna have three boats now. Rob was running Cathy 5 with Tommy Dolan and Janice, Ross was running Audy with Jay and Jen, and I was running Blue Mist with Mick, Dan, Rose, and Moms. We all crossed at night and it was good weather, Blue Mist ran like a top. Moms drank a few beers and crashed in the aft stateroom and slept all the way over to Gun Cay. As soon as we got to Gun and went through the Cut, we anchored about halfway down the island in close. Moms woke up and she was feeling pretty good about her first trip so far. She and Rose cooked breakfast for everyone and we ate in the cockpit under the Bimini Top. Then everyone sacked out and got some sleep until the noonday sun woke us up in a sweat. While we slept, my other two boats made it to Gun to my relief! We pulled the hook and went sailing on the Bank, listened to rock-n-roll on the tape deck, drank beer, smoked pot, and had a great afternoon of friendly racing with the other two boats. We ended up back at Gun Cay in time to cook steaks on the aft deck and watch a killer sunset, no green flash this time though. As soon as the sun had set, we cleaned up the cockpit, Rose and Moms tidied up the galley, and we began to tape down in preparation for loading.

As soon as we'd finished taping down, Mick and Dan pulled the hook and we got on a course of due East headed to the fishing hole. We motored for two hours at five knots to the fishing hole at 10 East of the Light. When we arrived, there were already two other boats there so that meant Jerry had five boats to load. About 2:00 A.M., Jerry called us on the radio and it wasn't long before the big Hatteras came out of the dark and pulled up to us to load. Jerry loaded the other two boats first and then he came and loaded my three boats. He loaded the other two boats with 5000 pounds each and then split 10,000 pounds between my three boats so each boat got about 3300 pounds each. Unless Blue Eyes had some pot leftover, I was gonna get shorted. As it turned out, all of Blue Eyes' scam boats showed up and he didn't have any pot leftover to load my boats. I was pretty upset and Jerry knew it!

After we finished loading, we cleaned up the cockpit, packed away the drop cloths, and ate a snack in the cockpit and tried to cool off. Everyone took showers and put on clean clothes as we motored back to Gun. We navigated the Cut as the sun was rising and got on a course of 300 degrees for Ft. Lauderdale. Some weather had moved in on us and it was rough in the Gulfstream, about 7-8 foot seas. We all took Bonine pills in hopes that nobody'd get seasick, especially me! Moms had on a life jacket sitting in the cockpit and she was scared to death. I'm behind the wheel and we're just off Bimini about 2 miles and we can see the lights of the houses off to our right. I'm thinking to myself *"Oh Lord, please let this boat run. Don't let it shut down in this rough weather, please God please!"* About 5 miles off to my left, there is a big powerboat coming right at us throwing up a big wave off his bow. I hope that sucker ain't a Coast Guard Cutter. The asspucker factor just increased by a power of ten and the damn thing is coming right at me. I thought *"What do you do now Scooter? Do you turn around and try to make a run for the shallow water at the south end of Bimini or do you keep going and hope for the best? Will the Coast Guard try to board us if it's this rough?"* My mind was racing a mile-a-minute and my adrenaline was pumping as I tried to figure out the best course of action. I finally decided to stay on my course of 300 degrees and see what happens because the motorboat is headed right at the south end of Bimini now, not directly at us. It isn't long before the boat passes off my stern about a mile or so and I can see that it is a big Burger motoryacht, about 70-80 feet, headed for the harbor at Bimini. Man, we all breathed a big sigh of relief! I decided to make a joke out of it and maybe it would cheer up my crew.

I said, "Y'all see, everything's allright, it's okay, it ain't the Coast Guard, we're okay."

Moms said: "Scooter, I'm scared to death. I sure wish it would calm down a little bit. I'd feel much better if it wasn't so rough."

I said: "Moms, you've gotta have faith. This boat is a good boat and it's not gonna sink. We've been working on it hard and heavy and it's running good. It hasn't quit on us yet so you've just gotta have faith."

She said: "Well, I've got faith in you and I've got faith in the boat but I just don't have faith in the sea."

I said: "You don't have to have faith in the sea, you've got to have faith in the Lord. You know the Bible says that Jesus can calm the wind and the sea. Why don't you ask God to calm the wind and the sea for you?"

She said: "Oh, I can't do that, he won't listen to me. I don't ever talk to God and I don't ever pray so if I were to ask him to do something for me now, he wouldn't listen to me. Why don't you ask him to calm the water down for you?"

I said: "Okay, I'll ask him." I thought to myself *"Okay Scooter, show a little leadership and make your crew feel a little better."* "Mick, take the wheel for me."

Mick took the helm and I climbed out of the cockpit onto the top of the Salon and grabbed the mast with both hands and hugged it to my chest. The boat was going up and down and it was rough! I thought to myself *"Okay Lord, I am just trying to make my people feel better. I do not mean to blaspheme you so please cut me some slack here."* My crew are all in the cockpit and they are looking at me with a real funny look on their faces.

In a real, loud voice, I said: "Lord, this is your humble servant Scooter here. The Bible says that you can calm the wind and the seas and I believe that you can calm the wind and the seas if you want to. If you could just find it in your heart to make the seas calm down a little bit and make the wind stop blowing so hard, we would be forever grateful. Thank you Jesus, thank you Lord."

I climbed down off the roof of the Salon, got back in the cockpit, and took the wheel back from Mick. My four-member crew looked at me like I was some kind of crazy man and nobody said anything for about five minutes. After about ten minutes, the waves had gone down to about 4-5 feet and the wind wasn't blowing near as hard as it was. In about fifteen minutes, the storm had passed completely through us, the waves were about 2-3 feet, and the wind was barely blowing at all.

Moms looked at me and said: "I don't know what kind of person you are but I'll never doubt you again." She thought that God had given us a miracle at my request but it was really just a local storm that blew through.

I said to Mick and Dan: "Why don't you guys put up the mainsail and we'll sail home. We might as well look good since the wind has calmed down. We'll have a good sail and we might pick up some speed and get home faster."

We all took the canvas cover off the mainsail and Mick and Dan climbed on the roof of the Main Salon and hauled up the main. The prevailing wind was now out of the Southwest so we let out the mainsail and trimmed it properly in hopes that we could get some more speed. By now, we've lost sight of Bimini, we're out in the middle of the Gulfstream, and the damn engine shuts down! I think to myself *"Son of a bitch! Now I'm gonna have to get down in the Salon and bleed those injectors and I'll get seasick and throw-up. I know it's that damned black algae, it hasn't sucked air, it's that black algae."*

I said: "Dan, you take the wheel. Mick, you come with me. Let's see if we can get this son of a bitch started without bleeding the injectors." Mick and I go down the stairs into the Salon and take the cover off the engine. I grab a can of Freon and take the breather off the engine.

I said: "Okay Dan, get ready to turn her over." I start shooting Freon into the breather intake and tell Dan: "Okay, turn her over."

That damn diesel engine is turning over and it's coughing and in about five seconds, the engine starts up and runs! Mick and I look at each other and we're thinking the same thing, I'm sure: *"Oh Lord, please let this thing keep running!"* I put the breather back on the engine, we put the cover back over the engine, and we go back up into the cockpit. The engine's running good for now and we go along another hour or so and the engine shuts down again!

I said: "Okay, Mick, let's do it again." We go through the routine again. I spray Freon into the breather intake, Dan turns the engine over, and the damn thing fires up and runs. Hallelujah!!

We sail on for another hour or so and we sight land. It's about 2:00 P.M. and we're about three hours out of the Port now. We go along for another thirty minutes and the engine shuts down again! SHIT!

I said: "Okay, Mick, let's do it again." I have no doubt that the damn thing is gonna start. I start spraying Freon in the breather intake, Dan turns it over, and the engine goes clickety, clickety, clickety, click, kicks over, runs for about ten seconds, and quits. I think to myself *"Oh Lord, I can't ask you for another favor today. Please just let this thing run."* I spray Freon in the breather intake again, Dan turns it over, and the engine goes clickety, clickety, clickety, click and fires off again and runs. This time it keeps running! I think *"Thank you Jesus, thank you Lord!"*

I decide that it's time to call Rita in the channel boat, check in with her, and let her know I'm having problems.

I grabbed the CB microphone and said: "Little Lady, Little Lady, Little Big Man, you got your ears on good buddy, kickit back."

Rita said: "Little Big Man, this is the Little Lady. What's your 20, good buddy?"

I said: "I'm about two hours out of the intersection. What's your 20?"

She said: "I'm right here at the intersection, right at the stoplight doing some fishing. You've got a big 10-10 good buddy, it's clean and green, bring it on home, comeback."

I said: "Roger that. Listen, I'm having mechanical problems and I may need you to tow me. I've shut down three or four times but I'm running okay for now. Don't you leave me out here alone, you hear?"

She said: "Roger that, good buddy, I won't leave you."

I said: "Good, I'll call you when I get closer to the intersection or if I shut down again. Little Big Man standing by."

She said: "Little Lady standing by."

We went on for about an hour and the Gulfstream had blown us north of the Port. We were off Oakland Park Boulevard about two miles off the beach and the damn engine shuts down again! Son of a bitch!

I said: "Mick and Dan, go downstairs and get that damn thing started, I'll take the wheel."

I grabbed the CB microphone and called Rita: "Little Lady, Little Big Man, you got a copy, comeback."

She said: "Roger that, Little Big Man, I copy."

I said: "I'm having problems, my engine has shut down again. Why don't you get on the highway and drive north and you'll see me 'cause I'm the only truck on the interstate."

She said: "I don't know if I want to do that, good buddy. It's pretty rough looking out there. Those hills look mighty big from here."

I said: "Roger that Little Lady, how'd you like to be broke down like I am? Listen honey, I'm not asking you, I'm telling you, you get on the highway and start coming north 'cause I need a tow."

She said: "Roger that, Little Big Man, I'm heading north, over."

I said: "Have you got an eyeball on me from where you are?"

She said: "Negative, I don't see anybody out there, comeback."

I said: "Well, I'm the only truck on the highway so if you'll look north about two miles off the beach, that's me."

She said: "Is that you way up north by the Pier?"

I said: "Roger that, we're south of the Pier around Oakland Park Boulevard."

She said: "Okay, I'm coming to get'cha."

I aimed the bow of the boat directly in toward the beach and tried to hold it there but with every wave that came through, it pushed the bow right or left and I had to fight to keep it aimed at the beach. The waves were building and getting bigger as we got closer to shore, they were about 7-8 feet now, it was rough!

I said: "Moms, howya doin', you scared?"

She said: "No, not as long as I can see land and I've got a life preserver, I can jump in and swim ashore if I have to."

I said: "Don't worry, the boat's not gonna sink and we're not busted so there's no need to worry."

Mick and Dan started shooting freon in the breather intake and I turned the motor over but the sucker wouldn't start, we were just draining the battery. That damn black algae had the injectors clogged up I was sure.

I grabbed the CB microphone: "Little Lady, what's your 20 now?"

She said: "I'm coming up on Las Olas Boulevard, comeback."

I said: "Look, we can't get the engine started, I'm broke down and drifting. I'm scared these waves are gonna knock us down and turn us over. I've got no control whatsoever. You put the peddle to the metal and get up here as quick as you can and give us a tow. I need you here right now."

She said: "Roger that, Little Big Man, I'm putting the pedal to the metal, I'll be there as soon as I can."

Mick took a fuel line off and tried to clear it, the fuel ran out on top of the fuel tank and there were big black globs of black algae, that was definitely the problem. Where was all that shit coming from? We'd pumped the tank twice, it ought to be clean you'd think. We kept trying to get the motor started but it would turn over but not fire off and run. In about ten minutes, here comes Lovely Rita in her 21 foot Boston Whaler Revenge with a lady friend named Wendy. Boy was I glad to see them! Rita brought her boat up to about ten yards off my port bow.

I grabbed the CB microphone and said: "Tell Wendy to get on the back of the boat and I'm gonna get on the bow pulpit with my longest line. I'm gonna throw it right over Wendy's shoulder so tell her to grab it when it hits her and tie it off to a cleat on the rear of your boat. Then, you can tow us to the dock if we can't get this damn thing started."

I went back up to the bow pulpit and coiled a line over my right shoulder into a big circle. Rita was laying off to our port but the sailboat would surf up high on a wave and then crash into the valley when the wave passed through. I could tell that Mick was having a helluva time keeping the bow pointed in toward the beach. Next time we surfed up high and then went down into the trough and stopped our forward motion, I threw the line to Wendy but it fell short into the water because Rita was too far away. I motioned to Rita to come closer and she brought the Whaler to about ten feet. After rolling up the line again, I threw it underhanded right across Wendy's shoulder, it hit her in her shoulder, she tried to grab it but missed, and the line fell in the water again. I quickly pulled the line out of the water again and motioned to Rita to come closer still. The waves were making it very difficult for Rita to control her boat but she was doing the best she could under the circumstances. I went back into the cockpit and grabbed the CB microphone.

I said: "Rita, I want you to pull up alongside the middle of my boat and I'm gonna jump onto your boat with the line, comeback."

She said: "It's too rough Scooter, we can't do it."

I said: "Rita, just get about three feet away from my port side and when we get in a trough, the boats will almost stop, that's when I'll jump in your boat."

She said: "Okay, Scooter, I'll try my best."

Mick said: "Scooter, you be careful, you can get killed doing this."

I said: "Roger that, good buddy."

I went up to the middle of the boat, climbed over the railing, and held onto the rigging with my right hand and had the line in my left hand. Rita brought the Whaler alongside and I got ready to jump. The next big wave came through, we surfed up high and then went down into the trough and our forward motion almost stopped completely. I jumped as hard as I could and landed spread eagle in the back of the Whaler, WHAM! I scrambled up and tied the line to a cleat on the stern of the boat. Rita and Wendy looked at me like I was a crazy man, maybe I was but that's what it took to get it done.

I said: "Rita, no hard feelings but I want to drive okay?"

She said: "No problem" and she gave me the helm.

I said: "Rita, you did real good, I'm real proud of you, you did a helluva job."

I towed Blue Mist in toward the beach until we were about 200 yards offshore and then I headed due south to the mouth of the Port. I towed her in the Cut and into the Port, 17th Street Bridge opened and we went through the bridge, up the river through the middle of town, all the way to the house off Riverland Road. When we got to our canal, I slowed the Whaler down to a dead idle and let the sailboat slow to a crawl. I ever so slowly pulled up to the dock and Mick and Dan jumped on the dock with lines and stopped all forward motion. They tied Blue Mist up with a bow, stern, and spring line as I pulled the Whaler alongside Blue Mist. I put the Whaler in neutral, grabbed the side of the sailboat, and jumped up on the deck. Rita got behind the helm of her boat and gave me a thumbs up.

I said: "Rita, you did damn good woman, damn good. Thanks a helluva lot, now you'd better get outta here."

She gave her boat some throttle, pulled out into the middle of the canal, cruised into the river, hung a left, and disappeared. I thought to myself: *"This fucking boat is gonna klll my ass before I can get it straightened out."* We got our seabags out of the Salon, locked the hatch and the doors, and went home and got some sleep so we could unload two boats in one night.

That night, I had one crew unloading Cathy 5 at Linda's house and another crew unloading Blue Mist at Moms' house. The next night, we unloaded Audy at Wen and WaWa's house off Cordova Road. We delivered the vans to Fu at the IHOP and everything went smoothly. I called my mechanic, Ron, and told him about the black algae in Blue Mist. He promised to call the guy again and have him come pump out the fuel tank again. Ron thought that the black algae was growing on the inside of the fuel tank and when it was rough, globs of algae would break off and clog up the fuel lines and the injectors. All we could do was pump it again unless we wanted to replace the fuel tank with a new one.

In a couple of days, Jerry called and he had green stamps. I had all my figures together and I ended up hauling about 9400 pounds net of sack weight. I drove over to his house, knocked on the door, walked into his kitchen, and he was sitting alone at the kitchen table.

I said: "Hey man, howya doin'?"

He said: "I'm fine as wine, man. Let's see what you got?"

I said: "I hauled 9400 pounds net sack weight. I'm really disappointed that I got shorted. I've been bustin' my ass to get three boats and when I finally get all three to the fishin' hole, I get shorted."

He said: "You know, I really didn't expect Blue Mist to run. I didn't think you'd have it ready for this trip."

I said: "Man, I told you that we were leaving a day early and crossing at night so that if we had any problems, we could sail the boat to the fishin' hole and still get loaded."

He said: "I really didn't think you were gonna get that boat to run this quick. I didn't think you'd have it ready."

I said: "Well look, it's gonna be ready next time. I've had my mechanic all over it, we're pumping the fuel tank again, we're working on it all this time and it'll be ready, so count on it."

He said: "Okay, no problem, I'll count on your three boats."

I said: "I don't want to get shorted no more, okay?"

He said: "I can't promise you anything but I'll do the best I can."

I said: "Okay, I guess that's all I can ask."

He said: "Allright, Fu is paying $220 per pound for this trip. You get 18% of that so that's $372,240. Now I gave Rita $10,000 for towing you, she said it was rough as a bitch." I guess Brad hadn't talked to Joe yet about getting me 20%.

I said: "Jesus Christ, Jerry, $10,000 is too fucking much! $2,500 would have been plenty."

He said: "Well, when Herb towed Blue Mist, it wasn't loaded."

I said: "Look, Rita did a helluva good job but $10,000 is overpaying her."

He said: "Don't be a greedy motherfucker, Scooter. You're making a ton of money so spread it around. You wanta tell Rita she's overpaid?"

I said: "What do you pay her to run the channel boat?"

He said: "Ten grand."

I said: "So, she made $20,000 this trip?" I was incredulous.

He said: "Yeah, that's right."

I said: "So that means she made more than my male crew members and they hauled the load, they brought it in the Port, and they took the chance of getting busted. That ain't right man."

He said: "Don't be an ass, Scooter."

I didn't know what to say, I just looked at him. There was a long, pregnant pause. Finally I said: "Okay Smith, give me a box for my money and let me get out of here. Next time we work, I don't want to get shorted. I want you to load all three of my boats with a full load."

He said: "I'll do my best, Scooter." I was not convinced.

He went into a bedroom and came back with a whiskey box. We put my money in the box, closed the top, shook hands not warmly, and I left. He knew that I knew that he was screwing me and he knew I didn't like it. He didn't like me calling him on it either. Working with my people felt like family. Working with Jerry didn't feel like family anymore.

Chapter 24
Workin' the Middle-The Big One
"Westbound and down, loaded up and trucking, we're gonna do what they say can't be done" – Smokey and the Bandit

I left Jerry's house and headed north back to my house but first I stopped at my bank of payphones on Commercial Boulevard and 18th Avenue. I called all my people that were local and told them that I had green stamps, everyone was excited. I drove home, got my box of money out of the car, and went into our bedroom in the back of the house. Pat was holding Sunshine and she followed me into the bedroom.

She said: "How'd it go with Jerry?"

I said: "It went, that's all I can say, it went. He charged me ten grand for the tow and I told him that was too much. He said I was a greedy motherfucker. Rita made twenty grand for the trip and she didn't even haul a load. I told him that wasn't right. He didn't pay me 20%, he paid me 18%. He forgot to charge me 3% for renting Linda's house and I didn't say anything. There were bad vibes when I left, I wasn't happy and he wasn't happy."

She said: "How much did we make this time?"

I said: "A little over $209,000. Jerry screwed us out of $150,000 net by shorting me 5000 pounds. That ain't no small change. Brad is right, Jerry doesn't appreciate me. I just don't get it, I've been good and I've been loyal and he just doesn't care."

She said: "What're you gonna do?"

I said: "I'm gonna go pay my people."

She said: "No, what're you gonna do about Jerry?"

I said: "We're gonna work the next trip and see what happens. If he loads all three of my boats with good loads, we should net out about $350,000. If he shorts me again, maybe it's time to split with Jerry and work with Brad. I just wish Jerry would do right."

I put my people's money in a brown paper bag and my box of money in our walk-in closet. I kissed Pat and Sunshine and went to pay my people and put a smile on their faces. That would put a smile on my face too! At least my people appreciated me and they knew that I appreciated them, and that was a good feeling.

The next couple of days, it was life in the fast lane. I went to see Chris to make sure all the legal things were completed and in order. Wen and WaWa had moved into the house off Cordova Road and we had gotten a lease for them and a lease for the fictitious owner of Audy. I was going to visit both my houses everyday to see my people and to check on my boats. Ron had gotten the guy to come and pump out the fuel tank on Blue Mist for the third time. He said that there was still a lot of gunk that came out and he thought that his theory about the algae growing on the insides of the fuel tank was valid. The guy said that the only way to know that the fuel tank was completely clean was to replace the fuel tank. Audy and Cathy 5 were running like a top so that wasn't a problem but we still didn't have much faith in Blue Mist, and that was a bad feeling. Also, Tommy Dolan hadn't shown up at the boats to work and when I called him, he told me that he wasn't working for me anymore, that he had his own boat now and Jerry was gonna load him. Well, I was flabbergasted at first but really not surprised, I should have seen it coming, in fact, I did see it coming from the gitgo. That <u>had</u> to mean that I was gonna get shorted again unless Blue Eyes would load one of my boats with a full load. That told me that Jerry had six scam boats now. I drove over to Jerry's house to talk to him about it.

I said: "What's going on, tell me what's happening, man. I don't understand, I think you owe me an explanation."

He said: "Why? What are you talking about?"

I said: "I called Tommy Dolan to tell him to go work on the boats and he tells me that he's got his own boat now, that he's working for you and not me, and that you're gonna load him. It would've been nice if I'd heard that from you and not him."

He said: "Oh well, I'm sorry, it just worked out that way."

I said: "Okay, what's the story, you owe me an explanation."

He said: "Tommy did three trips with you and he came to me and said that he wanted to run his own boat. I went to eat supper the other night over at Jim's house and Tommy was there. He said that he thought that he could do it on his own, that he'd learned everything from you and that he wanted to run his own boat. He asked me if I'd buy him a boat and let him run it. He and Jim kinda put me on the spot and I said I'd do it so I went out and bought him a trawler and that's how it happened."

I said: "I can understand that I guess. But we had an agreement Smith that you wouldn't do this and now you've done it and broken our agreement. It makes me feel bad because I've been loyal to you and I've busted my ass for you and tried not to let you down and here this guy comes along and works three trips with me and then you buy him a $100,000 trawler. I've been paying my way all along and now you're gonna load him and short me? That ain't right."

He said: "No, no, no, I'm not gonna short you."

I said: "How you figure that, who you gonna short? You gonna short the other guys, what about the other two scammers you been loading?"

He said: "No, listen, you know Blue Eyes? Me and Blue Eyes are gonna be working together. I like him and I like the way he works and he likes me. We've talked to Joe and whenever we do 40,000 pound loads, me and Blue Eyes are gonna be the middle boats and we're gonna use six scam boats. He'll load three boats and I'll load three."

I said: "Well okay, whose gonna load me, you or Blue Eyes?"

He said: "We haven't decided that yet. Does it matter to you who loads you as long as you get a full load? What difference does it make?"

I said: "Bottom line, it don't matter who loads me as long as I get a full load. But, I thought we had an understanding that I was gonna be your scammers exclusively. What happened to <u>that</u> understanding?"

He said: "You know, Blue Eyes is great. He's been in the business longer than me. I think you'll really like working with him. I like working with him."

I said: "Well, I've liked working with him and his people when they've loaded me before. I just wanta work, get full loads, and make money."

He said: "Well, you're gonna do that."

I said: "Fine, that's what I want. Listen, I've got three boats now and I've got three full crews trained with good captains on all three boats. I'd like to work the middle boat a couple of times and see what that's like. Can I do that?"

He said: "Yeah sure, next time we work a trip, you can work the middle boat on my boat. I'll pay you $20,000, that's what I pay my people. I think we've got two or three more and the next one should be here within a week. Then, we'll quit for the summer and that should be around the middle of July. You should make some good money before we quit for the summer."

I said: "I hope so, that's what I've been busting my ass for."

We shook hands, warmly this time, and I left his house and headed for my house on 18th Terrace. On the way home, I stopped by my houses and checked on all my people and told them to be ready, we would be working soon. I told them that I was gonna be working the middle boat with Jerry and that they'd be on their own crossing the Gulfstream and getting to the fishin' hole. They all said that they thought that they could handle it. I was pleased and so were they!

In three days, Jerry calls and it's time to go fishing. I called everyone and put my three crews together. I let Jay captain Cathy 5, Ross captain Audy, and I let Rob captain Blue Mist with Mick and Dan and Moms as crew. Jay left that night and Ross and Rob left the next morning. Pat drove me to Jerry's house and I rode with him to the dock where he kept his Hatteras. When we got there, the rest of his crew were all there and ready to go. The motors were warming up, the generator was running, and the air conditioning was blowing cold. This was gonna be fun. It wasn't long before Jerry backed us out of the slip at the dock, steered into the river and down to 17th Street Bridge. We let out the Outriggers and went under the bridge while it was closed, that was cool! We cruised out the Port at a dead idle and got on a course of 140 degrees for Bimini. I was on the flybridge with Jerry 'cause I didn't want to miss a thing. He pushed the throttles forward and we quickly got up to maximum cruising speed of 20 knots. We're boogeying along pretty well especially compared to the sailboats.

Out in front of us a couple of miles is a sailboat and I grab the binoculars to take a look, the sailboat is on a heading towards Bimini, the same as us. I can see that the mainsail is up but not the jib, the seas are kinda rough about 4-5 foot rollers, and the sailboat doesn't appear to be making too much headway. In a few minutes, we're off the starboard side of the sailboat and damn if it ain't Blue Mist! I grab the CB microphone and give them a call.

I said: "Homeboy, Homeboy, Little Big Man, you got your ears on good buddy, kickit back."

Rob answered: "Little Big Man, Homeboy, we copy, kickit back."

I said: "Howya doin', is everything allright?"

He said: "That's a negative, we've had the engine shut down twice on us already. We've got it started both times but I don't know if it's gonna run."

I said: "What do you think it is? Is it that black algae?"

He said: "Yeah man, that's it! It's all in the fuel lines. We pulled them off the fittings and let the fuel run out on the top of the fuel tank and there were big black globs of the stuff that came out. That's got to be it."

I said: "I can't believe that the guy's pumped the tank twice and he didn't get it all."

He said: "Man, it just shut down again!"

I said: "Take the Freon and shoot it in the breather and get it going."

He said: "Roger that, give us a sec."

About two minutes went by and then he came back: "It won't start, it turns over but won't kick off and run."

I said: "You're gonna have to bleed the injectors, can you do that?"

He said: "We've seen you do it but we don't think we know how to do it exactly."

I said: "Roger that, stand by."

Jerry's driving the boat standing right next to me and he's hearing the whole conversation. I said: "Do you think you could take me over there and put me onto my boat so I can bleed the injectors. It could've sucked air or it could be black algae. I'm sure that I can get it going."

He said: "Man, it's too rough. I can't pull up close enough so that you can jump from one boat to the other."

I said: "Okay, just pull over close and I'll jump in the water and swim over, they'll pull me out of the water."

He said: "You're a greedy motherfucker, ain't you."

I said: "No man, I'm not greedy, I don't think I'm greedy. I've just been bustin' my ass to get three boats and make money. If it's a minor problem then I want them to get it going so they'll get loaded because I want them to have a big payday too."

He said: "Okay, I'm just kidding." I was not convinced he was kidding. I think he was half-kidding and whole serious. "I tell you what we can do, I can get over there close enough to throw them a line and maybe you could hand walk the line over to them. Have you ever done that before?"

I said: "Yeah, I've done that at West Point before on maneuvers."

He said: "If you want to try it, I'll go over there for you."

I said: "Sure, let's do it!"

He said: "Okay, put on a life preserver." I got a life preserver out of one of the lockers on the aft deck and put it on, Jerry changes course, slows down to an idle, and heads for the port side of Blue Mist.

Jerry's new girl friend Joan is inside the main salon watching a video, feels the course change, and comes out on the aft deck.

She said: "What's going on?"

I said: "I'm gonna throw them a line and then I'm gonna handwalk over to them and see if I can get the engine started, it shut down on them."

She said: "Oh shit, you're kidding?"

I said: "No, I'm not kidding."

Jerry hollers down from the flybridge: "Tell Gary to come out and give us a hand."

Joan opens the door to the main salon, speaks to Gary, and he comes out on the aft deck with us. I fill him in on what we're doing. By now, we're close enough to Blue Mist that I can holler to them.

I said: "Rob, get on the bow and I'll throw you a line, tie it off to a cleat real good and make sure it won't come loose."

I throw the line to Rob, he catches it, puts it under the railing, and ties it off to the cleat. Gary is looking at me like I'm a crazy man. I climbed up on the transom, grabbed the line with both hands, dropped in the water with my feet and my legs, and then pulled my feet up over the line. I hung like a monkey with my feet and my hands and then handwalked backwards over to Blue Mist. As soon as I got to the sailboat, I let my feet fall off the line and I was hanging with my hands. Rob and Mick were on the deck of the sailboat. I let go with my right hand and locked wrists with Rob then I let go with my left hand and locked wrists with Mick. They pulled me up onto the deck of the sailboat and I was only wet from the waist down. The three of us went into the main salon of the sailboat and I got an adjustable wrench and bled the injectors while Rob and Mick watched. I made each one of them crack and bleed an injector so they'd know how to do it. I got the can of Freon, shot it in the breather as Dan turned over the engine. The damn thing started right up! I talked to my crew for a couple of minutes and the engine kept running! Success (maybe!)

I said: "Now look, if this thing shuts down again and you can't get it going, sail the boat to Gun Cay. When you get in sight of Gun, call one of the other boats and tell them your status and your location. We can come and load you in the Gulfstream if we have to so just get as close as you can, hopefully you can get to Gun or at least get close. Don't let me down guys."

Rob said: "We'll try our best, Scooter."

I went up to the bow of the boat, climbed over the hand railing, grabbed the line and hung, put my feet over the line, and handwalked back to the Hatteras. I let my feet loose and Gary grabbed me under the shoulders and pulled me over the transom and onto the aft deck. Rob untied the line from the cleat on the sailboat and Gary pulled the line in, rolled it on his shoulder, and stowed it in a locker. By now, I'm soaking wet and I take off the life preserver, Joan hands me a towel, and I dry off as best I can.

She said: "You know, that was a pretty incredible thing you just did. You put on one helluva show. I've never seen anybody do anything like that in all of my life."

I said: "Thanks, Joan, I appreciate that. I just want my people to have a big payday."

I went inside the main salon and got my sea bag, pulled out some dry clothes and put them on. The rest of the crew were laying on the floor watching Smoky and the Bandit on the video. I went into the galley and made myself a sandwich and got a can of Coke and then I went back up on the flybridge with Jerry. I sat on the bench seat in front of the dashboard and ate my snack. Neither Jerry or I said anything and when I had finished my snack, I tried to take a catnap. The sea had calmed down a little and the boat ran real smooth on autopilot. We came in right at Bimini in about two and a half hours and ran down the shelf to Gun Cay, went through the Cut at a dead idle, and then Jerry pushed the throttles forward and we quickly got back up to our cruising speed of 20 knots. Jerry aimed the bow east and got the Hatteras on a course of 98 degrees to Russell Beacon. The Bahamian Bank was flat calm and we were blasting across the Bank on autopilot with the efficiency of an Indy race car.

Jerry said: "Keep an eye on it for me, I'm gonna go downstairs and fix me a sandwich." He goes down the ladder from the flybridge to the aft deck and disappears into the main salon. I got up from the bench seat in front and sat in the Captain's chair and pretended that I'm running the boat, it was cool! It was a real good feeling like I was driving a quarter million dollar boat doing 20 knots. The Hatteras was moving a lot of water and throwing up a big roostertail wake behind us. Those 12V71TI Detroit Diesel engines were powerful! In about 20 minutes, Jerry comes back up the ladder to the flybridge and I move to get up from his seat.

He said: "No, no, that's allright, I'm gonna sit up front and eat my sandwich. You stay there." He sits up front on the bench seat and I continue to fantasize about running the boat.

I said: "Why'd you name your boat BJ?"

He said: "What do you think?"

I said: "I don't know, Blow Job, a fast ride and a cheap thrill?"

He laughed and said: "Everybody's named their boats after their wives or girlfriends. Joan's name is Barbara Joan, BJ is her nickname, so it's named after her. Pegleg's Smith boat is named Dolores, his wife, and Brad's Hatteras is named Sharon Lynn, his wife, pretty sinister, huh?"

By now, we're about 20 miles out of Gun Cay and it's around 1:30 in the afternoon. We hear an airplane coming, look behind us, and here comes this damn twin-engine airplane flying less than 100 feet off the water.

I said: "Oh shit, is that the heat?"

He said: "No man, that's the Colonel, that's one of ours."

I said: "Who's the Colonel?"

He said: "That's Joe's pilot. He's a retired Air Force bird Colonel who's a pilot extraordinaire. He goes and finds the freighters and tells us if it's there for tonight or if we're gonna have to wait until tomorrow night if it's not far enough up toward the Berry Islands. We won't know for a while if we're gonna party tonight or tomorrow night. All we can do for now is keep going toward the Berrys until the Colonel flies back over and tell us the status of the freighter."

Right about then, the Colonel flies by our port side at outrigger level, waggles his wings at us, we wave back at him, and in a few seconds, he's gone. What a rush!

Around 3 o'clock, we approach Russell Beacon and Jerry takes BJ off autopilot, turns to starboard, and puts the bow on a course of 112 degrees to Northwest Channel Light which is another 35-45 minutes from Russell Beacon at 20 knots. He puts BJ back on autopilot and leaves me in the Captain's chair. It's not long before we spot Northwest Channel Light and I start to see some islands out in front of us. Jerry takes the helm, sits down in the Captain's chair, takes the boat off autopilot, and begins driving the boat manually. We go right past Northwest platform and the water changes color from a clear, green-blue color to a dark blue color indicating that the water is very deep here.

I said: "How deep is the water here?"

He said: "This is the Tongue of the Ocean, it's a couple thousand feet deep here. The U.S. Navy does submarine maneuvers in this area 'cause it's so deep."

I said: "My Lord, it's that deep, huh?"

He said: "Yeah, like 3-4000 feet in the middle and more than a mile deep in some places."

I said: "What are those islands out there?"

He said: "That's the bottom tip of the Berrys off to port. That's Chub Cay right in front of us. That's Joulters over there to the right off to starboard. We were there last 4th of July when the freighter was broke down and got busted, remember?"

I said: "Yeah man, I remember. What's on Chub, do they have people living there?"

He said: "Yeah, they've got a marina there, you can get fuel if you need it. They've got people living there and an airstrip, it's nice, real nice. They've got a private club there, Chub Cay Club, we'll have to go there sometime, you'll really like it."

I said: "Man, I'd like that a lot."

Chub Cay is about 12 miles from Northwest Channel Light and as we're coming up on Chub, I can see a radio tower and a golf ball shaped water tower. Jerry tells me that's how you know it's Chub because it's the only water tower in the Berrys that looks like a golf ball on a tee. As we get closer, I can see houses and cottages and a nice white sand beach, it's real nice looking from the water. By now, it's around 4:30 or 5 o'clock and Chub is on our left and we're making a gradual turn to port. I look out about 1 o'clock and I see three Sportfishermen going from our right to our left.

I said: "Who are those guys, do you know who they are?"

He said: "Yeah, that's Joe and our other middle boats."

I said: "We're gonna have four middle boats this trip?"

He said: "Man, we're gonna have more than that."

I said: "How big is this load?"

He said: "Big!"

I said: "What's big?"

He said: "Well, it's supposed to be 140,000 pounds!"

I said: "My Lord, you're kidding me, right? How many boats are gonna be out here?"

He said: "Joe's got the whole fleet out here for this one. There'll probably be 50 boats out here tonight."

I said: "You have got to be bullshittin' me?"

He said: "No man, with all the middle boats and the scam boats, there'll probably be 50 boats out here. Everybody that works for Joe is working this trip. This is the biggest load that Joe has ever done. In fact, we're making history tonight. This is the biggest load that's ever been done by scam boats in the history of pot smuggling. Big Ed's done a barge trip with 200,000 pounds before but this is the most that's ever been done with scam boats." I was speechless!

We're gradually turning left around Chub Cay and are heading in a northerly direction now.

Jerry grabs the CB microphone: "Pegleg, Pegleg, Black Fin, Black Fin, kickit back."

Joe said: "Black Fin, Black Fin, Pegleg, Pegleg, kickit back."

Jerry said: "Hey buddy, howya doin'?"

Joe said: "Ah, pretty good, how you doin'?"

Jerry said: "We're doin' allright, you heard from the Colonel?"

Joe said: "10-4, it's on up the corner a little bit, just follow me."

Jerry said: "10-4, we'll be right on your tail."

Joe and his boats are off to our right and Chub is off to our left about a half a mile, they're closing in on us to our right. Jerry keeps gradually turning BJ to the left and pretty soon, we're headed almost due north up the chain of the Berrys which run north and south. Joe and his boats have pulled in front of BJ and we're about 100 yards behind them.

Jerry said: "Here, take the helm a minute" and I grabbed the wheel and steered directly at Dolores. Jerry got his binoculars out of the case and trained them on the boats in front of us.

I said: "What're you looking at?"

He said: "Man, all those guys are on the flybridge. Holy shit, you ain't gonna believe this. All them guys got on black pirates tee shirts."

I said: "You're pulling my leg?"

He said: "No man, I'll tell you right now, they are FUCKED UP!"

I said: "Whadaya mean?"

He said: "I guarantee you that they're all tooted up something fierce."

I said: "No shit, they do that and they work?"

He said: "Hell yeah, man, how the hell you think they make it through the night?"

I said: "Well shoot, me and my people don't do that."

He said: "Man, you guys are the only ones who don't."

Jerry comes back to the helm, takes the wheel from me, and says: "Go downstairs and tell everyone to start taping down."

I go down the stairs to the aft deck into the main salon and I said to nobody in particular: "Jerry says to start taping down."

All the crewmembers get up and start going like ants in a colony. They stow the furniture from the main salon in the forward V-berth. They get their drop cloths and cover the floor and the walls and start taping the drop cloths together. They break down the dinette table and stow it forward and get the boat ready for loading. One of the guys hands me a roll of masking tape and I help with the taping. It's the same as taping down the sailboats, just a little different 'cause it's the middle boat. I can look out the window and see as we pass Little Whale Cay and then Whale Cay. In about 30-45 minutes, everything is taped down and ready to go. I go up on the flybridge to tell Jerry.

I said: "Everything's looking pretty good, man."

He said: "Allright, good. You guys got to take the fighting chair off. Get some tools and get Gary to help you, unbolt it from the deck if you can."

I said: "Take the fighting chair off, how come?"

He said: "This freighter is so big, it's got cranes and it'll load us with cranes. They'll have cargo nets and the Colombians will load the bales in the cargo nets and the crane operator will put the cargo net full of bales right on our aft deck. If the fighting chair is there, it will destroy it. Stow the seat on the deck in the corner. If you can't get the base to come off, don't worry about it, we'll work around it."

I went back into the main salon and told Gary to come help me take the fighting chair off. We got two adjustable wrenches from the toolbox in the step to the main salon. The top of the step had been cut off and put on hinges and it was the main toolbox for the boat. We took the seat of the fighting chair off easily and then tried to unbolt the base from the fiberglass deck. The nuts were all frozen 'cause as we turned the bolts, the base stayed tight, it didn't loosen up as we turned the bolts. I told Gary that Jerry said that it was okay to leave it.

By now it's dark, probably around 7:30 P.M. and we're off Holmes Cay about halfway up the Berry Islands. The boats in front of us start slowing down and Jerry slows BJ down too. I'm on the bridge with Jerry and we can hear Joe talking to the freighter on the radio. The person he's talking to is speaking broken English and he's hard to understand. Jerry has his Furuno radar running and it's easy to see the freighter and all the middle boats. Everybody has their lights off including the freighter but you can see all the boats clear as day on the radar screen. There are nine boats on the radar plus the freighter. We've got six Sportfishermen and a big Burger Motor Yacht that are working this trip. There's another boat further north a couple of miles and we're not sure yet which one is the freighter.

I said: "Which one is the freighter?"

Jerry said: "We don't know yet, that's what Joe is trying to figure out, that's why he was talking to him and trying to find out his exact location. Hopefully, it's the closest blip on the radar to us."

There's a big blip on the radar screen that looks like it's about 8 miles off Holmes Cay. We see a boat heading for the big blip and assume that Pegleg is going to check it out. We sit there for about 20 minutes and watch the whole thing on the radar. Finally, Joe calls Jerry knowing everybody else is listening in on Channel 5.

Joe said: "Okay, this is it, I'm gonna bring it in closer to the island."

We watch on the radar as one small blip is in front of the big blip and the two of them are heading directly at all of the Sportfishermen. We're clustered together like a pack of hungry wolves about 100 yards off Holmes Cay in about 25 feet of water. We watch for about 30 minutes until Joe and the freighter are about a half a mile offshore. It is pitch black and you can't see anything past the front of your boat with the naked eye. The freighter captain gets on the radio and tells Joe he doesn't want to come any further.

Joe said: "How much do you draw?"

He said: "18 feet I think."

Joe said: "Man, you're in 40 feet of water, come on in a little closer. We need to get up here behind the island so it will block the radar from anyone on the inside." Joe wants us to hide behind Holmes Cay so anyone on the Bank side of Holmes Cay can't see us on their radar.

They come on a little further and get into about 28 feet of water and the freighter Captain said: "I'm dropping the anchor right here."

Joe said: "Okay, go ahead, that's good."

Then Joe said: "Okay you guys, come on out!"

Everybody pushes their throttles forward and start heading for the freighter about a quarter mile away. You can hear all the diesel engines on the boats as they rev up and it's a rush!

Everybody's adrenaline is really pumping and the whole thing is just unbelievable. It's like a James Bond movie but instead of watching it, you're in it! In a few minutes, out of the darkness comes this big, black form and here's this freighter and it's big. This thing is about 250 feet long and the deck of the freighter is higher than the tops of the Outriggers on the Sportfishermen. There's two big cranes and each one has a long boom with cables running from the top of the crane down to the booms. As we're coming up to the freighter, some of the boats go around to the other side to load. One crane will load one side of the ship and the other crane will load the other side.

Jerry and Blue Eyes are loading on the same side of the freighter. We've put huge bumpers on our port side and Jerry puts his port side to the freighter. Blue Eyes has his bumpers on his starboard side, he puts his starboard to the freighter, and BJ and Sharon Lynn are stern to stern with about 5 feet between the boats. As soon as we're both tied up to the freighter, another Sportfisherman comes and ties up to Brad's port side and rafts off him. Once we're tied up properly to the freighter, the Captains shut down their engines and we hear the diesel engines for the cranes crank up on the freighter.

It isn't long before a cargo net full of bales comes over the side of the freighter and the crane operator expertly sets down the net on the aft deck of the Sharon Lynn. Gary and Steve are on our aft deck and I am standing in the doorway watching in amazement. I think: "*If a bale fell out of the cargo net and hit you in the head, it could kill you. I'm glad I'm working the door!*" The other guys are in the main salon and the galley area in a fireman's line. The next load comes to BJ and Gary and Steve grab the cargo net, pull it to the deck, take one side of the net off the hook, and start handing bales of pot to me. I take each bale and hand it to the next guy in the fireman's line in the main salon. They filled up the guest head first, then the head in the master stateroom, and then the master stateroom. Then they packed the galley and the dinette all the way to the ceiling. You put the bales in like bricks as best you could because you got more in by packing them tight. Then we filled up the main salon all the way to the back door and all the way up to the ceiling. We definitely got a full load tonight. When we had the main salon packed all the way to the ceiling and to the back door, we all went out on the aft deck. The cool night air felt good after busting our humps in the heat of the main salon. We were all covered in sweat, burlap, and pot all over our skin, clothes and hair.

Joe was standing on the deck of the freighter watching the loading with a starry-eyed look on his face. Hell, this was history in the making, the largest trip ever done with scam boats. The crane operator put another cargo net full of bales on the aft deck and Gary and Steve started taking them out of the net.

I hollered to Joe: "Joe, we're full."

He said: "Take another 25 or 30 bales on your aft deck, we gotta get rid of all this pot." Man, we were gonna be loaded!

As it worked out, each Sportfisherman hauled about 22,000 pounds and the Burger took the rest, maybe 8000 pounds. We were loaded to the gills! Joe told us we could go ahead on so we untied BJ from the freighter and Jerry skillfully backed away, reversed the gears and did a 180, and we headed due south back towards Chub Cay. I took one final look at the freighter before it disappeared into the darkness and I tell you, that was one big mother! BJ was hunkered down in the water, the Detroit diesels strained under the load, and at full throttle, we could only make about 12 knots. By now, it was only about 10:30 P.M. and everyone grabbed a sandwich and a Coke out of the big igloo coolers. We half-sat and reclined on the bales on the aft deck and ate our snack, we were exhausted. I had a new appreciation for what the guys on the middle boat went through, and the night was only beginning. Now we had to go and find the scam boats and get them all loaded before the sun came up, we didn't want to have to lay over and sit on pot. I thought about my three boats and I hoped they all made it to the fishing hole, especially Blue Mist.

By the time we passed the southern tip of Holmes Cay, everyone had finished their snack and crashed on the bales for a nap, a couple of the guys snored loudly. It was a sight to behold. I closed my eyes and caught 40 winks too. I must have slept for about an hour, then woke up, got another cold Coke out of the igloo cooler, and went up on the flybridge. Jerry was driving in the Captain's chair and Joan was next to him in the Co-Captain's chair watching the radar screen in the dash in front of her. I stood next to Jerry and saw a beacon in front of us.

I said: "Is that Northwest or Russell?"

Jerry said: "It's Northwest." While I slept, we had come around the southern tip of Chub Cay and we were heading toward Northwest Channel Light. It was around midnight and I wondered if we were making good time? I sat down on the end of the bench seat 'cause Steve was crashed out on it and took most of it up. We came up on Northwest and Jerry steered a direct course for Russell Beacon. In about 15 minutes or so, we sighted Russell and there were a couple of boats anchored right next to it. They had all their lights on and they were lit up like broad daylight. We cruised past Russell and Jerry put the bow of the boat on 278 degrees, the reciprocal of 98, and put BJ on autopilot. We looked out over the Bank and there were boats everywhere all lit up, it was amazing, this was the entire fleet! It looked like a city all lit up at night like you see from an airplane or like that scene from the movie ET.

Jerry had me send my boats to 25 miles due east of Gun Cay because the word was that the heat was starting to watch the Gun Cay area and he wanted us to get further away for safety's sake. About 10 miles past Russell Beacon, Jerry starts talking to a boat on the radio and we're coming up on it. He takes BJ off autopilot and slows down to a dead idle.

He said: "Okay, go wake everybody up, it's time to go to work."

I said: "Who is this?"

He said: "This is my boat."

I said: "Oh, I didn't know you had a boat?"

He said: "Yeah, your three boats can't take all this pot, I had to have another scam boat."

I said: "I was hoping that my boats would get all your pot tonight."

He said: "There's no way your three Columbia's can haul 20,000 pounds, I had to have a fourth boat."

I said: "Shit, they can hold 18,000. How much you gonna put on this boat?"

He said: "Oh, about 4,000." I was beginning to see that I was gonna get shorted again but I could see why Jerry needed the fourth boat.

We pulled up to this trawler, put a big bumper on our transom, and we tied up stern to stern. There standing on the back of the trawler was Tommy fucking Dolan. Now I see the light! We loaded the trawler with the bales on the aft deck and then we made a fireman's line and started taking bales out of the main salon. We gave Tommy about 110 bales that was about 5,500 pounds. When we finished loading him, we untied, and got back on our course of 278 degrees for Gun Cay. When we got about 35 miles from Gun, we picked up three blips on the radar all clustered together. I was on the bridge watching the radar with Joan, she picked them up first and told Jerry to turn just a little bit left.

Then she said: "You're right on them now, they're about 10 miles in front of you."

I said: "Those are my boats, I know it. Can I talk to them on the radio?"

Jerry said: "Yeah, go ahead, give them a call."

I grabbed the CB microphone and said: "Homeboy, Homeboy, Little Big Man, you got your ears on good buddy, kickit back."

Rob said: "Roger that Little Big Man, this is Homeboy."

I said: "Howya doin'?"

He said: "Oh, we're doin' real good, how you doin'?"

I said: "Man, we're coming over to your house to have a party. Cut your porch light on." In front of us, a mast light came on. "We gotcha Homeboy, you got any friends with you?"

He said: "Roger that, my brother's here and another friend too."

I said: "Great, we'll see you in a short-short." I put the microphone down.

I said: "Well, Blue Mist made it!"

Jerry said: "Well good, I'm glad for you."

I said: "Me too, I'm glad for my people."

In about 10 minutes, Jerry skillfully pulled up to Blue Mist and we loaded her first. Then we loaded Cathy 5 and then we loaded Audy. We loaded them 1, 2, 3 just like that and finished about 5 o'clock in the morning, it was still dark.

As we pulled away from Audy, Jerry said: "Okay, let's get this thing cleaned up and eat some breakfast." We headed for Gun at about 1000 rpm's.

Joan said: "Boy, that's one of the easiest trips we've ever had."

I said: "Yeah, howcum?"

She said: "Because we didn't have to look for the scam boats. They were all where they were supposed to be."

She should have said: *"Thank you Scooter and thank your people."* I thought to myself: *"You're Welcome!"* I felt good!

I got a hose and hooked it up to a raw water outlet on the aft deck and started hosing down the outside of the boat. Burlap and pot residue was everywhere, on the flybridge, the catwalks, and the aft deck. The rest of the crew was inside, folding up the drop cloths and stowing them in trash bags. A couple of guys were putting Lemon Pledge on the woodwork, and somebody was running a Wet-n-Dry Vacuum getting the carpet and the floors cleaned. The crew is all over the boat like a bunch of ants cleaning it up and making it shine. When I finished hosing down the outside of the boat, my clothes were dripping wet so I stripped down to my underwear. I go into the main salon, get my seabag, and get some dry pants and a dry tee shirt. Joan is in the galley cooking bacon and eggs. Man, does it smell good, we're all ravenous! They've got a Jimmy Buffett tape playing, everyone is cleaning and singing along with the tape, they're happy campers. The reason they're happy is because they got rid of all their pot before the sun came up and they don't have to sit on pot until the next night. The guys look like they've got it under control so I go into the galley and ask Joan if I can help her cook.

She said: "No, you can just grab a plate and start eating because we've got to eat in shifts."

By now, Jerry has stopped the boat and we've dropped the anchor so everyone can eat. Jerry and I grab a plate, so does Joan and another guy. We serve up bacon and eggs, toast, and I get some coffee. They've got milk and orange juice too. This is better than the Waffle House! We sit in the dinette and wolf down our breakfast. When we're done, we throw our paper plates in the trash can and get out of the dinette so the next shift can eat. I feel really good but I'm really tired. I go up into the main salon and lay on one of the fold-out chairs. The guys have put Smoky and the Bandit back on the video. I'm still rushing from adrenalin while Jerry Reid is singing the theme song from the movie. "Westbound and down, loaded up and trucking, we're gonna do what they say can't be done. I thought to myself: *"That is our theme song for last night!"* The adrenalin has stopped flowing, the food has made me heavy, and in a minute, I'm fast asleep.

In about an hour, the engines crank up and I wake up. I feel the boat ease forward and wonder what's going on. I go up on the flybridge and Jerry is easing the boat forward as Gary and Steve are pulling up the anchor using the windlass.

I said: "Have you seen any of my boats?"

He said: "Yeah, one of them has already gone through the Cut and these are probably the other ones coming up now behind us."

I look behind us and there are boats everywhere. There were about 20 boats, sail and power, all heading towards Gun Cay Cut. I get the binoculars and look at two sailboats coming up on us. One sailboat is mine and the other one isn't.

I said: "Do you care if I talk to them on the radio?"

He said: "No, go ahead, just be careful what you say."

I said: "Gearjammer, howya doin', kickit back?"

He said: "We're doin' great. Is that you up ahead of us?"

I said: "Roger that, we're about to head for the house. Where's the other guy?"

He said: "Oh, he's back a ways. They decided to eat breakfast before they got on the highway. The rest of us, we were eating while we were on our way."

I said: "Good, but they're okay, huh?"

He said: "Yeah, they're fine no problems."

I said: "Good, okay man, have a good trip and good luck, I'll see you at home. You take care 'cause I care. Little Big Man standin' by."

He said: "We'll see you at home. Gearjammer standin' by."

Jerry has the boat headed toward the Concrete Ship and takes us through a passage between some small rock islands and some coral heads just north of Honeymoon Harbor and out into the deep blue water of the Gulfstream. He puts the bow of the boat on 300 degrees, pushes the throttles forward, and we quickly get up to our cruising speed of 20 knots. I went downstairs into the main salon and everyone is taking showers, the boat is shipshape and looking good. Smoky and the Bandit has finished and the guys are watching "Which Way Is Up?" the Richard Pryor movie. I get my turn at the shower and I go into the head in the master stateroom. It is wonderful to scrub off the sweat and pot and burlap residue and get clean. I feel like a new man only I'm getting really tired now. After I dry off from my shower, I put on clean clothes, go lay on the floor of the main salon, and I'm out before I know it. All the guys are crashed out on the furniture and on the floor and no one is watching the movie.

In about an hour and a half, we sight the smokestacks at Port Everglades and in two and a half hours, we're at the mouth of the Cut. Rita is sitting in the channel boat fishing just south of the Cut off Dania Beach, there are boats everywhere. We go down the Cut into the Port, let down the Outriggers and cruise under 17th Street Bridge at a dead idle. We cruise past the Gulf docks, go north up the Intracoastal, and Jerry docks BJ at a dock behind Joan's Condo at One Las Olas Circle. One of the crew gives me a ride home, I eat a quick sandwich, and get in my Oldsmobile 98 and drive south down A1A. I've got an in-dash CB radio and I listen to the scam boats talking to Rita in the channel boat. I find a parking space just north of the Yankee Clipper on the beach and sit and listen to the channel boat call home the scam boats. It is amazing to me that all of these boats full of pot are coming into Port Everglades and there seems to be no heat anywhere. It isn't long before I hear my three boats check-in with Rita and she gives them all "a big 10-10, it's clean and green!" They bring the boats to my houses, nobody gets busted, and we've done it again! This trip has really made an impression on me just how big the Joe Pegg Organization is, VERY BIG. It is truly unbelievable that we are able to smuggle 140,000 pounds of pot with 50 boats, nobody gets busted, and we're successful. Providence has smiled on us again.

That night, we unloaded two boats, Cathy 5 at Linda's house and Blue Mist at Mom's house. The next night, we unloaded Audy at Wen and WaWa's house. We delivered the pot to Fu at the IHOP on State Road 84, Pat got some ladies to clean up the boats, and we were done with The Big One. What a feeling of accomplishment I had finally getting three boats loaded. Like Jerry Reid sang in Smoky and the Bandit: "We're gonna do what they say can't be done." We'd done it, all 50 boats! My next payday was gonna be big. Lots and lots of green stamps!

Chapter 25
David, a Mooney, and Nassau
Let's take a plane and fly down south, we'll watch the weather straighten out,
We'll tan our bodies in the sun, oh girl, won't that be fun?

The next day, I went to see all my captains and got the paperwork for the three boats. As it turned out, the bales were not as heavy as we'd thought and Jerry ended up hauling about 19,500 pounds. Tommy Dolan got 5,500 pounds and that left my three boats with about 14,000 pounds. After deducting about 1,000 pounds for sack weight for the three boats, I ended up hauling about 13,000 pounds. When I realized this, I was a little disappointed because I had hoped to haul 15,000 pounds net after sack weight. Still, this was the biggest payday that I'd ever had for one trip, since the most I'd ever hauled before was 10,000 pounds on the three boats. I used $220 per pound and figured my gross to be $561,000 and my net after paying my crews to be $366,000. I was elated! The rest of the day, I spent quality time with Pat and Sunshine, we swam in the pool, had a great supper, and went to bed early.

The next morning, I got up, showered, ate some breakfast, and went over to Jerry's house. I knocked on the door, went in the kitchen, and Jerry and Brad were sitting at the kitchen table.

Jerry said: "Howya doin'man?"

I said: "Oh, I'm doing great!"

He said: "You know Blue Eyes, right?"

I said: "Yeah man, howya doin' Brad?"

He said: "I'm fine as wine man."

Jerry said: "Come on over here and sit down and let's see what you've got."

I sat down at the table, opened my leather Land Pouch which was a recent gift from Pat, and pulled out my yellow legal pad. I gave Jerry a copy of my figures for each boat along with a summary sheet for the three boats. We started and went boat by boat. I gave Jerry the number of bales, the gross weight, minus the sack weight, and the net weight for the boat. We did all three boats and then we did the summary for the three boats. Jerry wrote down the number of bales I hauled because he had to account to Joe for the bales he hauled. Joe was getting a bale count from every middle boat captain to make sure nobody was stealing from him. One bale was a lot of money and if people were keeping a bale for their personal stash, it added up to a helluva lot of money that Joe was losing. You didn't want to steal from Joe 'cause you wouldn't work anymore. That would be stupid!

Jerry said: "Okay, what's the total you hauled?"

I said: "Thirteen thousand pounds."

He said: "Fu is paying $220 per pound for this trip. You get 15% for Cathy 5, you unloaded at Linda's right?" I nodded. "You get 18% for your other two boats."

He got his calculator out and I got mine, we did each boat individually. Cathy's gross was $165,000 and the other two boats gross was $198,000 each, a total of $561,000 gross before my crew expenses. Jerry's 3% for house rental was $33,000.

He said: "Okay, your part of the surveillance fees is $26,000 so 561 minus 26 is $535,000."

I said: "How come I've got to pay $26,000 for surveillance?"

He said: "Well, you've got three boats, Tommy Dolan has one boat so you pay three fourths and he pays one fourth."

I said: "How the hell do you figure $26,000 for surveillance? What the hell is Rita getting?"

He said: "Rita's getting $15,000."

I said: "Last trip, she was getting $10,000, now she's making $15,000?"

He said: "Yeah man, she's worth it, isn't she? You ain't got busted yet, have you?"

I said: "No, I ain't got busted yet but I don't know if it's because of Rita. I think I ain't got busted yet because we're good. What's the inside channel boat getting?"

He said: "They're getting $7,500 and they had to go out there two days so I gave them $8,000, so that's $23,000."

I said: "Okay, fine, so how come I've got to pay $26,000?"

He said: "I had to pay our airplane surveillance $10,000. He had to fly two days and he gets $5,000 per day. That's $33,000 and you split that, three fourths is $26,000."

I said: "Jesus Christ, Jerry, this is unbelievable. My male crew make $15,000 and my female crew make $10,000. They go on the trips, they take the chance of getting busted, and they're only making fifteen and ten. Rita's getting paid $15,000 to sit on her ass and fish? That ain't right."

He said: "I'm sorry you feel that way about it but I think the surveillance is worth it."

I said: "Don't get me wrong, I'm glad they're out there looking out for us, but, you're just paying them too much for the chance they're taking, which is none. The people in the channel boats ain't taking a chance of getting busted."

He said: "If you get a boat busted, you ain't gonna get paid for what you hauled plus you're gonna have to pay the legal fees for your people. When you're on a percentage like you are, you have to pay your own legal fees. So, since you're the boss, you'll have to pay the legal fees for four or five people. The surveillance is a helluva lot cheaper than that. You shouldn't be bitching about paying $26,000 for surveillance because it's cheap insurance."

I said: "Okay, if you say so, but I just think you're overpaying them."

He said: "You can ask them if you want to, I'm paying them. I'm not keeping any of the money for myself, I'm not making nothing off the surveillance.

I said: "Look, if you tell me you're paying them, then, I believe you. I don't have to ask them, I just think you're paying them too much. Rita is good but all she's doing is sitting on her ass and fishing. If she gives us a tow, we pay for that too! I don't think it's fair but whatever."

He said: "Okay, I'm gonna get these figures to Joe this afternoon and as soon as I get some money, which I hope won't be too long, I'll give you a call and you can come get it."

I said: "Okay, great." I stood up and said: "Thank you very much." We shook hands and I said: "Blue Eyes, it's good to see you, I hope we'll be working together real soon." I took my Land leather pouch and left.

I left Jerry's house and went to check on my boats, my houses, and my people. When I got to Mom's house, my mechanic Ron was there and he was working on Blue Mist. I climbed into the cockpit and went into the main salon.

I said: "Ron, what's the matter with this damn thing?"

He said: "It's that damn black algae, Scooter. I think it's growing on the inside walls of the fuel tank and the Biobar we put in the diesel is killing it and making it flake off. That clogs up the fuel line and the injectors. I'll call that guy and have him pump it out again if that's what you want? That's all I know to do other than to replace the fuel tank."

I said: "Yeah, call him and let's pump it again."

He said: "The word is out on the street that y'all brought in a hundred thousand pounds, is that right?"

I said: "Yeah, it was actually a hundred and forty thousand pounds."

He said: "How many boats were out there?"

I said: "We had the whole fleet, it was fifty boats."

He said: "And nobody got busted?"

I said: "That's right, nobody got busted."

He said: "You guys are hot shit! A hundred and forty thousand pounds is a lot of fuckin' pot!"

I said: "Yes it is! It was a damn big freighter with two cranes that loaded the middle boats with cargo nets. It was amazing!"

He said: "You went to the freighter on the middle boat?"

I said: "Yeah, I'm going on the middle boat now and then loading my three boats. It was awesome to see the pot go from the freighter to the scam boats, to coming home, to getting unloaded, and then delivered to our dealer. It is an amazing process!"

He said: "Are you gonna get your own middle boat?"

I said: "Yeah, I think so, I think it's coming to that. First, I've got to get another scam boat so I can haul twenty thousand pounds. Then, I'll ask Joe if I can run my own middle boat, that's coming soon." I gave Ron $1,000 for his work and we shook hands.

I left Mom's house and headed for Wen and WaWa's to check on Audy. As I drove north up Riverland Road to Davie Boulevard, I began to realize that not only did I need to buy another scam boat, but I also needed to buy another house. That would give me four boats and three houses. I could flip-flop two sailboats at Mom's house or rent a house from Jerry if I had to. That meant I'd need somebody to live in the new scam house and that would be a problem. Oh well, I'd cross that bridge when I got to it.

When I got to Wen and WaWa's house, Mick was already there working on Audy. I visited briefly with him and he said everything was fine on Audy. Then, I went inside to talk to WaWa, Wen was at work. I told WaWa that I was going to buy another boat and I asked her if she thought she and Wen would want to run it for me. I could buy a trawler and all they had to do was drive it over to Gun Cay and get to the fishing hole. She said that she and Wen were impressed with my operation and with all the people they'd met that worked for me. She promised to talk to Wen and said they would consider it. Wen would have to be able to take a couple of days off to go on the trips but if they could work that out, they might be able to run the new boat for me. I told WaWa that I'd probably let Mom's go with them on the trawler and put a young guy on to help them load. I'd also give them a guy or two from the middle boat to help them load. I left WaWa's and headed for my house with a good feeling about getting a new boat.

In a couple of days, Jerry called and he had green stamps. I drove over to his house and went in the kitchen, there was a big case box for toilet paper on the floor near the kitchen table, I'm sure it was full of money.

Jerry said: "Okay, I owe you $535,000, right?"

I said: "Yeah, that's right. You'd better get me a box."

He went back into one of the bedrooms and came back with a case whiskey box. Then, he started counting bricks and putting them on the table. He counted out $535,000, there were some 50's and 100's but mostly it was bricks of 20's. This was gonna take two whiskey boxes or one big box. Jerry went back in the bedroom and got another whiskey box. I started putting the bricks in the boxes and counting at the same time. When I got all the money in the two boxes, it was exactly $535,000. I was pleased! I closed the lids on the two boxes by alternating the four flaps.

I said: "I'd like to talk to you about a couple of things, okay?"

He said: "Sure, what's the matter?"

I said: "I think I want to buy another boat and I want to buy another house."

He said: "Okay, do you want another sailboat?"

I said: "No, I think I'd like to get a power boat for my fourth boat. I've got some older folks that can run it for me. I was kinda thinking about a trawler. What do you think about that?"

He said: "They're good pot hauling boats, only thing is they've got to look real good coming in the port 'cause the heat looks at them pretty close."

I said: "I think I've got some people, a couple, who are about fifty years old, that could run it and take care of it for me. It's Pat's Mom and her boyfriend. I'd put some young people on there with them to help load and I'd help load too if I were on the middle boat. Do you know anybody that's got a trawler for sale?"

He said: "Maybe, let me check around. I'll get back with you on that."

I said: "Okay, good. I guess I'll just call Danielle and tell her that I'm looking for another house."

He said: "Well, I've got an appointment with her this afternoon. Do you wanta go with me? We're gonna go look at some houses that she's been looking at. I was gonna buy some more houses too."

I said: "Yeah, sure, I'd like to go with you guys."

He said: "Okay, why don't you meet me over here about 1:30."

I grabbed one box and he grabbed the other and walked me out to my Oldsmobile. I opened the trunk and we put the two boxes in. We shook hands and I drove home. I stopped at my bank of payphones on Commercial Boulevard and 18th Avenue, called all my people, and told them I had green stamps. I said I had a full afternoon but I'd try to see them sometime this afternoon or tonight. Everyone was excited! I drove to my house and took the boxes of money into my bedroom. I now had three whiskey boxes full of money in my walk-in closet, way too much money to have in the house. I needed to go offshore to the bank ASAP.

Pat said: "What're you gonna do now?"

I said: "This afternoon, I'm gonna go look at houses with Jerry and Danielle. Jerry is looking for a trawler for us so we're gonna need another house to unload. I talked to WaWa about she and Wen running the trawler for us. She said she'd talk to Wen tonight and they'd consider it. I'm gonna have to go to Cayman soon and get this money in the bank. I'm gonna call Jim Dolan and see if he can take me, maybe tomorrow. Listen, one of us has got to stay in the house at all times until I can get this money to Cayman. If I'm not here, you can't leave the house, okay?"

She said: "Yeah, that's okay, I don't leave the house much anyway. Why are you buying another boat?"

I said: "Because in order to haul 20,000 pounds, I've got to have four boats. That means we need another house to put the new boat behind. Then, sometime soon, I can get a Hatteras and run my own organization from top to bottom, we'll be vertically integrated. That would solve a lot of problems."

She said: "Howard, are you crazy?"

I said: "Hell yeah I'm crazy, this is all crazy. We passed the point of no return a long time ago. If I can run a middle boat and have my own organization from top to bottom, we can net $100,000 from each scam boat and $150,000 net from the middle boat. That's a net of $550,000 per trip. We'll work one more year and then retire and live happily ever after. How does that sound to you?"

She said: "Happily ever after sounds pretty good at this point. It can't come soon enough for me. Do you want some lunch?"

I said: "Yes, please, fix me a sandwich."

She went into the kitchen and I grabbed the phone, called the law firm, and asked for Jim Dolan. They told me he was out of town for a few days. I asked for Chris Fertig and they told me he was at lunch. I hung-up the phone and pondered the situation. Maybe I'd charter a Lear Jet and go to Cayman that way. In any event, I'd stop by the law firm this afternoon after I looked at houses and talk to Chris Fertig about it. Pat brought me my favorite lunch and a glass of Coca-Cola over ice. I went out by the pool, sat in the shade under the overhang, and wolfed it down. I gave Pat a big kiss and went out the door for Jerry's house.

I got to Jerry's right at 1:30 and Danielle was already there. We got in her car and drove over to the Las Olas Isles and looked at a beautiful house that was $260,000. Jerry liked it a lot and said he'd probably buy it. Then, we rode over to Riverland Road and went west about six blocks past Mom's house. We took a left and went all the way to the end of the street. The house was older and a little run down with an interesting floor plan. It looked like it could have been a small fishing lodge years ago. It was directly across from Broward Marine with a spectacular view of beautiful Broward Motor Yachts. I wondered how you could unload in this house? What was really cool was there was a family of peacocks that lived on the property. There was an inground pool and it was a nice piece of property at the end of the street on the River. We played it real straight with the other realtor. She told us the people were asking $165,000, were anxious to sell and that it had a real good assumable loan. All we had to do was put down $25,000 and move in. We got back in Danielle's car and headed for Jerry's house.

Jerry said: "Well, what did you think about that?"

I said: "Man, I don't know, it's right across from that marina. How could you unload a boat with that marina there?"

He said: "That wouldn't be a problem because there's no liveaboards in that marina. All they got is a night watchman that sits up at the guard house on the highway and probably sleeps all night."

I said: "Oh well, that would work then, and the price and the terms are great."

He said: "If you like it, you can have it. I'll just buy something else."

I said: "Okay Danielle, I want it, so make it happen." She shook her head in the affirmative. "Jerry, what about the trawler?"

He said: "Oh yeah, I know a guy that's got a 42 Grand Banks for sale. He'll sell it right away if you want it. He wants $120,000 and it's worth it."

I said: "Is it in good shape mechanically? I don't need another nightmare"

He said: "Yeah, he's got somebody taking care of it. It runs like a top and cosmetically, it looks pretty good. Its' woodwork could probably use a little varnish but it looks good all in all."

I said: "Can I see it?"

He said: "Sure, it's over in the Fruity Isles. We can go over there right now if you want."

I said: "Sure, that would be great."

Jerry told Danielle which way to go and she drove over to the Fruity Isles so named because all of the streets were names like Orange, Tangerine, Mango, etc. We stopped at this unimposing house and walked out to the rear to the dock. There was this beautiful 42 foot Grand Banks trawler. I fell in love with it instantly and was sure that Wen and WaWa would love it too. We crawled all over it and I was impressed with all the room in the fore and aft staterooms. You could leave the main salon open and the salon had lots of windows so the heat could see in if they passed you in the Port or the River. It had a Ford-Lehman diesel engine that looked like it had been well taken care of.

I said: "Jerry, I love the boat so tell the owner I want it. I'd like to keep it here until I can figure out where I want to put it. You think I can do that?"

He said: "Yeah, probably, you could keep it here as long as you wanted."

I said: "I'll move it to the marina if I have to but if I could keep it here for a while, that'd be great. Do we have any trips coming up soon?"

He said: "They're coming but we haven't heard anything for sure yet. It could be any day."

I said: "Do you think I have time to go down south to the bank?"

He said: "Yeah, you could probably go down there but come back the next day."

I said: "I'll probably just go down there and come back the same day."

He said: "Oh, if you're gonna do that then it's no problem. Go ahead and get it over with."

I said: "Okay, I'll probably go tomorrow or the next day at the latest."

We arrived at Jerry's house and after we all said our goodbyes, I got in my car and drove to the law firm.

I took the elevator up to the fourth floor, walked up to the receptionist, and gave her a big smile. She told me Chris was in his office and for me to go on back, he was expecting me. I walked down the hall and into his office.

He said: "What can I do for you today, Scooter?"

I said: "I need to make a trip to the bank and wanted Jim to fly me there. The receptionist said that he's out of town for a few days, right? I guess I could charter a Lear Jet but I was wondering if you had any ideas."

He thought for a minute and then said: "How soon do you want to go?"

I said: "Tomorrow if possible. I need to go and get back."

He said: "We need 24 hours to get clearance to fly over Cuba and it's too late today to get clearance for tomorrow. Why don't you fly to Nassau, make your deposit there at the Royal Bank of Canada, and wire transfer the money to the bank in Cayman. Have you met our new lawyer, David Bone? He's got his own airplane and he could fly you over tomorrow if he's not tied up."

I said: "No, I haven't met David but that would work for me if it worked for him. I never thought about going to Nassau, that's a good idea." Chris gave me a big smile.

He said: "Lots of people go over there to gamble. That could be your story. I think David is in his office now. Let's go check with him."

We walked across the hall and into David's office, Chris introduced us and we shook hands.

Chris said: "Scooter wants to go to Nassau to do some business and I thought you might want to fly him in your airplane. Jim is out of town and can't do it."

David said: "When do you want to go?"

I said: "Tomorrow if possible."

He said: "I've got a one o'clock appointment tomorrow that should only take a few minutes. I ought to be free by 1:30 and we could leave then. Will that give you enough time to do your business and then us be able to get back by dark?"

I said: "I think so, it should only take me two hours at the most to do my business. What time will we get there if we leave at 1:30?"

He said: "We'll get there around 3:00, maybe a little after."

I said: "I should be done by 5:00."

He said: "Then it's no problem. If we get in the air by 6:00 we'll be home by dark."

I said: "What kind of airplane do you have?"

He said: "I've got a Mooney. It's a single engine airplane but it's fast for a single engine. We can make it to Nassau in an hour and a half. The tail on the Mooney points forward, that's how you know it's a Mooney."

I said: "Okay, good, I'll meet you at the private aircraft terminal tomorrow at 1:30. You just come as quick as you can, I'll be ready to go."

He said: "I'll see you then." We shook hands and I left the law firm and drove home.

When I got to the house, I told Pat that I was going to Nassau to make the deposit and I explained everything to her. Then I went in my bedroom to figure out how much money I needed to take with me. I needed to keep enough to pay all of my people plus I needed to keep $120,000 to pay for the Grand Banks and $25,000 for the down payment on the Peacock House. I got my yellow legal pad out and did some figuring. After deducting my crew expenses plus $120,000 plus $25,000, that left me with $195,000 from this trip. I had $209,000 from the last trip so that gave me $404,000 that needed to go in the bank. I decided to take $400,000 and keep the extra $4,000 for mad money. I got my briefcase and my Samsonite suitcase and started packing them with bricks of 100's and 50's. After they were all packed, I started packing in the bricks of 20's. It was hard but I was able to get it all in my suitcase and my briefcase with very little room to spare. I was gonna have to get a bigger suitcase if I was gonna have deposits this big that were mostly bricks of 20's. I closed my briefcase and my suitcase and put them beside the bed up against the wall. Then I took one of the whiskey boxes, counted out what I needed to pay my people, and put all those bricks in a whiskey box and closed the cover. I put that box at the foot of the bed and went into the kitchen. Pat was cooking supper and it was almost ready, it was her special spaghetti that I dearly loved. We went in the den and ate in front of the television, it was a slow news night, nobody got busted for smuggling pot! When I'd finished eating my supper, I got my box of money and went to pay my people. I paid everybody that night except Rob in Miami. I stopped at a payphone and called him and told him I'd catch him in a couple of days. He said "no problem." I got home just before midnight, crawled in bed with Pat, and slept like a log until morning.

I slept in until nine o'clock the next morning and had my coffee out by the pool. I showered, put on some nice clothes, and ate some lunch. I kissed Pat goodbye, took my briefcase and my suitcase, got in my Oldsmobile, and drove to the private aircraft terminal. There was no airplane sitting on the tarmac when I arrived but in about five minutes, an airplane taxied up to the front of the building, and sure enough, the tail was tilted forward. This must be the Mooney. As soon as the pilot shut off the engines and the door opened, I could see that it was David Bone. I walked out to the airplane on the right hand side, climbed up on the wing, opened the door, and put my briefcase and suitcase in the floor behind the front seats. After fastening my seatbelt, David started the engine and we taxied out to the main runway and took off. The mainland of Florida quickly disappeared behind us and we flew at two thousand feet of altitude at roughly the same course that the middle boats took to Gun Cay. It was cool! We flew right over the Gun Cay, Cat Cay islands and then over the Bahamian Bank just north of Andros island and Joulters. It was really neat to see this area from the air. We got in the flight pattern for Nassau and it wasn't long before we landed and taxied over to the private aircraft terminal. David shut down the engines, I got my briefcase and suitcase, and we walked together over to the door to private Customs and Immigration in the terminal building. Standing just outside the door was a U.S. Customs agent in uniform watching us as we walked up. We entered the building and saw that the Bahamian agent on duty was working on some paperwork. We both knew him from prior visits and his name was also David.

He looked up, smiled, and said: "Ah, Mr. Bone and Mr. Alford."
David Bone said: "How you doing today, David?"
David said: "Oh, just fine. What you all up to today?"

David Bone said: "Oh, we just came over to do a little business."

David said: "You guys know each other?"

I said: "Yeah, we've been friends for a long time."

David said: "You all ain't never come over here together before."

I said: "No, this is the first time."

David finished the paperwork he was working on and he walked over to where we were standing. I had taken a $100 bill, folded it up, and put it in my right hand. I stuck out my right hand and David and I shook hands. He felt the money and took it from our handshake. He gave us a big Bahamian smile with lots of white teeth and began doing our paperwork. David Bone was filling out the paperwork for the airplane while I filled out an Immigration form. David put a chalk mark on my briefcase and my suitcase without asking me to open them. The $100 handshake always worked!

I said: "You want to go downtown with me, Bone?"

He said: "No, I'll just wait here. I'll get the airplane fueled up and wait here until you get back."

I said: "David, what's that U.S. Customs Agent doing outside?"

David said: "He's just snooping around."

I said: "How come he's not here in the office?"

He said: "Man, that guy has no jurisdiction over here. He's got to stand outside, I won't let him in the office."

I said: "You won't let him come inside out of the heat?"

He said: "No man, I won't even let him in the door."

I said: "You won't let him open my bags will you?"

He looked up from his paperwork, rolled his eyes, and said: "Over my dead body!" The three of us broke up laughing!

I picked up my briefcase and suitcase, walked out the door, took a right, and walked to the fence where a cab was waiting for a passenger. I got in the cab and told the driver to take me to the Royal Bank of Canada downtown. In about twenty minutes, we were sitting in front of the bank on the main street in downtown Nassau, the cab driver said he would wait for me. I went into the bank and told the receptionist that I had a large cash deposit that I wanted to make. She went into an office in the rear of the bank and came back with a male officer of the bank. He took me into a back room with a money counting machine and got a young male clerk to count the money using the machine. The process proceeded and the money was efficiently counted in just under an hour. It was exactly $400,000. I told the young man that I wanted to wire transfer the money to the Royal Bank of Canada in the Cayman Islands. He went and got the same officer, he took the account information and said the transfer would be completed that afternoon. He gave me a receipt for the deposit minus a 2% fee for counting and accepting the deposit, minus a $40 wire transfer fee. The total fees were $8,040 and the amount wire transferred to Cayman was $391,960. The fees seemed high to me but like Jim Dolan once told me, it was a lot cheaper than paying 40% in taxes to the IRS.

I left the bank, got in my cab, and rode in silence back to the private aircraft terminal. After paying the cab driver, I walked into the Customs and Immigration office and found David and David chatting like two long, lost friends. The U.S. Customs agent was still standing outside the door and as Bone and I walked across the tarmac to the Mooney, we could feel his eyes staring a hole in our backs. As we climbed into the plane, fastened our seatbelts, and prepared for takeoff, I was thinking that the war on drugs was heating up. If the heat was flying the area around Bimini and Gun Cay and a uniformed Customs agent was hanging out at the private aircraft terminal at Nassau International Airport, the war on drugs was definitely heating up. After being cleared for takeoff by the Tower, we took off and got on a direct heading for Ft. Lauderdale. In about twenty minutes, Andros and Joulters were off to our left and Chub Cay was off to our right, the golf ball water tower was easily recognizable. In about an hour, Cat Cay was off to our left, Bimini and the concrete ship to our right, and we flew right over Honeymoon Harbor on the northern tip of Gun Cay. In about an hour and a half, we landed at Ft. Lauderdale International Airport and taxied to the private aircraft Customs and Immigration building. Bone and I got out, went inside, and cleared Customs and Immigration in about ten minutes. I realized that I had gone offshore now three times in a private airplane and that this pattern was being recorded in the records at Immigration. Since I had gone down and come back the same day without spending the night all three times, I wondered if this pattern was suspicious and would it cause Immigration to red flag my name to watch for further suspicious activity. I'd better talk to Jerry and my lawyers about that. We got back in the Mooney and Bone taxied us over to the private aircraft terminal where I got out, got in my car, and headed for my house. As I drove home, I had an uneasy feeling that the war on drugs was indeed heating up and that our "cops and robbers" game of smuggling was going to become increasingly more difficult. We were going to have to be very careful and very good at what we were doing in order to continue to be successful and to not get anyone busted. I hoped that Providence would continue to bless us, protect us, and keep us safe.

Chapter 26
Blue Eyes, the Cookie Monster, & Another Big One
"The only thing that's for sure is that nothing's for sure, and that's for sure"
- Blue Eyes

When I woke up the next morning, I called Jerry and told him I wanted to come over and talk to him. He said: "No problem, come on over." After I'd had my coffee out by the pool, I put on some clothes, drove over to Jerry's house on S.W. 5th Place, and went in the kitchen. He was in the den in the back of the house and he came into the kitchen and we sat at the kitchen table.

I said: "I love the Grand Banks and I definitely want to buy it."

He said: "Okay, no problem. The guy said you could keep the dock space or you can move it to a marina if you want. Whatever you want to do is okay with him."

I said: "I'd just as soon keep the dock space for now."

He said: "You know you can't use it to unload."

I said: "No, I plan on putting it at one of my houses. I want to buy the Peacock House too. Pat is thrilled that we'll have a flock of peacocks as pets."

He said: "Well, I figured you wanted the house too. I told Danielle to go ahead and make an offer on it so if you want it, you can have it too."

I said: "Okay, no sweat, that's great! I went to Nassau yesterday with David Boone in his Mooney so that problem is taken care of." I said that like having money was a problem. "There was a uniformed U.S. Customs Agent standing outside the private Customs and Immigration building at Nassau International Airport. You know the Black Bahamian Customs Agent, David?" He shook his head "Yes". "David made him stand outside in the sun, he wouldn't let him in the building." We both laughed!

He said: "David's a good guy, he's a friend."

I said: "Yeah, I figured that out a while back. So, any word on the next trip?"

He said: "It could be any day so just be ready."

I said: "Man, I was born ready!"

He said: "When we get word the people have accepted our offer on the Peacock House, you'll have to give them $25,000 to assume the loan. Don't give them cash. Go to the bank and get Cashier's Checks."

I said: "Yeah, I've already thought about that. I figured that I could get three Cashier's Checks for $8,000, $8,000, and $9,000. That way, all three checks would be under $10,000 so the bank won't make me fill out the IRS form. I'll go to three different banks and get one check at each bank so it won't look suspicious."

He said: "That's good, you've got it figured out. Give the Cashier's Checks to Danielle and she'll give them to the Sellers. The house is free and clear and the Sellers are holding the paper. Chris Fertig will still have to represent you at the Closing but no money will be exchanged because they'll already have the Down Payment. You don't want to meet the Sellers and they don't need to meet you. That way, if anything happens and the Cops come to them asking questions or showing them a picture of you, they can honestly say that they never met you."

I said: "Okay, once we close, I've got to make monthly payments to them. Do I get a Cashier's Check every month and send it to them or what?"

He said: "You can do that if you want, that'd work. What I'd do is I'd let Chris Fertig pay them every month out of his trust account. That's what you pay him for. When he needs money, he'll ask you for it. Don't you have enough on your plate already? Do you want something else that you have to remember to do every month?"

I said: "I've got plenty enough to do just like you. That's a good idea, I'll let Chris do it."

I left Jerry's house and drove back to my house to get $25,000 so I could start getting the Cashier's Checks. When I got to my bank of payphones on Commercial Boulevard and 18th Avenue, I stopped and called Danielle. She said that the people had accepted our offer on the Peacock House and they were ready to close as soon as possible. I told her that I was getting her Cashier's Checks for the down payment and we arranged to meet later that afternoon. She sounded very pleased and rightly so, she was making another commission. I hung up with Danielle and called Chris Fertig. I told him about the Peacock House and the terms of the deal. We had already formed another corporation so we were ready to go with that. I told him I was giving the down payment to Danielle in three Cashier's Checks and that he should coordinate with her and get it closed as soon as possible. The Sellers were ready to close as soon as we could get it together.

In a couple of days, Jerry called and it was time to go fishing again.

He said: "You gonna run that Grand Banks this time?"

I said: "Yeah man, I've got four good crews and I'm gonna run it."

He said: "Blue Eyes is gonna load all four of your boats this time.

I said: "That's great! I like working with Blue Eyes, he's a straight-up guy. Who you gonna load?"

He said: "I'm gonna load Tommy Dolan and two other boats and another new boat that I just got."

I said: "That sounds good. Do you think Blue Eyes will care if I go on the middle boat with him?"

He said: "You'll have to ask him about that."

I said: "Okay, I guess I'll see you out on the Bank."

He said: "Yeah man, I'll see you out there. Good luck!"

I said: "Good luck to you too, man!"

I hung up with Jerry, drove up to my "office" at the payphones and called Blue Eyes. When he answered, I asked him if we could meet and we arranged to meet at the Carvel Ice Cream Parlor on Commercial Boulevard. I went in and ordered a chocolate milkshake with an extra shot of chocolate. In a couple of minutes, Blue Eyes drove up, parked and came inside. He ordered a milkshake and sat down at the table with me.

I said: "I understand that you're gonna be loading me on the next trip?"

He said: "Yeah, is that okay with you?"

I said: "Hell yeah, man. Does a wild bear shit in the woods? I wanta ask a favor. Do you have any objection if I go on the middle boat with you? You don't have to pay me if you don't want to."

He said: "No, I don't have any objection. I'll tell you what: if all my people go, then you'll be extra so I'll pay you half the fee, I'll pay you $10,000. If one of my people can't go, I'll pay you the full $20,000."

I said: "That's more than fair. When do we leave?"

He said: "Joe says that the freighter will be there in two nights, two nights after tonight."

I said: "When should I send my scam boats?"

He said: "You can send them tomorrow and let them lay over a day, or send them the next day and we'll load them that night. Whatever you want to do is okay with me as long as they all get there."

I said. "Will you be loading anybody other than my four boats?"

He said: "No, you'll get all the pot that I get off the freighter."

I said: "That's great man! How much do you usually get off the freighter?"

He said: "We usually get 18,500 to 20,000 pounds if we don't get shorted at the freighter."

I said: "Does that happen very often? Do you get shorted at the freighter very often?"

He said: "Some of the middle boat captains will fuck you if they get the chance. This is a big one and Joe'll be out there on the freighter. Joe makes sure everybody gets a good load when he's out there. We'll be okay."

I said: "Man, that sounds great! Any three of my boats can haul 20,000 pounds if push comes to shove. I hope I won't let you down."

He said: "There'll be plenty of boats out there to take any extra pot we've got left over. If any three of your boats can haul 20,000 pounds, then, I'll load all of your boats and be done."

I said: "I'm gonna send my Grand Banks to Russell Beacon and we can load them first and get rid of some pot early on. My three sailboats will all be together at 10 East of the Light, unless you want to do something different."

He said: "No man, that sounds good to me. If all your boats are where they're supposed to be, it'll be a piece of cake for us."

I said: "Okay then, I'm gonna go call all my Captains and tell them to leave tomorrow. This is for sure then?"

He said: "Scooter, the only thing that's for sure is that nothing's for sure, and that's for sure!"

I said: "Hey, that sounds like a t-shirt."

He said: "It's more like a motto that we live by."

I left Carvel and drove back to my office at the payphones. I called all my Captains and told them to put their crews together and to leave tomorrow. If this was another big one, the city would be abuzz with activity. With a 50 boat armada and 3, 4 or 5 people on each boat, I hoped that the heat didn't have somebody under surveillance or have our organization infiltrated. I said a silent prayer that Providence would smile on us again.

In two days, when it was time to go, Blue Eyes came by my house and picked me up. We drove to the marina where he kept his 53 foot Hatteras, the Sharon Lynn. He said they called her the "S-L" and his crew said that it stood for "Slave Labor". When we got on the boat, he introduced me to his crew, and what a crew they were. His right-hand man was a guy that looked like the Pillsbury Doughboy and went by the handle of the "Cookie Monster". When he got stoned, he'd go through a whole bag of chocolate chip cookies, thus, the "Cookie Monster". His kids' favorite television show was Sesame Street and he got his handle, the "Cookie Monster", from Sesame Street. The rest of his crew were a bunch of real characters, a little rough around the edges. As soon as we left the dock, they started smoking pot, drinking liquor, and snorting cocaine. They put an x-rated movie in the video recorder and watched the skin flick with much intentness. When the movie was over, they put on a Deputy Dog cartoon and watched it. When it was over, they put in another x-rated movie and then another cartoon, the Road Runner. It was histerical!

About an hour or so out of Ft. Lauderdale, I went up on the Flybridge with Blue Eyes. He had dual Captain's Chairs and I took the chair on the left in front of the radar screen. I could see Bimini, Gun Cay, and Cat Cay as plain as day in front of us about 20 miles out. Blue Eyes had the autopilot on with the bow pointed dead on to Gun Cay.

Blue Eyes said: "What's going on downstairs?"

I told him they were smoking pot, drinking liquor, snorting cocaine, and watching x-rated movies and cartoons. We both laughed!

He said: "They'll eventually pass-out and sleep until it's time to tape-down. When it's time to go to work, they'll turn into the pros from Dover. You'll have a good time working with us but when it's time to get serious, we're serious as a heart attack. I've done way more trips than anybody with the possible exception of Joe. This is the best crew I've ever seen."

I said: "I'm glad to hear that because looking at them now, you'd think they were a bunch of clowns. I just want to get my boats loaded with good loads."

He said: "Don't worry about that, my man. This'll be the most pot you ever hauled and your biggest payday."

I said: "That's good! That's what I've been working and busting my ass for, to get to this point."

We're coming up on Gun Cay now and Blue Eyes takes the S-L off of autopilot, pulls the throttles back, and slows down to a dead idle. He skillfully navigates Gun Cay Cut, puts the bow on 98 degrees to Russell Beacon, pushes the throttles forward, and we quickly get back up to cruising speed. When the boat gets up to full speed of about 20 knots, he puts the boat back on autopilot. He disappears down the ladder and into the main salon to get a sandwich. In a minute, the Cookie Monster comes up the ladder, and sits in the Captain's chair.

I said: "I'm gonna call my boats and see if everyone made it over." I grabbed the microphone to the CB radio and said: "Speedy Pete, Speedy Pete, Little Big Man, you got your ears on good buddy, kickit back."

In about 30 seconds, I heard: "Little Big Man, Speedy Pete, we got a copy, good buddy. What's your 20?"

I said: "We just came through the intersection and we're headed for Russell's house. You got any friends with you, kickit back."

He said: "Roger that, I've got two of my girlfriends with me and we're all excited about the party tonight. Is that you going by us right now off to the South, kickit back."

I said: "Roger that. You seen or heard from my mother in-law, kickit back."

He said: "That's a roger. She came through the intersection a little while ago and was going the same way you're going. We gave her a shout on the radio and spoke with her briefly, kickit back."

I said: "Is everything allright with her, kickit back."

He said: "Yeah, as far as we know. She didn't say they were having any problems, kickit back."

I said: "Good, I was kinda worried about her. I was hoping her car wouldn't give her any trouble, kickit back."

He said: "She didn't say anything about any trouble of any kind, kickit back."

I said: "Roger that. Okay, I'll give you a shout tonight when we're headed for your house. This is the Little Big Man, I'm eastbound and down and I'm gone."

He said: "This is Speedy Pete and I'm standing by."

The Cookie Monster said: "So all of your boats are here?"

I said: "Yeah, my three sailboats are sailing just east of Gun Cay and we'll load all three of them at 10 east of the Light. My Grand Banks is on the way to Russell Beacon and we'll load her at Russell. That way, we can get rid of one load with the Grand Banks and run a little easier to my sailboats at 10 east."

He said: "Aw man, that's great. Tonight is gonna be easy. So, how long you been smuggling?"

I said: "About a year and a half I guess, how about you?"

He said: "About twice that I think. So, you like it?"

I said: "Yeah, I like the boats and the money's great. What about you?"

He said: "It's a whole lot easier than being a Marine in Vietnam and getting shot at. I like the money too!"

I said: "How'd you get started with smuggling?"

He said: "I moved down here from Canada with my parents and my Dad had a huge paper route. We would start at 4:30 in the morning rolling papers and then I'd sit on the tailgate and throw the papers as my Dad drove the family station wagon. After a year or so of rolling and throwing papers, I was bored so I decided to join the Marines. They sent me straight to Vietnam after boot camp. It wasn't long before I was going on patrols, getting shot at, and shooting back. When my tour was up, they made me a deal I couldn't refuse so I re-upped for another tour."

I said: "That's crazy! Are you an American citizen?"

He said: "I am now. I wasn't then, I was a Canadian citizen here on a VISA."

I said: "So the U.S. Marines took you as a Canadian citizen?"

He said: "Hell yeah, they were taking anybody that could pass the physical and sending them straight to Vietnam. Here's an M-16, now go kill Gooks!"

I said: "So why did you re-up?"

He said: "Well, when my first tour was over, I had to make a decision. Did I want to come back to Ft. Lauderdale and start throwing papers again with my Dad or re-up. Other than getting shot at and a few close calls, it was fun."

I said: "What the hell is fun about war?"

He said: "Well, I guess I'm an adrenaline junky. When we'd get in a firefight, the adrenaline would rush and you could feel the blood pumping in your temples. When it was over and the adrenaline quit rushing, it was a great feeling of being alive. We'd go count the Gooks we'd killed, cut off an ear for the body count for the brass, and leave our calling card on the dead bodies. I liked the camaraderie among the guys too"

I said: "What does that mean, you'd leave your calling card on the dead bodies?"

He said: "We had playing cards with our units' name and insignia printed on the back of the cards. We'd leave a card on top of the dead bodies and all around the kill zone. Then, when the Cong's people would come back to bury their dead, they'd see our calling cards all over the kill zone. They'd know we were bad motherfuckers. We wanted to put the fear of God in them."

I said: "You are one crazy motherfucker!"

He said: "Yeah, that's what people say about me."

I said: "So when you came home from your second tour in Vietnam, how'd you get into smuggling?"

He said: "I met Blue Eyes and he was working as crew on a middle boat. When he started running his own middle boat, he drafted me. It was more money than the Marines, a whole lot more fun, and I wasn't getting shot at, and I didn't have to throw papers anymore."

By now, we're coming up on Russell Beacon. We passed to the left of Russell, he turns off the autopilot, and starts slowly turning the boat left to port. Pretty soon, we're heading due north and the chain of the Berry Islands is off to our right.

I said: "Man, where're we going?"

He said: "We're going up to the northern tip of the Berrys to Great Stirrup. That's where we're meeting this freighter, at Great Stirrup."

I said: "Oh, I've never been up there."

He said: "It's nice and real pretty. At night, you can see the glow of the lights of Freeport while you're loading from the freighter. We'll only be about 20 miles from Freeport."

I said: "No shit! That's far out, man. I'm looking forward to it. I ain't never been to Great Stirrup before."

Blue Eyes comes climbing up the ladder onto the flybridge and the Cookie Monster gets up to give him the Captain's chair. He takes the boat off autopilot and starts steering to the right and brings us in close to the back of Great Stirrup. He slows down to a dead idle and one of the crew goes up onto the bow pulpit and drops the anchor. We're in about fourteen feet of water and the anchorage and Great Stirrup are a picture postcard. As soon as the Danforth anchor has caught on the sandy bottom, Blue Eyes shuts down the big Detroit Diesel engines. SILENCE! It's about 4:30 in the afternoon, we're here.

Blue Eyes said to the Cookie Monster: "Okay, you guys start cooking supper and start taping down. Let's get this thing going."

The Cookie Monster goes down the ladder and I follow him onto the aft deck and into the main salon. One of the crew is already at the stove in the galley-up arrangement and he's got water boiling to cook rice. Another crewmember is opening up cans of Dinty Moore Beef Stew. The other guys are stowing the furniture from the main salon in the front v-berth. They've got it well under control and everyone works without talking. They've got some music on the sound system and we're sure they are singing just for us. When the rice has been cooked and the stew is hot, we all wolf down our supper with a piece of white bread and a cold drink, no beer now, only soft drinks. As we finish taping down, there is an air of anticipation that is building.

Chapter 27
Getting' Hurt on the Banks on the Bank
"I've been kicked by the rain, robbed by the sleet, had my head stove in but I'm still on
my feet, and I'm still, Willin" – Lowell George

Once we got through eating, we started putting the finishing touches on our
tape-down job. We heard the sound of an airplane flying directly over us and shortly,
Blue Eyes stuck his head in the door of the main salon and told us that the "Colonel" said
the freighter is out there heading our way. Everybody got real excited and began to work
fervently to finish up the taping job. The S-L is a galley up model with the kitchen area
in the main salon. Jerry's boat BJ is a galley down model with the kitchen area down the
steps to the right. I like the galley down arrangement better. Just then, the motors fire up
and we feel the boat ease forward as one of the crew pulls up the anchor.

I went up the ladder to the flybridge just as we're coming around the northern tip
of Great Stirrup. I looked out about a quarter of a mile and saw five Sportfishermen
sitting in close proximity to each other.

I said: "Are all those guys with us?"

Blue Eyes said: "Yeah man, they're all our guys."

I said: "This is another big one, huh?"

He said: "Yeah man, this is supposed to be 120,000 pounds."

I said: "How come they keep making us do these big ones. Isn't that dangerous?
If the heat were on to us, they could catch everyone in the organization in one fell
swoop."

He said: "Joe's got bosses too. Julio is putting pressure on Joe to do bigger trips
because he's got the pot in warehouses on the docks in Colombia. He says that the pot
gets wet from the humidity and that it is starting to rot. Rotting pot doesn't do anybody
any good. So, he wants to send it up here to us so Fu can sell it and make more money
for them. Julio is telling Joe what to do."

I said: "Who is this Julio?"

He said: "Julio is the largest pot broker in Colombia. He contracts with the
farmers to buy their pot. Then, he warehouses it on the docks, contracts with the
freighters, loads the freighters, and gets the freighters going from the docks in Colombia.
It's Julio's responsibility to get the freighter to the Windward Passage. Once the
freighter is through the Windward Passage and into the Bahamas, it is Joe's responsibility
to unload the freighter, get the pot to Fu, get it sold, and get our money. That's the
process!"

I said: "How do you know all of this?"

He said: " Julio is Big Ed's broker too. I do all of Big Ed's trips. Last year, Big
Ed did a barge trip with 200,000 pounds in the bottom of the barge. We unloaded the
barge at a shipyard in Pascagoula, Mississippi. We had 10 semi's full of pot that hit I-10
and went all over America. It was awesome!"

I said: "You're not bullshittin' me are you? 200,000 pounds of pot in the bottom
of a barge? That's hard to believe."

He said: "Believe it, man. I saw it. I was there! We had an electric conveyer belt
from the barge to the parking lot. We backed up the semi's to the other end of the

conveyer belt and filled up the semi's one by one. It was truly amazing! As soon as the sun came up, those semi's hit I-10 and fanned out all over America."

I said: "Where did you guys get the semi's? Did Big Ed coordinate that too?"

He said: "Big Ed knew a guy that was a freight broker. He got the trucks and the drivers for Ed. They were paid very well, hell, I was paid very well."

I said: "What did you do, what was your function?"

He said: "We had the Sharon Lynn in the Gulf and we met the barge about fifty miles offshore. I talked to the Captain of the tugboat and led the barge to the shipyard. Only thing was, when we got to the ten-mile limit, the fuckin' Captain called me on the radio and said he wasn't taking it any further. He refused to drive the tugboat inside the ten mile limit."

I said: "Oh man, what the hell did you do?"

He said: "I got on the tug and the Captain got on the S-L. I drove the tug and the barge to the shipyard and the S-L followed the barge in."

I said: "That must have been an experience?"

He said: "Yeah it was! It was a little tricky because it was windy. The barge had a big mountain of gravel on the top of it so it looked like it was a load of gravel. The wind would catch the gravel and it acted like a sail. The wind would catch the gravel and the barge would try to turn sideways."

I said: "What the hell did you do?"

He said: "We backed the tug up to the barge and snugged up the ropes. Then, I maneuvered the barge by driving the tug using the twin crews of the tugboat. It was a little tricky but I got the job done! Big Ed paid me very well!"

I said: "Fuck, he should have! What happened to the Captain?"

He said: "Ed said that Julio had him killed. Julio Nasser David is one very serious motherfucker."

We could hear Joe talking to the freighter Captain on the radio. We saw Joe's Smith Sportfisherman pull away from the pack heading east and he disappeared into the darkness. We could watch on the radar as the Smith approached the freighter. The blip on the radar that is the freighter is about twice as big as the blip that is made by the Sportfishermen. This thing is big! Joe steers the Smith in front of the freighter and leads it west towards Great Stirrup. About a mile offshore, the freighter stops and drops his anchor in about 40 feet of water.

Then on the radio, we hear Joe say: "Okay you guys, come on out!"

All five boats in unison push their throttles forward, black smoke comes out of the exhaust, and the S-L lurches forward under our feet. What a rush! Now this is an adrenaline rush!

The Cookie Monster is on the flybridge with us and he says: "Ah, Ah, Ah, Hatmania, Scammania, I love it!"

As we approached the freighter, Blue Eyes slows down to 1000 rpm's and then to a dead idle as we get close. This damn freighter is bigger than the last big one we did. This thing is about 350 feet long and there are no booms on this one. It looks like a fuckin' Cruise Ship it's so big! We're in luck because tonight there was a full moon and it was bright, just a gorgeous night to be on the water. It was so bright almost like broad daylight, you could have damn near read a book. This thing is enormous! On each side of the freighter near the stern, there was a cargo door about 8-10 feet above the waterline which they used to load their supplies when they were docked. We eased up to the cargo door and Jerry was right in front of us on BJ.

On the radio, Jerry said: "Blue Eyes, Black Fin, you copy?"

Blue Eyes said: "Roger that, kickit back."

Black Fin said: "Why don't we go stern to stern. I'll get a line from my bow to the freighter and you get a line from your bow to the freighter. We'll put a big bumper on my stern and we can tie up tight to each other. I'll use my throttles if I have to, to keep our sterns right on that cargo door. I think we can load that way, kickit back."

Blue Eyes said: "That's a roger. I'll do a 180 and then ease my stern back to your stern. Let me come to you, okay? Kickit back."

Black Fin said: "Roger that. I'll stay put and you come to me. When you get close, put it in neutral, have your guys throw us a line and we'll pull the two boats together so we don't do any damage. You're gonna have to tie two lines together to throw up to the deck of the freighter, kickit back."

Blue Eyes said: "Roger that. Okay, I'm gonna do a 180 and then ease back to you."

With that, Blue Eyes backed away from the freighter about 20 yards, reversed the throttles, and the Hatteras did a 180 degree turnaround in its' own length. Blue Eyes faced backwards with the throttles behind him with one hand on each throttle. He pushed the throttles forward, which was really backwards, and the boat eased back a little. Then, he put the throttles in neutral and let the headway stop. Then, he pushed the throttles forward again and continued this process until the stern of the S-L was about 3 feet from the stern of BJ. I was very impressed with the boat handling skills of Blue Eyes! Two of our crew threw two lines underhanded to two of Jerry's crew and they pulled the two boats together to the big bumper between us. On each corner of both boats, they tied the lines to the cleats. When Blue Eyes saw that we were tied up tight to BJ, He hollered to his crew on the bow of the S-L to throw their line to the deckhand on the freighter. Once that was done and the line tied off tight to the cleat on the bow, Blue eyes shut his engines down. We were lucky because in addition to a big, ole' bright full moon, the water was flat calm.

One of the crew stood on the stern at the corner of the boat by the cargo door. The Colombians on the freighter would hand a bale to him through the cargo door, he would hand it to the Cookie Monster at the corner of the aft deck, and he would walk it over to me at the door to the Main Salon. I would hand the bale to a crewmember in the Main Salon and they had a fireman's line going in the Main Salon. The crew inside the boat would fill up the Crew's Bedroom on the starboard, right, side first. Then, they'd fill up the Master Stateroom and the Master Head on the port, left, side. Then, they'd fill up the hallway downstairs all the way up to the ceiling. Then, they'd fill up the Main Salon all the way to the ceiling to the back door. This is how you got 20,000 pounds of pot on a 53 foot Hatteras Sportfisherman. The Colombians would give the S-L a bale and then they'd give BJ a bale so that each boat was loaded evenly.

As soon as we'd gotten tied up and started to load, another Hatteras pulled up to BJ and tied off to her port side. Holy shit, it was the Tin Man! Now, there were three Sportfishermen on each side of the freighter. The Cookie Monster said that he was glad they hadn't rafted off to the S-L because we would have had to help them load and it would have taken more time. It would have been more work for us and taken more time to get the two boats loaded. The other Hatteras came from the stern of the freighter and it was facing forward just like BJ was facing forward. So it naturally tied up to BJ and not the S-L since we were facing the stern of the freighter. That was good for us!

I asked the Cookie Monster: "What difference would it make?"

He said: "Shoot man, as soon as we get our load, we're gonna untie and get the hell out of here. Time is precious. We don't need to be spending another hour here at the freighter helping them load. Plus, it's double work for us if we've gotta pass bales across our aft deck to their aft deck. We'd do it if we had to but we really don't want to.

We got finished loading early, about 9:30 P.M. Blue Eyes and the Cookie Monster talked briefly and decided that we needed to get the hell out of Dodge. Joe was on the deck of the freighter all starry-eyed watching the loading procedure.

Blue Eyes hollered to him: "Hey Pegleg, we're all done down here unless you want us to take some more on the aft deck. Is it okay if we get outta here?"

Pegleg said: "Yeah man, go ahead. Everything's cool, everything's going good."

We get a Colombian deckhand to untie us from the deck of the freighter and we untie from the stern of BJ. Blue Eyes skillfully pulls away from the freighter and then makes a right hand turn to do a 180 and go around the northern tip of Great Stirrup. As the freighter disappears in the darkness, I am in awe of the process that I just witnessed. Blue Eyes takes the S-L around the northern tip of Great Stirrup and puts the bow on a course of 180 degrees, due south towards Russell Beacon. Great Stirrup and the chain of the Berry Islands is off to our left about a mile away. Russell Beacon is about an hour in front of us. My mother-in-law and father-in-law Wen and WaWa, are there at Russell Beacon waiting for us on my new 42 foot Grand Banks Trawler. Everybody grabs a sandwich and a soft drink out of a big Igloo Cooler on the aft deck. Me and the Cookie Monster climb the ladder to the flybridge, he sits in the left Captain's chair in front of the radar screen and I sit on the bench seat in front of the console. We eat our sandwich and drink our Cokes in silence. When I finished my snack, I closed my eyes and tried to catch a catnap.

In about twenty minutes, Blue Eyes said: "Hey Scooter, you awake?"

I said: "Yeah man, my eyes are closed but my mind is wide awake."

He said: "I see some lights up ahead. You wanta call your Grand Banks?"

I said: "Yeah, let's give them a shout." I got up and walked back to the two Captain's chairs and stood between them and took the microphone for the CB radio. I said: "Padre, Padre, Little Big Man, you got your ears on good buddy, kickit back."

In about five seconds, he said: "Little Big Man, Padre, we've got a copy on you, kickit back."

I said: "Padre, Little Big Man, howya doin' tonight?"

He said: "We're doing real good, howya doin'. You all coming over to see us tonight? Kickit back."

I said: "That's a big 10-4. We're on the highway and we're headed your way right now. Cut your porch light on and we'll be there in a short-short. We're gonna have a big party."

He said: "We got the porch light on and all the house lights on too. We're lit up like a Christmas tree. We just got finished eating, we cleaned up the kitchen, and we're waiting on you to come so we can party!"

I said: "Roger that, we'll be there in a short-short, we'll see you soon. Little Big Man standing by."

As soon as I signed off, Blue Eyes said: "Ah man, I'm glad to know those guys are there. That'll help us to drop a load quick. Do you think your sailboats are at the fishing hole?"

I said: "Yeah man, they're there. We saw all three boats daysailing when we came through Gun Cay Cut this morning. They'll all be together at the fishing hole."

He said: "Ah man, that's great. That'll make it easy."

I put the CB microphone back up in the overhead electronics box and went in front of the console and sat in the bench seat. I looked out the front windshield and I could see a lot of lights in front of us. There had to be other boats at Russell Beacon besides my 42 Grand Banks, there were just too many lights for one boat. As we came up on Russell Beacon, there's my 42 Grand Banks Trawler sitting there about 50 yards north of Russell all light up "like a Christmas Tree."

I said: "Bring me in close and let me get on the Grand Banks. I'll help us get tied up and then I'll stand on the aft deck and you guys can hand the bales to me and I'll hand them to my guys in the boat."

Blue Eyes said: "Okay good, that sounds like a plan."

I went down the ladder to the aft deck and stood on the catwalk on the starboard side of the S-L and held on to the handrail with my left hand. Blue Eyes eased the S-L up parallel to the port side of the Grand Banks about three feet away. Blue Eyes had his big, six foot long bumper on his port side from when we loaded from the freighter. It had been calm at the freighter but the weather had changed and now, the wind was blowing strongly out of the east due west. There was a pretty good chop on the Bank too. I told Wen to hang four small bumpers on his port side and we'd tie-up tight with the S-L and load that way. He and his other crew members started hanging the bumpers from the two-by-four wooden handrail. As soon as the bumpers were hung and in place, I went on the aft deck of the Banks and the Cookie Monster threw me a line which I tied off to the cleat on the port rear corner of the Banks. I walked up to the front of the Banks and one of the crew on the S-L threw me a line at the bow and I tied it off to the cleat there. The wind was really starting to blow and it felt like a storm was coming through. I could hear the waves lapping on the sides of both boats. Where the hell did this weather come from? Just then, it started to rain big drops of rain and they were hitting the decks and the Main Salons of both boats.

The wind was pushing the S-L up against the Grand Banks and waves were coming through that were making both boats go up and down in opposite directions. This was not good! The catwalk on the S-L went up to the bow at about a 30 degree angle and it crossed the wooden handrail on the Grand Banks right about in the middle of the boat.

The bumpers that we've got hanging from the handrail are hanging down between the hulls of both boats. A wave comes through and lifts the S-L up about two feet and throws it up against the Grand Banks. The catwalk barely misses hitting the handrail and I think "oh shit, that catwalk will destroy the handrail if it hits it. I'd better grab a bumper and pull it up to the handrail so the S-L will bounce off the Grand Banks. With my right arm, I reach over the handrail and grab the bumper. Before I could pull it up to the handrail, another big, rogue wave comes through and lifts the S-L up about three feet and throws the Hatteras into the Grand Banks. The catwalk catches my right bicep between the catwalk and the handrail and the two-by-four railing breaks about eight feet in from of me with a loud "CRACK!" The S-L pinches my right bicep on the handrail and it hurts like hell!

I screamed: "SHITMOTHERFUCKINGSONOFABITCH THAT HURTS LIKE SHIT!!" It hurt bad too!

My arm was caught for about fifteen seconds and it was a damn long fifteen seconds. Wen and another male crewmember saw what was happening and put their hands on the side of the S-L and tried to push the boats apart but the wind and the waves were too strong and held the boats together. Finally, the wave passed beneath the two boats and the S-L moved down and away from the Grand Banks and my arm was free. I pulled it over the rail to check the damage. I didn't think it was broken so I tried to move it. I couldn't bend my arm at all and I couldn't lift my arm up or it hurt like a son-of-a-bitch. The pain was damn near unbearable and I had a bruise on the inside of my bicep about the size of a baseball. My arm from the elbow down was numb and I couldn't move my fingers. My bicep was throbbing like a son-of-a-bitch every time my heart beat and pushed blood into the muscle. I grabbed my right forearm with my left hand and pulled my arm up against my stomach and held it there. I thought: *"Oh shit, this hurts, I don't know if I can stand it! You've really fucked up now Scooter."* I looked at the handrail and it was shattered. I guess if the handrail hadn't have broken, my arm would probably have broken so maybe the handrail breaking kept my arm from breaking.

Blue Eyes walked over to the port side of the flybridge of the S-L and said: "Are you alright?"

I said: "No, I ain't alright. I'm hurt."

He said: "Is it broken? Is that your arm that I heard crack?"

I said: "No, I don't think it's broken. It hurts like hell but I don't think it's the level of pain of a broken bone; but, it hurts like a son-of-a-bitch! Look at the handrail, that's what you heard crack. It's broken."

He said: "Alright, why don't you come up here on the flybridge with me. We've got plenty enough people to load."

I said: "No, that's okay. I think I'll just stand here on the aft deck and lean up against the railing. I want to tell my guys how to load. They've never loaded this boat before."

The Cookie Monster climbed over the railing and got on the aft deck of the Grand Banks. His guys started handing him bales over the railing. The Master Stateroom was aft with a door that opened to the aft deck. The Cookie Monster would hand a bale through the door to Wen and he packed the bales into the Master Head and Stateroom.

Then, the Cookie Monster would give a bale to a male crewmember who would walk it up to the door into the Main Salon. WaWa and Mom's would drag the bale forward to a male crewmember who was packing them in the front V-Berth. The Cookie Monster would alternate one bale in the back and one bale in the front. We continued that process until we'd given them about 6,000 pounds. That left us with about 14,000 pounds to split between the three sailboats so that meant that each sailboat would get a little less than 5,000 pounds each. That was good! Nobody would be loaded heavy so they should look good coming into Port Everglades.

I hugged Wen and WaWa, Mom's, and the other crewmembers as best I could. I told them I'd see them back at home, that they'd done a great job. Everyone beamed but I could see concern on their faces for my condition. The Cookie Monster had already said his goodbyes and climbed back on the S-L. I walked to the aft deck and began to climb over the handrail while wincing with pain. He grabbed my left arm and helped me onto his aft deck. We untied our lines and pulled slowly away to the rear of the Grand Banks.

I slowly climbed the ladder to the flybridge as Blue Eyes put the bow on a course of 278 degrees to Gun Cay. It was around midnight and we were doing good with time since we were the first boat to leave the freighter. My arm was starting to throb real bad every time my heart beat and pushed blood into my bicep.

Blue Eyes said: "Man, are you okay?"

I said: "No man, I ain't okay. This son-of-a-bitch is starting to hurt really bad."

He said: "We ain't got nothing for pain except some pot. Do you want me to roll you a joint?"

I said: "I've got some Excedrin in my shaving kit. I think I'll take two Excedrin and drink a beer. If it's still hurting, maybe I'll smoke some pot."

The Cookie Monster said: "Where's your shaving kit? I'll get it for you."

I said: "I don't know, where's my seabag?"

He said: "It's stowed up here, upfront under the dashboard. I'll get them for you." He opened the two doors to the dashboard, pulled out my seabag, found my shaving kit, and got me two Excedrin. He walked to the back of the flybridge and hollers down to the guys on the aft deck: "Hey, throw me up a beer." One of the guys goes into the big, Igloo cooler, gets a cold Budweiser, and throws it up to him. He gives it to me, I pop the Excedrin in my mouth, and wash it down with the beer. I basically chugged the beer so I could get the alcohol into me as quickly as possible. I went forward and sat on the bench seat in front of the console, put my head back, and closed my eyes. The pain was starting to ease-up just a little bit, something was working.

I said: "When you see my boats, wake me up if I'm not awake."

He said: "Okay man, go ahead and go to sleep, everything's under control."

I said: "Okay, I'm gonna shut my eyes and try to take a catnap but I don't know if I can sleep."

I must've fallen asleep because I felt the S-L hit a wave, the boat shook, and I woke up. My arm was starting to throb again and hurt worse.

I said: "I'm gonna call my boats and tell them we're on the way."

Blue Eyes said: "Go ahead. How's the arm?"

I said: "It's starting to throb and hurt bad again. I think I'll drink another beer and smoke that joint."

I grabbed the CB microphone and said: "Speedy Pete, Speedy Pete, Little Big Man, you got your ears on good buddy, kickit back."

In about ten seconds, I heard: "Little Big Man, Speedy Pete, we copy, kickit back."

I said. "Are all my friends with you? Kickit back"

He said: "That's a big 10-4! We're all sitting right here together waiting on you to party. Kickit back."

I said: "Alright, that's great I'll see you in a short-short, maybe 45 minutes. Kickit back."

He said: "Alright, we'll be here waiting on ya. Speedy Pete standing by."

Blue Eyes said: "That's great that they're all there together. Here's another beer and a sandwich. The guys downstairs have rolled some joints and it's pretty good stuff. When you get through with your sandwich, we'll smoke this joint."

I said: "Man, I hate to get screwed up before we load my boats."

He said: "Don't worry about it. If your boats are there, I'll find them and get them loaded. We got it under control, you just relax."

I ate my sandwich and drank the beer and the pain subsided some but it was still hurting like a motherfucker.

Blue Eyes said: "You ready for that joint now?"

I said: "Sure, fire that mother up!"

He has the joint behind his right ear so he pulls it out, lights it up, takes a few deep tokes and hands it to me. I take a few tokes, hold my breath, and pretty soon, I've got a good buzz going. Lo and behold, the pain has subsided enough to where it's tolerable. How about that shit? Marijuana for medicinal purposes! It sure as hell worked because the pain had subsided somewhat. I handed the joint back to Blue Eyes and told him that I'd had enough, he takes a couple more tokes and then throws it overboard. For some reason, I had the Little Feat song "Willin" going around in my head, it seemed to be appropriate for these circumstances. Lowell George was singing: "I been kicked by the rain, robbed by the sleet, had my head stove in but I'm still on my feet, and I'm still, Willin'. And if you give me weed, whites and wine, and you show me a sign, I'll be Willin', to be movin'." I didn't have weed, whites and wine but I did have weed, Excedrin and beer, and it worked just fine! I didn't have my head stove in but I did have my arm mashed up but I'm still Willin'! Yep, I know how Lowell George was feeling when he wrote that song.

The Cookie Monster is staring at the radar screen and he sees three boats together about ten miles east of Gun Cay.

He said: "I got three boats right together. You reckon they're yours?"

I said: "Yeah man, that's got to be my boats, they gotta be mine."

Two of the boats are side-by-side and the third boat is behind the two in a triangle formation. We're about 10 miles away from them or about 30 minutes running time. I grab the CB microphone.

I said: "Speedy Pete, Speedy Pete, Little Big Man, you copy good buddy, kickit back."

He said: "Little Big Man, Speedy Pete, we copy, kickit back."

I said: "You got your porch light on?"

He said: "That's a negative. You want me to turn it on?"

I said: "Roger that. We're coming atcha and we'll be there in a short-short, maybe 30 minutes. You all ready to party?"

He said: "That's a roger, we're ready to get the party going."

Just then a light goes on in front of us. I said: "Okay Speedy Pete, we gotcha, see you soon. Little Big Man standing by."

He said: "Speedy Pete standing by."

I said to Blue Eyes: "I want to load Speedy Pete first because he's the slowest of the three boats. Once he's loaded, he'll hit the road for Gun Cay and the other two boats can catch up."

All the crewmembers are on the flybridge now, some are sitting on the benchseat and some are standing.

One of the guys said: "Are all these boats yours?"

I said: "Yeah man, all three of these are mine, these are the ones we're gonna load."

He said: "Shoot man, we'll get rid of all our stuff with these three guys, won't we?"

Blue Eyes said: "Yeah man, this is it."

He said: "Man, this is unbelievable, let's go get it done."

All the guys got real excited. They went down the ladder to the aft deck and started getting the lines and the bumpers ready to load my sailboats. Speedy Pete is the boat that is behind the front two. Blue Eyes has slowed the S-L down to a dead idle and we are coming up to Speedy Pete from behind and to the port, left side. Blue Eyes come in at about a 15 degree angle and a crewmember throws a line to someone on the bow of Speedy Pete. Blue Eyes then puts the right throttle in forward and the left throttle back in reverse and the aft deck swings right until the S-L is parallel with Speedy Pete. Somebody throws them a line, they pull the boats together, and tie off the lines to a cleat. Blue Eyes shuts down the engines and there is silence!

He said: "Don't you worry about it, we've got it covered. We don't need your help. You just sit up here and take it easy."

I said: "I feel kinda bad that I can't help."

He said: "Why don't you come sit in the Captain's chair and count the bales as they go on your boat. You can be the counter."

I sat in the Co-Captain's chair, turned around facing to the rear overlooking the aft deck, put my feet on the railing, and watched as the crew loaded Speedy Pete. They loaded her with about 110 bales, about 4,700 pounds. When we were done with her, we went and loaded the other two boats, bam, bam, and we were done by 4:30 in the morning. We were lucky because by the time we got to my sailboats, the storm that we loaded in at Russell Beacon had blown through and it was calm. I had told all my Captains that we would cruise back to Gun Cay, drop the hook, and wait for them to come through the Cut just to make sure that nobody had any problems. Blue Eyes wanted to be anchored back at Gun Cay when the sun came up in case the heat was flying the Bimini-Gun Cay area looking for smugglers. A serious Sportfisherman like the Sharon-Lynn should be near the deep water where the big game fish were hunting to eat. If a Sportfisherman were on the Bank, they better be moving like they were going or coming from somewhere. It wouldn't look right if they were way out on the Bank and they were anchored. Blue Eyes had the S-L at cruising speed headed for Gun.

The Cookie Monster and the rest of the crew have started to clean up the mess of hauling 20,000 pounds of pot. The first thing they did was pull the drop cloths off the walls and the floors and stuff them in garbage bags. Then someone starts vacuuming every square inch with a Sears Wet-n-Dry vacuum cleaner. Someone else is washing all the woodwork with Pine Sol and another person is coming behind him with Lemon Pledge. The Cookie Monster is in the galley butt naked cooking bacon and eggs with a joint hanging out of his mouth. What a sight this was, it was hilarious! Everybody is working like a bunch of worker bees in a hive. I can smell coffee brewing and music is playing over the sound system. Like Blue Eyes said: when it's time to work, they're serious as a heart attack. I ask the Cookie Monster what I can do?

He said: "Man, you just relax. This is about the easiest night we've ever had."

I said: "No kidding, how come?"

He said: "Man, because your boats were all together where they were supposed to be. It's really nice working with somebody that's got their shit together. Usually, we've got to drive all over the Bank looking for the scam boats. They get lost and don't know where they're going and a lot of times, they don't even know where they are. They're lost and we've got to find them. We're lucky if we get everybody loaded by the time the sun comes up. Man, we were finished by 4:30. We ain't never had it this easy. Just because you've got you shit together and your people are so good, it makes it easier on us. So, don't worry about it, especially since you're hurt. We'll take care of the cleaning up."

I said: "Okay man, I just wanta do my part."

He said: "Don't worry about it, you did your part."

I said: "Okay man, thanks."

I sat down on a chair in the main salon and put my head back, closed my eyes, and tried to take a catnap but sleep won't come. There's too much going on around me and besides, there's loud music coming out of the sound system.

The Cookie Monster said: "Hey Scooter, we've got the Master Head and the Master Stateroom cleaned up. Why don't you go take a hot shower and put your clean clothes on, it'll make you feel better. By the time you're done, we'll have this thing completely cleaned up and breakfast will be ready. Then, you can eat some bacon and eggs."

I said: "Man, that sounds great!"

I've taken off my dirty clothes that are covered in pot and burlap residue and left them on top of my seabag on the aft deck. I'm walking around in my underwear and I go in the Master Stateroom and get in the shower in the Master Head. The hot water feels great and I let it hit my right bicep to see if that will help ease the pain. The weed, whites and wine have helped the pain but the hot water helps too. I do the best I can with the soap considering I've got to do everything with my left hand. If I try to raise my arm away from my body, the pain shoots up my arm into my shoulder joint. I decide I've got to keep my arm pressed against my body. Somehow, I manage to shower one-handed, get clean, and then dry off. I silently thank the Lord for two arms and two hands even if one is hurt. I walk naked through the main salon out to the aft deck and get some clean clothes out of my seabag. I go into the main salon, sit down in a chair and try to put my clothes on with one arm. This is an adventure! I pull on a clean pair of underwear and that goes pretty well. Now, how do I get this t-shirt on? I take the t-shirt and put my right hand in the opening and then pull the shirt up over my right arm. Then, I pull the t-shirt over my head and put my head and left hand in the holes and pull it down to my waist, all with my left hand. Okay, that wasn't so bad. Now I get a pair of khaki boat shorts, put my feet in each side and pull the pants up over my hips. I can barely use my right hand enough to help me get the waist snapped together. Then, I zip up the zipper with my left hand. Done! Wow, what an ordeal.

The smell of the coffee and bacon makes me realize I'm hungry. The Cookie Monster has cooked three pounds of bacon and he has an electric frying pan full of scrambled eggs. I put two pieces of bread in the toaster as the Cookie Monster hands me a paper plate of bacon and eggs. I get a big mug of coffee, grab my toast, and sit in a chair in the main salon. I'm wondering if I can eat lefthanded? I start with the bacon because that's easy, just put it in your mouth. I grab the fork with my left hand and stab a glob of scrambled eggs. That works! I put the scrambled eggs in my mouth. Oh boy, this is gonna work! I take a sip of coffee and boy, is it good. While I'm eating the scrambled eggs, I remember hearing Paul McCartney tell the story of how he wrote his hit song "Yesterday". He said he was eating scrambled eggs for breakfast one morning and he came up with this little ditty: "Scrambled eggs, all I want to eat is scrambled eggs, but all we've got to eat is big pancakes, oh all I want is scrambled eggs." So while I'm eating, I'm singing in my head: "Scrambled eggs, all I want to eat is scrambled eggs." True story. It's funny what your mind remembers sometimes. I wolf down my breakfast, drink my coffee, and that's about the time my tired hit me. I threw away the plate and put my fork and mug in the sink. I sit back down in the chair, close my eyes and crash.

It isn't long before we're coming up on Gun Cay. I felt the S-L slow down to a dead idle and figured that Blue Eyes was getting ready to anchor. I woke up and walked out on the aft deck to the starboard side, looked forward, and could see Gun Cay about thirty yards away. Blue Eyes puts the boat in neutral, its' headway stops, and I hear a SPLASH as the Danforth anchor falls into the water. It's almost 6 o'clock in the morning and it's starting to get light. I look behind me out over the Bank and I can see about fifteen boats, sail and power, spread out all over the Bank. It looks like Grand Central Station! It looks to me like it would be obvious that a pot smuggling trip was happening if the heat were to fly over. I climb up the ladder to the flybridge and one of the crew is hosing down the flybridge washing off the pot and burlap residue which is everywhere.

I ask Blue Eyes: "Is everything okay, any problems?"

He said: "Yeah man, everything's going good. We're gonna hang out here for about an hour or so. Your boats ought to be coming through here pretty soon. Soon as they come through, we'll get on the road and head for home. It'll give us a chance to eat and get the boat cleaned up."

I said: "Okay, that sounds good to me!"

Blue Eyes goes down the ladder and disappears into the Main Salon to get some breakfast. I sit in the Co-Captains chair facing the Bank, put my feet on the railing, and put my head back to catch a catnap. I can't sleep because there's too much talking on Channel 5 on the CB radio. It isn't long before I see a powerboat coming our way so I grab the binoculars for a look. Damn if it ain't Padre! He's passed my three sailboats and is gonna beat them to the Cut.

I grabbed the CB microphone and said: "Padre, Padre, Little Big Man, you got your ears on good buddy, kickit back."

He said: "Roger that, kickit back."

I said: "Howya doin', is everything okay?"

He said: "We're fine as wine, man, we're doing good. Howya doin?"

I said: "I'm doing okay, just okay. You be safe goin' home."

He said: "Is that you parked over there by the stoplight?"

I said: "Roger that." We were the only Sportfisherman anchored at Gun. I said: "I'll see you back at the house. You take care 'cause we care. This is the Little Big Man standing by."

He said: "Padre standing by."

He goes on through the Cut and disappears behind the east side of Gun Cay. I look west and can see a bunch of sailboat masts and a few powerboats. In a little less than an hour, I see two sailboats running together so I grab the binoculars and take a look. It's Gearjammer and HomeBoy. I don't see Speedy Pete so I hope he's not having any trouble.

I grabbed the CB microphone and said:" Gearjammer, Little Big Man, you got your ears on good buddy, kickit back."

He said: "Roger that, kickit back."

I said: "HomeBoy, you copy?"

He said: "That's a roger, kickit back."

I said: "You guys look like you're doing alright. How 'bout Speedy Pete, is he doin' okay?"

Gearjammer said: "He's doin' fine, he's just back a little ways. He'll be coming along soon, kickit back."

I said: "Speedy Pete, you got a copy, kickit back."

He said: "Roger that, Little Big Man. We're coming as hard as we can, we're just a little slow this morning, kickit back."

I said: "Okay, you guys be safe goin' home. I'll see you back at the ranch. You take care 'cause we care. This is the Little Big Man standing by." That let them know I was watching out for them as best I could.

I went down the ladder to the aft deck and into the Main Salon. Blue Eyes and the rest of the crew were sitting around the Main Salon and the Cookie Monster was rolling joints.

I said: "Okay, all my boats have come through and everything's alright. We can hit the highway and take it back to the house whenever you're ready."

Blue Eyes said: "Okay, let's pull the hook and get on the road."

One of the crew goes out the door of the Main Salon to pull the anchor up and Blue Eyes goes up on the flybridge, starts the engines, and eases the boat forward to get some slack in the anchor line so it'll come up easy. As soon as the anchor is up and secured on the bow pulpit, Blue Eyes points the bow at the Concrete Ship and we cruise at dead idle to just south of the Ship. Blue Eyes takes the S-L between some coral heads going due west and then turns the bow north to the right and we idle right along the drop off where the water turns to a deep blue color. One of the crew puts two lines in the water from the big Penn International Reels and secures the poles in the rodholders on the fighting chair. We troll north right along the dropoff until we get to the northern tip of Bimini but get no bites.

Blue Eyes hollers down to the crewman on the aft deck: "Pull the lines in, let's go home." The crewman pulls the lines in and puts the rods and reels away in the main salon in the overhead rodholders. Blue Eyes puts the bow on 300 degrees for Ft. Lauderdale, pushes the throttles forward, and it's not long before we get up to cruising speed of 21 knots. We're boogeying! We blasted across the Gulfstream passing about a half a dozen scam boats from the trip and got just offshore of Florida about eleven o'clock in the morning. It's a little early to go in the Port because the half-day charters don't come in until noon. Blue Eyes stamps his foot on the deck and one of the crew comes out on the aft deck.

Blue Eyes hollers to him: "LET'S FISH!"

The crewman goes into the Main Salon and comes out with the two rods again. He puts the lines in the water and Blue Eyes keeps the S-L heading north just off the dropoff in the deep blue water. I can see about six other Sporfishermen that are trolling north and south along the dropoff. We troll north until we get to the Pier on the end of Commercial Boulevard which is easily recognizable from the water. Blue Eyes does a 180 degree turnaround and we troll south along the dropoff. By the time we get to the Yankee Clipper Hotel, it is right at noon and the charter boats are starting to go into the Cut at Port Everglades. We pull the lines in and the S-L falls in line with the other charter boats. We cruise at dead idle west into the Port, take a right, put our outriggers down, and cruise under the 17th Street Bridge while it is still closed. We cruise north up the Intracoastel Waterway to Bahia Mar Marina and into the slip that Blue Eyes rents for the S-L. The crew skillfully get the boat tied up properly with a bow, stern, and spring line and Blue Eyes shuts down the engines. Blue Eyes and I grab our seabags, walk to his car in the parking lot, and he drives me home. I thought to myself: "Man, other than getting hurt, this is the best trip that I've had so far. I like working with Blue Eyes a whole lot better than working with Black Fin." I can't wait for payday, it's gonna be big, VERY BIG!!

Chapter 28
Gettin' Screwed without Gettin' Kissed
Paying way too much for surveillance.

Blue Eyes pulls out of Bahia Mar Marina, heads north on A1A to Commercial Boulevard, and then west to my house on 18th Terrace. Pat hears us drive up in the circular driveway and meets me at the front door holding Sunshine.

She gave me a big wet kiss and said: "How'd it go with Brad?"

I said: "Other than getting hurt, it went great."

I gave her a detailed account of how I hurt my arm loading Wen and WaWa on the Grand Banks. As she listened, she had a look of horror on her face. I showed her the bruise on the inside of my right bicep and of how I couldn't raise my arm any higher than half-way without it hurting like a son-of-a-bitch.

She said: "Dammit Howard, the whole time you were gone, I had a funny feeling that something was wrong. I was worried to death and couldn't shake it!"

I said: "I'm gonna be okay, it's just gonna take a couple of days for me to get my arm back to normal. Brad gave us a full load on all four of my boats. We're gonna have the biggest payday yet. That helps to ease the pain. Listen, I'm gonna get in the Oldsmobile and drive down the beach and listen to Rita call in the scam boats. As soon as all my boats are in, I'll come home."

I left my house, went east on Commercial Boulevard to A1A, turned right, and drove south down the beach road. I had the in-dash CB radio on Channel 5 and I could hear Lovely Rita calling in the scam boats. She was giving them a "Big 10-10, it's clean and green" as the powerboats came in ahead of the sailboats. I drove past Las Olas Boulevard and then the Yankee Clipper, went west on 17th Street Causeway to Pier 66, and did a u-turn in the parking lot 'cause I didn't want to cross the bridge and get caught if the bridge opened up. Around 2:00 P.M., I heard Wen on my Grand Banks call Rita and she told him it was "clean and green" and to bring it on home. There seemed to be no heat anywhere. Pegasus was flying and he'd told Rita that he didn't see any Candy Stripers in the ocean. With the whole fleet of 50 boats coming in this afternoon, it was great that there was no Heat anywhere, not in the Port, the River, or in the Ocean.

As I passed the Yankee Clipper Hotel going north on A1A, I found a parking spot across from Bahia Mar so I parked, cut off the engine, got out of my car, and sat in the sun on the hood of the car. Around 3:00 P.M., Gearjammer was close to the Port and the Little Lady called him home. It wasn't long before HomeBoy checked in and she brought him in. Around 5:00 P.M., Speedy Pete was given a "big 10-10" and I breathed a sigh of relief. Everybody was in the Port, in the River, or at the house.

I backed out of my parking space, made a u-turn on A1A and went south, and then west on 17th Street. I drove north on Cordova to 8th Street and went east to the park so I could see the back of Wen and WaWa's house on 7th Street. Audacious and the Grand Banks were behind the house so I drove over to Mom's house and Blue Mist was at the dock there. I drove west on Riverland Road to the Peacock House but Cathy 5 was not there so she must still be in the River coming west.

I got on the CB and said: "Speedy Pete, Little Big Man, you got your ears on good buddy, kickit back."

In a couple of seconds, he said: "Little Big Man, Speedy Pete, we copy, come back."

I said: "Howya doin'? What's your 20?

He said: "We're doin' fine. We're in the middle of town on the main road heading for the house, come back."

I said: "Roger that. I was just lookin' forya and was a little worried."

He said: "We're okay, just a little slow, come back."

I said: "Roger that. Okay, I'll talk to you later on. You take care 'cause I care, Little Big Man standing by."

That night, we unloaded Audacious at Wen and WaWa's house and Blue Mist at Mom's house. Cathy 5 was behind the Peacock House and we let her sit because I didn't have three crews to unload and I wasn't ready to unload at the Peacock House yet. The next morning, we delivered the pot from the two boats to Fu at the IHOP on State Road 84 and I told him we had two more boats to unload that night. The next night, we unloaded the Grand Banks at Wen and WaWa's house and we flip-flopped Blue Mist and Cathy 5 and unloaded Cathy at Mom's house. We delivered the vans to Fu at the IHOP and I was done! What a relief! This is the first time I'd ever had four boats and it's the most pot I'd ever hauled. It was gonna be a big payday! Thank you Blue Eyes!

After we delivered the last van to Fu, I went home and started working on my figures. I got a yellow, legal pad and did a summary for each boat. Then, I took another sheet of paper and did a summary for the four boats. I got a gross total of 19,000 pounds and 450 bales. I multiplied 450 times 3 pounds sack weight and got 1350 pounds sack weight. I subtracted 1350 pounds sack weight from 19,000 pounds and got 17,650 pounds of pot that I'd hauled. I multiplied 17,650 times 20% and got 3,530. I multiplied 3,530 times $220 per pound and got a gross of $776,600! That was awesome! Jerry had been getting 20% from Joe and was paying me 18% so he was screwing me out of 2%. Blue Eyes didn't take the 2% so I got 20% because Blue Eyes loaded me and I unloaded all my boats at my houses. I didn't rent any of Jerry's houses so I saved 3% for that.

The next morning, I went to Jerry's house and gave him copies of each of my four boats' summary and the summary sheet for the four boats. He had a funny look on his face when he saw that I hauled 17,650 pounds. I could tell he was jealous and green with envy. In three or four days, Jerry called and said "Come on over, I've got green stamps." I went over to his house, Blue Eyes was there, and the three of us sat down at his kitchen table. We went over each one of my boats, boat by boat, and then went over the summary sheet. The numbers for my boats agreed with Fu's numbers perfectly. We multiplied by 20% and multiplied that by $220 per pound and came up with $776,600 that I was owed.

He said: "Now, you've got to pay for surveillance."

I said: "Okay, how much?"

He said: "I paid Rita $20,000. I paid the inside channel boat $15,000, and I paid the airplane $7,500 so that's $42,500. Since you had four boats, you've got to pay all of it."

I said: "You mean nobody is paying for surveillance but me?"

He said: "Nobody used the surveillance but you."

I said: "What about your boats?"

He said: "They didn't use the surveillance."

I said: "Smith, that is bullshit! I sat on the beach by the Yankee Clipper in my car and listened on my car CB radio to Rita call them in. She called your two boats in because I heard her with my own ears. In fact she called in every fuckin' boat in the whole fleet. Why isn't everybody paying their share of the $42,500? Why am I the only one paying for the surveillance?"

He said: "Don't be an ass, Scooter. You just made over three-quarters of a million dollars and you're bitching about $42,000?"

I said: "I'm not being an ass, Jerry, I'm being a good businessman. You're the one being an ass by fuckin' me out of $42,500."

He looked at me and didn't say anything. Then he took his calculator and deducted $42,500 from $776,600 and got $734,100.

He said: "This is what I owe you" and turned the calculator so I could see it.

I said: "Okay motherfucker, get me a box."

He said in a shitty voice heavy with jealousy: "You know, you made more money than I did this trip."

I said: "Well you know, all you did was run a middle boat with two scam boats. I had four scam boats. Maybe you need to get you some more scam boats. I've been busting my ass to get to this point so that I could be your only scammer and uphold the commitment I made to you. And all you've done is fuck me at every opportunity. You haven't upheld the commitment you made to me. What's up with that, Smith?"

He didn't say anything but pulled the box of money over close to him and started counting bricks and putting them on the table. When he finished counting, I counted behind him and got the same thing: $734,100.

I said: "You'd better get me a big box."

He went in the downstairs bedroom and came back with a big case box for toilet paper. I put all my bricks in the box and had very little room left over. Through this whole process, Blue Eyes just sat there and didn't say anything.

I stuck my hand out and said to Blue Eyes: "I enjoyed working with you, man. I hope we can do it again real soon." We shook hands warmly and I ignored Jerry. "You wanta help me carry my box out to my car?"

Blue Eyes said: "Sure man" and we both picked up my box full of money and walked it out to my little red Honda. We put it through the hatch in the back and I drove home like a little ole' lady without saying goodbye to Jerry. He knew I was pissed!

I got home and parked by the front door, went in the house and hollered to Pat: "Honey come here, I need your help." She came into the living room and I walked out the front door to the back of the Honda. We took the box out of the car, walked it clumsily into the master bedroom, and dropped it on the floor in the middle of the room.

I said: "Come here and take a look at this!"

She looked in the box and said: "Holy shit, is that all ours?"

I said: "No, I've still got to pay my people but over half of it is ours."

She said: "How much is it?"

I said: "SEVEN HUNDRED THIRTY FOUR THOUSAND, ONE HUNDRED DOLLARS!!" She was speechless and incredulous!

I rode up to my "office" at the bank of payphones and called all of my people that were local and told them to stay home because I had green stamps. Everyone sounded very pleased! I went back to the house and figured that my total crew expenses was $257,500. That meant that my net for the trip was $476,600!! If Jerry hadn't fucked me out of $42,500 for surveillance, I would have netted over a half-a-million dollars. Now that was awesome! I got a whiskey box and put the bricks for my crews in the box. I dragged the toilet paper box into my walk-in closet and left to pay my people. I put a big smile on their face and of course, I had a shit-eating-grin on my face from ear-to-ear because I made almost a half of a million dollars! Working with Blue Eyes and getting four full loads was good! I liked it, I liked it a lot!

Chapter 29
Sailin' Home a Load
The thing about a sailboat, if your motor quits, you can sail the boat home.

By now, it's getting into the end of August 1979 and we've worked trips all summer long. We didn't quit at the end of June, beginning of July, like we did in 1978. Julio must be cleaning out the warehouses in Colombia and sending the pot up to Joe 'cause we've damn sure been working. I've made another trip to Nassau with David Bone in his Mooney, made a big deposit at the Royal Bank of Canada, and wire-transferred the money to Grand Cayman. We're coming up on Labor Day, the first Monday in September, and Jerry calls: it's time to go fishin' again! This is supposed to be the last trip of this smuggling season. Jerry is going to load my boats this trip instead of Blue Eyes and that makes me feel apprehensive, a premonition that I'm gonna get shorted. Jerry says that he's got a full crew on his Hatteras and doesn't need me to go with him on the load boat. I told him that I'd cross over to Gun Cay on one of my sailboats and after he loaded me, I'd ride home with him. I had bought me a 25 foot Mako center console boat with the intention of having my own surveillance next year to keep Jerry from screwing me out of surveillance fees. I wanted to come home and cruise the Port and the Cut to watch over my people myself. I was gonna pay Jerry the surveillance fees one more time but this was gonna be the last time! Next year, I was gonna have my own channel boats.

I was on Cathy 5 with Rob, Ross was running Blue Mist, and Mick and Dan were on Audacious. Blue Mist had actually been running pretty well and it looked like we <u>finally</u> had the black algae problem solved, maybe!?!? The Perkins 4.154 diesel engine shut down once or twice from sucking air but my Captains were able to bleed the injectors, clear the air, and get the thing running. We were leaving in the morning, crossing the Gulfstream, and getting loaded that night. That seemed to be working pretty well since all the boats were running good.

Before we spotted Gun Cay Light, we saw a bunch of lights that we thought were the houses on Bimini. Since we'd gone south to Government Cut in Miami and turned left, I couldn't understand how we'd gotten blown so far north. We put the lights at about 11 o'clock off our bow and figured that we were heading directly for Gun. It wasn't long before we spotted Gun Cay Light and it was right in the middle of all the lights! That meant that the lights weren't the houses on Bimini, they were boats at Gun Cay for the Labor Day weekend! There must have been at least a hundred boats on both sides of Gun, the most I'd ever seen. Cathy 5 is about 10 miles from the intersection with Blue Mist back about 5 miles.

The radio crackles and it's Ross: "Little Big Man, Little Big Man, Homeboy. You gotta copy on me good buddy, kickit back."

I said: "Homeboy, Little Big Man, I copy good buddy, kickit back."

He said: "I'm shut down and pulled over on the side of the road, kickit back."

I said: "Roger that. Have you tried Freon in the breather, kickit back."

He said: "Roger that, it won't kick off and run, kickit back."

I said: "Have you tried bleeding the injectors, kickit back."

He said: "That's a roger, I'm not sure I'm doing it right, but I did it and it still wouldn't kick off and run, kickit back."

I said: "Roger that. Okay, I'm gonna turn around and come to you and see if I can get it going. Get your spotlight and give me a wink. Count to three and tell me when you're gonna do it, kickit back."

He said: "One, two, three, now!"

I looked behind me away from Gun Cay light and I saw his spotlight light up the night sky behind Cathy 5.

I said: "Okay Homeboy, I gotcha'. As soon as I can do a u-turn, I'll be heading your way and I should be there in a short-short. Put your bumpers on one side and we'll raft off when I get there, Little Big Man standing by."

Homeboy was on a heading of almost due east and in about an hour, we dropped our sails, and rafted off to his starboard side. I climbed on Blue Mist, got a can of Freon, and sprayed it in the breather. The damn thing turned over but wouldn't kick off and run. *Son-of-a-bitch* I thought. I grabbed an adjustable wrench and started going through the procedure to bleed the injectors. Sure enough, air bubbles came out of one of the injectors and I thought *Aha! There's the problem.* I purged all of the air bubbles and felt sure that the damn thing would run now. I sprayed Freon in the breather, Ross turned it over, it caught and ran about twenty seconds and shut down again! I said: "Son-of-a-bitch, motherfuckin' shit!" I went through the procedure to bleed the injectors again and found air bubbles again. I purged all the air bubbles, got the Freon, and sprayed it in the breather. Ross turned it over, it fired off, ran about thirty seconds this time, and quit again! I said: "Motherfuckin' shit! Why won't this motherfucker run?"

By now, it's around 10 o'clock at night and I'm thinking that I don't want to miss getting loaded with two boats. I told the crew of Homeboy to get on Cathy 5 and go to the fishin' hole. Jay and I were going to sail Blue Mist as far as we could and hope we could somehow get loaded in the Gulfstream around Gun Cay. I told Ross to tell Jerry what was going on when he got loaded and to tell Jerry to load me in the area of Gun Cay. We'd sail the boat as far as we could. That was one good thing about sailboats, if the motor wouldn't run, you could sail 'em! We untied Cathy 5 and Ross headed for Gun Cay light. The mainsail was up on Blue Mist, Jay turned her into the wind, and I put up the jib. Jay turned her off the wind on a starboard tack and we were zipping along about 6 ½ knots, that was pretty good without the motor! I bled the injectors again, got air bubbles again, and felt sure I'd solved the problem. Jay turned over the motor, it fired off, ran about thirty seconds, and quit again! I was starting to feel a little quesy from breathing diesel fumes and from being hot in the main salon so I went upstairs into the cockpit to cool off.

I said: "Son-of-a-bitch, man, it's gonna be one of those trips. It seems like every trip, something happens. We hardly ever have a trip where everything goes right."

Jay said: "We're making good time in this wind. We wouldn't be going any faster with the motor. We oughta' be at Gun around one o'clock, maybe. Jerry can load us at one or two miles east of Gun and we should be okay."

I said: "You're probably right. That'll be the plan, Stan!"

Jay has the bow aimed right at all the lights on the boats at Gun Cay with the bow directly on Gun Cay light. There must be at least a hundred boats at Gun Cay on both sides of the island. As we come up on Gun, we can hear the load boats talking to the scam boats on channel 5 on the CB radio.

It's about one o'clock in the morning and I hear Black Fin call one of my scam boats and pull up to load him. It's Audacious at ten east of the light.

I grabbed the CB microphone and said: "Black Fin, Little Big Man, you copy, kickit back."

He said: "Roger that, I gotcha' Little Big Man, kickit back."

I said: "I'm about three blocks east of the intersection. Can you come see me here when you're done doing what you're doing?"

He said: "I'll be all out when I finish with your buddy here. Blue Eyes will come over to you, kickit back."

I said: "Okay, what's his twenty? Kickit back."

He said: "He's about ten out from me seeing another friend of his, kickit back."

I said: "Can I talk to him or is he too far out? Kickit back."

Blue Eyes said: "Little Big Man, I copy the last transmissions. What's your twenty? Kickit back."

I said: "I'm about three blocks on the other side of the intersection from you. When you come through the intersection, give me a shout and I'll blink my headlights at you. I'll be easy to see, kickit back."

He said: "That's a big 10-4. We should be there in about an hour, kickit back."

I said: "Roger that, we're coming, we're just coming slow, Little Big Man standing by."

In about an hour, Blue Eyes is coming through the Cut and he calls me: "Little Big Man, Blue Eyes, you copy, kickit back."

I said: "Roger that Blue Eyes, I copy, kickit back."

He said: "Give me a wink."

I grab my spotlight, point it right at Gun Cay light, turn it on, and wave it around about fifteen degrees.

He said: "I gotcha Little Big Man. We'll be right over."

In about five minutes, he pulls up to my port side, throws us some lines, and we get tied up.

I said: "Howya doin' tonight?"

He said: "Okay, only okay, could be better. We're doin' better now."

I said: "Who you loading tonight?"

He said: "I'm loading some other boats. One boat didn't show up, that's why I've got pot left over. I wish I were loading your boats."

I said: "Who's Jerry loading?"

He said: "He loaded two of his boats and then your three boats."

I said: "So, what does that mean?"

He said: "Your boats ain't gettin' full loads, you're gettin' shorted."

I said: "So, how much you got for me?"

He said: "Lucky for you, one of my boats didn't show up so we've got 80 bales for you."

I said: "That's fine with me, I'll take 80 bales."

The Cookie Monster got on Blue Mist and worked the cockpit. Jay loaded the rear, Master Stateroom and I loaded the v-berth upfront. We got the job done in about 45 minutes and were finished around 4:00 A.M.

Blue Eyes said: "So, what are you gonna do?"

I said: "Me and Jay are gonna sail this sucker home."

He said: "No shit? How you gonna get in the Port?"

I said: "When we get to the mouth of the Port, the channel boat will have to tow us to the dock. You make sure you tell the channel boat that I'm gonna need a tow when you go by them."

He said: "Okay, we'll tell them when we're going in. We'll see you at home." With that, we untied the boats and Blue Eyes pulled away at a dead idle going north towards Bimini.

Jay was at the helm and I told him to steer about 270 to 280 degrees instead of 300 degrees. That way we should come in south of Ft. Lauderdale and that should compensate for the Gulfstream pushing us north. I slept for an hour in the cockpit 'cause I was exhausted and then I took the wheel and Jay slept. The sun came up behind us out of the east and it was a beautiful day with good wind out of the southwest. We got on a port tack and stayed there all the way to the Florida coast. Around 3:00 P.M., we were about 10 miles offshore around Hollywood and we were going dead downwind. We tried to go wing and wing with the sails but the jib kept flip-flopping so we got back on our port tack and let the sails out about halfway.

About 4:30 P.M., Pegasus flies over us, waggles his wings, and said: "Little Big Man, you got your ears on good buddy, kickit back."

I said: "Roger that, Pegasus. Howya doin?"

He said: "Somebody wants to shout atcha" and Jerry got on the radio.

He said: "Little Big Man, Black Fin, howya doin'?"

I said: "We're doin' good it's just slow going downwind like this."

He said: "Roger that! Listen, my brother's out there waiting for you and he's gonna hang around until you get there and he'll give you a tow."

I said: "That's great! Tell him it'll be two and a half to three hours maybe."

He said: "Okay, we'll give him the word. We were really worried about you since we hadn't heard anything from you so I wanted to come and find you."

I said: "I appreciate you looking out for me good buddy."

He said: "Okay, we'll see you at home. Give me a call when you get to the house."

I said: "Roger that good buddy and thanks again!"

By 7:30 P.M., the sun is going down and we're around Dania Pier. I call Steve and he asks me my location, my 20. I tell him just off Dania Pier and he says that he's coming to get me. In about ten minutes, he shows up, throws us a line, we drop the sails, and he tows us into the Port. As soon as the bridge opens, we go through the Port, up the river, and all the way to Mom's house. As soon as we got the boat tied up, we locked the doors and the hatch, took our seabags, got in my car, and left. I took Jay to Riverland Shopping Center and he went in the Floridian Restaurant and called Rose to pick him up. I drove up U.S. 1 to Commercial Boulevard then to 18th Avenue to home. I called Jerry as soon as I got home and told him that I was unloading two boats at two houses that night and then doing the same thing the next night. He said for me to call him in the morning when the vans were all ready to go. I hung up with him, grabbed a bite to eat that Pat had fixed me, and then called my crewmembers and arranged for my crews to unload the boats. My people are all good and experienced so I don't have to unload the boats any more with them. Once my unload crews were set with lookouts at both houses, I took a shower, got in bed, and crashed.

About 4:30 A.M., the phone rang and woke me up, it was my crew at Mom's house. They had all the pot in the house. I sat on the couch in the bedroom and waited about five minutes to hear from the crew at Wen and WaWa's house. Finally, I called them and when they answered, I asked them how they were doing. They said they had about ten more bales to go and they'd be done. I told them to call me when they were done. In about ten minutes, the phone rang and it was Mick; all the bales were in the house. I told him to call me when the van was packed and ready to go. I climbed in bed and went back to sleep.

About 7:30 A.M., the phone rang and it was Rob at Mom's house.

He said: "Okay man, we got everything weighed and the list made and everything's cool. The van's loaded and ready to go."

I said: "How much did you haul?"

He said: "We got 90 bales and 3,500 pounds, that's all Jerry gave us."

I said: "He shorted us bad, didn't he? I knew it was gonna happen. Oh well, there's nothing we can do about it now. You sit tight and I'll call you right back and we'll see if we can get the van delivered soon."

He said: "We asked Jerry for more but he said he didn't have enough for everybody and he was gonna split it up evenly between all the boats to be fair to everybody."

I said: "Yeah, right!"

In about fifteen minutes, the phone rings and it's Mick at Wen and WaWa's house.

He said: "Okay, we're all done and got the van loaded. We're ready to go."

I said: "Good, how much did you haul?"

He said: "Man, we only got 3,200 pounds, 85 bales. What's going on?"

I said: "Jerry just decided to screw us. There ain't nothing we can do about it now. You sit tight and I'll call you right back and hopefully we can get these vans delivered and be done 'till tonight."

I called Jerry and told him that we were ready to go with two vans at my two houses. Jerry called Fu and called me right back and told me to bring the vans to the Huddle House on U.S. 1. I called both houses and told my guys to bring the vans to the Huddle House on U.S. 1. I left my house and drove south on U.S. 1 to the Huddle House. I found Fu and his guys sitting at a big table eating breakfast. In about five minutes, Mick comes in from Wen and WaWa's house and shortly, Rob comes in from Mom's house. They give Fu the keys to their vans and Fu gives them keys to empty vans. Mick and Rob leave and go back to pack up what's leftover. In about thirty minutes, Mick comes back with the second van and it isn't long before Rob comes back with his van. Fu and his guys leave, we order breakfast, and I give Rob and Mick instructions about unloading the Grand Banks at Wen and WaWa's and Cathy 5 at Mom's.

When we finished our breakfast, I drove them back to the houses and everyone went home to get some rest. That night, we unloaded the other two boats and delivered the vans to Fu. Everything went smoothly and it was a good trip except for getting shorted. When I got home, I took the lists from each boat, got my yellow legal pad, and did my summary for each boat and then a total for the four boats. We hauled right at 14,000 pounds with 335 bales so I netted out about 13,000 pounds net sack weight. That was a disappointment! By being shorted 6,000 pounds, it cost me a net of a quarter-of-a-million dollars because my crew expenses remained the same for the four boats. That wasn't small change!

I think that this was the straw that broke the camel's back in my relationship with Jerry. I was gonna have to talk to Joe and get his permission to buy my own middle boat and run my own organization. If he wouldn't let me buy my own middle boat, I was gonna tell him I only wanted to work with Brad. I was sick of being screwed by Jerry. Brad was a straight-up guy and Jerry wasn't. Enough was enough!!

The next morning, I took my figures and went to see Jerry. We sat down at his kitchen table and settled up. Fu was paying $210 a pound for this trip 'cause the pot wasn't quite as good as it had been. We multiplied 13,000 pounds times $210 per pound times 20% and got my gross to be $546,000. Jerry knew I was pissed off so he "only" charged me $25,000 for the surveillance and $5,000 for the tow. That gave me a net from Jerry of $516,000.

I said: "You know I was real disappointed that I didn't get a full load."

He said: "That's just the way it worked out."

I said: "How come it worked out that way?"

He said: "Joe made Brad load some other people and I had to load Tommy Dolan and another boat. I tried to split up the load evenly among everybody."

I said: "How do you figure you split it up evenly?"

He said: "Well, my boats hauled 10,000 pounds and your boats hauled 10,000 pounds, that's evenly."

I said: "Yeah but you loaded six boats, your two and my four. You didn't split it up evenly between the six boats. I figure I got shorted."

He said: "You oughta be glad you got 10,000." I thought that was a pretty shitty thing for him to say.

I said: "When do you think we're gonna get paid?"

He said: "It'll probably be three or four days, maybe a week. Do you need the money that bad?"

I said: "No, but I want to go back to the bank and get my financial affairs in order so I can take some time off and go see my Mom and Dad in Georgia. That was the last trip for awhile, wasn't it?"

He said: "Yeah, that was the last one for this season. We're gonna probably start back up around the middle of November, maybe Thanksgiving. We ought to be off for about two months."

I said: "That's good, I could use some rest."

There were bad vibes in the air and Jerry knew I wasn't happy about what had gone on. He tried to act like it was no big deal but it was a very big deal to me! I left his house without shaking hands with him so he'd have no doubt that I was pissed off. I drove home in silence listening to WSHE: "She's Only Rock-N-Roll" in hopes that some good music would cheer me up. After three days, I hadn't heard from Jerry so on the fourth day I called him and asked him about green stamps. He said he hadn't heard anything but that he'd call Joe and get back with me.

In about ten minutes, my phone rings and it's Joe's nephew, Chuddy.

He said: "I hear you want to get together?"

I said: "Yeah, I'm planning a trip to the bank and I'd like to get all that's owed me so I can go on vacation and not have that hanging over my head."

He said: "We were just about to leave town to go to my sister's high school graduation. Can you meet me right now?"

I said: "Sure, I can meet you right now. Where do you want to meet?"

He said: "You know that shopping center on the corner of Highway 441 and Broward Boulevard. I'll just be in the parking lot so look for me. I'll beat you there and I'll see you when you drive up."

I said: "Okay, fine. I'll be there in ten or fifteen minutes."

I get in my car and drive west out Broward Boulevard to Highway 441, pull in the parking lot, and see Chuddy standing at the back of his car. I pull up to him, he opens the trunk, picks up a whiskey box that is duct taped closed, and hands it to me. He points to a figure written in pen on the duct tape in the upper right hand corner of the box.

He said: "This ought to be what we owe you."

I said: "That looks like it's a little short."

He said: "If it's short, we'll make it up next time you get paid."

We shook hands, got in our cars, and went our separate ways. Damn, if I hadn't been shorted again! I was getting sick and fuckin' tired of getting shorted!

When I got home, I called my mechanic, Ron, and told him that Blue Mist was sucking air. I told him the story of the trip in detail and of how I had bled the injectors four times and she still sucked air. He couldn't believe that we sailed the load home with no motors! That afternoon, he went by Mom's house and went over the Perkins 4.154 engine with a fine-toothed comb. He found that one of the fittings that connected the fuel line to the top of the motor had cracked, probably because we had bled the injectors so much. He replaced the fitting, started the engine, and sat in the cockpit for thirty minutes while she ran like a top. Hopefully, no more black algae and no more air!

I wanted to put all four of my boats in the yard and do a bottom job on them. I told my Captains what yard to use and to make the arrangements themselves. When we started back up in November, I wanted every boat to be shipshape. There were a couple of things I needed to clean up around Ft. Lauderdale and I needed to make another trip to the Bank. As soon as that was done, Pat and I were going to go visit my parents in Georgia and I was gonna tell them that we'd been smuggling pot and that I was a millionaire. I hoped that their sense of unconditional love would override their displeasure that I was doing something that was illegal. I really needed a vacation to recharge my batteries.

Chapter 30
New York, the Soccer Bowl, & Grease
"Well, I know that you're in love with him, 'cause I saw you dancin' in the gym, you
both kicked off your shoes, and I dig those rhythm and blues" – Don McLean

My Captain, Mick, had a friend named Roman that was a pot dealer in the New
York/ New Jersey area. Mick approached me and asked if I would take part of my pay in
pot for the last trip and deal it to Roman. Fu was paying us $210 per pound and Roman
was willing to pay $270 per pound. He wanted 1000 pounds so that would be an
additional $60,000 that we would make and Mick and I would split the extra money,
$30,000 each. Since Jerry had shorted me, I was looking to make the extra money and it
was like Mick had worked another trip. So, I agreed to do the deal with Roman. He was
gonna get the pot from me and sell it in Florida to someone else from New York. We
were gonna get paid in New York so that was a bit of a problem but for an extra $30,000,
it was worth it. I was planning on buying a 53 foot Hatteras and figured that I needed
about $250,000 for that. I would get $270,000 from Roman, give Mick his share at
$30,000, and that would leave me with $240,000 from the transaction. That ought to just
about cover the purchase of the Hatteras.

I had way too much money in the house, so I called David Bone and asked him
to fly me to Nassau again. We left the next day right after lunch, flew to Nassau
International Airport, cleared Customs and Immigration with David (I gave him the $100
handshake), took a cab to the Bank, made the deposit, and wire-transferred the money to
Grand Cayman. There was no U.S. Customs agent this time and that made me breathe
easier. We departed Nassau, flew the slot between Joulters and Chub Cay, right over
Honeymoon Harbor, and into Ft. Lauderdale International Airport. I was getting to be an
old hand at this money laundering thing! My Certificate of Deposit at the Royal Bank of
Canada in Grand Cayman was now just over a million dollars!

By now, it was the middle of September 1979 and the Soccer Bowl was coming
up in New York City. Vancouver had beaten the Ft. Lauderdale Strikers in the semi-
finals and they were playing the New York Cosmos for the league championship at
Giants Stadium in the Meadowlands. My friend John Chesterfield from my Dolphins day
had gotten us tickets to the game and he and his wife Peggy flew in to Newark from
Tampa. I flew to Newark on Delta from Ft. Lauderdale, we arrived within twenty
minutes of each other, and we met at the baggage claim. I rented a car and drove us to
the Marriott Hotel close to the stadium. Mick and I had called Roman and told him to get
a room in the same Marriott Hotel and I would get the money from the deal from him at
the hotel. We checked in to the hotel mid-day, grabbed some lunch, and went to the
game that afternoon. The Cosmos beat Vancouver pretty decisively and we felt like the
Strikers could have played as well or better than Vancouver did. When the game was
over, we went back to the hotel and when I got in my room, I called the front desk and
asked for Roman's room. When he answered, I told him I was coming to his room to
settle up and he said "come on". When I got to his room, we called Mick on the phone
and Mick told me "that's Roman, it's okay". Roman pulled out a briefcase full of money,
I counted the bricks, and it appeared to be $270,000. Roman said he'd counted it twice
and it was right so I took his word for it. I put the money in my briefcase, went down to

the front desk, got a safe deposit box, and put the money in the box. I went back to my room, laid down on the bed, and took a nap 'cause we had a big night ahead of us.

John had gotten us tickets to the Broadway Musical "Grease" through the company that printed the tickets for the Tampa Bay Buccaneers. It just so happened that Brad was in New York City with his business partner from California along with both their wives and John had gotten tickets for all of us. I had called Brad after the soccer game and we'd agreed to meet at the theatre that night. I drove us into New York City to the Port Authority Bus Terminal, parked in the parking garage, and we took a cab to the theatre arriving about ten minutes before showtime. Brad, Sharon, and the other couple were standing on the sidewalk when we arrived and there were hugs and handshakes all around.

I asked Brad: "Have you got the tickets yet?"

He said: "Yeah, I just got them."

I asked: "Did you have to pay for them?"

He said: "No, they were free, the man said they were complimentary!"

I said: "Far out! That's great!"

He said: "Are you guys going to go with us to eat when this is over?"

I said: "Sure man, we don't have any other plans except to spend some time with you."

He said: "Listen, we need to have a real serious talk, just you and me, that'll probably take 30-45 minutes.

I said: "Okay, there's a 30 minute intermission in the middle of the show and we can talk then. If we don't get done at the intermission, we can just go off in a corner somewhere and talk until we're done talking."

He said: "Okay, that sounds good.

We went in the theatre, walked up to the usher in the center aisle, handed our tickets to him, and asked "Where are our seats?" He said: "They're down front, follow me" and he brought us to the sixth row, center section, front and center. We were only in our seats a couple of minutes when the lights went down and the play began. It was great! The music, dancing, costumes, the stage, and the set were just terrific! I was the only one in the group that'd seen a Broadway play before and my friends were mesmerized. Intermission came and Brad and I went upstairs to the Balcony Lobby, got a rum and Coke from the bar and found a seat on a sofa.

Brad said: "Are you happy working for Jerry?"

I said: "Well, yes and no. Mostly no I guess. I'm a millionaire because of Jerry but I'm sure tired of being shorted and I'm tired of him screwing me on the channel boats and surveillance."

He said: "Jerry's been fucking you really bad."

I said: "Yeah I know, I've finally come to that conclusion. I started with Jerry and I've tried to be loyal to him but he just keeps screwing me. I've come to the conclusion that Jerry doesn't give a shit about me."

He said: "First time I was there when y'all settled up and he only paid you 18%, I couldn't believe it. He shouldn't be taking 2% from you to load you. That ain't kosher, believe me, it ain't kosher. There's a lot of other things too. Why don't you buy your own houses and stop paying him for house rentals?"

I said: "Oh, you don't know, do you? I've bought three houses and I'll probably buy another one or two. I'm all set up now to unload my boats at my houses."

He said: "That's good, I didn't know that. Look, I don't want to badmouth Jerry too much because I like working with him. He knows a lot about boats and a lot about electronics and he can Jury-rig anything and get it going. I've seen him do some amazing stuff, so, I like working with him. But, how would you like to work with me?"

I said: "Man, you know I wanta work with you so how can we make it happen? Will Joe let us work exclusively with each other?"

He said. "I don't have any fulltime scammers that work for me and I don't own any scam boats, but, that's gonna change. I've been working a long time and I've never seen anybody as good as you and I've never worked with any scammers as good as your people are. When I load you, it's a real easy night because you've got your shit together, your people know what they're doing, and they're where they're supposed to be. My people couldn't believe how easy it was the night we loaded your boats. We had never been done at 4:30 in the morning before. We've had many trips where we hadn't loaded our first boat at 4:30 in the morning. I'd like for you to work for me every trip and let me load you every trip. I'll guarantee you 20,000 pounds every trip. On top of that, you'll work more if you work for me than you would if you worked for Jerry."

I said: "How could that be?"

He said: "I work for other people other than Joe. Jerry only works for Joe. Believe me, next year there is a lot of pot coming in. What I'm doing right now is I'm going around talking to all these people that I've worked for in the past and I'm making sure that I have a place as one of their importers when the stuff starts coming in next year. Joe hauls more pot than anybody else, he's the biggest there is. We call him the King of the Bank. Joe brought in over 950,000 pounds of pot last year. But, he's not the only game in town. There's a lot of other people that haul a lot of pot too. I work for almost everybody. The only people I don't work for are people I don't want to work for. If you come to work for me and you let me load you, I'll guarantee you 20,000 pounds every time, because I won't be loading anybody else but you. You'll work every time you'd normally be working a trip for Joe plus you'd be working trips with me for other people too."

I said: "That sounds almost too good to be true. It sounds like a pretty good proposition. Will you pay me 20%?"

He said: "Hell yeah, I'll pay you 20%. I don't want something to load you, that's bullshit! I made my money last year. Big Ed paid me very well for that barge trip in Pascagoula. I'm going to be buying my own boats and getting my own scammers but it's gonna take a little time. That's another thing I want to talk to you about. Why don't you get your own middle boat and run your own organization from top to bottom?"

I said: "Man, I'm glad you mentioned that because I've been wanting to meet with Joe and ask him if I can do just that."

He said: "Hell man, Joe would let you do that in a minute."

I said: "He would, how do you know that?"

He said: "Look, there's plenty of people like me that want to just run a middle boat because you're not taking much of a chance running pot from the freighter to the scam boats. The people who take the chance are the scammers."

I said: "Hell, don't I know that. I think the scammers are the ones who ought to be making the big money because they're the ones who are taking the biggest chance."

He said: "That's right! There's plenty of guys like me that just have middle boats. I'm just about the most senior guy around. Everybody knows me from three and four years ago. This thing goes by seniority with these people. People know me and trust me. They know I'm honest and I won't steal bales from them. There's a lot of people with middle boats but there ain't very many people that've got their own houses and boats and good people like you. If you ask Joe to let you run your own operation, to have your own middle boat, he won't turn you down because that's helping him. That's less of a headache for him but right now, he's got too much to worry about. We need to take stuff off of Joe and let him concentrate on getting the freighters up here. When I go and talk to Joe about next year, I'll just tell him that you're working with me exclusively. I'm gonna set up my own organization like you've got. I'm gonna start buying houses and boats and getting my own scammers. You see, I do a lot of loads for people other than Joe. Most of the loads are 40,000 or 60,000 pounds, that's two or three middle boats. Until I can get my own houses and boats and scammers trained, I'll load you exclusively. I'll guarantee you 20,000 pounds. In the meantime, I've got a middle boat that I can sell you. If a 40,000 pound trip comes up for Joe, we can work it and you can run your middle boat and I'll load some of Joe's people. If we work a 40,000 pound trip for somebody other than Joe, we can do the same thing. You can run your middle boat and load your people. I'll get my own scammers to load. We're gonna have plenty of work. We're probably gonna have more work than you want when it's all over with."

I said: "Gee man, that sounds awful good. It sounds too good to be true because that's exactly what I've been wanting to do. What about this middle boat, is it a Hatteras?"

He said: "Hell yeah man, it's a 53 footer just like mine."

I said: "Is it galley up or galley down?"

He said: "No man, it's galley down. I made a mistake getting a galley up. I should've gotten a galley down."

I said: "How much do you want for it?"

He said: "I'll sell it to you for $200,000."

I said: "Man, that's cheap, howcum so cheap?"

He said: "Look man, you'll be helping me out."

I said: "Well shit, if you'll sell it to me for $200,000, I'll take it. I just wanta look at it and make sure it ain't a piece of junk."

He said: "No man, it ain't a piece of junk. It just came out of the yard. I had a lot of work done on it and I had it painted. I've got a $40,000 yard bill but I won't even make you pay for that. I'll show you the receipts."

I said: "Shit, that's a good deal Brad, thanksalot! Okay, when I get back to Lauderdale, I'm gonna go see Jerry and tell him that I'm getting my own middle boat and that I'm gonna be working with you. I hope this won't cause any hard feelings."

He said: "Okay, as soon as you talk to Jerry, let me know and I'll talk to Joe."

I said: "Okay man, that'll be real good."

The House lights blink and it's time for the second half of Grease. We find our seats and our friends and enjoy the rest of the play tremendously. When the play is over, we all pile into a taxi and go to Mama Leoni's Spaghetti House just off Columbus Circle. We have an all-American pigout of Italian Food, a couple of bottles of wine, and good company among good friends. When we finished eating, Brad and his partner paid the bill for us, and there were good vibes all-around.

I asked: "Do you guys want to go have a drink somewhere or do you have to call it a night."

Brad said: "We've got to go halfway out Long Island to our motel so we'd better call it a night. What're y'all gonna do?"

I had told Brad about the money I had so I asked: "What do you think I should do about going home?"

He said: "Well, you should not fly commercial so either drive the rent-a-car or charter a Lear Jet. I'd charter a Lear Jet if it was me."

I said: "I don't want to drive New York to Ft. Lauderdale in a car so who do I call to get a Lear Jet. Do you have somebody you use that we can trust?"

He said: "Yeah, call Tom Boye at National Jets in Ft. Lauderdale. He's cool, he won't ask any questions, and his pilots are the best! You can pay them cash too. They're discreet." He gave me the number for National Jets in Ft. Lauderdale.

We said our goodbyes, flagged down two taxis, and they headed off to Long Island and we headed for Port Authority Bus Terminal to get our car. Once we'd gotten our car, I drove us to the hotel back in New Jersey.

The next morning, I got a 9:00 A.M. wakeup call and the first thing I did was call Tom Boye. I told him I needed a Lear Jet to return to Ft. Lauderdale from Newark Airport around 2 o'clock that afternoon. He told me to go to the private aircraft terminal at Newark and the Lear would be waiting for me. John and Peggy and I had breakfast, checked out of the Marriott, and drove to Newark Airport. I dropped them off at the main terminal, turned in the rent-a-car, and took a cab to the private aircraft terminal arriving around 1:30 P.M.

When I walked in the door of the private aircraft terminal, this older gentleman walked up to me and asked: "Are you Mr. Alford?" When I answered "yes" he said: "We're your transportation to Ft. Lauderdale."

I said: "Great! I didn't expect you to be here."

He said: "We've been here about an hour. Are you ready to go?"

I said: "Yes, let's go."

He took my suitcase and hangup bag, I kept my briefcase, and we walked out the door to the Lear Jet that was parked about ten steps from the door. They had literally "rolled out the red carpet" for me and I was pleased and impressed! We walked up the fold-out steps and I sat in the first seat on the right. The pilot closed the door and sat down next to me.

He said: "Can we take care of the bill right now before we take off?"

I said: "Sure, I'll be glad to."

I opened my briefcase and took out a pack of $2,000 and took $400 from another pack. I paid him all in 20's.

They started the engines, we taxied out to the runway, turned right onto the main runway, and were ready to go.

The pilot turned his head toward me and said: "Everything okay, Mr. Alford. Are you ready to go?"

I said: "Yeah, let's go" and gave them a thumbs up.

He pushed the throttles forward, we bolted down the runway, he pulled the wheel back, and we went straight up like the space shuttle. It was a rush! When we got up to cruising altitude and leveled off, I got me a glass of ice and a Coke and I could see the pilot counting the 20's. We must have been on auto-pilot. I'm thinking to myself that this is unfucking believable because it was like riding on a bullet. I could feel the Lear Jet hurtling through space and it was cool! I guess it was smart to spend $2400 to get $270,000 home safe. Brad was right! Mick and I lost $1,200 each to get $30,000 more out of the trip. That was just the cost of doing business. We flew down the east coast of the U.S. which I could see out of my right-side window. When we got near south Florida, I felt the pilot pull back on the throttles and slow the plane down, then make a right-hand turn and start his final approach into Ft. Lauderdale. In about two and a half hours, we land, taxi over to the private air terminal. No Customs this time since we didn't leave the country. The attendants are waiting for me with the red carpet and they roll it out for me as I descend the stairs. Boy, did I feel important! The pilot had radioed ahead and told them I needed a taxi and it was waiting for me at the terminal. The taxi came through the double gate and pulled up to the front of the Lear Jet so I only walked about ten steps from the plane. Life was good and it was getting better every day!

Chapter 31
Socrates, Pegleg the Pirate, & the Colonel
Getting promoted to an Admiral in the Navy of Pegleg.

The next morning after I got up, I had my coffee out by the pool, ate a bowl of cereal, and went to see Jerry. When I got to his house, he was out back on an old boat that was at his dock behind the house. He was inside the boat painting it by hand.

I said: "Listen man, I want to have a serious talk with you."

He said: "Okay, let's talk."

I said: "I want to buy a middle boat and run my own operation from top to bottom. I'd like for you to get me a meeting with Joe so I can ask him if he'll let me do that."

He said: "Okay, no sweat. I kinda figured that's what you wanted to talk to me about."

I said: "Oh yeah?"

He said: "Anything else you want to talk to me about?"

I said: "No, not really. I'd rather not get into any other stuff with you because it'll probably cause us to have an argument and then there'd be hard feelings, and I don't want to have any hard feelings with you. I appreciate what you've done for me and I appreciate the money I've made working for you. I think it's better if we don't get into specifics. I'd like for us to have a parting of the ways that is cordial and for us to both go on to bigger and better things. I hope I won't be letting you down by going off on my own?"

He said: "Don't worry about that, I've got plenty of scammers now. It seems like everyone wants to work. Don't worry about letting me down."

I said: "I was worrying about it and I'm glad to hear you've got plenty of scammers. I just feel like I deserve to run my own operation."

He said: "You're pretty good and you really do deserve it. I can understand how you feel like at this point in time, the best thing for you to do is to run your own operation. I'll call Joe and tell him you want to talk to him and I'll give you a good recommendation, so don't worry about that. We'll still be friends."

I said: "I hope we'll still be friends. You know I'd do anything for you except kill somebody. If you told me to go to hell, I'd grab a shovel and start digging because I think that much of you. If you ever need anything that I can do for you, don't hesitate to ask because I'd do damn near anything for you."

He said: "That goes double for me."

I said: "I hope we'll still see each other a lot and you know, you can come over to my house and visit me and my wife anytime. Let's don't let this fuck-up a good relationship."

He said: "No man, there ain't no problem with that."

We shook hands warmly then gave each other a hug. I left his house on S.W. 5th Place, drove to a payphone on Davie Boulevard, and called Blue Eyes.

I said: "I just left Jerry and we've had a cordial parting of the ways. Go ahead and call Joe for me and set up a meeting. Now, what about that Hatteras? Would it be possible for me to take a look at it?" He said: "Give me your phone number and let me call up and find out where it is 'cause I don't even know where it is. My Captain's taking care of it for me."

I gave him the phone number of the payphone and in about five minutes he called me back.

He said: "Listen, they should be there right now working on it. It's down off Las Olas Boulevard in the Las Olas Isles. If the people's car isn't there, don't stop. The people who live in the house are kinda funny about a lot of people coming to the boat. If the car is there, you can go on back to the boat. You'll know my people 'cause you've worked with them before. They'll let you on the boat to take a look at it."

I said: "Great! I'll give you a call when I'm done looking at it."

I drove from Davie Boulevard to U.S. 1 and then north to Broward Boulevard and to Las Olas. I found the street address and the car was parked in front so I pulled in behind it. I walked through the yard on the left hand side of the house to the dock at the rear. There at the dock was this beautiful 53 foot Hatteras named "Socrates". I climbed on the aft deck, went into the main salon, and sure enough, I knew the two guys that were there.

One of them said: "Hey man, coming over to take a look at your new boat?"

I said: "Yeah man, I hope it's gonna be my new boat."

He said: "Come on and take a look at this thing, it's mighty pretty."

My first impression was that I was just blown away, it was so pretty! The boat had obviously been very well taken care of. The main salon had beautiful furniture with custom, wooden cabinetry built for a television, VCR, and a stereo system. I went down the stairs into the dinette and kitchen on the right. On the left was the Master Stateroom and Head. The bedspreads and pillowcases were made of expensive cloth. There was expensive art on the walls. I went forward to the crew quarters in the V-Berth passing another Head on the right. This boat was NICE! I went back into the Dinette, pulled off the stairs, opened the door, and went into the engine room. It was clean and bright! I was impressed. I came out of the engine room, closed the door, and put the stairs back on the latch. The air conditioning was blowing cold and it felt good.

I asked: "This boat looks like it's in pretty good shape. Were the people that owned it working it?"

They said: "Hell yeah, man, they worked the hell out of it, but they had two guys that worked on it fulltime. If it got the least little nick, they'd have it fixed immediately as soon as they got back from the trip."

I said: "It looks like a mighty fine ride to me. I'd be real proud to own this thing. I'm gonna talk to Blue Eyes and work out a deal."

They said: "He don't need it. He's glad for you to have it 'cause he knows you need it."

We said our goodbyes, I left, and drove up to the convenience store to the payphones to call Blue Eyes.

I said: "I just looked at Socrates and it's about the prettiest boat I've ever seen. I want it so let's do the deal."

He said: "That's good, I knew you'd like it. I'll sell it to you for what I told you, is that okay?"

I said: "Hell yeah, man, that's better than okay. What about the name, can I change it?"

He said: "Yeah man, you can name it anything you want. Have you got a name you want to use?"

I said: "Yeah, I want to name her "PattySunshine" after my wife and daughter"

He said: "That's a good name! Do you want me to have a painter come over and change it for you?"

I said: "Man, that'd be great! I'd love to bring Pat and Sunny over to look at it and have "PattySunshine" already painted on the transom. When do you think you can get it done?"

He said: "I'll call the painter now and tell him to do it tomorrow morning. If you bring them over tomorrow afternoon, it should be done."

I said: "Brad, that is awesome!"

I left the payphones on Las Olas and drove to Wen and WaWa's house to check on Audacious and the Grand Banks. Then, I drove to Mom's house to check on Blue Mist and on to the Peacock House to check on Cathy 5. All my boats and all my people were good. I called it a day and drove home to tell Pat about "Socrates". "PattySunshine" would be a surprise!

The next day, I got a phone call and it's Pegleg the Pirate.

He said: "How about if we get together?"

I said: "Sure man, tell me where and when."

He said: "Can you meet me in about an hour?"

I said: "Sure, where do you want to meet?"

He said: "Do you know that fishing pier off the end of Commercial Boulevard?"

I said: "Yeah man, I eat there all the time."

He said: "Why don't I meet you there."

I said: "Fine, I'll be driving a little red Honda."

He said: "Okay, I'll look for you."

I drove east on Commercial Boulevard to the beach, found a parking space, parked, and went in the little restaurant and got me a large Coke. I walked back out to the street to my car and stood and watched the people coming and going from the beach. Joe drives up in a Jeep and he's got an older man with him, he looks about 55 or 60 years old. He pulls up and parks in a parking space, I walk over to his Jeep before he gets out, and he sees me.

He said: "Where is your car? Do you wanta ride around and talk?"

I said: "I live real close by. Do you guys wanta come over to my house?"

He acted kinda surprised and said: "That'll be fine if you don't mind me knowing where you live."

I said: "Well, I don't guess I mind you knowing where I live, I know where you live."

He said: "Yeah, I guess you do, don't you?"

I said: "Man, if I don't trust you and you don't trust me, then, we're in a heap of trouble."

He said: "Yeah, I guess you're right."

I said: "Why don't you follow me. I live just on the other side of U.S. 1."

I got in my Honda and drove west on Commercial Boulevard and then north on 18th Avenue to my house. We both parked in my driveway and the three of us went in my house. When we all got into my living room, I locked the door behind us.

Joe said: "You ever met the Colonel?"

I said: "No, I don't believe I've ever had the pleasure."

Joe said: "The Colonel is my pilot and he spots the freighters for me; he finds the freighters for us."

I said: "I've heard all about you but I've never met you." We shook hands warmly. "Why don't you come in the back and we can talk."

The Colonel said: "I'll just sit here in the living room until you guys get finished."

Joe and I walk to the back of my house into the Master Bedroom, I close the door, and we sit on a sofa together.

He said: "I hear you want to run your own operation."

I said: "Yeah, I'm all set up to have my own operation. I've got the houses, the boats, and the scammers to haul 20,000 pounds. I'd like to buy my own middle boat and go to the freighters and then load my own boats. That way, I wouldn't get shorted. I don't want to badmouth Jerry but he was shorting me almost every trip last year. The few times that Brad loaded me, I got a full load every time on all four of my boats. Jerry and I have talked and we've come to a mutual parting of the ways, but we're still friends I hope. Blue Eyes wants to load me until he gets his own scammers but I'd rather have my own middle boat and load my own boats myself. I wanta run my own organization from top to bottom."

He said: "I've been told that you're real good and you're real professional and I've never had any problems with you that I know of. I don't have any problem with you buying your own middle boat. In fact, I'll buy you a middle boat and you can pay me back."

I said: "Well, I've already agreed to buy a 53 Hatteras from Blue Eyes. He made me a good offer on it and I've agreed to buy it from him. So, I really don't need for you to buy me one too, but, I appreciate the offer."

He said: "Listen, I'm having a little bit of a problem with Blue Eyes."

I said: "What do you mean? What kind of problem?"

He said: "Blue Eyes works for other people besides me."

I said: "Yeah, I know, that's what he told me."

He said: "Okay, what's gonna happen when you and Blue Eyes are out on a trip for somebody else and I've got a freighter that's out there and I need you guys to work my trip? You guys are out working somebody else's trip and can't work for me and I'm short people, what am I gonna do?"

I said: "I don't know what to tell you because I promised Blue Eyes that I would work with him and he could load my boats until he gets his own scammers. So, all I can tell you is that I'll always be ready and I'll never let you down."

He said: "If you work for Blue Eyes, you won't be able to promise me that and that's why I want to buy you another middle boat. Suppose you're out there working a trip for somebody else and you've got to layover with pot. A trip comes up for me and you can't work my trip. If you've got two middle boats, you can work my trip and bring my pot in and then finish up the other trip later."

I said. "Look, I don't want to get involved in politics with you guys at the upper level. All I want to do is run my own organization from top to bottom. I want to go to the freighter and get a good load. I want to load my own scam boats. I want to unload them at my own houses, and, I want to deliver the pot in my own vans. I can do all that right now. That's all I want to do. I've got the best people as my scammers. They're very serious about what we're doing and a lot of them don't even do drugs. But, they're very serious about making a lot of money. I don't know what's going on, if there's a power struggle or what, but I just wanta be left out of the politics of it all."

He said: "What I'd like for you to do is promise me that you won't work for anybody but me."

I said: "Joe, you're putting me on the spot because I've already promised Brad that I would work with him. I can't promise you that without going back on my promise to him."

He said: "You'd better talk it over with Blue Eyes because you might wind up not working at all for me."

I said: "Let me talk to Brad and I'll get back with you on that. What I can promise you is that I'll never let you down. I promised that to Jerry and I'll promise that to you. I've got the boats, the houses, and the people to do 20,000 pounds. That's what I'm looking to do. I do feel loyalty to you and I'd like to do what you're asking me to do but I've already promised Blue Eyes that I'd work with him. I hope that we can work this out."

He said: "All right, I'll be waiting to hear from you but I would prefer to buy you another middle boat and just let you have two middle boats."

I said: "Joe, I think it's just crazy for me to have two middle boats when I feel like one can do the job."

He said: "Okay, I'll be waiting to hear from you but, listen man, we've got a lot of pot coming. I want you to be ready to go because when it starts coming, I'm gonna work your ass off."

I said: "I don't really want to work my ass off, I just wanta work steady, but, if you need me, you call me, and we'll go. I won't ever say no to you and I won't ever turn you down."

He said: "You talk with Blue Eyes and you get back with me."

I said: "Okay, I'll get with you tomorrow."

He said: "I'll be waiting to hear from you."

We walked out of my bedroom into the living room, I shook hands with the Colonel, they got in Joe's Jeep and drove off.

As soon as they'd left, I went and got me a glass of Coca-Cola over ice and sat in my den to gather my thoughts. I was a little overwhelmed by what had just taken place. First of all, Pegleg the Pirate and the Colonel had just come to my house for a meeting.

That, in and of itself, was overwhelming. These people were like folk heroes to me and to everyone who'd ever heard of them. Pegleg was the King of the Bank and the Colonel was, well, the Colonel! I was kind of blown away that I'd gotten to this point and that Pegleg trusted me enough to let me go to his freighters and haul over $4,000,000 worth of pot. I'd been blessed by Pegleg and brought into his inner circle of five middle boat Captains. I guess I was now the sixth middle boat Captain. For me to be included in this inner circle was very flattering. I thought to myself : *Scooter, you must be pretty fucking good!* When I'd finished my Coke, I decided that I'd better talk to Brad so I rode up to my "office" at the bank of payphones. When he answered, I told him that I'd just met with Joe and that we needed to talk. He said for me to come over to his house which wasn't too far away from mine. I drove straight over to his place.

I said: "You want to tell me what the fuck is going on because I don't understand about these power struggles. I don't want to get involved in the power struggles if I can help it but it seems like Joe wants to pull me into them. So, why don't you explain to me what's going on. "

He said: "Do you know Ed?"

I said: "No, I don't know Ed. Is that Big Ed?"

He said: "Yes, they are one and the same person."

I said: "Is that what the power struggle is all about, a struggle between Big Ed and Joe?"

He said: "Yeah, it's a power struggle between Ed and Joe. Joe used to work for Ed, he used to bring in his pot for him. Then, Ed had some problems and got hot and he had to lay low for a couple of years. Joe sort of stepped into the void and grew his organization to be the biggest there's ever been. Now, Ed wants to come back and do trips and Joe doesn't want him to come back. Joe's trying to stop Ed from coming back and doing trips. Ed's always done mostly big trips in marinas and boatyards, he's never had an organization of middle boats and scammers. Ed has come to me and asked me to work for him and I've agreed. That's why Joe doesn't want me and you to work for Ed, it's an ego thing. Each one of them wants to be the biggest marijuana smuggler that's ever been."

I said: "Wow, so that's it in a nutshell! Why don't you go back to the beginning and tell me the whole story so I'll know."

He said: "How far back do you want me to go? Ed is from California and he got started by crossing the border into Mexico, buying pot directly from the farmers, and backpacking it across the border back into California by foot. He would sell the pot himself and keep all the money. Ed became a millionaire backpacking pot into California. Then, Ed somehow got hooked up with Julio in Colombia and Julio would send boats full of pot up to the Bahamas and anchor them at Gun Cay. This was like the early 1970's. There was no heat anywhere back then and nobody knew anything was going on. Joe would get in a fast boat like a Sea-Ray and blast over to Gun and fill up the Cuddy Cabin and bring it back to Ft. Lauderdale. Fu was the Dealer and he would meet Joe at the public boat ramp with a trailer. As Joe was coming up the River, he would call Fu on the CB radio and Fu would put the trailer in the water. Joe would drive the boat right up on the trailer and they would haul the boat out of the water and take it to a warehouse out in West Ft. Lauderdale. Joe and Fu would unload the pot in the boat into a van and Fu would drive away from the warehouse and sell the pot to Dealers he knew. Joe would go home and get some sleep, then, wake up the next day and blast over to Gun again. They repeated this procedure for as many days as they needed until the boat at Gun was empty. As the pot kept coming in, Fu was getting more and more Dealers from all over the U.S. He was growing his contacts and his business. Other people starting calling Joe and getting him to bring in their pot and Joe was getting a helluva reputation. And the three of them were getting very rich! Then, Ed got hot and he had to go underground for awhile."

I said: "How did Ed get hot, what happened there?"

He said: "I'm not exactly sure. I think somebody got busted in California that had connections to Ed. They got Ed's name and they were looking for him so Ed had to lay low for awhile."

I said: "So, Joe stepped into the void left by Ed. Is that what happened?"

He said: "Sort of, and this is where it gets kinda weird. Joe knew Julio's name from Ed but he'd never met him and didn't know how to contact him. So, Joe being the brash and brazen young man that he is, got in his private airplane and flew to Colombia with $2,000,000 in cash in a suitcase. He checked into the Bogota Hilton and went out behind it where the drug dealers were and told them that he was here to see Julio. He told these low-level drug dealers to get the word to Julio that he was in such-n-such a room at the Bogota Hilton. He waits and waits and in a couple of days, his phone finally rings and someone says "This is Julio, I hear you want to see me." Joe invites him up to his room, they meet, and Joe gives the guy the $2,000,000! Only thing, it ain't the real Julio. The next day, the phone rings and it's the real Julio. He comes up to Joe's room and convinces Joe that he's the real Julio by telling him of his relationship with Ed and all the pot that he's sent up to Gun Cay. Joe tells the real Julio that he's given $2,000,000 to a fake Julio. The real Julio leaves and puts out the word that he's been robbed and offers a reward for the name of the culprit. It doesn't take too long for someone to contact Julio with the name of the thief, a mid-level drug dealer. Julio takes a bunch of his guys with automatic weapons and they go to this guys house, bust in, kill thirteen people, and find the money. Julio goes back to the Bogota Hilton with the money and has a meeting with Joe. Joe tells Julio that Ed is hot and will have to lay low for awhile and that he, Joe, wants to continue their operation. They discuss smuggling and come up with the idea for Joe to unload the mother ships all in one night with a larger boat and then for Joe to offload to smaller boats to bring the pot into Florida. Joe returns to Ft. Lauderdale and buys a Sportfisherman to use as the middle boat and he recruits people to be scammers on smaller speedboats and sailboats. They rented some waterfront homes to use to unload the scam boats and Julio started sending up 20,000 pound loads in boats he contracted with. The first year that they worked together, Joe Pegg brought in more pot than Ed ever thought of. Fu had the network of dealers and together they grew the business to where it is now. Joe Pegg has the biggest organization that there's ever been. Last year, Joe brought in just under a million pounds of pot and the people in Colombia are very, very impressed with Joe Pegg. I guarantee you that Joe will bring in more than a million pounds this year that's coming up. Julio will see to it!"

I said: "Wow! That's quite a story! This thing is very complicated, ain't it?"

He said: "Yeah, it could be but it doesn't have to be. Now, Ed wants to come back and he's asked me to work for him and I've agreed. Joe doesn't want me to work for Ed and that's why he asked you to only work for him. Joe wants to try to stop Ed from coming back because he sees Ed as a threat. You see, Ed started me off, Ed bought me my first boat, and I made most of my money under Ed. When Ed quit to lay low, I started working for Joe but I was working for a lot of other people too. Now, Joe is going around and asking everybody that has worked for him to only work for him this upcoming year. In that way, he's hoping that he'll lock-up all the independent contractors, or most of them, and Ed won't have anybody to bring in his pot. If I'm gonna work for Ed then you're gonna work for Ed and there's no way Joe can stop him from coming back."

I said: "Joe said if I didn't agree to work for him exclusively that I might not work at all."

He said: "No man, that can't happen because when I talked to Joe, I told him that I wanted to work every trip for him and that if I found out that he'd done a trip and I hadn't worked it, I wouldn't work for him at all. I'd work for Ed exclusively."

I said: "Man, it seems like he's got enough people that he can cut you off."

He said: "No man, he doesn't have enough people, that's the point. In order for Joe to bring in all the pot they want to send him from Colombia, he needs all the middle boats he had last year, which is five middle boats, plus one or two more. That's why your middle boat is number six and a friend of his nephews will be number seven. So that's 140,000 pounds that seven middle boats can haul and he'll still have the Burger to take the extra if there's any left over. He needs you and he needs me so he can't cut us out."

I said: "I feel loyalty to Joe but I don't have any loyalty to Ed."

He said: "I understand that but what it boils down to is this. Whatever money you made last year, you'll make twice as much this year working for Joe and Ed and a lot of other people too. There's a lot of pot coming up this year because they are supposed to be having a good crop in Colombia. Those folks down there want to get it up here. Joe and Ed are the two biggest guys that have ever worked. They've brought in more pot in one year than anybody else has ever. They've just been doing it different ways. Ed has always done big loads and Joe has done smaller loads but just as much quantity. Now, Joe is going to start doing bigger loads with scam boats and he needs both of us to do bigger loads."

I said: "Okay, it's all beginning to make sense to me now, but, all I want to do is work and make money. I want to stay out of the politics."

He said: "You've got to make up your mind what you want to do. Do you want to be an independent contractor or do you want to work for someone else and get jerked around like Jerry did you?"

I said: "I want to be an independent contractor. I'm tired of being shorted and I'm tired of being jerked around."

He said: "Okay, if you want to be an independent contractor, then, you've got to be an independent contractor. All you've gotta do is what's right for you. I always do what's right for me and my people. That way, people know how to approach me if they want to make a deal with me. You know, if people like you, they say you're a good businessman. If they don't like you, they say you're a greedy motherfucker. It really doesn't matter. The name of the game is making money. I always do what's right for me and my people."

I said: "That's a good philosophy if you can do it that way. Okay, my mind is made up if you're sure Joe's not gonna cut us out."

He said: "I'm sure man, I've already talked to him about it. He can't cut us out because he needs us both. You just trust me."

I said: "Okay, I'll call Joe and tell him that I'll try not to let him down and that I'll do the best I can."

He said: "Man, that'll be good enough. Don't you worry about it."

Brad and I shook hands and I left his house and headed for home. I stopped at my "office" at the payphones and put in a call to Joe. He gave me a payphone number and said to call him there in ten minutes. In ten minutes, I called him and told him that I'd talked to Blue Eyes and that I was gonna keep my promise to him to work with him.

He said: "If you've got your mind made up."

I said: "For the time being, that's just the way it's gonna have to be. I hope you understand."

He said: "We'll just see what happens."

I said: "Okay, I'll be waiting to hear from you. I'm ready anytime."

He said: "Okay, it shouldn't be too much longer."

We hung up and the knot in my stomach started to unwind. I couldn't wait to see my two beautiful ladies, Patty and Sunshine. Only thing was, now I had three beautiful ladies: Patty, Sunshine, and PattySunshine!

Chapter 32
Comin' Clean with Mom and Dad
There's no place like home.

I was past ready to take a vacation, but I still had a few loose ends to tie-up. The people that lived in the house where the PattySunshine was kept had started to act a little weird so I decided that it was better if I moved her to a new dock. My real estate agent and friend, Barry B., found me another dock behind a house off Las Olas Boulevard on the north side of the street so I went ahead and moved the "PS" to the new dock. Now, I needed someone to take care of her for me. My Captains, Mick and Dan, knew a Captain that had a 100 Ton License and he was running a crew boat down in the oil fields off Campeche, Mexico. They contacted him for me and got him to come to Ft. Lauderdale to talk with me about a job. We met and I liked him right off. I showed him the "PS" and he was blown away at how nice the boat was. When I told him that I'd pay him $500 per week to take care of the boat for me plus I'd pay him $20,000 for each trip, he was thrilled to death. We made a list of all the things we needed for the boat and Captain Jim set about getting what we needed. We got fishing rods and reels from Beach Bait and Tackle. We got big, six-foot long bumpers and a scuba tank to blow them up, and, we got drop cloths, masking tape, and all the paraphernalia we needed to "tape-down" in preparation for loading from the freighters. It was about the middle of October 1979 and we still had about a month before we worked our first trip of the season. Brad said that it was about time for the harvest of the new crop and that it was expected to be big. As soon as Julio could get the pot harvested and packaged in bales, he would start sending it up hot and heavy. We were looking forward to a big year!

Pat got us passes on Delta to fly to Georgia so we could finally tell my parents that we'd been smuggling. I called home, talked to my Mom, and told her we were coming for a visit. She was thrilled! I told her that we were flying into Atlanta and renting a car, then, driving to Callaway Gardens to stay at the motel at this very nice resort that was seventeen miles from my hometown of LaGrange. She said that we didn't need to rent a car, that she'd get someone to pick us up, and, she wanted us to stay with she and Dad in their house. I insisted that we would rent a car and stay at Callaway Gardens and that I was getting them a room also as a treat. I'm sure she was perplexed because the last time we'd visited them, money was tight and we were looking to save money, not spend it.

We flew into Atlanta about midday on a Sunday, rented a Lincoln Town Car, and drove to LaGrange. We went straight to their fast-food restaurant because they would both be working this time of day. When we arrived, the lunch rush was just dwindling down, and there were hugs and kisses all around. After visiting and chatting briefly, Dad fixed Pat and me a plate of his special barbeque and Sunny got a cheeseburger and french fries. When we'd finished eating, we visited some more with Mom and then we drove the seventeen miles to the motel at Callaway Gardens. I got us two adjoining rooms so we could stay in one room and my Mom and Dad could stay in the other. We relaxed around the pool and enjoyed the weather which was unseasonably warm. We ate supper that night in the restaurant there and waited for Mom and Dad to close the restaurant and join us. The restaurant was closed on Monday so that would be a free day for us to do our best visiting.

My parents closed the restaurant at 9 o'clock and they were at the rooms by 9:30 P.M. We fixed everyone a mixed drink, sat on the beds, and talked and visited until past midnight. I wasn't sure exactly how I was going to tell them about smuggling but I figured it would come out tomorrow at sometime. We slept in 'till past 9 o'clock then went into the restaurant for breakfast. After breakfast, we checked out and headed for LaGrange. I rode in the Toyota Leisureliner with Dad and Pat drove the Lincoln Town Car with my Mom and Sunny.

Not long after we were on the road, I said something about "my lawyer" and my Dad said: "Why do you need a lawyer?"

I said: "Well, Dad, since I last saw you, I <u>have</u> been working for Jerry Smith but not in the Detective Agency. We've been smuggling marijuana from the Bahamas to Florida by boat. This past year or so, I've made one point eight million dollars."

My Dad ran off on the right shoulder of the road and then regained control of the car. He said: "JESUS CHRIST, SCOOTER, HOW MUCH?!?!"

I said: "One point eight million dollars!"

He said: "You're not joking me are you?"

I said: "No, Dad, I'm not joking you. To show you this is real, I've brought you something." I had my briefcase in the back seat, which I retrieved and put on my lap. I turned to the combinations on the briefcase and opened the top so he could see. "This is a hundred thousand dollars which I want you to keep for me. If I ever have to run, this will be my running money. I hope I don't ever have to get it back from you. If you or Mom need anything, you can take what you need and next time I see you, I'll replace it and get it back to a hundred thousand dollars. I don't want you guys to ever have to do without again. If the transmission on the car needs to be fixed, fix it. If the air conditioner at the house goes out, fix it. I don't want you guys to ever have to do without anything ever again."

Dad looked straight ahead and drove without saying anything. Finally, he said: "Where is the rest of your money?"

I said: "I've got a little over a million dollars in a secret bank account in the Cayman Islands. I've got a safe deposit box at our bank in Ft. Lauderdale with a quarter million dollars in it, and, I've got a floor safe in our house that's got about a hundred thousand dollars in it. I own three sailboats, a trawler, and three small Mako boats, and, I own three waterfront homes where we unload the boats."

He said: "You're not kidding me about this, are you?"

I said: "No Dad, I'm serious as a heart attack."

He said: "Is that why you need a lawyer? Are you in trouble with the law now?"

I said: "No, I'm not in trouble with the law so far. I've actually got four lawyers in Ft. Lauderdale and one lawyer in Grand Cayman."

He said: "Why do you need so many lawyers?"

I said: "Three of the lawyers are at the same law firm. The senior partner, Jim Dolan, got me set up offshore in the Cayman Islands, offshore is one of his specialties. His partner, Chris Fertig, formed the dummy corporations for me when I started buying houses to unload my boats. Chris represented me when I closed on the houses. The other lawyer, David Bone, has his own airplane and he flies me to Nassau to launder money when I don't have enough time to fly to Grand Cayman. I make a deposit in Nassau and then wire-transfer the money to my secret bank account in Grand Cayman. The fourth lawyer in Ft. Lauderdale is Lou DeReuil, a tax attorney who advises me on how to get the money back from Grand Cayman without getting in trouble. The lawyer in Grand Cayman formed the Cayman Corporation for me and he takes care of everything that needs to be done in the Cayman Islands."

He said: "It sounds like you've been busy this past year."

I said: "Very busy. It's been a whirlwind. My life has changed dramatically."

He said: "It sounds like you and Jerry are pretty organized."

I said: "Yeah, we're pretty damn organized! I think the authorities would consider us organized crime. That sounds funny like we're the mafia or something. But we are organized and we're committing crime so I guess that makes us organized crime."

We drove on for awhile in silence as Dad pondered what I'd just told him.

Finally, I said: "I'm gonna give you the combination to the safe in the house, and, I'll get you a key to the safe deposit box and a signature card so you can get in the safe deposit box. I'll also give you Jim Dolan's phone number and the name and phone number of the lawyer in Grand Cayman. That way, if something happens or if I'm killed, you and Pat won't have any problem getting access to the money and y'all can sort things out as best you can."

He said: "That sounds good, I guess, but just don't get yourself killed."

I said: "I don't plan on it but it's a dangerous business that I'm in and shit happens."

We drove on in silence and I could see my Dad thinking about everything that I'd told him. We got to LaGrange and went through Lafayette Square and headed for the house.

I said: "Do you think Mom will be okay with this?"

He said: "Yeah, she'll be okay with it. We were talking in the room last night before we went to sleep and we knew something was up, we just didn't know what. She'll be glad you're not doing something stupid like robbing banks." I thought: *"Yeah, like smuggling pot isn't doing something stupid."* "I think she'll be okay with it, especially when you show her the hundred thousand dollars in the briefcase."

When we got to the house, we parked the cars and went inside.

Mom gave me a big hug and a kiss and said: "Pat told me what you've been doing this past year. It was one heckuva story. I want to hear all about it!"

We sat in the den and I proceeded to tell them all about smuggling, money laundering, and growing my own organization. They both sat there with this stoic look on their faces. I got my briefcase and showed Mom the hundred thousand dollars and she was truly amazed! She teared up and almost cried when I told her that I didn't want her to ever have to do without anything ever again. We spent the rest of the afternoon talking and laughing and having a great visit. I was relieved that they had taken the news of my latest career move with such aplomb!

The next two days, I played golf one afternoon and we went horseback riding the other afternoon. I found some of my old friends from high school and we reminisced about the days of our youth. When asked, I told everyone that I was working for the

Smith Detective Agency as a Private Detective doing mostly repossessions, skip-tracing work, and serving subpoenas. I didn't give anyone even a hint that I was doing something illegal or that I was a millionaire. We flew back to Ft. Lauderdale on Thursday and I had a newfound peace about me now that my parents knew about the smuggling. We had a great visit but I was glad to be back in Ft. Lauderdale.

Chapter 33
Breakin' Up with Jerry
"They say that breaking up is hard to do, now I know, I know that it's true"
- Neil Sedaka

We landed in Ft. Lauderdale about mid-afternoon, got our bags from baggage claim, and retrieved our car from long-term parking. I wanted to check-on my boats, my houses, and my people so we drove over to Riverland Road and checked on Mom's house and then the Peacock House. From there, we went to Wen and WaWa's off Cordoba Road near Southport Raw Bar. From there, we drove over to Las Olas Boulevard to check on PattySunshine. Captain Jim was there and he was pleased as punch to see us and to show us the progress he'd made. He had just gotten new canvas made for the flybridge and the front windshield that was a pretty royal blue color. He had already replaced the white canvas and the "PS" really looked good. What I wanted to do was keep the blue canvas on the boat when we were in Florida waters and put on the white canvas when we were in the Bahamas. That way, we could change the "look" of the boat in case the heat flew over us in the Bahamas and then were watching for us coming home. Captain Jim had also gotten made for us a transom cover with the name "MasterBaiter" to further disguise our appearance when we were in the Bahamas. So, if the heat were flying on the Bank or around Gun Cay and they photographed the boat and the transom, hopefully, if they were looking for a boat with white canvas and named the "MasterBaiter", when we came in the Port with blue canvas and the name "PattySunshine", they wouldn't recognize us and we'd slip through. Captain Jim and I had quite a chuckle about the transom cover and I was very pleased at how good the "PS" looked. As we drove north up A1A headed for home, I was very pleased and satisfied with my organization and with the fact that we were ready to go to work when the trips started coming.

We had a big weekend coming up, our favorite minstrel was in concert at the Miami Jai Alai Fronton and everyone was looking forward to that. My captain Rob, worked for the Promoter as his accountant and he ran the box office on the day of the shows. He got me forty tickets in the center section, rows two through eight, so I could take everyone that worked for me as well as Jerry and Rita and Linda. We had great seats and I felt like the singer was doing a private concert for my organization and all the pot smugglers in South Florida. I called a local transportation company and chartered a Greyhound Bus with forty-four seats and a bathroom for all of us to travel together from Ft. Lauderdale to Miami. We all met at Riverland Shopping Center, boarded the bus, and made the trek to the Fronton. We were drinking liquor and champagne, smoking pot, and snorting cocaine and by the time we got to Miami, our heads were in the right spot and we were ready for a good concert. The singer came on promptly at 8:15 and proceeded to play all of our favorite songs. All in all, it was a religious experience and truly a night we'd never forget. The singer played for two and a half hours and when the show was over, we were all spent! On the bus ride back to Ft. Lauderdale, I had brought us a cooler with a gallon of milk, chocolate chip cookies, and brownies. Everyone ribbed me for bringing milk before the show, but now, they looked at me knowingly and enjoyed their snack. Ah, MILK! On the bus ride back, Jerry asked me if I wanted to eat breakfast when we got back and have a talk and I said "Sure, why not?!?! When we arrived at Riverland Shopping Center around midnight, I sent Pat home with Jen, and, Jerry and I went in the Floridian Restaurant and ordered breakfast.

Jerry said: "Whaddaya wanta talk about? Anything you wanta say to me?"

I said: "There's a lot of things that I wanta say to you, but if I say them, it's gonna cause us to have an argument and there'll be hard feelings. Like I told you the last time we talked at your house, I don't wanta have hard feelings with you so maybe it's better if we just let things lay and go on from here."

He said: "Okay, let's just talk and try not to lose our tempers. How much money have you made working for me?"

I said: "One point eight million dollars."

He said: "So what are you unhappy about?"

I said: "I'm unhappy about you charging me too much for surveillance. You paid Rita more than my scammers made. That ain't right. If you wanted to overpay Rita, then, you pay her but don't pass it on to me. Don't make me overpay her. Plus, you charged me for tows. Brad says that ain't right. He says that towing in a broken down boat is just part of smuggling, you don't get charged for it. I figure you've screwed me out of at least a hundred thousand dollars for surveillance and tows."

He said: "So, you've been talking to Brad about this?"

I said: "Brad's been talking to me about this. He's been wanting to load my boats for the last three or four trips. He promised to always give me twenty thousand pounds. But I said "no" and remained loyal to you. And how did you reward my loyalty? You shorted me every trip. Brad said you've shorted me out of at least a million dollars. I should have at least three million dollars now instead of one point eight. The only trip I got all my boats loaded full was when Brad loaded me that one trip. You never loaded all my boats full, not once. What does that say, Smith?"

He said: "It sounds to me like Brad's been stirring up the shit."

I said: "I was unhappy long before Brad approached me. He just confirmed what I already knew. He says that you don't appreciate me. He and the Cookie Monster tell me that me and my people are the best scammers that they've ever seen and they say they've seen 'em all. Me and you had an agreement that I'd be your exclusive scammers and you broke that agreement. When you gave me Tommy Dolan, we had an agreement that you wouldn't take him away from me. You broke that agreement."

He said: "That just worked out that way. Jim Dolan asked me to buy Tommy a boat and let him run it so he could make some big money. I couldn't say "no" to Jim Dolan." I said: "Yes you could have, Smith. You should have said "no" to him. If you appreciated me like you should, you would have said "no" to him. But you don't appreciate me, Jerry, that's the point!"

He said: "Well, I'm sorry you feel that way."

I said: "I'm sorry I feel that way too. But, that's the way I feel."

We ate our breakfasts in silence for awhile. Then, he said: "Okay, what else?"

I thought: *"Dare I broach the subject of my wife with him. Oh, what the hell. If we're airing everything out, then let's air it out."*

I said: "What do you think you're doing by taking <u>my</u> wife on trips with you on <u>your</u> boat? Pat and I talked about it and I wanted her to stay home and take care of Sunshine. She agreed to stay home. She wasn't happy about it but she understood. So you pull up to load me on your boat, and I look up and <u>my</u> wife is sitting on the flybridge of <u>your</u> boat. And I'm thinking "What the fuck, over!" Now, you wanta explain <u>that</u> to me?"

He said: "Pat and I were talking once and she told me you didn't want her to go on trips anymore. She said that she'd agreed with you because she didn't want to have a fight with you. But, she really wanted to keep going on trips. So, I told her she could go on the load boat with me if she wanted. I'd pay her to count bales and to cook and clean up with my crew. That way, she could go on trips, make some money, and there wasn't much chance of her getting busted. So, I took her on a couple of trips with me on BJ. What's the harm in that?"

I said: "I'll tell you what the harm in that is. You have gotten in the middle of my relationship with my wife. You have, in effect, fucked with my marriage. That is inexcusable, Smith. I have been a good friend to you, I have been a good scammer for you, and I have been loyal to you. And this is the way you reward my friendship and my loyalty, you fuck with my marriage?!?! That is inexcusable."

He said: "Aw, Scooter, it ain't no big deal. She got to feel like she was still a part of this, she made some money, and she was only gone one night. Y'all have got a good baby sitter, so that's no problem. Nobody got hurt."

I said: "Jerry, I got hurt. You hurt <u>me.</u> Don't you get it? You fucked with my marriage, you hurt me. Oh God, let me ask you this. Did you fuck my wife? You've got Rita and Linda and Joan and all the women in Ft. Lauderdale. Don't tell me you fucked my wife."

He looked at me with a blank stare on his face and didn't say anything. I felt like I'd caught the kid with his hand in the cookie jar. We finished our breakfasts without saying anything else.

Finally, he said: "Look, I'd like to tell Joe that if there's a 40,000 pound trip, that you and I will work it together with our two middle boats. And, if there's a 60,000 pound trip, we can work it with Brad. Is that okay with you? Can I tell Joe that? Do you have any problem working with me?"

I said: "No, I don't have any problem working with you. But, I've already agreed to work 40,000 pound trips with Brad. But, I have no problem working with you. I'll help you any way I can and I hope you'll help me if I need it."

He said: "Man, when we're on the water, we need to help each other anyway we can."

I said: "Well, at least we agree on that."

Jerry paid the bill, I left a tip, and I asked the cashier to call me a cab. We went outside to wait on my cab and in a couple of minutes, my cab showed up, we shook hands, and the cab drove me home.

When I went into my bedroom, Pat was sitting up in bed reading.

She said: "Well, how did it go with Jerry?"

I said: "Well, it went, not real good, but it went."

She said: "Did either one of you lose your temper?"

I said: "No, we didn't but I'm sure it was hard on both of us."

She said: "Did you settle anything?"

I said: "No, not really. Jerry doesn't think he's done anything wrong. Jerry ain't gonna change. Jerry's Jerry. You know that old Neil Sedaka song "Breaking Up is Hard to Do"? Well, me and Jerry are officially broken up and it was definitely hard to do. We've agreed to work together on the water but our friendship has been damaged. Can it be repaired at some point in the future, I don't know. Maybe, maybe not. We'll have to see. I wish it wasn't so late, I'd call Blue Eyes."

She said: "C'mon, crawl in bed with me and let's get some sleep."

I got in bed singing Neil Sedaka: "They say that breaking up is hard to do, now I know, I know that it's true." We slept until Sunshine woke us up at 8:30 in the morning.

Pat made a pot of coffee and we sat out by the pool under the overhang and woke up slowly. As soon as I'd gotten my second cup of coffee, I called Brad and gave him the lowdown on my breakfast with Jerry. He was all ears! When I'd finished telling him everything, he said that he was glad that there were no more hard feelings than there were and that he was glad we parted friends. He said it was only gonna be a couple more weeks before we started back working and we were gonna make enough money to buy Ft. Lauderdale! I told him I couldn't wait!

I was about as ready as I could be for the upcoming marijuana smuggling season. I had three luxury, waterfront homes to unload my boats. I had three 41 foot Columbia sailboats, a 42 foot Grand Banks trawler, a 25 foot Mako, two 20 foot Makos, three Chevy vans, and a 53 foot Hatteras Sportfisherman. The key to the success of my organization was the fifty-five people I had as my scammers that were as good as they came. From March 1978 to July 1979, I had done seventeen trips and made $1,800,000! I had three lawyers in Ft. Lauderdale advising me and helping me with dummy corporations, purchasing real estate, and doing offshore banking. I had a tax attorney advising me on how to launder money without getting caught, and, I had an attorney, a Cayman Corporation, and a secret bank account in the Cayman Islands. All in all, it was quite an empire that I'd grown in the last eighteen months.

Pegleg had agreed to let me get my own middle boat and go to the freighters and get twenty thousand pounds of pot. I was now an Admiral in the Navy of Pegleg and a trusted member of his inner circle! I had the boats, the houses, the vans, and most importantly, the people, to run my own organization from top to bottom. Being vertically integrated would theoretically allow me to avoid the problems of being shorted and thus I should be able to make a ton of money. If things went well, I was hoping to make another three to five million dollars, then, we'd retire and live happily ever after. What I didn't and couldn't know was that things would not go well. If I'd had a crystal ball, I would have seen that boats would get busted, people would be arrested and go to prison, people would be killed in plane crashes, and someone would be shot and left for dead in the Everglades. The Organized Crime Bureau (OCB) and three Grand Juries would investigate us, my home telephone would be legally tapped, criminal charges would be filed, I'd become a wanted man, and I'd flee to Jamaica and the Cayman Islands to hide and avoid prosecution.

In the upcoming season, Joe Pegg and his associates would smuggle 1,200,000 pounds of pot into South Florida, the most ever by any one group in a twelve month period. This is the intense and unbelievable story of the rise, fall, and demise of a member of the Joe Pegg Organization, the largest group to ever smuggle marijuana into the United States. The saga of Pegleg, Black Fin, Blue Eyes, and the Little Big Man continues in **Pot Smugglers II – The Blue Jean Millionaires,** coming soon to a bookstore near you.

Reflection

In your reflection in the water, you don't look too well,

Your voice is trembling softly, with stories you couldn't tell,

Stories of times when we didn't have a dime or care.

Living in a small town, dreaming all day long,

Never doing real work, my folks they think I'm wrong,

We stay out all night while the feeling is right,

And we drink us a beer or two,

When the feeling is gone, you just can't go on, us too.

Now I'm living in the real world but the real world's such a mess,

I close my eyes try to run away, the real world makes me stay,

Trying to hide is just like suicide, it'll drive a man to drink,

And running that smoke, it just ain't no joke you know.

Acknowledgements

All song lyrics reprinted with Permission.

Breaking Up Is Hard To Do
Words and Music by Howard Greenfield and Neil Sedaka
© 1962 (Renewed 1990) SCREEN GEMS-EMI MUSIC INC. and UNIVERSAL
MUSIC- CAREERS
All Rights Reserved International Copyright Secured Used by Permission
Reprinted by Permission of Hal Leonard Corporation

East Bound And Down
From the Universal Film SMOKY AND THE BANDIT
Words and Music by Jerry Reed and Dick Feller
Copyright © 1977 USI B MUSIC PUBLISHING and VECTOR MUSIC
CORPORATION
Copyright Renewed
All Rights Controlled and Administered by SONGS OF UNIVERSAL, INC.
All Rights Reserved Used by Permission
Reprinted by Permission of Hal Leonard Corporation

Renegade
Words and Music by Tommy Shaw
Copyright © 1978 ALMO MUSIC CORP. and STYGIAN SONGS
All Rights Controlled and Administered by ALMO MUSIC CORP.
All Rights Reserved Used by Permission
Reprinted by Permission of Hal Leonard Corporation

Man In The Wilderness
Words and Music by Tommy Shaw
Copyright © 1977 ALMO MUSIC CORP. and STYGIAN SONGS
Copyright Renewed
All Rights Controlled and Administered by ALMO MUSIC CORP.
All Rights Reserved Used by Permission
Reprinted by Permission of Hal Leonard Corporation

Acknowledgements

All song lyrics reprinted with Permission

American Pie
Words and Music by Don McLean
Copyright © 1971, 1972 BENNY BIRD CO., INC.
Copyright Renewed
All Rights Controlled and Administered by SONGS OF UNIVERSAL, INC.
All Rights Reserved   Used by Permission
Reprinted by Permission of Hal Leonard Corporation

Willin'
Words and Music by Lowell George
Naked Snake Music
Reprinted by Permission of Elizabeth George

Beatin' the Odds
Words and Music by Molly Hatchett
Mister Sunshine Music, Inc.
Reprinted by Permission of Patrick J. Armstrong

Front and Back Cover Photo
Reprinted by Permission of Marinas.com

Author Photo taken by Patricia Clark Photography
Reprinted by Permission of Patricia Clark

Made in the USA
Coppell, TX
24 June 2021